Down
& out,
on the
Road

Down & out, on the Road

THE HOMELESS IN AMERICAN HISTORY

Kenneth L. Kusmer 1945 –

OXFORD
UNIVERSITY PRESS

2002

OXFORD
UNIVERSITY PRESS

Oxford   New York
Athens   Auckland   Bangkok   Bogotá   Buenos Aires   Cape Town
Chennai   Dar es Salaam   Delhi   Florence   Hong Kong   Istanbul   Karachi
Kolkata   Kuala Lumpur   Madrid   Melbourne   Mexico City   Mumbai   Nairobi
Paris   São Paulo   Shanghai   Singapore   Taipei   Tokyo   Toronto   Warsaw

and associated companies in
Berlin   Ibadan

Copyright © 2002 by Oxford University Press

Published by Oxford University Press, Inc.
198 Madison Avenue, New York, New York 10016

Oxford is a registered trademark of Oxford University Press

Library of Congress Cataloging-in-Publication Data
Kusmer, Kenneth L., 1945–
Down & out, on the road : the homeless in American history /
Kenneth L. Kusmer.
    p.   cm.
Includes bibliographical references and index.
ISBN 0-19-504778-8
1. Homelessness—United States—History.   2. Homeless persons—
United States—History.   I. Title.
HV4504 .K87 2001
305.569—dc21   00-140074

Material in text previously published in articles in *Amerikastudien*, Volume 40 (December 1995) and
in "The Underclass in Historical Perspective: Tramps and Vagrants in Urban America, 1870–1930,"
in Rick Beard, ed., *On Being Homeless* (New York, 1987). By permission of the Museum of the City
of New York: *Reconstructing American Literacy and Historical Interpretations*, Günter Lenz, Hartmut
Keil, and Sebine Bröck-Sallah, eds. (Frankfurt: Campus Verlag, 1990). Quotations from letters in the
text between William Aspinwall and John J. Cook by permission of the McCook Collection, The
Antiquarian and Landmarks Society.

9 8 7 6 5 4 3
Printed in the United States of America
on acid-free paper

To

JOHN HOPE FRANKLIN

JOHN HIGHAM

STANLEY KATZ

AUGUST MEIER

Teachers, scholars, friends

Preface

When New York Mayor Rudolph Giuliani announced in December 1999 that he would require the homeless to work before they could receive a bed in a shelter, he probably was unaware that his proposed policy revived a very old historical tradition. For a time in the 1820s, persons convicted of vagrancy in New York City were forced to labor on a treadmill, and from the 1880s to the 1930s it was common throughout the country for men staying in homeless shelters to have to chop wood or break stone for two or three hours before receiving a meal and a bed for the night.

Throughout American history, such policies have been based on the assumption that the homeless are lazy and irresponsible—a deviant group, perhaps incorrigible, but in any case outside the boundaries of mainstream society. There is much evidence, however, that these views are fundamentally biased. Negative stereotypes about the homeless have often functioned to justify persistent class or racial inequalities in American society. In reality, the homeless have always had much in common with other Americans, especially the working class. The primary characteristic that has set them apart from the mainstream is their extreme poverty or vulnerability to economic change.

The history of the homeless is intrinsically interesting in its own right, but its broader significance lies in its connection to economic, social, and cultural trends that affected the entire society. In this book I approach the history of the homeless from three distinct but interrelated perspectives. I address the causes and nature of homelessness, both "on the road" and in the cities. I also examine the response of municipal officials, social workers, and private charities who dealt with the homeless as a social problem. Finally, I explore the ways in which Americans of different class, religious, ethnic, racial, and regional backgrounds perceived and reacted to the homeless. My aim throughout is to demonstrate that the homeless have been an integral part of American civilization for well over two centuries.

I WAS NOT born a historian. As an undergraduate, I studied mathematics and physics until the inspiring teaching of Geoffrey Blodgett, Richard D. Brown, Robert Soucy, and the late Leon Soulé convinced me to change majors and pursue a career in history. In graduate school, I had the good fortune to work with August Meier at Kent State University and with John Hope Franklin, John Coatsworth, and Neil Harris at the University of Chicago. If there is any value in this history of the homeless, a good deal of the credit must go to the high intellectual standards that these professors set for me when I was a student.

No scholar can accomplish anything without the assistance of good librarians and archivists. Of the many institutions I visited while researching this study, I would especially like to express my appreciation to the librarians and archivists at Temple University (especially Margaret Jerrido, director of the Urban Archives), the University of Chicago, Princeton University, the University of Pennsylvania, the Wisconsin State Historical Society, the Salvation Army Archives, the Philadelphia City Archives, the Museum of the City of New York, the Free Library of Philadelphia, the Western Reserve Historical Society, and the National Archives.

I owe a special thanks to David McAllister, my research assistant during 1998–99; to Pamela Haines, who helped collect quantitative data; to Gang Luo, whose knowledge of computer programs was so helpful; and to Susan Ferber of Oxford University Press, whose expert editorial advice greatly improved the quality of the manuscript. I also want to thank the following individuals, who in many different ways provided moral support during the years I worked on this project: Nancy Anderson, Robin Saul Raab, Paul

Finkelman, the late Elizabeth Fogarty, Alison Price, Karen K. Bradley, Martha Saxton, Brett Williams, Al Camarillo, Dirk Voss, Barbara Titus, Bettye Collier-Thomas, Waldo Heinrichs, Hermann Wellenreuther, the late Marie-Luise Frings-Wellenreuther, Judy Hill, Karsten Poehl, Claude Guillaumaud-Pujol, Brigitta Hoth, Gail Farr, and Diane Maleson. Four friends were particularly helpful in reading and commenting on the manuscript or providing intellectual input: Nando Fasce, Kim Hopper, Jim Borchert, and Susan Borchert. I also want to thank Dorothy Kusmer, Robert Kusmer, Debra Carner, and Madeleine Lord, whose warm encouragement during the final phase of work on the book was so important in helping me bring it to fruition.

Only two of the scholars to whom this book is dedicated were literally my teachers. All of them, however, have been teachers in the deeper meaning of that word.

Contents

Down
& out,
on the
Road

PHOTOGRAPHS OF SOUP LINES AND destitute farm families making their way to California during the Great Depression have been indelibly etched on the American imagination. Long before the 1930s, however, the homeless were an important element on the American scene. Known during the colonial era as "the wandering poor," "sturdy beggars," or simply as vagrants, the homeless first became noticeable in the late eighteenth century, then grew significantly in number after 1820, when urbanization and industrial development began to take hold in the young nation. By the 1840s and '50s, municipalities were setting aside rooms in police stations for overnight lodging of the destitute, and organized charities began to grapple with the problem of the homeless for the first time.

Chapter 1.
The Problem of the Homeless in American History

Homelessness emerged as a national issue in the 1870s. During that decade the homeless population increased dramatically in size and assumed a distinctive form. A new, more aggressive type of homeless man emerged—the tramp. Tramps rode the railroads without paying, joined together in threatening bands, and frightened farmers while incurring the wrath of law enforcement officers. In the cities, meanwhile, the number of destitute persons forced to stay overnight in privately run shelters or police station "tramp rooms" increased, while those who were not completely penniless sought accommodations in cheap lodging house districts like the Bowery in New York.

During the post-Civil War decades, some of the homeless went "on the road," while others gravitated to the cities. There was considerable overlap between the two groups, but those who traveled in search of work (or, sometimes, adventure) were generally younger than those who remained permanently in one locale. This dual aspect would continue to define homelessness until the 1940s, when the effects of war and structural changes in the economy led to a sharp decline in the number of persons riding the rails. After 1945, homelessness would undergo a drastic change as an aging population of destitute men became confined, for the most part, to the deteriorating skid row areas of cities. Homelessness, which in the 1930s had reemerged as an important national issue, now reverted to what it had been before the Civil War—a strictly urban problem. Even in the cities, the homeless became largely invisible to all but the police. The lack of concern for this impoverished group made the skid rows ripe for urban renewal, and in the 1960s and 1970s most of the old lodging house districts in American cities were demolished.

The level of significance we ascribe to homelessness very much depends on how the term is defined. In conducting the first census of the homeless in 1933, sociologist Nels Anderson identified a homeless person as "a destitute man, woman or youth, either a resident in the community or a transient, who is without domicile at the time of enumeration. Such a person may have a home in another community, or relatives in the local community, but is for the time detached and will not or cannot return." This succinct definition recognized that a homeless person could be either a permanent resident of a community or a traveler, that the condition of homelessness could either be voluntary or involuntary, and that family relationships were significant in determining whether or not a person became homeless.[1] All of these aspects are important for understanding the phenomenon historically.

Counting only those "without domicile," however, implies that only persons literally without a roof over their head, or forced to sleep in public or private shelters, are genuinely homeless. Such a restrictive definition seriously underestimates the level of homelessness in society. People sleeping outdoors are difficult to count, and even diligent investigators will miss many, as census enumerators discovered in 1990. Anderson's definition also sidesteps the fact that homelessness is often a transitory condition. A person can be temporarily domiciled at one point yet still be functionally homeless. Recent studies have shown that many persons living on the street or sleeping in shelters are able, from time to time, to find accommodations with family or friends. These arrangements are almost always temporary, however, and in most cases such individuals are back on the street in a relatively short time. The best contemporary estimates indicate that for every person in a shelter or on the street on a given night, three or four times as many have been homeless at some point during the previous year. Finally, the word "domicile" itself is open to varying interpretations. Too narrow a definition artificially understates the size of the homeless population. Until the 1970s, it was common for destitute men to rent six-foot-square cubicles in skid row hotels. Quite properly, people living in such circumstances were always considered homeless, as were those in the 1930s and earlier who survived by building makeshift structures in shantytowns.[2]

In the past as today, a flexible definition of homelessness that takes these factors into account makes the most sense.[3] Homelessness has assumed a variety of forms throughout American history. Especially during the industrial era, many homeless persons took part in tramping or worked as seasonal laborers (sometimes called hobos) during part of the year. Others traveled little and lived for decades in the poorest sections of cities, surviving on intermittent wages from odd jobs, begging, and occasional meager support from family members. Homeless women, especially, have always been more likely to live for long time periods in one city. What all these groups shared was the lack of a fixed abode, an impoverished lifestyle, and, in most cases, weak or nonexistent family support.

How the term *homeless* is defined brings up the far more difficult question of how to measure the level of homelessness at different times. Impressionistic evidence strongly suggests that homelessness was relatively insignificant prior to the 1730s but increased substantially in the late eighteenth century and again in the 1820s. This initial growth of the homeless population took place primarily in the nation's small but growing cities. The main source of data on the homeless during this period, however, consists of records of vagrancy convictions. While it is safe to assume there is some correlation between the number of people charged with vagrancy and the size of the entire homeless population, vagrancy convictions may also be influenced by the size and function of the police force, as well as by the attitude of the authorities toward the homeless. This is especially true for the period prior to the 1840s, when police forces were modest in size and still organized around the informal constable-watch system.[4] Vagrancy incarceration data provide valuable insight into the social characteristics of the early homeless population, but they are much less useful for estimating the size of this outcast group.

In the 1850s, officials in some cities began recording the number of persons who lodged overnight in police station rooms for the homeless. Because those who stayed there did so voluntarily, this is a much better general source for estimating the level of homelessness at the time. Extrapolating from statistics of men who stayed in these facilities, historian Eric Monkkonen has plausibly suggested that between 10 and 20 percent of American families in the late nineteenth century had at least one member who "had experienced the hospitality of the police station." There were, however, many other places where the destitute could sleep besides the station house "tramp rooms." As an estimate of families' experience with homelessness, then, the figure of 10–20 percent is probably conservative. Between the mid-nineteenth and mid-twentieth century, a substantial portion of the American public joined the ranks of the "down-and-out" at some point in their lives. Although we will never know exactly how many homeless people existed, their numbers must surely be measured in the millions.

Homelessness fluctuated in relation to a variety of factors, but even at low points the number of destitute persons without shelter was substantial. World War II marked an important turning point in this regard. During the three decades following the war, the usual cyclical pattern disappeared, and homelessness receded to its lowest level since the mid-eighteenth century. The postwar decline proved temporary, however, as mass homelessness reemerged in the late 1970s. Although the homeless population today is not nearly as large as it was at the beginning of the twentieth century, it is still much closer to the historic "norm" than was true of the skid-row era of the 1950s and '60s.[5]

Numbers alone cannot adequately convey the significance of homelessness as an aspect of American civilization. Especially during the industrial era, uncertainty about who was or might become homeless magnified the impact of homelessness well beyond what any isolated "head count" could measure. In addition to those who actually became homeless, there existed a substantially larger group—family members, friends, and fellow workers —who today would be described as an "at-risk" population. In his study of the homeless of the postindustrial era, sociologist Peter Rossi notes that the line between the "literal homeless" and impoverished individuals with homes is often tenuous. Today, of course, there is at least some public assistance available to the destitute. The vulnerability of the poor was even greater during earlier times, when government aid to the impoverished was almost nonexistent. For urban manual laborers in the nineteenth and early twentieth century, an awareness of the porous line between the down-and-out and the working poor profoundly influenced their understanding of the emergent industrial order and their precarious place in it.[6]

Although not everyone feared falling into homelessness, by 1900 most Americans were in some way affected by the phenomenon. The increased mobility of the homeless, who after 1870 were as likely to travel by train as on foot, potentially brought the specter of homelessness to the doorstep of every family in the country. The homeless were more visible, and far more assertive, during the industrial era than at any other time in American history. Prior to World War II, tramps and beggars could scarcely be avoided. Most Americans regularly encountered people begging for a handout, either at their back doors or on street corners, and stories about the homeless were common in magazines and daily newspapers.

Despite its pervasiveness as an aspect of American history, homelessness has received relatively little attention from scholars.[7] Social mobility studies, despite their claim to represent "history from the bottom up," have always ignored the underclass of homeless people. Few of the myriad histories of specific communities, works that have enriched our understanding of the American past in so many other ways, even acknowledge the existence of the homeless. If mentioned at all in general histories of the United States, tramps and beggars are usually categorized as simply another effect of the business cycle.[8]

The homeless cannot be traced in city directories or manuscript census schedules, traditional sources for documenting social change at the local level, since almost by definition these were persons who had broken loose from settled society. To ignore such a large group of destitute people, however, presents an incomplete—and in some ways quite false—view of the evolution of the American social order over the last two centuries. Who were the tramps and beggars? How did they become homeless? What were their lives like? With whom in society did they interact? Answers to these questions, hopefully, can help to reclaim an important part of the American experience.

Equally important to the history of the homeless is the public's response to this impoverished group. No other element of the population, with the exception of African Americans, has generated such strong reactions over such a long time period. Attitudes toward work, idleness, inequality, and benevolence have all been connected in some way with the homeless, who in different guises have represented alienation and failure in a society that has long worshiped upward mobility and success. To some extent, this was true almost from the beginning of American society, as evidenced by the early passage of harsh antivagrancy laws and the construction, in the eighteenth century, of the first workhouses for the "idle poor."

Homelessness did not spread uniformly to all parts of the country at the same time. On the eve of the Civil War, much of the South and many rural areas in the North had managed to avoid the "plague" of homeless persons already commonplace in Philadelphia, New York, and other northern cities. That was one reason that so many people were shocked when they first encountered vagabonds riding the rails in the 1870s. Especially to farmers and residents of small towns, these newly assertive homeless men were deeply subversive of the established order, still rooted at that time in the Protestant ethic. "He is at war in a lazy kind of way with society," an 1875 *New York Times* editorial on the tramp declared, "and rejoices at being able to prey upon it." This was a mild statement compared to the vitriolic commentary about "criminal, lazy vagabonds" that would pour forth from the press during the next decade.[9]

In every age, the homeless have been anathema to many Americans because of their alleged laziness, but the tramps of the 1870s and '80s also threatened another core American value: community control.[10] Of unknown origin and designs, the homeless suddenly appeared in communities across the country, sleeping in barns, pestering citizens for handouts, and leaving as mysteriously as they arrived. Prior to the Civil War, the "wandering poor" were few enough in number that town officials could usually control them. But forcing the homeless to "move on" became futile when the next train only brought more vagrants to their community. The class dimension of homelessness presented yet another cause for anxiety. The tramp came into prominence at the same time that freewheeling entrepreneurs like Jay Gould and Jim Fisk were amassing their ill-gotten gains. Both types seemed to indicate a betrayal of the ideal of a society where there was a direct relationship between work done and benefits received.

Urban beggars and train-riding vagabonds were visible signs of the breakdown of local control that accompanied the rise of urban industrial society in the nineteenth century. Those who responded most antagonistically to the homeless refused to accept this explanation. Instead, they sought scapegoats, the most convenient of whom were the waves of immigrants pouring into the country. Prior to World War I, a common theme in the literature on the homeless was that they were foreigners who had not assimilated American values. Initially, there was an element of truth in this image. In the mid-nineteenth century, the foreign-born, especially the impoverished Irish, made up a disproportionate share of the homeless population. By the early twentieth century, however, this stereotype was out of step with the facts. An increasing majority of the homeless were native-born, and few of the new immigrants from southern and eastern Europe ever became tramps or beggars. Whatever its causes, homelessness was an indigenous phenomenon, not something imported from the outside.

The tramping phenomenon and the responses to it must be understood in the context of the industrialized, increasingly organized society that came into being in the post–Civil War decades. As giant enterprises, routinized factory work, and a new bureaucratic management structure emerged, the distance between the ideal and the reality of the American values of self-help and individualism began to widen. The new industrial system placed severe limitations on workers, forcing them into rearguard strike actions in an attempt to retain as much control over the work process as possible.[11] Forced layoffs were not the only cause of homelessness; rather, unemployment operated in conjunction with a host of other factors influencing the lives of workers. Economic depressions, automation, and industrial accidents could all lead to homelessness. Workers, aware of the inherent instability of the economy and more prone than the middle class to suffer because of it, came increasingly to sympathize with the homeless class. They realized that they might have to join it, whether they wanted to or not.

It would be a mistake, however, to conclude that all the workers who became tramps did so because they had no alternative. Many young workers voluntarily left their jobs and took to the road, either because they sought jobs elsewhere or because they had decided to temporarily "opt out" of the industrial system. The memoirs of more than two dozen former tramps indicate that, for many, their experience represented an incipient rebellion against the new work disciplines and institutional strictures of industrial society. While riding the freights, transients congregated in hobo "jungles," camps strategically located within walking distance of railway terminals but outside the jurisdiction of town police. One appeal of this environment was release from the constraints of a rapidly modernizing social system. At a time when youths unable to obtain an education saw only dead-end factory labor ahead of them, tramp life, at least as a temporary expedient, could be attractive, despite its acknowledged dangers and inconveniences.

The rebellious aspect of tramping was fundamentally different from attempts to preserve "traditional" peasant values in an industrial environment, a subject that has become a staple of ethnic and labor history during the past 30 years.[12] Tramping, in fact, seemed to have something in common with what one historian has identified as the anarchist streak in the American character.[13] Coxey's Army of 1894 and the Bonus Marchers of 1932 illustrated some of these qualities. By adopting extralegal forms of government, both of these groups carried forward a tradition long associated with the American frontier, where communities often preceded formal government. The hobo jungles, with their unwritten rules of conduct, reflected a similar mentality. African Americans had other reasons for going on the road. For a young, impoverished black man of the post-Reconstruction era, escape via the freight car was one means of rebellion against the white South still open to him, and the lifestyle of transients was surprisingly free of overt racism.

Regardless of the racial background of the homeless, it is somewhat misleading to categorize them as unemployed. The homeless have usually been intermittently employed, often at low-paying "odd jobs." Throughout the American past, including the immediate post–World War II era, such work usually involved unskilled manual labor. Since the 1960s, service jobs in restaurants, hotels, or offices have been more common. Historically, unskilled workers have been overrepresented among the homeless, but homelessness was something that could and did happen to Americans from a wide variety of educational and occupational backgrounds.

The railroad-riding tramp was a new phenomenon of the post–Civil War period, but urban vagrants and beggars have existed as long as there have been cities in America. Like the tramps, their numbers grew dramatically in the late nineteenth century. This trend coincided with the development of specialized areas in cities, later known as skid rows, where the homeless were able to find temporary shelter in "cage" hotels or crowded dormitory-style lodging houses. In the 1950s, skid rows came to be identified with elderly homeless men, but this had not been the case earlier in the century. Prior to the 1920s, most lodging-house occupants were relatively young men who survived through a combination of casual labor, begging, and seasonal work in the farmlands and forest areas of the upper Midwest. The "main stem" (as the lodging house district was called by those who lived there) was usually situated in the most run-down section of the city, often adjacent to the red-light district. Nevertheless, to some extent the cheap lodging houses, noisy saloons, and second-hand clothing stores located there provided a protective environment for the down-and-out.

Prior to the 1870s, women made up a significant fraction of the homeless population of urban America. By the end of the nineteenth century, however, the world of the homeless had become an overwhelmingly masculine realm. This was not because women were less at risk to become homeless; indirectly, the same forces at work creating male homelessness could and did have an impact on women as well. Rather, it was mostly a consequence of the gender ideology of the Victorian era, which assumed that women were weaker and less able to care for themselves than men. As sociologist Theda Skocpol demonstrated in her pathbreaking study, *Protecting Soldiers and Mothers*, this mentality led to the establishment of numerous institutions to assist indigent women and children and ultimately to the passage of protective labor legislation and "mothers' pensions" laws in the early twentieth century.[14]

Men were much less likely to receive charitable help of this nature. Regardless of unemployment, accident, or illness, they were expected to be the primary breadwinners. Success manuals of the day repeatedly argued that financial achievement resulted from the development of "masculine" traits.[15] Part of the extraordinarily hostile reaction to tramps and beggars in the late nineteenth century was outrage over the fact that these outsiders had seemingly rejected male responsibility by embracing a vagabond lifestyle free from the bonds of marriage and family.

From the colonial era to the early twentieth century, municipal officials and mainstream charities often exhibited barely concealed contempt for the homeless. Beginning in the 1840s, organized charities sought to separate the "worthy" poor from the growing hordes of urban beggars. After the Civil War, the Charity Organization Society attempted to replace the police station facilities with the more controlled environment of privately run shelters, where homeless men were required to submit to a contrived "work test" before receiving food or lodging. Charity officers also joined forces with the police in an attempt to suppress street begging. At the turn of the century, younger social workers began to promote a more humane approach to homelessness. No significant change in the treatment of the homeless would take place, however, until the crisis of the Great Depression led the federal government to become involved for the first time.

The views of reformers and social welfare experts, however, were not always shared by ordinary citizens. Class, ethnic, and religious differences led to wide variation in the way the homeless were treated. During every period of American history, the working class was probably more sympathetic to the homeless than people of higher economic strata. In the nineteenth century, domestic servants often provided the homeless with food pilfered from their employers, and in some immigrant neighborhoods beggars were considered objects of sympathy, not derision. Despite their own difficult financial straits, racial minorities were also more willing to assist the homeless.

Even at the height of the antitramp hysteria, the societal response to the homeless was not totally negative. There were a great many "sentimentalists," as Yale sociologist William Graham Sumner derisively called them, who believed that it was immoral to withhold food from the destitute until their character was investigated. Concerned citizens set up soup kitchens and dispensed free bread during depressions, carrying on a tradition that dated to the late colonial period. Despite constant admonitions against "unscientific almsgiving," many middle-class persons were also prone to give to beggars.

By the beginning of the twentieth century, the negative impression of tramps and beggars conveyed by organized charity leaders was also out of step with the image of the homeless man as popularized in various entertainment media. Writers like William Dean Howells and Josiah Flynt introduced new perspectives on the homeless to their readers, helping to undermine some of the old stereotypes. By the eve of the Great Depression, the mainstream image of the tramp in middle-class literature and magazines was milder, but no closer to reality than the earlier, vicious stereotype had been. With its nostalgic overtones, the new image deflected attention from the real problem of homelessness, which continued to exist and even grow during the "prosperity decade" of the 1920s. In contrast, the tramp persona in media favored by the working class, such as vaudeville, music, and early motion pictures, was more likely to contain a subtext critical of the new industrial order. The image of the homeless man served many functions for many audiences.

As both social fact and cultural icon, the homeless receded from public consciousness after World War II, and, except for the social scientists who studied skid-row conditions, they would remain largely forgotten until the late 1970s. Only then did the unexpected emergence of a younger, more racially diverse population of "street people" again draw attention to a problem which had never really gone away, but only changed form, many times, over the centuries.

THE HOMELESS HAVE BEEN A PART OF American civilization almost since the founding of the first English colonies four hundred years ago. As early as 1640 "vagrant persons" were listed among the social outcasts that peace officers in Boston were charged with apprehending. By the mid-eighteenth century, "sturdy beggars" had become a fairly common sight wandering along backcountry roads, but they were much more likely to congregate in bustling seaport towns like Philadelphia and Baltimore. The decades immediately before and after the American Revolution witnessed a substantial increase in homelessness. After 1820, accelerating economic change forced many more individuals into the ranks of vagrants and beggars, prompting the first concerted attempt by private charities to deal with this problem. By the depression of 1857, every substantial urban center was grappling with throngs of homeless persons. This trend was not equally evident in all sections of the country, however. On the eve of the Civil War the homeless problem, and responses to it, remained local in nature.

As in later years, during America's first two centuries people entered the homeless class for a variety of reasons and stayed in it for widely varying periods of time. Many homeless persons were

Chapter 2.

The Origins of Homelessness in Early America

unemployed workers; others were people whose lives had been disrupted by the catastrophes of war, plague, or natural disaster. Still others were "footloose adventurers or social misfits" who for one reason or another could not adjust to the emerging social order.[1] It is probable that, even during the colonial era, there existed a core group among the homeless unemployed whose displacement from normal society was so severe that they formed a kind of counterculture to the dominant values of the social system. It is unlikely that members of this outcast group were as cohesive in America as they apparently were in Europe at this time, where beggars' "guilds" were well organized and even required initiation rites.[2] The small scale of American cities compared with London or Paris probably would have made such activities difficult. The mere existence of a homeless population, however, was enough to arouse the concern of authorities and generate a debate about what to do with them. It is a debate that would recur again and again during the next two centuries.

During the early colonial period, the effects of warfare were probably the most important cause of homelessness. The first dramatic upsurge in vagrancy in New England occurred in the wake of King Phillip's War of 1675–76, an Indian uprising that disrupted much of the Massachusetts and Rhode Island countryside, forcing settlers from their farms and into coastal towns. Bostonians complained that among some people "the sin of idleness (wch is the sin of Sodom) doeth greatly increase," and constables reported in 1679 that during the past three years 62 newcomers to the city had become public charges. Shortly thereafter Massachusetts passed an act requiring those who lived an "idle and riotous life" to be bound out as servants. Newport, Rhode Island, suffered even more from refugees, many of whom stayed on and had to be cared for by public or private charity. For decades, periodic conflict with Indian tribes or the French would continue to devastate frontier areas in New England and New York, forcing families into the ranks of the homeless. This would also be a major, unforeseen consequence of the French and Indian Wars of 1756–63 and the American Revolution.[3]

The beginnings of the business cycle added another important factor influencing the growth of homelessness. The colonies were little affected by industrialism, a prime cause of nineteenth- century poverty, but fluctuations in trade and the price of commodities created periods of hard times, especially as the colonial economy became more closely linked to the world market. Before 1700, historian Robert Cray, Jr., notes, poverty in New York City and its surrounding environs "was a decidedly minor problem," and there were no beggars to speak of in the city. In the 1720s and '30s, however, New York began for the first time to experience the negative effects of economic downturns. In 1734 one newspaper correspondent complained that "many beggarly people wander about the streets" and urged the construction of a public building to incarcerate such individuals. A year later the city erected its first institution for that purpose, a combination "Poor House, Work House, and House of Correction."[4]

In the eighteenth century, especially, the immigration of poor people to the colonies also led to homelessness. Philadelphia was little troubled by vagrants early in the century; one observer stated in 1724 that there "are people who have been living here for 40 years and have not seen a beggar." The influx of indigent newcomers into that city soon thereafter, however, rapidly made this statement outdated. In 1729 a new law allowed local authorities to expel indigent migrants from other provinces or Europe who might become charges. Six years later another ordinance limited public welfare of any kind to legal residents of the city. In Boston, the arrival of hundreds of impoverished Scotch-Irish immigrants, many of whom were unable to obtain jobs, also led authorities to take stern action. In 1719, the selectmen ordered the 49 destitute inhabitants of one ship arriving from Ireland to leave the community at once.[5]

While the homeless could be found throughout the colonies, it was in the cities that the "wandering poor" were most conspicuous. By the end of the seventeenth century, Boston was already known as a haven for those without legal settlement. Despite stricter laws, the growth of the transient population of seamen, immigrants, and people who had moved or been expelled from smaller towns made it increasingly difficult for Puritan officials to keep close watch over the behavior of all inhabitants. By the 1730s, Philadelphia, New York, Providence, and Charlestown were undergoing similar experiences. During the last half of the eighteenth century, inequalities of wealth grew rapidly in all colonial cities, and the number of poor and destitute increased substantially. "Laboring people," says Billy Smith in his study of Philadelphia's lower classes, "often lived a hand-to-mouth existence, struggling to maximize their family income and to cut the cost of basic necessities." Those unable to make ends meet might find themselves sleeping in back alleys and begging on the street.[6]

Among the working class, former indentured servants were particularly likely to become homeless. Until the early eighteenth century, servants had considerable opportunity to acquire land. Upward mobility became constricted after 1730, however, and ex-servants lived an increasingly marginal existence. At one time or another in the late eighteenth century, 80 percent of former servants in Pennsylvania received public assistance. Escaped slaves and runaway servants also augmented the homeless population. Especially after the Revolution, the number of such individuals willing to risk almost certain destitution in their quest for freedom increased dramatically. A majority of those sentenced to the Philadelphia county prison for vagrancy in the 1790s were former or escaped slaves, runaway servants, or apprentices who had absconded from their masters. In one typical case, a slave listed only as Harry was sentenced in 1791 to 30 days hard labor for "disorderly behavior, getting drunk and absenting himself day and Night from the service of his Master William Lewis." No sooner was Harry released than he again ran away, was immediately recaptured and sentenced to another 30-day prison term. This pattern would be repeated two more times during the next three months. For slaves like Harry, a life of intermittent homelessness and incarceration was preferable to waiting for Pennsylvania's gradual manumission law to take effect.[7]

The poverty and disorder that followed the British evacuation of New York City in 1783 left that city particularly open to vagabonds. In 1784 Mayor James Duane complained of the "abandoned Vagrants and Prostitutes whom the ordinary Process of Justice hath not awed nor reclaimed" and argued that "the Discipline of the Bridewell or House of Employment vigorously administered will alone be effectual to correct and restrain those shameful Enormities." A harsher policy toward sturdy beggars failed to have much effect, however. Duane's successor, Richard Varick, noted in 1788 that "Vagrants multiply on our Hands to an amazing Degree." Overcrowding in the jails and workhouses led officials to place many vagabonds in the city almshouse, until the city was forced to erect a new, four-story building in 1796. By 1800 New York was the new nation's largest city. It was also becoming the metropolis where the vagrant and beggar class was most noticeable.[8]

Despite the growth of homelessness at the end of the eighteenth century, especially in the nascent urban centers, the problem was less severe at that time than it would be after 1820, and much less important than after the Civil War. There are several reasons for this. First, homelessness was greatly reduced in the South as a result of the development of slavery. Prior to Bacon's Rebellion in 1676, when slavery still played a rather minor role in Virginia's labor system, that colony suffered from bands of roving young men who lived without work. The rise of the institution of slavery to prominence by the early 1700s changed all that. It effectively harnessed a permanent proletariat to the labor system in a way that was impossible in England. This, coupled with the social and political elevation of the smaller white landowners, meant that the southern colonies (and later, states) would have much less vagabondage than provinces to the north.[9]

The legal history of vagrancy in colonial Virginia gives some indication of its insignificance there and in the South in general. Like most other provinces, Virginia passed its first vagrancy legislation toward the end of the seventeenth century. The act of September 1672, noting an increase in the number of vagabonds, charged "that the justices of [the] peace in every county doe put the lawes of England against vagrant, idle and desolute persons in strict execution." It can hardly be a coincidence that this law was followed immediately by an "act for the apprehension and suppression of runawayes, negroes, and slaves." The Assembly, recognizing "that many negroes have lately beene, and now are out in rebellion in sundry parts of this country," was fearful of the "very dangerous consequence [that] may arise to the country if other negroes, Indians, or servants should happen to fly forth and joyne with them." Many of the vagrants against whom the first act was aimed were disgruntled former servants unable to obtain land after completing their term of indenture. What the gentry feared was exactly what happened in 1676—a union of the propertyless lower-class elements against the planters. Although Bacon's Rebellion was violently suppressed, its underlying cause was extinguished only by expanding the importation of slaves, which by the early eighteenth century made the class division in Virginia increasingly a racial one as well.[10]

Thus, in the South a large portion of what a later slaveholder would call the "mudsill class" was effectively controlled by thousands of masters, whereas in the North even the harshest codes could not eliminate the "masterless men." While Virginia legislators passed numerous laws for the control of slaves and their capture if they escaped, they took little interest in the small number of white vagabonds, who no longer posed even a symbolic threat to the established order. The legislature did not even address the problem until 1723, when it included a reference to vagabonds within an all-purpose "Act for the better Securing the payment of Levys, and restraint of Vagrant and idle people, and for the more effectual discovery and prosecution of Persons having Bastard Children." Equally revealing was the clause empowering the county courts "to bind every such Vagabond to Serve on Wages for the Space of One year, or to Order him or her to receive Twenty Five Lashes on his or her back well laid on at the Common Whipping Post, at the Choice of such Vagabond." To allow such discretion to the criminal was extraordinary. Obviously, Virginians at the time did not take the crime of vagrancy very seriously—provided the offender was white, of course. Contrary to proslavery propaganda of the antebellum period, the existence of slavery did not eliminate poverty among whites. By the mid-eighteenth century some southern cities had erected almshouses for indigent, sick, and homeless persons. Partly because it was a seaport, Charleston attracted a larger number of vagabonds than most southern communities. Yet, even there, the response was much milder than in New York or Philadelphia. Charleston's paternalistic elite acknowledged a degree of responsibility to poor whites. The increasing proportion of blacks in the colony made the planter class much more anxious to control runaway slaves than homeless whites.[11]

In the New England and Middle Atlantic sections, other factors kept the growth of homelessness within manageable proportions. Growing class divisions and increasing commercialization during the post-Revolutionary decades did not in and of themselves lead to the emergence of a sizeable sub-proletariate. The vagabonds and wretchedly poor street beggars that so disturbed the urban middle class were much less common in small towns and rural areas. There too, wealth holding became more stratified after 1750, and the number of propertyless laborers increased, especially between 1780 and 1820. By working in family units and combining farming on leased land with small-scale home manufacturing, however, they were able, to some extent, to share in the general prosperity of an expanding society. Furthermore, property ownership, though less common than in the seventeenth century, remained more widespread in the rural North in 1800 than anywhere else in the western world. It was still possible for the children of eastern farmers to migrate to Ohio, Indiana, and Illinois, where land could be purchased fairly reasonably.[12]

It is a mistake to equate the increasing geographic mobility of many workers during the 1760–1820 period with poverty, much less with the desperate search for work that would define much of the "tramp" class of the late nineteenth century. In the expanding commercial and agricultural economy of the early 1800s, geographic mobility of artisans and farm workers was often due to a quest for higher wages. A diversified, growing economy made itinerant laborers more valuable and allowed them, to an extent, to choose their place of employment. The dispersed nature of American settlements in the eighteenth century and early nineteenth century also insured that itinerant peddlers, artisans, printers, clergy, and even doctors and lawyers existed in large numbers. Hat finishers, for example, had a tradition of traveling. They were seldom destitute, however, and the unemployed could always count on assistance from fellow craftsmen in other cities. In the words of one scholar, migration was often "an act of renewal" rather than a prelude to poverty. Compared to England or France, "where the number of beggars reached massive proportions" in rural areas, itinerant beggars were not yet a serious problem in eighteenth-century America. The growth of homelessness in urban areas was much more significant. But young America had no equivalent of London or Paris, and as late as 1820 only 7 percent of its population resided in cities. To a considerable degree, the problem of homelessness still lay largely in the future.[13]

The moderate level of homelessness in America prior to 1820 did not necessarily lead to public indifference. Colonial era attitudes toward the homeless would continue to influence public policy toward this group throughout the nineteenth and twentieth centuries. The preeminence of Protestantism in the British colonies insured that here, as in England, attitudes toward the homeless would be quite different from that of Catholic Europe. Throughout the Middle Ages, social custom and Catholic theology promoted a lenient attitude toward begging, and during the thirteenth and fourteenth centuries the mendicant orders even raised begging to the level of a spiritual principle, as one way of imitating Christ. In many ways, Protestantism was very far from being a complete break with the medieval worldview, but its new emphasis on the efficacious spiritual value of work set it apart from Catholic views.[14]

To the English Puritans, the homeless unemployed represented a kind of negative reference group. William Perkins, a leading Calvinist theologian, argued vehemently that "wandering beggars and rogues" were not only a plague on civil society, but should "bee taken as ennemies of this ordinance of God." This image of the rogue vagabond, part criminal and part ne'er-do-well, became commonplace in sixteenth-century England. During the Tudor Stuart period, as the number of "masterless" men increased, punishment for the now criminalized status of beggar grew steadily harsher. Sturdy beggars were whipped, mutilated, sometimes deported, or even hung.[15] The colonists who founded New England brought similar attitudes with them. The Puritans of Massachusetts Bay drew sharp distinctions among different types of destitute persons. The poor, the sick, and those unable to care for themselves because of age or debility were considered part of the community, and it was the responsibility of godly Christians to care for them. The wandering poor, however, were different. They had broken the bonds of community and rejected the idea of diligently working in a calling. The earliest instruction of Governor John Endicott to the Massachusetts Bay Company in 1629 admonished that "Noe idle drone bee permitted to live amongst us." The Quaker founders of Pennsylvania had a similar conception of the importance of work, even if they differed with the Puritans in many other ways. William Penn criticized the "lazy" monks who were "burdensome to others to feed their Idleness," while Israel Pemberton, a leading eighteenth-century Philadelphia Friend, wrote that "the Principle

of True Religion . . . never disposes the Mind to Indolence or Sloth."
Charles Chauncey, speaking in 1752 before the Boston Society for Encouraging Industry and Employing the Poor, made his own point of view clear in the title of his sermon: "The Idle Poor secluded from the Bread of Charity by the Christian Law."[16]

Early poor relief in America, copying the Elizabethan code of 1601, made the parish, county, or town directly responsible for its own poor. The Puritan emphasis on a covenanted community and family government militated against single people living alone, much less wandering the highways, and in the seventeenth century people found living by themselves were required to board with families. If this concept of community demanded care for those within the bounds of the social order, however, it also allowed townspeople to disregard those defined as outside the community. As early as 1658 the process of "warning out" was instituted by selectmen in New England towns. By formally warning out a newcomer, a town was able to deny all responsibility for caring for the person in question, should he or she need aid or care. In the seventeenth century, such a policy meant physical banishment from the town; in the eighteenth century it increasingly became merely a legal maneuver to keep the towns' poor rates down. In the late seventeenth and early eighteenth century the colonies began to pass laws that dealt specifically with the homeless unemployed. One way in which vagrants were distinguished from most others receiving poor relief was that they were much more likely to be institutionalized. In 1658 Plymouth colony was the first to pass a law establishing a house of correction for vagrants, rebellious children, and stubborn servants who refused to work. In 1699 Massachusetts also moved to suppress "Rogues, Vagabonds, Common Beggars and other Lewd and Disorderly Persons" by allowing towns to establish workhouses, where inmates could be whipped if they refused to labor. In a society that was extremely family centered, this treatment indicated that vagrants were outside the moral order of the community.[17]

Other colonies dealt with vagabonds and beggars in a variety of ways. In 1680, the governor of Connecticut stated that "beggars and vagabond persons are not suffered, but when discovered [are] bound out to service." It was not until 1713, however, that the colony clearly distinguished between paupers and vagrants, requiring that the latter be kept at hard labor while in jail. The court could also order offenders "to be chastened by whipping on his or her naked back." Whipping or payment of a fine were common punishments in most colonies in the seventeenth century; by the early eighteenth century the workhouse was becoming more popular. In most cases, workhouses were nothing more than local jails in which provision for labor of some kind was made. By the mid-eighteenth century, however, Boston, New York, Philadelphia, and Charlestown had erected larger facilities or converted part of the almshouse specifically for this purpose. In the colony of New York, it was customary throughout the colonial era to inflict various types of corporeal punishment on convicted vagrants, including the stockades, pillory, ear-cropping, and branding, in addition to whipping, although some town officials might simply warn out wandering strangers.[18]

On rare occasions, a habitual vagrant might even be sold into slavery. This happened in 1677 in Boston to one John Smith, "a Vagrant idle Person who hath formerly been whipt out of Town for a Vagabond" but who persisted in returning. That such a thing could happen shows that in the minds of many Englishmen at this time there was not a great deal of difference between slaves and the "idle poor." Both were perceived as unlikely to labor unless forced to do so, which is perhaps why early vagrancy codes were unusually broad in scope, and often included under the rubric of "vagrants" recalcitrant or runaway servants or slaves. At an early stage, then, the vagrancy statutes functioned as a means of controlling the labor force as well as punishing deviant behavior—and no behavior was considered more alien to a well-ordered community than idleness.[19]

Surprisingly, however, widespread antagonism toward vagrants did not lead to a consistent policy to discourage such behavior. Especially in the seaport towns, implementation of vagrancy statutes was harsh but uncertain, confined mostly to a periodic lashing out (sometimes literally so with the use of the whipping-post) during periods when the nuisance became too great. Such behavior was consistent with the general belief that poverty and crime could never be completely expunged from the social order and sometimes even served a religious purpose. Vagrancy and begging could not be completely eliminated any more than could sin. As a result, even when the "idle poor" increased in number, colonial officials did not necessarily feel impelled to launch a concerted attack on the problem.

In the late eighteenth century, the stern language of the vagrancy codes was mitigated by class solidarity and traditional practices of charitable giving, as well as by changing religious values. In 1788, when Philadelphia's mechanics paraded in celebration of the ratification of the new Constitution, they distributed bread, meat, and flour to the poor without making any investigation into the moral character of the recipients. For different reasons, some middle-class individuals exhibited similar behavior. During the late colonial and early national period, charity was still understood largely as a religious duty, and the private obligation of the prosperous to the poor was not satisfied merely by the payment of taxes for poor relief. This was particularly true of periods of distress, such as epidemics or depressions. At such times, especially in urban areas, it was common practice for wealthier citizens to set up ad hoc committees to dispense food, fuel, and clothing to the poor and unemployed. In distributing this largesse, charitable individuals paid relatively little attention to the distinction between the "deserving" and "undeserving" poor that would become the hallmark of some charitable organizations in the mid-nineteenth century. To inquire too much into the object of charity, in fact, would have been viewed with suspicion. The giver, the prominent Puritan minister Jonathan Ashley stated in 1741, should avoid sitting in judgment on others for their condition; for the charitable man "knows it is by the Grace of GOD, that he is what he is." Charity, Ashley concluded, "unlocks our Hands to distribute our Wealth to such as want our Alms."[20]

After 1750, the idea of charity as disinterested benevolence gained increasing acceptance as theologians came under the influence of Jonathan Edwards's writings. Edwards stressed that virtue was not a matter of reasoned thought but of being controlled by the proper emotions. The views of Edwards and other post–Great Awakening "New Light" ministers helped to create greater sympathy for the downtrodden.[21] They gave a religious motivation, as well as a certain intellectual respectability, to the traditional practice of assisting the poor. It was in the person of the beggar that this charitable impulse conflicted most directly with the Puritan work ethic. In the late eighteenth and early nineteenth centuries, especially in cities, the hostile official attitude toward beggars was not matched by an equally negative response on the part of the general populace. The conflict of principles may have led many to give to beggars with "a half formed resolution," as one observer noted in 1812, but since many still believed that beggary or poverty in general would never be completely expunged from society, the impulse to give alms often won out. Provided beggars had no apparent criminal or violent intent, some religious writers even viewed them positively, as examples of humble poverty and patience in the face of the will of an all-knowing deity.[22]

THE DECADES BETWEEN 1820 and 1860 were years of transition from a preindustrial society to one dominated by the mill and the factory; from a fundamentally agricultural nation to one in which cities, if not yet dominant, were assuming a new importance—especially in the North. By the eve of the Civil War, New York City's population (if Brooklyn is included) was approaching one million, Philadelphia had over half a million, and Boston, Baltimore, and other cities emerged as major metropolises. Although these cities grew rapidly, they often did so chaotically. In this era of the "walking city," many neighborhoods typically contained a heterogeneous and shifting mixture of homes, businesses, small factories, taverns, even illicit gambling houses and places of prostitution. Within this confused pattern of development, however, some distinctly working-class sections developed, and the elite began to separate themselves out, residentially and socially, from the city's poorer inhabitants, especially immigrants.[23]

At the same time, the intrusion of new technologies into the production process began to upset the traditional lifestyle and economic status of many artisans. With the exception of northern textile mills and a few large factories like the Springfield Armory, in most enterprises these changes were incremental and incomplete prior to the 1840s, a situation that created deep social tensions. The growth of productivity was accompanied by falling wages and sharp decline in artisanal independence. In the late antebellum period, change came more rapidly in many industries. The manufacturing of firearms, clocks, locks, and safes now used interchangeable parts, and by 1850 factory labor had replaced the artisan in the production of shoes, sugar, beer, glass, and other products. Simultaneously, the telegraph and the railroad were beginning to transform the distribution process. These changes inaugurated the shift to a national distribution network that would be completed after the Civil War. By 1860, the groundwork for the creation of modern business enterprise in America had been laid.[24]

This transformation made cheaper goods possible, but it also led to increased economic insecurity, especially for the working class. The 1820–60 period was marked by growing inequality in income and wealth, especially in large cities.[25] In Philadelphia, Baltimore, and elsewhere, seasonal unemployment forced hundreds to seek temporary shelter in the city almshouse each winter, including many widows unable to get by on a combination of intermittent, poorly paid work and meager public assistance. The embargo of 1807–08 and the economic downturns of 1817–23 and 1837–43 left many of the laboring poor destitute and increased the number of homeless persons significantly. Wretched poverty was already a conspicuous element of New York life as early as 1800, but by the 1830s the slums in the northern part of the city were the largest of any city in the country. The Corlear's Hook and Five Points sections became particularly notorious, with thousands of impoverished immigrants crammed into unhealthy, poorly ventilated tenements. The city attracted native-born migrants as well, mostly from nearby declining farming areas, who flocked to the metropolis with expectations that jobs would be available there. Instead of finding suitable employment, however, many wound up on the relief roles or, worse yet, ended up on the street.[26]

At the beginning of this transitional period, newly freed African Americans in the North were disproportionately represented among the homeless. Between 1823 and 1826, African Americans in Philadelphia made up 40 to 50 percent of all people imprisoned for vagrancy and about 20 percent of those admitted to the county almshouse, at a time when blacks comprised only a tenth of the city's population. One cause of this may have been Pennsylvania's gradual manumission law, which forced hundreds of unskilled, illiterate, or elderly slaves to suddenly fend for themselves in a racially hostile environment. More probably, it was a combination of economic depression and the steady influx of impoverished black migrants from nearby states, the South, and the West Indies that produced widespread destitution in the black community. Beginning in the late 1820s, however, homelessness among black Philadelphians began to decline, until by 1850 their numbers (5 percent) were roughly similar to their percentage of the city's population. Considering the rampant discrimination most African Americans suffered throughout the antebellum North, the small number of black homeless on the eve of the Civil War was a remarkable testament to the ability of the black community to survive adversity. By that time, vagrancy had become identified in the public mind with immigrants, especially the Irish, who in a number of cities made up a disproportionate share of the homeless.[27]

Whatever the cause, vagrants and beggars became an increasingly common sight on city streets in the early nineteenth century. From time to time the problem became onerous enough in New York for the city's marshals to round up numbers of these persons and have them committed to the city's new penitentiary for 60 days. Beginning in the 1820s, the authorities were assisted in their efforts by the passage of new vagrancy laws, providing harsh penalties for street begging. It was largely because of the vagrancy problem that the city constructed two treadmills in 1823. The treadmills, which required prisoners to spend about 8 minutes laboring, followed by 8 minutes of rest, produced 40 bushels of grain per day and saved the city $1,900 per year. The machinery proved so disastrous to the prisoners' mental and physical health, however, that enlightened citizens began to protest, and in 1826 it was discontinued. Even before then, however, the treadmill had failed as a deterrent. Despite the "acknowledged terrors" of this form of punishment, "vagrancy continued to increase at an alarming rate."[28]

By the mid-1840s, police stations in New York had begun to provide rooms for lodging homeless people overnight, and the number requesting these austere accommodations was rising, especially in the Sixth Ward, where the Five Points was located. Over a six-month period in 1853, almost 25,000 individuals made use of these police station shelters; thousands more slept in Battery Park. The phenomenon that shocked the middle class most, however, was the sudden appearance of thousands of homeless children, especially boys. Reformer Charles Loring Brace wrote retrospectively that many of these young people "had no settled home, and lived on the outskirts of society, their hand against every man's pocket, and every man looking on them as natural enemies." During the antebellum period the number of homeless children also increased in Philadelphia, as unmarried women and impoverished widows abandoned their offspring when they could no longer afford to care for them. All too often these women themselves became homeless. On the eve of the Civil War, more than a fifth of the city's police-station lodgers were female.[29]

Along the eastern seaboard, more of the homeless now moved from city to city. As a result, the old settlement laws, requiring nonresident paupers to be transported back to their place of origin, became more difficult to enforce. In New York, efforts to reduce welfare costs by removal of non-resident poor proved futile, and their numbers steadily grew. Increasingly, towns in Massachusetts were forced to care for destitute strangers, and almshouses that had originally been designed for the local poor filled up with vagabonds. The proportion of all relief given by towns to people without legal settlement rose steadily during the late antebellum period, from 36 percent in 1839 to 44 percent in 1845 to 65 percent in 1854. Meanwhile Boston, like New York, also suffered from increasing numbers of homeless children, who slept in alleyways and lived the life of scavengers. Nor were these conditions limited to eastern cities. In Cleveland, a thriving frontier community in 1842, one observer commented derisively on the whiskey-drinking "loafers" who were in the habit of sleeping in barns, especially in the city's "Flats" area along the Cuyahoga River.[30]

In some ways, the 1850s witnessed a genuine prelude to the massive vagrancy problem of the 1870s. In Detroit, homelessness grew apace after 1850, and even after the crisis of 1857–58 subsided, observers complained of the numerous "dock loafers" who could be found "living by no visible means, sleeping in boxes, barns, stairways, and under sheds on the docks." In 1859, the city approved the construction of a House of Corrections to incarcerate these offenders. In Philadelphia, the number of vagrants per thousand population during 1855–60—though not as great as it would be 20 years later—was higher than at any time since the 1820s.[31] In Massachusetts, the number of "state poor" (without legal settlement), which had remained fairly constant at about 8,000 between 1837 and 1855, increased to 10,000 in 1856 and then, during the depression of 1857–58, jumped to 13,000. The opening of three state almshouses in 1854 helped "relieve local [alms]houses of a horde of infants and disabled adults. The wandering poor . . . went workless and unscathed," however. The *Cleveland Leader* complained in 1855 that the "swarms of beggars are becoming more numerous daily. Perfect clouds of them infest the doors and dwellings of our citizens." In New York there were so many mendicants demanding alms during the 1857 depression that the *New York Times* urged the police to arrest "every person, man, woman, or child who may be found begging in the streets." The homeless poor in New York were forced to choose between one of the lodging houses in the lower wards of the city where beds could be had for 3 to 12 cents a night and the police station lockup, where as many as 60 men might be jammed into a 16-foot-square room. In the winter of 1858, hundreds were turned away nightly from overcrowded station houses and left to "walk the streets or find repose in the public markets."[32]

THE PUBLIC RESPONSE to homelessness was not limited to the actions of the police and the courts. For decades, private individuals and local charities had attempted to aid the homeless or to provide assistance to the poor on the verge of becoming homeless. It was traditional for well-to-do citizens to dispense food and fuel to the poor during the winter months, and philanthropists usually increased such activities during periods of high unemployment such as the embargo of 1807 and the depression of 1817–19. A changing mentality about urban poverty, however, led philanthropists to develop larger, more highly organized welfare institutions after the War of 1812. Strong religious beliefs motivated many of these organizations' founders, but as time passed the concern for social order and fears about the weakening of the work ethic among the poor played a more important role in their thinking. Organizations such as the New York Society for the Prevention of Pauperism (NYSPP), founded in 1817, desired "not just the amelioration of the condition of the poor, but the prevention of pauperism itself." The "sentimental approach" to poverty, they believed, should give way to "a more hard-headed attitude." The middle class became increasingly suspicious of the poor, viewing them "as weak individuals who had given in to temptations." By the 1840s, large bureaucratic charities like the Association for Improving the Condition of the Poor (AICP), espousing a harshly moralistic interpretation of poverty, dominated public debate over how best to deal with the increase in poverty and homelessness.[33]

The leaders of the new charities often expressed the fear that poor people would not labor unless forced to do so. Bostonian Ward Stafford argued that "if people believe, that they shall be relieved when in distress, they will not generally make exertions, will not labor when they are able and have the opportunity." Here, in embryo, was a theme that would retain its saliency throughout the century: All poor people were potential vagrants or beggars. As early as 1821, the NYSPP campaigned to outlaw outdoor poor relief altogether and replace it with a workhouse to which all able-bodied paupers, street beggars, and drunkards would be assigned. Boston Unitarian minister Joseph Tuckerman sharply criticized soup kitchens, which he believed only attracted "idlers and vagrants" from nearby towns. The New York AICP refused to have anything to do with vagrants or the homeless at all; their aid was designed only for the "worthy poor." Charles Loring Brace, who founded the Children's Aid Society, believed that the tendency to live a vagrant life must be nipped in the bud, before adulthood. His organization devoted itself to reclaiming young New York City vagabonds by sending them to Midwestern farm homes. "It is true sometimes," Brace assured skeptical readers, "that the habit of vagrancy and idling may be too deeply worked in him for his [the vagrant boy's] character to speedily reform; but, if of tender years, a change of circumstances will nearly always bring a change of character."[34]

The historical literature on nineteenth-century charitable programs for the poor still focuses largely on the large bureaucratic philanthropies. To be sure, the leaders and supporters of such organizations were a highly articulate (and often wealthy) group of people, who in the 1820s and '30s were in the vanguard of changing attitudes toward work, idleness, and charity. By the 1850s their ideas were increasingly influential in the North and were readily compatible with the emerging Republican party ideology of "free soil, free labor, free men."[35] Organizations like the AICP, however, do not tell the whole story. Alternative conceptions of charity continued to exist, providing a counterpoint to the approach favored by the large philanthropies. In southern cities, for example, the treatment of destitute whites continued to be informed by the more personalized and casual approach favored by the slave-holding elite. In Charleston, few wanted to embark on a moral crusade against the "idle poor," partly because idleness per se was not necessarily considered a sin in the mind of the slaveholder. As late as the 1840s, the city almshouse remained an all-purpose institution that housed the sick, the indigent, the homeless, and the insane, much as it had a hundred years before. Free blacks and transients, as well as local whites, received assistance there.[36]

In northern cities as well, the tendency toward harsh, moralistic positions in dealing with the poor by no means completely superseded older patterns of benevolence. In focusing on the first large-scale, citywide welfare organizations, historians have too often ignored a vast network of smaller associations, often at the neighborhood level and sometimes of an ad hoc nature. These societies were much less bureaucratic and professionalized than the larger philanthropies. For this very reason they left few records, and often what knowledge we have of them is filtered through the eyes of officials or reformers who viewed them as unnecessary or even pernicious. There were a great many New Yorkers who practiced what charity reformer Robert Hartley scornfully called "impulsive" almsgiving.[37] Such individuals rejected the new "scientific" approach to poverty and were much less concerned than the more prominent reform groups with modifying the behavior of the poor to conform to a particular ideological agenda. The participants in these small associations believed that citizens should give to the poor out of a sense of civic or religious duty without questioning the motives or morality of the recipients.

The AICP complained that few of the myriad small charitable organizations in the city studied the needs of the poor systematically and followed up their aid with a plan to improve their lives, physically and morally. The association had partly been founded to combat soup houses and other "false and dangerous methods" of charity that, in the words of the directors, promoted "mendacity, vagrancy, and able-bodied pauperism." In the 1850s, however, these views still contended with strong popular opposition. Opponents feared that the bureaucratic techniques favored by the new philanthropies would deny the individual the opportunity to take a personal interest in the objects of charity. No amount of organized effort, *Harper's Weekly* editorialized, could eliminate the need for the "secret charities of the Christian almsgiver."[38]

In spite of rising unemployment during the depressions of 1855 and 1857–58, the AICP continued to maintain its rigorous standards of "worthiness"; in the latter year only one-fourth of those who applied for assistance received it. New Yorkers with a more traditional approach to charity took up the slack. In 1855 relief committees in 12 wards sprang up to distribute clothing and fuel and to establish soup kitchens. These committees received support throughout the city, with people from a wide range of class backgrounds contributing. In other cities the depressions of the 1850s also rejuvenated the traditional approach. In 1857 in Philadelphia, independent "ward associations" to aid the destitute were organized all over the metropolis. Soup kitchens in the city stepped up their operation during the last half of the decade. Their only nod to the more modern methods of organized charity was a limitation on the distribution of free bread in 1857.[39]

An unpublished chronicle of the Western Soup Society of Philadelphia (the organization's activities were limited to the western section of the city) provides a rare glimpse into the operations of a charity that carried forward a traditional attitude toward the destitute. It is unlikely that such an informal history (written in 1948) would have been produced at all had not the society, unlike the vast majority of similar associations, survived and evolved into a more broad-based organization in the twentieth century. Ironically, it is only because the society ultimately became "modern" that a record of its premodern roots has been preserved.[40]

Like many such charities, the Western Soup Society was established during a depression year, 1837, by several anonymous "gentlemen" who believed that the best way to address "the sufferings of the poor" was through the establishment of a soup kitchen. During its first winter the kitchen, open every day but Sunday from 11 A.M. to 1 P.M., provided 15,000 quarts of soup to over a thousand local residents and a "considerable quantity of transient applicants." Undeterred by critics who claimed it was feeding "unworthy, lazy people," the society expanded its operations in 1842 to augment soup with potatoes and rice. In 1845 the association was placed on a better financial footing when it received a bequest from philanthropist Paul Beck. Apparently Beck was anxious that the association not be deterred from its original purpose, because he stipulated that his money be used only to feed the destitute. Four years later—in what surely was an extraordinary activity for the time—the society began a school lunch program for 50 African American students at a nearby school. Throughout its existence, the society's charitable activities would be interracial. In 1863, about 15 percent of those assisted by the society were blacks—over twice their proportion of the population of Philadelphia at that time.

The Western Soup Society was probably one of the best-funded such associations in the city. It was doing well enough financially in 1849 to lend $300 to the Moyamensing Soup Society, and in 1860 it erected a new soup house at a cost of $5,300 (no small amount at the time) and hired a matron to live in it year round. By 1870 it was dispensing fuel and clothing, as well as food, and holding some free night school classes in the building. In the late nineteenth century, the society rejected an offer by the Philadelphia Society for Organizing Charity (PSOC) to take over its operations and turn its building into a "wayfarers' lodge" for homeless men. The association did, however, begin to adopt at least some of the language of the PSOC by calling for closer investigation of applicants for aid and, in 1901, appointing an officer whose job partly involved cooperating with other charities. By 1910 the society had become involved in so many community outreach programs that the dispensing of food became secondary, and in the 1920s the organization changed its name to the Western Community House.

The story of the Western Soup Society is part of the hidden history of urban philanthropic endeavors. Soup societies did not only serve the homeless. Like some later, religiously oriented charities, they also fed the working poor to prevent them from becoming homeless. Unlike the AICP and, after 1878, the Charity Organization Society, soup societies received little publicity. Considering that many such societies existed in a single city, however, their impact was far from insignificant. In Philadelphia, by 1862 they were large enough in number to require a meeting of representatives to define geographic boundaries for their activities.[41]

The resiliency of these local philanthropies in the face of strong public criticism was only one example of the failure of proponents of the new "scientific" charity to carry the day. Another was the strong backlash against attempts to eliminate public outdoor relief—the dispensing of money, food, or fuel by local government to poor people, often with little or no investigation of the "worthiness" of recipients. Only in Philadelphia between 1827 and 1839 and Chicago between 1848 and 1858 was outdoor relief abolished. In the 1820s the New York Society for the Prevention of Pauperism met repeated rebuffs in its efforts to end outdoor aid and place all paupers in a workhouse. In Baltimore, a resolution to give "a decided preference to the deserving poor over the vicious" in the distribution of fuel by the city was defeated by the city council. The increase in the numbers of almshouses after 1820 did not mean that such "indoor" relief was replacing the outdoor variety. In Massachusetts, for example, the number of people granted outdoor relief doubled between 1839 and 1852 and then, after a modest decline, more than doubled again, reaching a total of over 35,000 by 1863. During this same time period, only slightly more than 3,000 paupers per year received aid in local almshouses, and the number staying in state almshouses was even smaller.[42]

Charity reformers criticized local governments' dispensation of outdoor relief as politically motivated, and it undoubtedly was. As Michael B. Katz notes, both before and after the Civil War an effective defense of public relief was carried out by a "coalition of the poor, their friends and relatives, and the merchants who enjoyed their business."[43] Yet this would not have been so politically popular had not many favored a philosophy of benevolence that was distinctly at odds with that of the new charity theorists.

A similar conflict over values was revealed by the continued practice of giving to beggars. Already, in the 1850s, advocates of "scientific philanthropy" were urging citizens to avoid giving money or food to beggars. There is no evidence, however, that such admonitions had much practical effect. Especially during periods of depression or when disaster struck, newspapers urged Christian generosity on their readers. "Better to be a pauper in purse than a pauper in heart," the Cleveland *Daily True Democrat* counseled its readers in 1849. "Better to be an outcast in society than an outcast of God. And we shall make ourselves one or both, whenever or wherever we shut our ears or eyes against sinning or suffering humanity." Such statements were often contradicted—especially during good times—by hostile commentaries on the "undeserving poor." Yet this very inconsistency, during a period when the press was attempting to appeal to a larger and more heterogeneous clientele, may have reflected the uncertainty of its audience as much as that of the editors.[44] The growth of a sentimental attitude toward poverty in popular culture at midcentury further contributed to this ambiguity. Romantic novelists like Charles Dickens encouraged compassion for the poor and sensibility to their suffering, as did melodramatic plays dealing with the themes of disparities of wealth in American cities. Impoverished children elicited a particularly sympathetic response. Both before and after the Civil War, the romanticized image of the homeless child was popular in illustration, art, and fiction. During a period when vagabond "street urchins" were common, such images undermined the sharp divisions between the worthy and the unworthy poor that organized charity tried to establish.[45]

This softening of Victorian moralism was greeted favorably because almost everyone realized that at least some poverty resulted from circumstances beyond the control of the individual—accident, sickness, or adversity of various sorts. As literary scholar John Cawelti notes, "the curious incidence of providence or luck" in early didactic novels raised some doubts about the conventional belief in success through perseverance and sobriety. Just as Horatio Alger's protagonists had an "astounding propensity for chance encounters with benevolent and useful friends," so too in the novels of Alger's predecessors of the 1830s and '40s did a happy ending result when the hero "falls in love with a charming young lady who turns out to be the governor's daughter; or discovers that he is the long-lost heir to a great fortune."

If success was partly the result of chance, might this not also be true of failure? The thought undoubtedly gnawed at many a reader of the following poem, entitled "Homeless," which appeared in *The Knickerbocker* during the depression of 1858:

I sit in the Park alone,
The dead leaves are round me blown; . . .
I once had houses and lands,
And friends with generous hands,
And a Love who sung
With a honeyed tongue
When I had houses and lands.
Now I have not even a hut,
And the generous hands are shut
And my Love's proud eyes
Cannot recognize
Him without even a hut.

The dark side of the success myth—the fear of falling, even to the level of the beggar class—was not a prominent theme in American literature of the nineteenth century, especially during the antebellum era. Yet during the depressions of the 1850s, which shook the nation's economy more severely than earlier financial panics, it must have been on the minds of many people. In Philadelphia, vagrancy convictions reached a new high of 2,747 in 1855, then skyrocketed to 7,488 two years later. The city established a special mendicancy squad (the "beggar detectives") to deal with the problem, but the officers found it difficult "to keep our streets clear of adult vagrants whilst the inspectors of the prison are obliged, from want of room, to discharge them, thus thwarting our exertions to perform our duty." Destitute beggars were a constant reminder that economic mobility was a two-way street, that—in a society with no safety net—losing everything and slipping into homelessness was far from impossible, even for the middle class.[46]

Although by the 1850s the problem of the homeless unemployed was already severe in many cities, the issue of vagrancy did not attract national attention as it would two decades later. This was not solely because the looming struggle between North and South made such an issue seem insignificant. To a much greater degree than would later be the case, vagrancy was still a local problem, and the solutions (such as they were) to it and arguments about it remained local. The unsafe nature of railroad travel before the Civil War, when "flimsy tracks, hazardous curves, unstable bridges and dangerous inclines" were common, discouraged the homeless from riding the freights.[47] Equally important, the relatively short length of trains made it easy for railroad crews to detect nonpaying passengers. It was infeasible for the poor in search of work to travel long distances, and except along the New York to Baltimore corridor, the geographic mobility of vagabonds usually encompassed a fairly small radius. Most probably never left the vicinity of their hometown.[48] Wherever they went, the homeless had to go on foot. Travel along the plank roads connecting the far-flung towns of upstate New York, western Pennsylvania, and much of the Midwest was difficult.[49] As a result, the problem of vagabondage and begging was largely restricted to the emerging large cities and to smaller communities in New England and the Middle Atlantic states, where the roads connecting towns were well developed.

The frequent encounter of city dwellers with the homeless during the antebellum era was not an experience shared by all Americans. In 1860, over 80 percent of the nation still lived in rural areas and small towns, many of which were vital communities with relatively little poverty. Although in the 1850s the upward path to farm ownership that had been open for agricultural laborers earlier in the century was disappearing, property ownership in rural areas and small towns in the North was still much more widespread than in urban centers, and on the eve of the Civil War there were a great many small communities like Kingston, New York, that were still undergoing vigorous expansion and relative prosperity.[50] These communities did not suffer much from vagrants or beggars. A study of one rural Wisconsin county during the first 20 years of its existence, 1846–66, found that only 4 of the 117 individuals received into the county poorhouse during this period were "transient paupers." In his retrospective *Life on the Mississippi*, which dealt with the antebellum period, Mark Twain described an incident of a "poor stranger, a harmless whiskey-sodden tramp" (he would not have been known by that term then) who had wandered into Hannibal, Missouri. The vagabond was viewed as something of an oddity by the townspeople, and "a troop of bad little boys followed him around and amused themselves with nagging and annoying him." Rare was the vagabond, one memoirist later recalled, who "used to hobo through Nebraska and Wyoming before there were any railroads."[51]

By 1860 the Republican party's free-labor ideology, emphasizing the economic independence of workers and the opportunity to achieve middle-class status, was triumphant in the very areas of the North where homelessness was least significant. Conditions in the nation's rapidly growing cities indicated that the social and economic foundation of the Republican philosophy—in which the work ethic and mobility through land ownership were still largely taken for granted—was already being undermined. But the citizens of the rural and small-town North, focusing upon the "slave power" as the chief enemy of their way of life, scarcely comprehended this. They did not believe that any major reorganization of northern life was likely—or necessary. Although they recognized that the nation would, of course, continue to expand westward, they felt the future would be very much like the present: a predominantly agricultural, locally controlled society with small-scale industry, where diligent workers could obtain economic independence, either as farmers or as small capitalists.[52]

The emergence of the tramp in the 1870s was one of the first indications that they were mistaken.

ONE POSITIVE EFFECT OF THE CIVIL WAR,

an author commented in the *United States Service Magazine* in 1864, will be the development of "an orderly spirit and a settled regard for law. . . . Men trained in the stern, unyielding discipline of the camp, knowing by experience its power and value, will not be apt hastily to violate the law of the land themselves or excuse its violation in others." It is likely that a new respect for discipline was one of the most important lessons learned by the average soldier. Yet the effects of the Civil War in inculcating order were far from unambiguous. Not all habits born of the wartime experience—even those that involved organized and regulated behavior—could be readily adapted to civilian life. If the war made some men more settled and orderly, perhaps even more accepting of the new mechanized factory work that was coming into being, it produced in others precisely the opposite result. Indirectly, the war helped to transform the experience of homelessness in the late nineteenth century.[1]

Chapter 3.

The Emergence

of the Tramp,

1865–1880

The Civil War gave large numbers of men their first opportunity to use the railroad. Especially for the North, the movement of troops by rail was a significant part of the war effort and contributed substantially to the Union victory. Soldiers normally traveled in boxcars or cattle cars, herded together much like the animals for whom the conveyances had been designed. A similar experience awaited them after the general demobilization in the spring of 1865. "Many rode in cattle cars, as they had done going up to the front," noted one observer. "Others on the Baltimore and Ohio going west were put in coal cars, so packed that they could neither lie down nor stretch out." Some rode on the roofs of cars or even "lashed themselves and their blankets to the footboards." Their experience in riding trains during the war would bear a close resemblance to that of the men who became tramps in the decades following the war.[2]

There was another way in which army life helped lay the groundwork for tramping: it gave many soldiers the opportunity to engage in foraging expeditions in small groups. Under the discipline of experienced officers, foraging was a perfectly valid military maneuver, often necessary to obtain food to supplement the inadequate diet of army rations. "Peaches and apples were plentiful and orchard fences easy to climb," noted a historian of one Union regiment operating in Mississippi, and officers sent wagons into the country every other day to gather corn and fruit. Southern soldiers depended to an even greater degree upon foraging to obtain food, as well as other necessities. As the conflict wore on, noted Union soldier John Billings, the line between legitimate expropriation of essentials and the theft of valuables gradually disappeared. "[C]onscientious scruples stepped to the rear, and the soldier who had them at the end of the war was a curiosity indeed." Farms near main roads in the South were stripped by both armies. During Sherman's march through Georgia and South Carolina, foraging frequently degenerated into a rampage of pilfering and property destruction. Yet the activities of Sherman's troops were hardly unique. The general's "traveling picnic," Billings astutely observed, simply illustrated "in a *wholesale* way the kind of business other armies did on a *retail* scale." The Confederates, too, became increasingly undisciplined as the war proceeded. In western Virginia in 1864, soldiers of both armies pillaged and plundered, despite orders not to do so.[3]

This behavior hardly reflected the "unyielding discipline" conservatives hoped army life would produce. It was, however, an education of sorts, and one that was put to good use by many of the men who became tramps in the 1870s. Only a few memoirs of tramp life actually mention individuals who went from the army into a life of tramping, but this is probably because most of these reminiscences were published after 1900, by which time a new generation of vagabonds, born too late to have participated in the war, were now on the road.[4] But the parallels between life in the army during the war and life on the road after its conclusion are too numerous to be mere coincidence. The tramp "colonies"—later called "jungles"—had many characteristics of army camp life, and tramps living in these colonies often foraged for food from surrounding farms in much the same manner as soldiers had during the war. It should come as no surprise that the annual "encampments" of the Grand Army of the Republic (the Union veterans' organization) always attracted a large number of tramps.[5]

Even the words "tramp" and "bum," as applied to the homeless, can be traced to the Civil War era. Billings spoke of small bands of soldiers going off "on a tramp" of their own. In 1871, Massachusetts state charity officials were using the word as a noun to refer to wandering vagabonds who roamed the rural areas of the commonwealth. By 1875 the term was being applied more specifically to railroad-riding vagrants, especially those of a violent disposition.[6] "Bum" was derived from "bummer," defined by British visitor James Burn as a soldier "keen on the scent of rebels, or bacon, or silver spoons, or corn, or anything valuable." Even before the end of the war, "bum" was sometimes substituted for "bummer" and was first used as a term of derision against foraging soldiers. In 1868 the *New York Times* used "bummers" as a synonym for vagrants for the first time, identifying them as "men who hate the discipline of life, detest marching in the ranks of workers, and hold industry in abomination." The definition neatly connected the ideas of rebellion against military discipline with a supposed rejection of the work ethic. By 1872 Charles Loring Brace was using "bumming" to refer to urban vagrants' habit of sleeping outside during mild weather, and in 1877 newspapers broadened the use of the term even further, calling striking railroad workers and their sympathizers "the bummer element."[7]

The negative effects of serving in the war led some veterans down a path that could end in homelessness. Physically wounded ex-soldiers often received assistance in soldiers' homes or from charities or friends, but the psychically wounded, or those who simply found civilian life difficult to adjust to, were accorded less sympathy. The three-year postwar recession did not help veterans to adjust. Some soldiers reenlisted in the army to serve in the West, where they exhibited the same undisciplined behavior common among the bummers of the Civil War, but the postwar army was far too small to absorb more than a fraction of the discontented or unemployed.[8]

In the immediate postwar period, a considerable number of former soldiers slid into a life of vagrancy or petty crime. Prison officials in Massachusetts, Pennsylvania, and Illinois found that two-thirds of their charges in 1866 and 1867 were veterans. "Vagrancy—which was checked by the war, now seems to be largely on the increase," said F. B. Sanborn, secretary of the Massachusetts State Charities Board, in 1867. Sanborn noted that the number of homeless wanderers in the state using public facilities had doubled in just one year. The commonwealth passed a new vagrancy law in 1866, but it had little effect on the small towns, where vagabonds continued to use local almshouses. If anything, the number of homeless persons using local facilities increased, because vagabonds now avoided the state almshouses for fear of being sentenced to a term in the workhouse. In the cities, too, the number of dislocated people seeking temporary lodging in police station houses increased sharply following the war. During the summer of 1867 over 1,400 "indigent persons" received lodging at the central station house in Cleveland, and by the following winter the overcrowding of that facility was even worse, "there being an unusual number of homeless, moneyless wanderers found without a place to lay their heads."[9]

Despite the postwar increase in homelessness, the problem occasioned little public debate. With the exception of Massachusetts, which may have suffered more from this phenomenon than other states, public officials did not exhibit much concern, and even there the comments that were forthcoming were often rather subdued. One official there stated that, among the homeless receiving aid from the commonwealth in 1871, there were "many honestly seeking work, though of the more shiftless class." Though hardly objective, such comments were far more conciliatory than would later be the case. The relative size of the homeless population immediately following the war, after all, was not much larger than it had been during the depression of 1858, and by 1870 the latest upsurge seemed to be subsiding. Reassuringly, Massachusetts officials predicted at that time that "the vagabond class has reached its maximum, and may be expected to materially diminish."[10]

Far from being the end of the vagrancy problem, however, the 1870s marked its beginning as a recognized national issue. The depression that commenced in the fall of 1873 and steadily deepened during the next three years produced widespread unemployment. Wage cuts and layoffs fueled worker discontent and led, in 1877, to the most violent confrontation between labor and management that had occurred until that time. Accompanying the economic decline and social turmoil of these years was a dramatic increase in the size of the homeless population. "The most significant thing in the year's returns seems to me to be the figures relating to vagrancy," noted the secretary of the State Charities Board of Massachusetts in 1874. Excluding the police station "lodgers" in Boston, the number of reported vagrants was 98,263, more than three times the number reported in 1872. The number of "lodgings" in Boston for the year was 57,014, compared with 35,667 two years before. The actual number of persons receiving lodging in almshouses, jails, or police stations was much smaller than these numbers indicate since many men received assistance or lodging more than once, but they do accurately measure the relative growth of the homeless population during these years.[11]

The increase during 1873–74 was only the beginning. Between 1874 and 1878, relief was provided to the homeless over 200,000 times each year by city and town authorities in Massachusetts. During the same period, vagrancy arrests grew by 50 percent in New York City, while the number of men and women using the police stations for overnight lodging in Philadelphia increased almost fourfold.[12]

This increase was not only greater in magnitude than that of previous depressions, it also affected a wider range of communities. Writing in 1875, the *New York Times* editorialized that 10 years earlier only a few rag-tag "cadgers" could be seen tramping the country roads; now, however, they had become a cause for concern among both citizenry and public officials in many rural areas. Data from three representative Massachusetts towns indicate that, proportionate to their populations, vagrancy had become as much of a problem in outlying communities as in major urban centers (see table 3.1). The relative effect on small Midwestern communities was even greater. There, because of the distance between villages and the lack of adequate roads in many areas, vagabondage had been even less of a concern before the Civil War.[13]

What made the spread of homelessness to small towns and the countryside possible, of course, was the railroad. The period between 1865 and 1880 saw a vast expansion of the rail network in the United States. "The railroads are doing wonders for this country," one traveler wrote in his diary in 1871. "Facility of travel makes people homogeneous and a man in Bloomington or Quincy is just as well posted as in Chicago." Travel became easier not only for legitimate passengers but also for those who wished to ride illegally. The increasing length of trains and greater variety in the types of cars made it easier for a man to stow himself away undetected. Standardization in the construction of cars also made it possible for him to

TABLE 3.1.   Number of Times Selected Towns Gave Relief to Vagrants, 1868–1878

	1868–69	1870–71	1872–73	1874–75	1877–78
Dedham	562	764	829	1,539	3,161
Abington	61	76	122	308	505
Brookfield	89	94	166	415	350

Source: *Annual Reports* of the State Board of Charities of Massachusetts, 1869–1878 (Boston, 1869–1878).

gain a kind of rudimentary knowledge of trains that he could utilize regardless of what "line" he was riding on. Illegal train-riding was never a safe practice, but by the 1870s the risks that it entailed had at least become more predictable. These factors, and the increasing interconnectedness of rail lines, made possible the emergence of a new type of mobile homeless man. Vagabonds did not cease entirely to walk from town to town, but increasingly they would view travel on foot more as an adjunct to train riding than as an acceptable alternative to it. "From Maine to 'Frisco' the railroads are at the tramp's disposal, if he knows how to use them," journalist Josiah Flynt observed in the 1890s, "and seldom does he take to the turnpike from any necessity."[14]

The sudden increase in the number of homeless, coupled with their adoption of the railroad as a means of travel, lifted the vagrancy issue to a level of social significance that it had not previously been accorded. No longer was the idle beggar a stereotyped bit-player in the drama of the evil big city. Now, unexpectedly, he was a palpable reality even in small-town and rural New England and the Midwest. This situation insured that many Americans would respond with deep antagonism to the new vagrancy. The conflict that arose was heightened by the aggressive and sometimes violent behavior of tramps in the 1870s and 1880s, which called forth an equal if not more hostile reaction on the part of railroad workers and rural communities. The phrase "army of the unemployed," widely used during the last quarter of the nineteenth century, was more than a convenient metaphor. Compared to a later generation of homeless men, the tramps of the 1870s were much more assertive in declaring their "right" to free transportation, much more willing to use the threat of force. Especially in the late 1870s, tramps commandeered trains and fought pitched battles with authorities, inducing fear in isolated communities, even if the vagabonds seldom actually attacked inhabitants.

"Tramps are reported very numerous and troublesome on the railroads in Wisconsin," the *Railroad Gazette* noted in 1876. "They travel in gangs and ride on the freight trains, in many cases being too numerous for the trainmen to deal with, and they are careful to leave the train before reaching any place with a police force large enough to take care of them." Train crews everywhere had similar experiences. A correspondent from Ohio told of a large gang of men who "captured" a train and forced the engineer to take them to another destination. Acting much like Civil War bummers, before boarding they "appropriated a lot of boots and shoes to their own use from a country store." The tramps, a *New York Times* reporter observed, "are fierce fellows [who] jump on engines and direct engineers to stop, manage brakes themselves, and stop in country places and raid on farm houses for food, returning to [the] trains when satisfied. They threaten to destroy property if inter-fered with." Some tramps were quite willing to carry out such threats. Two men ejected from a train attempted "out of sheer spite" to wreck the follow-ing train by placing obstructions on the track.[15]

The response of train crews to tramps at this time was hostile and fre-quently violent, often justifiably so. Brakemen and conductors carried pis-tols and were not reluctant to use them, and nothing was more common than to read of fistfights or an exchange of shots between train crews and "surly" tramps. On numerous occasions one or more of both groups were injured or killed.[16] The reaction of trainmen, however, was sometimes unnecessarily vicious. The abiding antagonism of many railroad workers was reflected in a series of darkly humorous stories in the *Railroad Gazette* that told of vagrants being accidently locked in a refrigerator car and "half frozen"; of tramps in a cattle car being "perfectly at home with swine"; of a tramp who was almost asphyxiated when he started a fire in a sealed boxcar. Some train crews looked forward to confrontations with tramps as an opportunity to relive old glory days. Unwanted passengers, one railroad worker stated, could make a trainman's job "as exciting and almost as dangerous as that of a cavalryman during the war."[17]

These violent confrontations led to a series of court decisions regarding ejection of people from moving trains, but the fine legal distinctions drawn in many cases had little effect on railroad workers' conduct. A carrier owed no duty to a trespasser on a train and could eject him at any time. If the per-son in question was injured in the process, he could not recover damages except in the rare instance that the train crew had attempted to "wantonly" or "recklessly" injure him. Nor, in most cases, was a trespasser justified in resisting ejection. Not until 1920 did the Utah Supreme Court rule that a trainman's "threats of violence" to a trespasser, if it caused him to lose his "self-control" and injure himself in falling or jumping from a train, would be grounds for recovery of damages. All of this, of course, presumed an injured plaintiff. Dead men brought no law suits. "If a brakeman throws a tramp off a train and he is killed," one correspondent observed in 1883, "you will generally read an item about an unknown tramp, while trying to steal a ride, having fallen between the wheels or something of that kind, but we know better."[18]

The danger that tramps posed to people living close to railroad lines was frequently exaggerated, and vagabonds were probably accused of many crimes they did not commit. "If a barn is burnt," one tramp related to social reformer John J. McCook, "the first theory is some tramp set it on fire, when it was some of the drunken careless hoodlums of the community more careless than a tramp ever thought of being." Professional thieves operating in towns along rail lines could also count on blame being placed first on tramps and "bums" in the vicinity.[19] Although tramps seldom engaged in violence against individual citizens, however, the assertive demeanor of some vagabonds could be frightening, especially to people in isolated settlements. The *Times* editorialists were justified in claiming, in 1875, that there were many men on the road who begged for food "in a masterful, threatening way." In 1877 there were reports of tramps descending on summer resorts in New England, "camping together by scores in the woods, begging, stealing, drinking, and fighting." In his retrospective novel *The Vacation of the Kelwyns: An Idyl of the 1870s*, William Dean Howells captured the nebulous fear of the residents of these communities when rumors spread of men in ragged clothing wandering along little-used local roads. Another Howells novel, *The Undiscovered Country* (1884), portrayed a man and his daughter as terrified when, while walking through the woods, they come upon a group of tramps sitting around a campfire:

> One [tramp] held a tilted bottle to his mouth, and another clutched at it; the rest were shouting and singing. As Egeria and her father came into the range of the firelight, the men saw them. They yelled to them to stop and have a drink. The one with the bottle snatched up a brand from the fire with his left hand and ran toward them. [He tripped and fell, however, and the pair] fled into the shadows beyond the light.

Farmers living near the Erie Railroad line north of New York City may have found much to identify with in this passage. In 1884, a group of tramps who regularly camped in the woods in Rockland County became "unusually bold and desperate." The men "roamed among the villages and among the farmers, demanding food in [the] daytime and breaking into farmhouses and out-buildings at night." The tramps sometimes avenged themselves against farmers who refused them food by killing livestock.[20]

This type of behavior resulted in a series of fierce confrontations between tramps and the residents of towns and smaller cities. In July 1877, for example, a large group of tramps were run out of Altoona, Pennsylvania, only to descend upon Harrisburg. In a pitched battle, police there finally "routed forty of them from the stockyards." A similar incident occurred the following year near Fulton, Kentucky. Throughout the eastern states in the late 1870s and 1880s there were reports of vigilante committees being formed, threatening to lynch vagrants. In 1885 citizens in Anderson, Indiana, removed four tramps from the local jail, "whipped [them] until they bled," and chased them out of town. Continued depredations by tramps in the farming areas in Westchester County, New York, finally led authorities there to raid the vagabonds' hideout. The resulting free-for-all was dubbed "The Battle of the Tramps" by the New York *Tribune*.[21]

In 1877, the Clarion, Pennsylvania, *Democrat* declared that tramps were "leeches, fastening themselves on the vitals of society, sucking its life blood from it, producing loathesome and festering sores that cannot be healed." The "alien" nature of the new class of vagrants, as much as their aggressive demeanor, inspired such rhetoric. The *Democrat* might console itself that the tramp phenomenon was increasing "especially in the South and in our cities," but the real problem now lay closer to home. As early as 1871 the Pennsylvania State Charities Board had noted the "large number of vagrants" who were in the habit of using the county almshouses, "sometimes in such numbers as to render it difficult to accommodate them. They remain over night, receive a meal or two and depart in the morning and apply again in the evening for admission in an adjoining county." The tramp represented an unwanted intrusion of the urban industrial world into rural America, and he was a not very subtle reminder to those who lived in rural areas or small communities that they were no longer immune from urban problems.[22]

The harsh initial response to the tramp, however, was not limited to the hinterland; it was widespread throughout American society, especially the middle class. It is impossible to overstate the hostility of the educated public to the tramps in the 1870s and '80s. "They are like the barbarians who came down like wolves upon Rome!" exclaimed the *New York Tribune*. The editors of *Scribner's* likened them to lepers. William H. Brewer, writing in the *New Englander*, came close to advocating the extermination of this "dangerous element" through any means necessary. The *Chicago Tribune*, not altogether with tongue in cheek, seemed to promote just such a solution: "The simplest plan, probably, where one is not a member of the Humane Society, is to put a little strychnine or arsenic in the meat and the supplies furnished the tramp." In a similar vein, the protagonist in *The Vacation of the Kelwyns* asks a gun dealer at one point what kind of weapon would be "good for tramps."[23]

Behind this humor there lurked a scarcely concealed urge to strike back against what was perceived as "the most dangerous class in society." "The tramp," one writer argued, "is a man who can be approached by no other motive but pain—the pain of a thrashing or the pain of hunger." The dehumanization of the homeless unemployed in articles and stories of the 1870s helped to justify such sentiments. It may not be a coincidence that the literature on tramps and vagrants in libraries was shelved between books on poverty in general and those dealing with the rights of animals. The new vagrants were often perceived as something subhuman or, at best, uncivilized. Yale Professor Francis Wayland called the new type of homeless man "a lazy, shiftless, sauntering or swaggering, ill-conditioned, irreclaimable, incorrigible, cowardly, utterly depraved savage." In 1882 the *New York Tribune* described the tramp as a "creature, midway between the vegetable and animal world," similar to "primeval man," and not unlike "reptiles in general." The behavior of tramps, said Brewer, was "very analogous to that of a hardy, prolific, warlike tribe of Indian savages" planning an attack on a "settlement of peaceful, industrious whites." At a time when the annihilation of General George Armstrong Custer's regiment by Sioux warriors was still fresh in people's minds, such language almost invited a violent response to the new class of homeless men. In effect, the comparison racialized unemployed workers on the road, equating them with "primitive" people who themselves were often portrayed as drunken and lazy.[24]

Another theme popular in newspaper accounts and fiction was the tramp as criminal. Much like contemporary reports of black men in the South accused of assaulting white females, alleged tramp violence against women received sensationalistic coverage in the press, helping to create an image that demonized the homeless man. Many commentators portrayed tramps as "treacherous, cowardly, brutal" men who would rob, rape, and kill when they were not begging or drinking. Lee Harris's novel *The Man Who Tramps* (1878) portrayed the homeless as "drawn from the most vicious classes of society." Harris's fictional tramps were eager to "gratify their desire for destruction and plunder." In one scene, two tramps kill an innocent farmer and steal his hard-earned savings, only to be robbed in turn by another tramp. Horatio Alger's *Tony the Tramp* presented a similar image. The sinister Rudolph, an older tramp who forces the young Tony to travel with him, has no qualms about robbing a farmer who befriends them. Later in the novel he tries to murder his companion by throwing him down a well. Throughout the story, vagabond life is depicted as synonymous with a life of crime.[25]

The perception of the tramp as violent or dangerous was widespread in the 1870s and '80s, but there were many who believed tramps had the desires of genuine criminals but lacked the will. Professor Wayland's vicious portrait of the typical tramp was tempered somewhat by his conclusion that the homeless man was also "lazy" and "cowardly," hence not fully able to act upon his malicious tendencies. *The Nation* spoke of a growing "half-criminal element," composed not of the violent but of "the shiftless, the fickle, the irresolute, and the characterless." By the turn of the century this view of the homeless man predominated. Most vagabonds, Josiah Flynt wrote in 1902, were "discouraged criminals." The typical tramp could never succeed as a professional burglar or bank robber because he lacked "criminal wit."[26]

It was taken for granted that the vast majority of the new class of vagrants were foreign-born. "The New York beggars are mainly foreigners," stated one author in 1871. "Scarcely an American is seen on the streets in this capacity." The native-born were often given the benefit of the doubt in this regard. A Wisconsin charity official, commenting in 1876 on the tramps in his state, admitted he had no data on the nationalities of these men, but this did not stop him from adding that "almost all were evidently of foreign birth." Even after statistical information discrediting this idea became available in the 1890s, there were those who continued to cling to the myth of an "imported" vagabond class.[27]

Until the arrival of immigrants from southern and eastern Europe beginning in the 1880s, most Americans believed that the foreign-born would ultimately assimilate American values. Likewise, most held that the poor in general, however degraded, were capable of improving their condition and entering the mainstream of American life.[28] It is an indication of the depth of the hostility to the new class of homeless men, then, that many commentators believed that tramps were "incorrigible." Homeless men, said one writer in 1877, were "incurable" in their habits; the return of good times would thus have little effect in reducing their numbers. "As a rule the tramp is irreclaimable," echoed the New York *Tribune*, "as he does not take to the road until civilization has become too much for him." Although there was little evidence for it, the idea persisted into the early twentieth century that a workman who tramped for as little as two or three weeks would degenerate rapidly into a permanent vagrant. "Tramping is a vice, that, first endured, is finally embraced and adopted as a vocation," the Massachusetts State Charities Board stated, "and many persons who took to the road originally from real or fancied necessity, will undoubtedly remain vagabonds to the end of their days or until they get into prison."[29]

From this idea it was only a short step to the belief that vagrancy was hereditary. In *The Dangerous Classes of New York City* (1872), Charles Loring Brace came close to arguing that the "disease of pauperism" was hereditary. Five years later, Richard Dugdale's influential study, *The Jukes*, provided a more scientific justification for this conclusion by purporting to show how both pauperism and criminality could be transmitted from one generation to another. Dugdale reflected the common belief that paupers and criminals were two poles on a single spectrum of deviant behavior. While he did not specifically use the word "tramp," that was undoubtedly what he had in mind when he spoke of a median type that was too weak to engage in normal criminal behavior, yet too strong to live the life of an almshouse inmate for any length of time. Authors like William Brewer were quick to apply Dugdale's hereditarian theme to the tramp problem.[30]

Although the "scientific" basis for identifying criminals by physical characteristics was little known in the United States prior to 1890, popular writers were already applying such stereotypes to tramps as early as the 1870s. Descriptions emphasized the "brutal" features of the new vagrants. "His eyes were small and piggish," said Harris of one of his fictional tramps; "his nose was flat, and his mouth was large and sensual. His complexion was exceedingly florid, and he had that appearance of filthy dilapidation common to the worst class of tramps." Animalistic features were often combined with vague ethnic stereotypes that reinforced the notion that the new vagrants were immigrants. In Alger's novel Rudolph is depicted as having black, "piercing" eyes; he is "tall and dark-complexioned, with a sinister look . . . [and] a low, receding brow." Alger implies that Rudolph's propensity to wander is inherited, since he is "of gypsy blood." On the other hand, the hero of this maudlin tale, Tony, bears "not the slightest resemblance" to the older man. Underneath the dirt and grime "his features were regular and strikingly handsome," and he had chestnut hair and blue eyes. Tony's features mirror a finer moral sense, which allows him eventually to break away from Rudolph's way of life. Andy Offitt, the tramplike "labor organizer" in John Hay's anonymous 1883 novel *The Bread-Winners*, is described in terms similar to those that depict Alger's villain. He had a "low and shining forehead covered by reeking black hair, worn rather long" and a countenance "which could change in a moment from a dog-like fawning to a snaky venomousness."[31]

Criminality and immigrant background were key aspects of the emerging image of the homeless man, but the characteristic stressed most often was the tramp's "utterly hopeless laziness—a laziness so all pervading and controlling that the wretched being possessed by it is actually incapable of memory, hope, ambition, love and gratitude." Many middle-class commentators claimed that tramps were not "honest laborers in quest of work, but knaves who have determined, if possible, to live without it." "It cannot be alleged," the *New York Times* editorialized, "that the cause [of tramping] is in lack of employment, and that a revival of business activity will correct the evil, for not one tramp in a hundred will accept any sort of situation." Not to be outdone in hyperbole, the *Tribune* claimed that "the proportion of really unfortunate persons" among the men on the road "is not more than one in a thousand."[32]

The tramps' alleged failure to adhere to the work ethic resonated strongly with northerners because it challenged deeply held values over which, many believed, the Civil War had been fought. In the wake of Union victory, something of a sectional consensus had emerged, identifying the virtues of work, productivity, and self-denial as superior aspects of northern society. Such views were not limited to the middle class but were found among the working class as well, especially among laborers who adhered to a more "modern," individualist ethos. Chief among these were the railroad workers, who saw their jobs as offering substantial upward mobility. New York State welfare officials spoke for more than themselves when they stated that "man is so constituted, bodily and mentally, that happiness is found only in connection with constant and systematic labor." "Steady, plodding work," said Dugdale, "is the characteristic not only of honest and successful individuals, but also of all nations that have made a mark in history." The end of slavery and the aristocratic pretensions of the South, achieved at such a terrible cost, would be futile unless the free labor doctrine and "the primacy of work" remained strong in areas outside the vanquished Confederacy. It was vitally important, then, that the tramp "menace" be suppressed.[33]

If work was one's salvation and idleness a vice, it is no wonder that the tramp was portrayed as he was. In a nation comprised, ideally, of sturdy yeomen, small capitalists, and upwardly mobile working men, he seemed a footloose, goalless wanderer, living not by his hands but by his wits and—worst of all—in the dissipation of idleness. It was the factor of idleness that made it possible for some to condemn the tramp while approving—even glorifying—newsboys, despite their many vagabond traits. Brace praised the boys' "sturdy independence" and saw them as incipient capitalists, "independent dealers." The tramp, on the other hand, said popular author Elizabeth Oakes Smith, "hates work; he has no respect and no shame." This, more than any other characteristic ascribed to the homeless man, justified extreme methods for dealing with him. As one writer put it, "by counting himself permanently out of the productive and self-supporting forces of society," the tramp "counts himself out of his rights." He urged legislators to "throw away all sentimentality" and establish workhouses exclusively for vagrants. Another commentator, believing tramps were "incurable," recommended that they be placed in lunatic asylums.[34]

If, in the nation that above all others honored and rewarded productive labor, some seemed to prefer idleness, this was not seen as a weakness in the society or the economic system. Rather it was a sign of depravity in the class of men who became vagrants. After the riots of 1877, however, a number of writers came forward with another possible explanation: the tramp was a subversive, a carrier of alien ideas. This concept was particularly appealing to those who, through selective memory, believed that before the war "there was hardly any beggary in all the country." The sudden appearance of men riding the rails in the 1870s was perplexing, and a conspiratorial view helped put to rest doubts that there might be deeper causes of the phenomenon.[35]

What amounted to America's first "red scare" occurred in the 1870s. As Nell Irvin Painter has pointed out, the violence of the Paris Commune of 1871 haunted the imagination of Americans as the depression deepened and labor conflict intensified. With little proof for their allegations, businessmen and newspaper editors saw the "spectre of Communism" behind every strike.[36] Without ignoring other aspects of the image of the tramp, some commentators began to focus on what they perceived as the political radicalism of the new vagrants. A prime cause of the increase of tramping, the *Tribune* editorialized, was "the growth of that communistic literature which flatters the indolent with the assurance that the world owes them a living." According to this view, the new, mobile homeless man was a semicriminal, communistic agitator whose goal was nothing less than the overthrow of American democracy through devious means. If unchecked, the tramp "tribe" would "gather strength enough to threaten our political system, if not, indeed, our civilization." A Westport, New York, resident believed the new vagrants had "become a guild, and it is by no means sure how nearly they have approximated a rude and modified form of secret association. In time they will be prepared for combination and for leadership, and the latter will be in superabundant supply."[37]

In fulminating against subversives, some observers conflated the images of the criminal, the labor agitator, and the tramp. Allan Pinkerton, who for the most part was careful not to confuse these types, nevertheless spoke of "the hundreds of thieves, communists, and tramps, too cowardly to fight, but just shrewd enough to be on hand for prey" during the riot at Pittsburgh, while the Chicago *Times* pictured immigrant trade-unionists in terms similar to those used to describe tramps—"sallow Bohemians and Poles, dirty and ragged renegade Frenchmen, stupefied by idleness, and Germans, outcasts from the society of their own nation, mingled in a filthy snarling crowd."[38]

This confusing, conspiratorial image of the tramp was exemplified by two books published in 1878: Lee Harris's *The Man Who Tramps* and a short volume by Frank Bellew, *The Tramp: His Tricks, Tallies, and Tell-Tales with All His Signs, Countersigns, Grips, Pass-Words, and Villainies Exposed.* Though written as a novel, *The Man Who Tramps* was a thinly disguised polemic against tramps, designed to "arouse the people to the danger of longer ignoring the evil." Harris portrayed the typical vagabond as an unemployed ne'er-do-well who, "having tasted of the fountain of indolence," had "lost all wish to labor." According to Harris, many tramps were recent immigrants, their heads filled with a crude ideology that somehow managed to combine socialism with burglary. "I tell you they're after no good," related one "honest" mechanic of the tramps. "I stumbled onto a camp of 'em once and there was a feller there makin' a sort o' speech to 'em, and he told 'em that things was a goin' to be fixed up so's they'd all git rich. They was goin' to divide up things, he said, and they'd all git a share."[39]

There were three types of tramps, according to Harris: the indolent vagrant; the criminal tramp; and the "political tramp," who spread inflammatory doctrines that "threatened the very life of the nation." Many of the latter, Harris announced, were "vicious agitators, who had tasted the intoxication of anarchy and bloodshed" during the Commune of 1871 and "when driven from France found a refuge here." Tramps readily impersonated workers seeking employment, but their real goal was more sinister. The tramp "commits deeds of violence in the name of workingmen only that he may plunder from rich and poor alike." Far from being disorganized and impoverished, the vagabonds were actually well-fed members of a "fraternity" that was "regularly organized and officered." The fraternity was not a union of equals, however. The political tramps gave orders that the men under them "dare not disobey." Tramps, one of these leaders predicted, "are the beginning of a new order of things, and the time will come when they will be no longer vagrants, but rulers in this land."[40]

Bellew focused even more intensely on the conspiratorial theme. The tramps, he claimed, were "under a most perfect system of organization, and ready at any moment, when the opportunity arises, to hurl their power at the throat of organized society." The vagrants were required to swear a "blood oath" of comradeship and secrecy, and they used passwords and secret handshakes. They also had "a certain set of signs, or hieroglyphics, which they mark up, with chalk, on houses, fences, trees, &c., as a guide to others" who travel down the same road. Bellew portrayed the tramp organization as hierarchical; local leaders kept in contact with a "grand central lodge somewhere out West." As many as half a million tramps across the country, Bellow claimed, "could be concentrated at various points in less than a week." During any labor conflict, they would "aid the revolutionary party, strikers, or what not, and reap a large harvest of plunder."[41]

The conspiratorial designs of the tramps, as painted by Harris, Bellew, and others, were in most particulars inventions of the imagination. Tramps certainly participated in the mob violence associated with the railroad strikes of 1877, but their behavior was as haphazard and unplanned as that of most strikers. Tramps often traveled in large groups, but these groups seldom remained intact for very long, and it is unlikely that they engaged in any ongoing organization. Even criminal tramps, two Massachusetts detectives discovered, planned no further ahead than where to meet after each "job" was completed. Men became tramps for many reasons but seldom for explicit ideological motives. Their behavior may have entailed an element of rebellion, but it was almost entirely prepolitical in nature.[42]

The more extreme examples of antitramp propaganda bore a marked resemblance to the "countersubversion" literature, aimed at Masons, Catholics, and eventually the "Slave Power," that had been so popular before the war.[43] The northern war effort, uniting diverse groups against the slavocracy, helped to still these fears, but victory may have helped stimulate a paranoic attitude toward the homeless. Tramps incurred much hostility because they seemed to be rejecting the ideology of the northern way of life just at its point of high triumph. An added problem, perhaps, was one of timing. The tramps emerged most visibly and dramatically during 1875–77, the very years when Reconstruction was coming to an end. Just at the time when sectional differences seemed finally to be subsiding, in other words, they entered as a new divisive symbol to challenge the theme of consensus.

THOUGH WIDESPREAD, THE negative reaction to the new homeless population was not uniform throughout American society. Fractures occurred along class lines. Regardless of whether they had "traditional" or "modern" attitudes toward the work ethic, men forced out of work because of layoffs had much less reason to view men on the road as lazy or depraved. Some artisans had always had a tradition of traveling; during the depression of the 1870s they were joined by others who normally were less mobile. In 1876–77 the phrase "on tramp" was often used by ironworkers and cigarmakers with no sense of disparagement.[44] When, in 1874, the Chicago *Times* described strikers as vagabonds who were too lazy to work, a striker replied that there was no work to be had. Labor newspapers quickly picked up this theme. "A tramp is a man, an unfortunate man," said the *National Labor Tribune*, "because he can find no work." "No doubt there are naturally bad men" who become tramps, stated the *Weekly Worker*. "But does it follow that every tired, ragged, foot-sore, dirty and hungry wretch who comes to the door to ask for something to eat is a vicious fellow? By no means." Expressing a religious theme that would become common in the labor movement, the paper reminded its readers that "Christ was a tramping vagabond." In a letter to the editor of the *New York Tribune*, one unemployed worker complained that it was an injustice to label as "tramps" the many "honest and industrious men out of work and starving." Quite properly, many labor journals saw the "antitramp" laws hastily passed in the wake of the 1877 riots as punitive class legislation. "Only the man who stands utterly alone," said Terrance Powderly, future head of the Knights of Labor, "friendless, moneyless, ill clad, shelterless and hungry, looking at the sun sinking red in a mid-winter snow, can know what it is to be a real tramp." Blacklisted during the depression of 1873–74, Powderly would list his months on the road as one of the main experiences that motivated him to become a labor organizer.[45]

Nor was hostility to the homeless equally strong in urban as in rural areas. Although overseers of the poor in small towns sometimes complained of "the willingness of private citizens to feed tramps," it is clear that most inhabitants of rural areas and small communities were united in their antagonism to the new vagabonds. Most of these communities had little experience with vagrancy prior to the 1870s, and even if newspaper accounts of tramp violence were exaggerated, the sudden appearance of so many homeless wanderers induced fear.[46] This was not as true of urban areas. In many cities, traditional, unsystematic giving to the poor in general and the homeless in particular remained popular among segments of all classes. This moderated some of the antipathy to the tramps, even while it engendered a backlash from charity reformers who believed the new vagabonds were a threat to well-ordered communities.

As during earlier depressions, many neighborhood organizations sprang up in the 1870s, offering free soup, meals, or lodging to the unemployed without regard to the moral "worthiness" of the recipients. In New York City alone 34 soup kitchens, lunch units, lodging houses, or other temporary agencies were opened, many of them by religious organizations. "Business at the soup house continues lively," a Troy, New York, newspaper reported in the winter of 1874, "and every day proves more and more the necessity of the institution." Although the Indianapolis city council refused to set up municipal soup kitchens, authorities in Boston, who had been distributing free soup through the police stations since 1868, discontinued the practice for only one winter (1873–74) before resuming it again. In Detroit, the city remodeled the police station rooms for the homeless to provide more space for those seeking shelter there.[47]

In the crisis atmosphere of the 1870s, however, both the private associations and public officials who carried out these measures found themselves under vigorous attack. The proponents of "scientific" charity condemned such traditional means of assisting the poor more harshly than ever. Paranoia about tramps added an edge to their message. The New York Association for

Improving the Condition of the Poor deplored the "outgush of morbid sympathy" that free lunches and lodgings represented. The *Nation*, observing in 1876 that several large metropolises had begun making a "daily or tri-weekly gift of a dinner of beef-soup or fish-chowder to every poor person who might apply for it," described such a policy as "communistic." Reformers blamed those who opened soup kitchens for enticing "into the city the floating vagrants, beggars, and paupers, who wander from village to village." "One thing is certain," editorialized the Cleveland *Leader*. "Individual charity promiscuously bestowed is, in a great majority of cases, worse than thrown away."[48]

Reformers almost without exception failed to see any connection between economic conditions and the growth of tramping. They focused instead on the "immoral" habits of the men who took to the road. An 1875 New York State Board of Charities report stated that vagrancy was caused by "idleness, improvidence, drunkenness or other forms of vicious indulgence." The solution to the tramp problem, the Philadelphia *Inquirer* argued, was "to hold over the heads of chronic able-bodied paupers the terror of work, and so reduce their number."[49] To accomplish this objective, charity reformers argued, four things were necessary: elimination of almsgiving to beggars; termination of the municipal policy of "outdoor" relief; centralization of urban charities under leadership that supported "scientific" benevolence; and more stringent vagrancy laws. The latter two items were especially important if the tramp was to be successfully forced to labor, or required to pay a penalty for not having done so.[50]

Partly due to the tenacity of traditional attitudes toward charity and relief, much of the initial campaign against the tramps was a failure. As Philadelphia's Society for Organizing Charity lamented in its 1881 annual report, vagrants "prefer to prey upon the people who don't believe in Organized Charity and who think we ought to help the poor 'without asking so many questions.'" Charity reformers were successful in getting public outdoor relief abolished in 1879 in Philadelphia and Brooklyn, but other large cities rejected this idea. There was also a continuing resistance, born as much out of hostility to incipient bureaucracy as to newer conceptions of benevolence, to the idea of centralizing charitable endeavors. An attempt to unite New York City's charities in 1873 failed as a result of "suspicion and jealousy among the co-operating agencies and the refusal of many to surrender their list of clients to the central registration office." In Brooklyn, a similar umbrella organization met the same fate in 1876. In 1877, several cities set up Charity Organization Societies, but recalcitrant smaller groups in Philadelphia, Chicago, and elsewhere continued to hamper the drive to unify and systematize charity.[51]

Reformers attained more immediate success on the legislative front. In 1876 New Jersey passed the nation's first "antitramp" law, and by 1880 a number of other states also had statutes that lengthened the terms of commitment for vagrancy or sought to distinguish the wandering poor from the less mobile (and presumably less dangerous) local mendicant. New Hampshire, for example, passed a "very strict law against vagrancy, making it a State-prison offence, and requiring little evidence to convict a tramp." Charity reformers, however, greatly exaggerated the effects of the new laws. The claim that these laws were chiefly responsible for the substantial decline in the number of vagrants after 1878 overlooked the fact that the enforcement of the new laws coincided with a general revival of industry in the country.[52]

The experience of New Jersey, one state that passed a tramp act before the depression had bottomed out, illustrated the difficulty of any attempt to legislate the homeless out of existence. New Jersey was particularly troubled by homeless men wandering along the roads between New York and Philadelphia. In many towns, one newspaper reported, it was "impossible to walk more than a mile without encountering one of these peripatetic pilferers, creeping from house to house." The legislature responded in February 1876 with a law defining tramps broadly as persons without legal settlement who

> live idly and without employment, and refuse to work for the usual and common wages given to other persons for like work in the places where they then are, or shall be found going about from door to door, or placing themselves in the streets, highways or roads, to beg or gather alms, and can give no reasonable account of themselves or their business in such places.

Local sheriffs were required to apprehend and bring such individuals before the justice of the peace to be "examined." If the magistrate determined the suspect was a tramp, he could sentence the vagabond to a jail term of as much as six months. The act aimed not only to rid the state of vagabonds, but to make the work ethic universal. It admonished jailers and poorhouse officials to set such individuals to work in some fashion or bind them out to do labor for private individuals. To that end, all almshouses and correctional institutions in the state were declared to be workhouses.[53]

In the spring, New Jersey authorities began to enforce the new law. By May, reports of "wholesale arrests" were being noted in the local press, as magistrates dutifully committed one wanderer after another to 30 or 60 days at hard labor. Overcrowding and the excessive cost and difficulty involved in finding suitable work for the tramps, however, soon made a shambles of the drive to eliminate the new vagabonds. By the third week of June the Camden county jail was so crowded with tramps that the sheriff informed local judges that "he could not furnish room for any more, and consequently no [more] commitments were made." By the end of the month most of the vagrants had been released. Smaller towns, too, were reaching the limit of their capacity to house the vagabonds arrested under the act. Authorities in Gloucester directed the police to simply "warn them out of the city limits" if they encountered any more tramps. It was impracticable for most towns to turn local almshouses into workhouses. It may have been possible to set the local poor to work, but it was too easy for transients from outside the area to abscond. Twenty-six of the vagrants in the Camden jail were taken to the almshouse at Blackwoodtown, which maintained a farm for the inmates; within four days the steward reported that 10 of them had already run away. The Tramp Act remained on the books, but its enforcement in the future would be sporadic.[54]

Perhaps the New Jersey experience made Massachusetts officials wary about trying too hard to eliminate the tramp. At the end of 1876 a new statute authorizing overseers of the poor to require, at their discretion, a "reasonable amount of labor" from the nonresident poor was being put into effect in only a third of 150 Massachusetts towns, with fewer than 20 communities carrying out the policy "persistently." Boston overseers ignored the law, claiming they had "no means to set so large a number at work" and that they could not "see our way clear at present to introduce any system of profitable employment." Smaller towns rejected the work requirement because they believed it would simply lead vagabonds "to avoid overseers of the poor and beg at private houses, and lodge in barns or sheds." Towns that forced the homeless to labor did experience a gradual decline in vagrancy, but Boston overseers complained that the effect of this was not to reduce the problem throughout the state but to drive tramps into the metropolis.[55]

"The question, What shall we do with them?" one observer commented, "is more easily asked than answered." Those most hostile to the new class of homeless men could not effectively channel widespread public antagonism toward tramps into a campaign to combat them. While many people supported the idea of imposing the work ethic on vagrants, a majority of the population opposed the cost and the degree of centralized power that would be needed to attain this desirable goal. To involve government in a coordinated effort to "reform" tramps through the establishment of special reformatories and an enlarged bureaucracy was anathema to Americans of the Gilded Age, who glorified local control as much as they did the work ethic. When Brace suggested the development of a federal "pass" system, akin to that which some European nations used to validate the status of traveling workers, few people took him seriously. If New York and Massachusetts welfare officials could not agree about the law of comity regarding the expulsion and transportation of nonresident paupers across state lines, there was little reason to expect them to unite in a larger campaign against vagabonds.[56]

Ironically, the free-labor doctrine itself made it difficult to carry out a vigorous program against the homeless population. The labor press was on strong ground when it argued against any restrictions on the right of unemployed laborers to travel in search of work, and except during the crisis years of 1876–77, even the most hostile critics grudgingly admitted that some bona fide workers, honestly seeking jobs, were among the men who had taken to the road. As the Illinois State Charities Board observed, if a man "cannot obtain work at home, he must seek it elsewhere." In 1883, a justice of the New York Supreme Court criticized the magistrates of Westchester County for arresting tramps, arguing that "poverty is their only crime; [and] they are traveling presumably from town to town in search of employment." But if some homeless men were not criminals, this called into question the general policy of treating them all as such. Massachusetts welfare officials succinctly stated the problem they faced: "The difficulty of denying relief or in instituting prosecution lies in the want of sufficient evidence as to the character of the applicant, whether he is a vagabond or an honest laborer."[57]

A temporary solution was to provide only the most minimal level of assistance to the homeless. Most large cities continued to allow overnight lodging in police stations until at least the 1890s; many smaller communities maintained such facilities as late as the 1930s. The men and women who stayed overnight in these "tramp rooms" did so under the most primitive conditions. In Philadelphia, each station house had two poorly ventilated rooms, usually above the cells, in which the homeless were allowed to lodge—"or rather," as one observer put it, "store themselves for the night." In New York in the 1870s the "casuals" slept on tiers of planks. The atmosphere was described as "foul," the rooms "filthy in the extreme." In Boston, an investigation found lodgers "huddled together in their damp, reeking clothes, no bed but a hard bench, no food if hungry, turned out at daybreak into the snow of a winter morning." In addition, the destitute people who used these facilities were often allowed to stay only one or two nights a month in any given police station. Thus was born the "revolver," a person "who passed in pilgrimage from one station-house to another, and in the course of a month returned to the point" from which he began. In smaller cities conditions were no less primitive, but the space allotted the homeless was sometimes much less adequate.[58]

The degrading nature of police station accommodations was not accidental. Such a policy at once kept state intervention to a minimum, punished the vagrant attempting to avoid work, and served as a goad to the legitimate, unemployed laborer. It came close to William Graham Sumner's dictum that the man "in the gutter is just where he ought to be." In many ways barbaric, such a policy nevertheless placed a high premium on personal liberty. Reformers recognized the dilemma. "Mobility of labor is a good thing," wrote Amos Warner in his classic textbook, *American Charities*, "but it is having some unfortunate results." In 1878 an editorial in the *Nation* neatly summarized the dilemma when it stated, with no little frustration, that "the immutable natural right of persons to travel about for the purposes of obtaining employment cannot be curtailed, . . . and yet the sturdy beggar should be restrained."[59]

In the decades ahead, municipal officials, social welfare specialists, and railroad managers would grapple with this issue. They would do so, however, in the context of a much different society than that which had originally encountered the tramp.

PLEASE GIVE ME A PENNY.

Street beggars became a major problem in urban America in the nineteenth century. In this scene from an 1882 urban guidebook, a beggar approaches a wealthy New Yorker. *Source:* James D. McCabe, *New York by Sunlight and Gaslight* (Philadelphia: Hubbard Brothers, 1882).

Cheap lodging houses for homeless men proliferated between 1870 and 1915. For 7 cents, a man could sleep overnight on a hammock in Uncle Jack's Canvas Palace, located on Pell Street in New York. *Source:* The Jacob A. Riis Collection, © Museum of the City of New York.

Police station "tramp rooms," such as these facilities in New York's Oak Street station house, provided free overnight lodging for the destitute as early as the 1850s. *Source:* The Jacob A. Riis Collection, © Museum of the City of New York.

Homeless women were often much older than homeless men, as this scene of women at mealtime at an almshouse in the 1890s illustrates. *Source:* The Byron Collection, © Museum of the City of New York.

Especially during its early years, the Salvation Army attempted to reach out to poor women and blacks as well as homeless white men. *Source: Harper's Weekly,* April 3, 1880. Courtesy of Salvation Army Archives and Research Center.

Until the 1940s, homeless men often rode the trains illegally. Riding between cars (on the "bumpers") or beneath them (on the "rods") was particularly dangerous. *Source: The Century*, February 1894.

By the mid-1920s, a romanticized view of the homeless had replaced the earlier hostile image in middle-class periodicals. The quaint hobo in this Norman Rockwell illustration seems quite harmless. *Source: The Saturday Evening Post,* April 1924.

Charlie Chaplin's movies presented a complex image of the homeless. In depicting the "little tramp" as a father figure, Chaplin's *The Kid* (1921) was particularly subversive of traditional stereotypes of the homeless. *Source:* The Museum of Modern Art/Film Still Archives.

This 1932 Reginald Marsh drawing ("Breadline—No One Has Starved") was typical of writers and artists in the 1930s, who often presented the homeless as an anonymous, downtrodden mass. © Museum of the City of New York.

(above) This rare 1962 photograph of the lobby of a cheap lodging house in Philadelphia shows an element of camaraderie among the homeless that was often missed by commentators who focused on negative aspects of skid row. *Source:* Urban Archives, Temple University.

(facing page, top) The Great Depression led to a massive increase in homelessness. Shantytowns, like this one in Philadelphia near the Pennsylvania Railroad tracks, sprang up in every major city. *Source:* Urban Archives, Temple University.

(facing page, bottom) After World War II, "cage" hotels became the most common type of private dwelling for the homeless. The cubicles, with chicken wire on top, resembled cages for animals. *Source:* Urban Archives, Temple University.

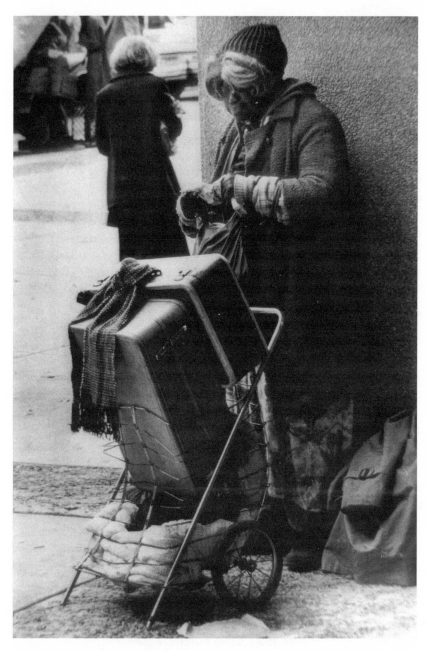

After 1975, racial minorities, women, and families became much more common among the homeless. This homeless woman in Philadelphia carries all of her possessions with her. *Source:* Urban Archives, Temple University.

THE RETURN OF PROSPERITY IN 1879
reduced the numbers of homeless unemployed,
temporarily calming the anxieties of those who
viewed the ragged squadrons of vagabonds as the
advance guard of revolution. But it could not end the problem.
Homelessness in its various forms was too intimately connected to
major changes in American society and its economic structure for

that to happen. From time to time,
especially after the return of prosperity following a period of financial depression, editorialists might
talk hopefully about "the end of the
tramp," but railroad workers and
communities near major transportation routes knew better. "The tramp

Chapter 4.
Tramps, Trains,
and Towns,
1880–1915

problem shows no sign of letting up," observed one railroad journal
in 1913, and the prediction was borne out during the next two years,
when the number of men on the road reached new heights.[1] By the
beginning of the twentieth century, however, both the nature of the
phenomenon itself and the response of Americans to it were undergoing significant change.

In the 1880s, public fear of tramps was only slightly less intense
than it had been during the crisis-ridden seventies. With the onset of
another economic downturn in 1882, violence between roving bands
of men and train crews broke out anew. Twelve vagrants captured a

freight on the Chicago and Ohio and ordered the conductor to take them to Lexington, Kentucky. In another incident a brakeman who attempted to dislodge three tramps from the top of a car was severely beaten.[2] Disturbing articles about raids by tramps on isolated homesteads again filled the columns of newspapers, and the Haymarket bombing of 1886 renewed fears of the "subversive" tramp. The revival of business activity in 1887 had little effect on the hostile attitude of social welfare officials toward the homeless. W. M. F. Round, secretary of the New York Prison Association, stated jocularly that the only reason tramps should not be killed was that it was "impracticable." C. G. Truesdale, head of the Chicago Relief and Aid Society, related that many "burglaries, and not a few murders and outrages of all sorts, are justly laid to these vagabonds." It was a mistake to be kind to such persons, said Truesdale, because "they are thereby encouraged in their viciousness."[3]

At first it appeared that the onset of another depression in the fall of 1893 would lead to a revival of intense conflict over the tramp issue. The year 1894 brought a short-lived wave of hysteria over Coxey's Army, groups of unemployed men who traveled to Washington to petition the government for assistance.[4] Dispensing with legal niceties, the dean of the Yale Law School called one contingent of Coxeyites "soap-shunning and vermin-haunted rabble," while a former Civil War general, O. O. Howard, compared them to the Marseilles regiment that marched on Paris in 1792. As a new rash of stories about vagabonds commandeering trains and destroying property made their appearance in the daily press, moralists once again began to demand "the whipping post for tramps."[5]

Yet the depression of the nineties, though more serious than the relatively mild economic downturn of the previous decade, did not generate another period of confrontation over the issue of homeless men. In fact, by the turn of the century the dominant public mood on this question was undergoing a significant change. After an initial flare-up in 1893–94, there was a dramatic decline in overt conflict between tramps and trainmen. The number of stories about aggressive tramps in newspapers and in the *Railroad Gazette* was smaller in the 1890s than in the 1880s and much smaller than in the 1870s. After the turn of the century, such stories appeared very infrequently, and only occasionally did one read of farmers "in fear of their lives."[6] During the succeeding depressions of 1907–08, 1911, and 1914–15, there was no indication that tramps forced train crews at gunpoint to transport them. The rare confrontations that did occur were between vagabonds and railroad detectives, not trainmen.[7] Despite a continuous campaign by railroad officials to prevent homeless men from riding the freights, by the

World War I era a kind of modus vivendi had emerged between tramps, on the one hand, and trainmen and local communities, on the other.

Why did this change occur? Ironically, the continued expansion of the homeless population in the late nineteenth century may have contributed to a general softening of the public's attitude toward homeless men. During the 1870s, vagabonds were feared partly because they were a new, unknown factor—a body of men whose behavior seemed unpredictable and whose goals and motivations were the subject of dark conjecture. By the 1890s— much to the chagrin of charity officials—they were becoming an established part of the American scene, and many people who came in contact with them realized their previous fears were largely unfounded. Such contact became increasingly common. Rural and small-town America, which in most areas was little troubled by vagabondage prior to 1870, now found itself imposed upon by a growing number of homeless wanderers. In Johnstown, Pennsylvania, notes one historian, "there were always tramps about, drifters, who came with the railroad, heading west nearly always, knocking at back doors for something to eat." One man who lived outside of the town amused himself by recording a daily "tramp count" in his diary. William Aspinwall, a tramp who reported on conditions in the small towns of Ohio and Indiana in 1895, found "more hobos on the road than ever before."[8]

As early as 1879 some people exhibited more curiosity than apprehension about the new vagabonds. Robert Louis Stevenson related the following incident during his trip across the western United States at that time:

As we were standing, after our manner, outside the station, I saw two men whip suddenly from underneath the cars and take to their heels across country. They were tramps, it appeared, who had been riding on the beams [rods] since eleven of the night before; and several of my fellow passengers had already seen and conversed with them while we broke our fast.

By 1883, trainmen had come to expect the tramp to appear in March or April, for "the approach of Spring generally starts him out of the city where he has wintered, and trainmen will have plenty of his company soon." In May 1885, the "usual Spring army of tramps" may have been "worrying Western railroad men," but at least the problem had assumed a predictable pattern. If familiarity with tramps bred a degree of contempt, it could also foster a measure of toleration.[9]

The marked reduction in the level of tramp violence was partly a result of the demographic profile of the men who rode the freights. By the 1890s, most of the men on the road were too young to have served in the Civil War, and this may have contributed to a decline in organized violence among tramps. Ben Reitman, who tramped intermittently for 20 years prior to World War I, claimed that throughout his experience on the road "the hobos never fought back" when confronted by railroad police.[10] This did not mean, of course, that tramps were totally passive in the face of antagonism from others. Given the tramps' rough-hewn lifestyle, it is not surprising that violent men continued to travel on the road, and a number of tramp memoirs provide examples of "toughs" who would not hesitate to pick fights with trainmen or, for that matter, fellow tramps.[11] But such individuals were not typical, and the aggressive gangs of vagabonds who had first appeared in the 1870s were mostly gone by 1900.

A more important cause of declining violence between tramps and trainmen lies in the changing attitudes of the railroad workers. During the strife-torn 1870s, railroad workers usually sided with their employers in the struggle to keep the tramps off the trains. Their behavior was rooted in a vigorous adherence to the free labor ideology and identification with middle-class values. P. M. G. Arthur, the austere president of the Brotherhood of Locomotive Engineers (BLE), stressed that the engineers' organization had been founded for moral rather than economic reasons, to reform or eliminate railroad workers who "were given to habits of dissipation and vice." The BLE regularly expelled members for drunkenness, "neglect of duty," or "unbecoming conduct." Engineers and conductors, who exercised considerable independence in their work, thought of themselves as aristocrats of labor.[12] Articles in the engineers' monthly journal praised the railroad magnates in the 1860s and 70s, making the railroad companies seem like large extended families rather than corporations. The engineers, firemen, and conductors (whose organization remained a fraternal order until 1890) pursued a conservative policy toward employers and usually eschewed the strike as a weapon. "Much has been said and more written concerning the antagonism between capital and labor," said Arthur in 1886. "To my mind there is no such thing."[13]

Few workers accepted modernization more thoroughly or glorified the Protestant work ethic more fervently than railroadmen. Self-help, "bootstrap" advice filled the columns of the railroad workers' journals in the 1870s and '80s. "He who squanders time is prolifigate of God's most precious gift," said one fireman. Another found a "large element of fact" in the theory of the "self-made man." The only way to overcome poverty, an engineer claimed, was through "self-denial and economy." Workers' views of the railroads were largely positive; they were heralds of "modern civilization" and "progress."[14] Little wonder, then, that most railroadmen found tramps highly objectionable. The vagabonds were more than a nuisance. They represented the very antithesis of the trainmen's value system. The homeless man was of a piece with "the lazy, the languid, and the indifferent," who blame "bad luck" for their own failures. The "indolent, careless, improvident, and unambitious," said one fireman, taking a page from the Social Darwinists, deserved to fall behind in the race for success.[15]

Despite a number of negative features (especially irregular employment and long hours),[16] prior to the 1880s employment on the railroads seemed to justify a good deal of the railroadmen's ideology. Mobility was not a myth. As Walter Licht points out in his study of nineteenth-century railroad workers, the men who moved up were seen as "symbols of the basic beneficence of the system—objective proof that diligence and loyalty had their rewards." Wages of railroad workers were high compared to those of other manual workers, although the hours of work fluctuated greatly from one month to another.[17]

However, the conditions of railroad labor seriously deteriorated in the last two decades of the nineteenth century. In the mid-1870s, major companies introduced continuous running engines, which meant that specific trains would no longer be the responsibility of particular enginemen or crews. Longer work stints interfered with the family life of trainmen. By the end of the latter decade trainmen were complaining that insufficient rest was causing an increasing number of accidents. Railroad management offered few concessions to employees after the great strike of 1877, and the owners' victory in the 1888 Burlington strike led to the imposition of new technologies and work rules that undercut railroad workers' positions. Accompanying these changes was a gradual decline in wage rates for most railroad labor.[18]

The increasing insecurity of railroad labor gradually undermined the railroadmen's adherence to the free-labor ideology. As Shelton Stromquist has shown, a growing "congestion" in the higher-skill positions increasingly limited the opportunities of younger railroad workers for advancement. The dramatic slowing of railroad growth beginning in the 1890s exacerbated this situation.[19] Simultaneously, the physical safety of trainmen deteriorated. Railroad work, of course, had always been hazardous, especially for brakemen, who regularly lost fingers in coupling accidents.[20] Beginning in the 1880s, however, the number of railroad injuries grew dramatically. In Massachusetts the annual number of trainmen killed or injured increased steadily from 68 in 1878 to 300 in 1887; total coupling accidents went from 24 to 122.[21]

Increasingly long trains (which made signaling difficult) and the failure of companies to repair equipment led to a new wave of injuries. In Iowa, a representative state, the number of nonfatal injuries per thousand railroad workers increased almost sixfold between 1898 and 1911. Railroad workers everywhere complained bitterly of short crews, inadequate lighting, and dangerously long trains. The memoir of one railroad engineer published in 1913 is little more than a chronicle of accidents—runaway locomotives, exploding boilers, collisions, and derailments.[22] While the number of accidents rose, the average cash settlement for injured workers or their families plummeted. Although the chances of disabling injury increased, disability protection was highly uncertain as a result of the "fellow servant" rule in effect until 1908.[23]

As trainmen gradually lost their sense of identification with the corporations for which they worked, their attitude toward the tramps and hobos who rode the freights underwent a striking transformation. Perhaps worker and vagabond had more in common than railroadmen had believed. "Many a poor fellow," wrote conductor Charles George in 1888, "has faithfully worked for a railroad during long years, on poor pay, only to be dropped from the roll when old or disabled." Despite their "faithful service," such unfortunate men were left "to the charity of the world." As early as 1883 some railroad workers were, as a result of this type of treatment, beginning to doubt the strictly moralistic interpretation of tramping:

> Some men are born to be tramps, and they may be found in every
> class and calling; but it is a fact that railway management, in a greater
> degree than all other influences combined, is responsible for the
> development of this unfortunate propensity. . . . Under the rules in
> force on most lines, there is not a trainman, however faithful, how-
> ever intelligent and skillful, however devoted to service of his com-
> pany, who can confidently assert, that in a day he may not be com-
> pelled to abandon his home and be sent out to tramp in search of
> employment elsewhere.

The loss of the strike on the Burlington line in 1888, which drove many engineers and firemen out of work, brought home such fears in a particularly direct way. In 1895, even the staid *Railway Conductor* printed an article arguing that "as improved methods of production and labor-saving machinery have increased, the number of tramps have also increased in exact proportion." Men will tramp, the author stated with grim humor, unless they "are educated to patiently starve in the locality of their last employment."[24] By

1915 sympathetic statements about the homeless were the norm, not the exception. "Suppose you didn't have any money ahead, and could not find a job, what would you do?" one worker asked rhetorically in the *Railroad Trainman*. "Would you lie down and meekly starve or would you do as thousands of others have done: go down to the railroad yards, climb into an empty box car and start touring the country, looking for work?"[25]

For purely financial reasons railroad workers found it useful to take a more lenient approach to tramps. Beginning in the 1880s, some trainmen began to disregard railroad regulations and allow tramps and hobos to ride on their trains in return for a small "consideration." In 1888 the *Railroad Gazette* indicated that while most vagabonds still used tactics of intimidation to deal with recalcitrant trainmen, others found this was no longer necessary. "Some conductors are indifferent to the presence of the intruders and to the rules requiring their expulsion, and others are doubtless bribed, by cigars or favors of some kind, to wink at their presence on the train." During the 1890s the system became firmly established, although the amount that trainmen exacted from illegal passengers varied widely. "On lines where money is demanded of them," said Josiah Flynt, "ten cents is usually sufficient to settle for a journey of a hundred miles, and twenty cents often secures a night's ride." "Jack Black," however, found the going rate to be fifty cents per person, and train crews "flourished by carrying [migratory workers] over their entire division in the box cars at a dollar each." By the first decade of the new century fifty cents was fairly typical, and by the 1920s one dollar was not unusual.[26] Some brakemen were much less demanding and were willing to accept payment in kind. Flynt claimed that "to get across the Missouri River," he actually traded shoes with one trainman. Another observer noted that brakemen "will accept as tribute anything the hobo has to offer, from a corkscrew to a glass eye. Pennies, a jack-knife, a mangled piece of chewing-tobacco, anything at all will purchase immunity from a shack."[27]

In some cases the practice of demanding "fares" from tramps riding the freights took on an organizational aspect that oddly mimicked the methods of the railroad corporations. One journalist who "beat" his way across the country in 1903 to investigate tramp life found that brakemen's efforts to extract payment were almost universal and that some had gone a step further by sharing such "fares" with the other trainmen. In this way, the amount of "boe money" that each railroadman would receive over the long run became more predictable. "So recognized is this graft," the writer explained, "that I seldom took the trouble to hunt up my own hiding place on a train but at division points I would hang around the yards, carefully avoiding the 'bulls' or yard police, until one of the train crew hunted me up, asked me where I wanted to go and whether I had the price, and stowed me carefully away in the proper car." As one hobo song put it,

> I walked up to the brakeman
> To shoot him a line of talk.
> He says, "If you've got the money
> I'll see that you won't walk."[28]

The relationship between tramps and trainmen was more than a business proposition. There is evidence that after 1900 class solidarity began to play an increasingly important role. The brakeman's "standard tariff" might be "reduced somewhat by the tearful eloquence of the victim and altogether remitted if the fortunate traveler has a card and book of any reputable labor union, stamped with receipts for dues to date." In legend, the Industrial Workers of the World received special treatment from trainmen; in actuality, it is doubtful that they were viewed any differently than other unionists. "The expression, 'wot cha ridin' on?'" one writer who tramped in the 1920s explained, "is the shack's invariable greeting everywhere. It means, "'Do you carry a union card?'" Those who did were not required to "pay tribute." In other ways, too, trainmen became more sympathetic with the passage of time. "When times are hard and jobs are scarce," noted one observer, "the good will of the train crew increases proportionately." During the depression of 1921, he found that "provided one keeps out of sight, the brakeman seldom objects."[29] Regardless of the state of the economy, it was common practice for train crews to regularly allow former or unemployed railroadmen to ride for free.[30] Trainmen assisted homeless men in other ways as well. Switchmen were known to help vagabonds locate outgoing trains, and railroad hands would often direct tramps to the nearest hobo jungle. A friendly stationmaster in a town on the New York Central line informed Flynt and the tramps he was traveling with when their train was due to arrive. When the locomotive pulled into the station, he called out, "'Boys, don't miss your train.' We followed his advice."[31]

Of the various types of trainmen, brakemen were the most friendly to tramps. "There can be no question," said John J. McCook in 1893, "that many a brakeman has a very tender spot in his heart for a tramp, and that he finds ways of helping him along in spite of the universal reprobation of the management. . . . Engineers, firemen and conductors are far more stern." Some brakemen claimed to have never "kicked off a bum" during their careers, and tramp memoirs are rife with stories of "friendly shacks."[32]

Why? "Our tramps have the instinct of brakemen," said McCook, "but without the industry and laboriousness of the better part of them." Behind this author's conservative moralism lay a valuable insight. The "shacks" and the tramps did indeed have much in common. Brakemen tended to be younger, rowdier, and more often single than other trainmen, and they shared many of the same hazards of railroad travel as did the vagabonds.[33]

Brakemen had even less reason than did the engineers and conductors to support the free labor ideology. Not that upward mobility was not possible for brakemen—clearly it was.[34] But it is likely that such mobility slowed drastically after 1890 at the same time that unemployment resulting from physical injury became a greater threat than ever before. "Wary feet, an alert mind, and chilled nerve were needed every instant," said one brakeman in his reminiscences. Brakemen may also have been part of a more traditional working-class culture than were other railroadmen. Glen Mullin, writing of his tramping experiences in the 1920s, noted that one brakeman readily accepted a "hearty swig" of liquor from a communal flask when a group of hobos offered it to him. One can hardly imagine an engineer or conductor doing that. Brakemen, perhaps, knew what it was like to be down and out and were more willing to help those in a similar situation. Said one brakeman to Flynt: "I hate to see a lad get pulled for ridin' a train, because I've been broke myself, and I know what it is to be on the road. I'll always carry a man on my train if I can."[35]

Sympathy for tramps was not universal among train workers. Some crews remained "at war with the tramps" and made a determined effort to keep them off the trains. News of "hostile" lines circulated through skid rows and hobo jungles, and the vagabonds learned to "steer shy" of them.[36] Conductors, perhaps less willing to tarnish their exalted sense of self-importance by helping a vagrant, were consistently less friendly than other railroad workers.[37] Yet specialization in railroad employment sometimes worked to the benefit of the tramps. "I'm not a policeman for the road," one conductor told Flynt. "I'm a conductor, and I only draw a salary for being that, too. . . . It's the detective's business to look after such people." "Don't the engineers look out for tramps?" one investigator asked. "Not they," replied the trainman. "That is no part of an engineer's duty. He'd just as soon haul a tramp as not, and he hates the trouble of having to stop to put them off."[38]

Status rivalries were at the root of some of these attitudes, but so too was a growing disenchantment with the railroad corporations. The new conditions of labor on the railroads had dimmed the luster of the work ethic for most trainmen, and in this area as in many others, they no longer saw the need to carry out every instruction ordered by a distant manager. Even among the railroad detectives, who were much feared by tramps, there was little desire to do more work than necessary. They preferred to hunt for vagrants in the safety of the station yards.[39] With "'regulations' staring them in the face," said McCook, "it is curious how tolerant most crews are of their uninvited passengers." What seemed strange to the outside observer, however, may have made perfect sense to the trainman.[40]

IN THE 1870s the towns and villages of America had been as adamant in their hostility toward the tramp as had been the railroad workers. Yet by the end of the century the views of the residents of many of these communities had undergone a similar alteration. Certainly there remained, even in the 1920s, towns that were known as particularly hostile to vagrants—"tough burgs," in the parlance of the road. In 1909 a sheriff in Delanco, New Jersey, was accused of "cruel and unusual punishment" because he regularly chained tramps to trees. Poughkeepsie had a reputation as a place "where vagrants were hunted like rats," and Cheyenne, Wyoming, was known for its notorious and legendary "hobo stalker," Jeff Carr. Periodically, the constables of villages near rail lines would invade hobo jungles to round up "impudent vagrants."[41] As time passed, however, such behavior became much less common. For public officials who had to deal with the problem, the tramp was gradually downgraded from menace to nuisance, and by the turn of the century there was much less interest in arresting tramps. A survey of 184 towns and cities in Massachusetts in 1900 revealed that 109 communities never brought tramps before a court, only six always did so, and the remainder did so "occasionally." County court records from California in 1914 indicate that there were almost no arrests for vagrancy in the 20 most rural counties. Furthermore, the proportion of convictions and average sentence served for vagrancy were both substantially lower in less urbanized areas.[42]

Smaller communities that continued to prosecute vagrants often utilized the fee system, by which sheriffs were paid a certain amount for the upkeep and, sometimes, the apprehension of tramps. This method of dealing with vagrants, however, was never very satisfactory. Fees that were too high led to corruption and actually attracted tramps to a locality instead of driving them away. In 1900 Port Chester, New York, residents learned that many of the tramps imprisoned there were "repeaters" who had "no other occupation except appearing before the local courts as many times a year as is possible and sharing the fees with the constables." A minor scandal rocked Camden, New Jersey, in 1894 when it was discovered that justices and constables, who shared a seventy-five cents per person fee for capturing tramps, were bribing vagabonds with whiskey and tobacco to get them to submit to the authorities. The men were then released after 10 days to be recruited anew. While in jail "the tramps loll in idleness in hammocks . . . or spend their time smoking and playing cards." The jail was soon packed with 175 vagrants. What gave the game away were the actions of 40 additional vagabonds who were brought to the jail by a constable, only to be told that they could not be committed. The men then "attempted to force their way into the building, and it took the united efforts of the wardens to drive them away"![43]

Revulsion against the soft treatment of "tramp boarders" and a need to cut costs led many communities to terminate the fee system at the turn of the century. This, however, was hardly an ideal solution. "In more than one instance," one observer noted, "convictions have almost literally ceased the moment rewards or liberal fees for arrests were abolished." Constables refused to raid "tramp camps" in the vicinity of New Brunswick, New Jersey, for example, claiming that the fee of fifty cents per person was often not enough to pay for the cost of bringing the prisoner to the county jail.[44] Any effort to enforce vagrancy laws in rural areas was hindered, additionally, by the lack of a strong state police force prior to the 1920s.[45]

The gradual softening of the enforcement of vagrancy laws in the rural North found no equivalent below the Mason-Dixon line. The South produced less vagabondage of the kind that troubled so many northern moralists in the 1870s and '80s. Vagrancy in the post-Civil War decades was largely a product of urban, industrializing society, and the South remained overwhelmingly rural. With few exceptions, southern cities had substantially less unemployment in the 1890s than did urbanized areas elsewhere, because most southern cities still lacked an industrial base. Except for a small contingent from the steel center of Birmingham, the former Confederate states produced no Coxeyite "army" in 1894.[46]

Still, tramps did use the railroads in the South to some extent, especially in the winter, when large numbers of unemployed, homeless men congregated in a few Gulf seaport cities. New Orleans, Jacksonville, and St. Augustine were favorite haunts of vagabonds during the colder months. "Many hobos had pictured New Orleans to me as possessing a kind of tropical lure," tramp memoirist Glen Mullin wrote. "To hear them talk it was a kind of paradise for tramps."[47] The problem, however, was getting there, for the intervening territory lacked the easygoing ways of the old, predominantly Catholic seaport communities. A former Confederate soldier could tramp through the southern states without fear of arrest; northern vagabonds had to be much more careful. As one elderly tramp warned Harry Kemp in Texas: "You'd better beat it out of the South as quick as you can;

they're hell on a bum down here, and harder yet on a Yankee. No, they haven't forgot [*sic*] *that* yet—not by a damn sight." "The Bible Belt John Laws," said one investigator, "like nothing better than to raid a hobo jungle and shoot holes through the pots and pans and then chase the hobos through the cane brakes. Getting caught is a serious calamity. If they don't send you to the piney woods, you go to the turpentine swamps." A South Carolina law made hoboing punishable by 30 days on the chain gang. In Alabama, the threat of similar harsh punishment sharply reduced the number of train-riders on the lines between Montgomery and Mobile, where tramps had "camped along the right of way and foraged on potatoes, peas, chickens, and other farming products." Although northern as well as southern communities could be antagonistic toward tramps, the latter were dreaded most by men on the road. McComb, Mississippi, for example, had a well-earned reputation for punitive treatment of vagrants. All trains stopping there were searched thoroughly and tramps caught were sentenced to hard labor on road gangs.[48]

The hostility of the white South to tramps was to some extent a product of the region's entrenched localism, which promoted an insular view of the world. The white South's commitment to "place" and the "primordial" values that lay beneath the conscious level of ideology brought with it an enmity toward outsiders—and no one was more of an outsider than the train-riding tramp. If the vagabonds were the offscourings of northern industrialism, so much the worse for them.[49]

In both sections, vagrancy laws had been used for decades to control a variety of deviant or criminal behavior, including prostitution.[50] Except when occasionally used against strikers or harvest workers, however, in the North these laws were relatively unimportant as a means of disciplining labor. The assault of the Buffalo police in 1894 on Rybakowski's Army, a Coxey-like band of 140 unemployed immigrant workers, was as exceptional as it was vicious. Most tramps were not organized enough even to pursue the modest political goal (petitioning Congress to assist the unemployed) of Coxey or Rybakowski, much less take part in strikes, and rounding them up did no damage to organized labor.[51]

Vagrancy statutes in the South, however, functioned in a much more draconian fashion. For the most part, their thinly veiled purpose was to keep blacks in a state of economic subjugation. Used in conjunction with the convict lease system, the statutes sometimes allowed the return of a type of involuntary servitude not far removed from slavery. In 1882, for example, a Louisville judge sentenced a black convicted of vagrancy to be sold as a laborer to the highest bidder for one year. Seven years later, four vagrants in

Missouri were auctioned off in a similar manner for six-month terms. In Georgia at the beginning of the twentieth century, some municipal courts worked hand in glove with local white farmers, who paid the fines of convicted African Americans and in return obtained use of their labor. Others convicted under the law were sent to chain gangs. "Threat of enforcement," notes one historian, "was often enough to force unemployed blacks to take undesirable, low-paying jobs as servants and common laborers." Between 1890 and 1920 Birmingham, Alabama, police periodically waged "unrelenting war against the vagrants," and they would sometimes "descend on black saloons and arrest every Negro who could not account for himself." Convicted vagrants were frequently leased to Alabama coal mining corporations. Both during and after Reconstruction, African Americans often had to struggle to maintain the elementary right of free movement.[52]

In contrast to the South, the response of small towns and rural areas of the North to homeless men was much more hesitant. When purely legal solutions to the vagrancy problem failed, communities reverted to the old practice of lodging tramps temporarily in almshouses. This approach, however, produced a conflict between the desire to control and the need to economize. In Massachusetts, the State Board of Charities complained that too few towns "undertake the disagreeable duty of a prosecution," but the board had no power over local institutions. At the end of the 1890s almost half of the almshouses in the commonwealth admitted vagrants, in all but two instances providing them with lodging as well as food. Of the 96 institutions that received vagrants, 82 found some means of separating tramps from the rest of the inmates. Despite the admonition of state charity officials, however, only four out of ten required any kind of work from the vagrants. When the towns that did not house tramps in poorhouses are taken into account, less than a quarter of the municipalities required work of vagrants before giving them assistance. Financial exigency was the determining factor. As an overseer from Midford explained, "it would cost us a dollar to get twenty-five cents work out of them." Frustrated poorhouse officers in Bridgeport tried to make the homeless work, but given the time expended in finding suitable work for them, "in showing them how to do the work, and in looking after them to see that it was done, the investment proved a poor one."[53]

A fundamental ambivalence remained. Though officials from 165 communities answered "yes" when asked whether "tramps should be compelled to work," few were willing to enforce this in their own town. Each year the number of vagabonds increased, and so too did the reluctance of communities to pay for their upkeep, much less expend funds to reform them (see graph 4.1.). In 1900, one investigator noted with exasperation, rural areas

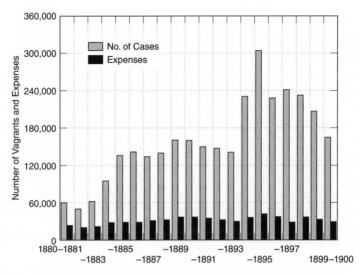

GRAPH 4.1. Number and Cost of Vagrants Receiving Aid in Massachusetts Towns and Cities, 1880–1900. *Source*: Massachusetts State Board of Charity Report, 1901 (Boston, 1901).

and villages across the country either failed to enforce the work test or did so only sporadically. Tramp facilities were even worse than those provided for the more permanent almshouse residents. "[T]hese tramp rooms are of the most forbidding description, as a rule," the inspector of the Massachusetts State Board of Charity reported to John J. McCook in 1896. Conditions in the poorhouse at Rehoboth were typical: "The well-patronized accommodations for tramps in the attic are very objectionable, introducing vermin and interfering with proper discipline." The rooms provided for tramps in New York State almshouses at this time were equally repugnant.[54]

In 1905, the Massachusetts State Board was finally able to obtain what it had called for in its 1900 *Annual Report*: "some common and consistent method of dealing" with tramps. New laws mandated a work test as well as the separation of vagrants from other almshouse inmates. The number of vagrants using poorhouses in Massachusetts dropped suddenly, from 23,341 in 1905 to 3,127 during 1907. "So far as the almshouses are concerned," the State Board stated with satisfaction, "the old rounder has practically disappeared, and with few exceptions the vagrants now cared for seem to be really honest laborers looking for work." In reality, however, all these numbers signified was that local communities were solving the tramp problem by washing their hands of it once and for all. Faced with the potential expense of building new facilities or paying officials to guard the tramps and keep them at work, one Massachusetts community after another found it more expedient to simply refuse to board the homeless at all. Eighty-nine almshouses provided assistance to the homeless in 1905. Eight years later, a total of 17 almshouses cared for a mere 149 tramps.[55]

The new approach of the towns to the homeless, two historians of New York State's welfare policies note, "was to provide the transient poor with a night's lodging and a meal or two and to pass them on to the next community as the easiest expedient for getting rid of them." This strategy saved money, but it also revealed a good deal of latent hostility toward the railroads. Local communities refused to take on a burden that they felt rightly belonged to the corporations that brought the tramps to their doorstep. In 1909 a railroad journal reported that railway detectives were having increasing difficulty getting officials in Pennsylvania towns to cooperate with them by punishing vagabonds. Railroad managers, complaining bitterly of increased thefts and accidents caused by tramps, argued that the method of passing vagrants on from one town to another was not a "rational policy."[56] The towns and villages along major rail lines, however, did not see it that way. As social investigator Alice Willard Solenberger noted, "[T]he community in which the tramp is brought into court and convicted is responsible for the cost of his maintenance in the jail or workhouse, and the feeling is everywhere common that this is benefiting the railroads at the expense of local taxpayers." It was largely because the railroads could not expect help from small municipalities that they organized their own force of detectives.[57]

A growing antagonism toward the railroads in other ways may have compelled a measure of sympathy for the vagrant population. Disputes over unfair railroad hauling rates, of course, helped fuel discontent among farmers in the late nineteenth century. At one level, Alan Trachtenberg has indicated, ambiguity about the railroads was part of a larger cultural insecurity resulting from the rapid pace of technological innovation that was transforming American life. The enclosed space of railroad cars, with passengers (in the U.S., at least) required to sit in long rows, induced a sense of loss of control.[58] Some of the negative consequences of railroad development hit home in a more visceral way, however.[59] The railroads frequently killed livestock that wandered onto the tracks and injured or killed thousands of people who were crossing the tracks or walking upon them. Each year hundreds were killed at unguarded railroad crossings, reputed to be the most dangerous in the world. A 1914 survey of 11,000 accident victims injured or killed while trespassing on railroad property revealed that almost 60 percent were local residents.[60] It was difficult for plaintiffs to win damages, except in cases involving fires caused by sparks from locomotives.[61] When the injured party did win a judgment, the settlement was usually either insignificant or was overturned on appeal. Not without cause, perhaps, citizens believed the free passes given judges and legislators biased them toward the railroads.[62]

All of this undoubtedly increased sympathy for the homeless men on the road who—now that they were no longer considered violent—seemed to be asking very little of the powerful railroad corporations. Animus against the railroads was obvious in 1894, when the various groups of Coxeyites riding the freights to Washington received considerable material assistance from townspeople along the way, much to the consternation of railway officials. In 1913 the *Scranton Times* observed that some people in northeastern Pennsylvania believed that "as long as men endanger their lives by jumping on or off moving trains . . . and ride in the most uncomfortable manner, one would think they are sufficiently punished, without the railroad authorities hauling them before the courts and locking them up at public expense." The reluctance of the towns to "cooperate," social worker Orlando Lewis noted sadly, was partly due to the fact that they "frequently have no love for a railroad." It was not unusual for townspeople to go a step further, as did many railroad workers by the 1890s, and actively *sabotage* railroad policy toward vagrants. "Along the Big Four lines," said Lewis, "some town authorities warn vagrants not to get off the trains," while along the Chicago, Burlington, and Quincy "some town officials even assist tramps aboard trains, to facilitate their departure."[63]

By the turn of the century, traveling beggars, once feared, were being received more hospitably by the residents of small towns. One charity worker complained that, instead of turning such people over to the authorities, "citizens are much more likely not only to feed them, but also to assist them in evading the officers." If a single railroad served a town, it might be able to bring some pressure on local officials to enforce vagrancy statutes, but even then the town police often did so reluctantly. "Jack Black" related how a constable who jailed him for vagrancy told him he had to serve 10 days because of "company's orders." He then "apologized for having lost his temper and treating me so roughly, asked me if I wanted tobacco, and made a special trip back to his house for some old newspapers."[64]

No wonder the railroads despaired of ever ridding themselves of the tramp nemesis! By the 1920s, controlling the homeless who rode the rails would mostly be a task for the railroads' own detectives, who could expect little assistance from either train crews or townspeople.

IF THE OFFICIALS OF VILLAGES IN THE NORTH
and West adopted a minimalist policy toward
tramps and beggars in the late nineteenth century,
the same cannot be said for the large urban charities
that grappled with this problem. While rural dwellers were becoming more sympathetic to the homeless, urban social welfare specialists often remained antagonistic well into the twentieth century.
Building on the foundation of similar societies like the AICP, the Charity Organization Society (COS) movement, founded in 1877, quickly took the lead in social welfare reform. COS leaders hoped to use modern, bureaucratic means to reduce poverty by re-creating an

Chapter 5.

Organized Charity,

Social Workers,

and the Homeless

idealized sense of urban community where class lines were less rigid and where moral values—especially the quintessential Victorian virtue of work—were unquestioned. The tramp and the beggar were the very negation of the charity reformers' cultural system, and charity professionals expended a great deal of time and energy attempting to combat them.[1]

The COS hostility to tramps was partly based on the fear that many more people might learn from the vagrant's example that it was possible to survive in industrial America without work or discipline. Tramps also represented a more extreme case of what reformers perceived to be a general problem: the existence of a class of people—denominated "paupers"—who attempted to get by with as little labor as possible by living off public aid or private charity. The Cleveland COS affiliate made the reduction of "vagrancy and pauperism" its primary goal, and one exponent of scientific philanthropy claimed there were only "slight differences" between "insane criminals, the tramps, and the chronic paupers." "Ordinary relief seekers," said Josephine Shaw Lowell, a leading charity reformer, were already well on the way to becoming tramps. Nevertheless, the tramp was more dangerous—and more depraved—than the ordinary pauper because his mobility made him more difficult to deal with. In his textbook on the "dependent, defective and delinquent classes," Charles Richmond Henderson defined the tramp as "a vagrant beggar, in whom the roving disposition which characterizes defective natures is highly developed." Vagrants not only scorned the virtues of hard work and thrift, they had no commitment to family or community. "The tramp," Henderson concluded, "is a distinct social peril," requiring special treatment.[2]

The key innovation in the charity reformers' strategy for dealing with the homeless was the wayfarers' lodge. Run under private auspices, usually by the local COS, the wayfarers' lodge was designed to give alternative shelter to the homeless man (and, sometimes, woman) who had previously had to choose between sleeping outside or on the floor of a police station-house. Those who used the lodges usually received breakfast and, in a few cases, supper. In return for room and board, however, the lodger was required to do a certain amount of work, usually chopping wood or breaking stone. In lodges that admitted both sexes, women were also required to work, either doing laundry or scrubbing floors. A few of the largest lodges built sewing workrooms for the women. The first wayfarers' lodge was opened in Boston in 1879. During 1883–85, Harrisburg, Newport, Indianapolis, Brooklyn, Trenton, Cincinnati, and Detroit opened similar institutions; by 1885, Philadelphia had two lodges. Two of the nation's largest metropolises lagged behind in this trend; New York did not begin operating a wayfarers' lodge until November 1893, and Chicago never had a private facility of this type, although it established wood yards where a homeless man could earn a small amount of money. The wayfarers' lodges were found almost exclusively in large or medium-sized cities; only rarely did communities like Ann Arbor, Michigan, or Glenwood Springs, California, set up lodges. With the exception of Louisville and Baltimore, cities in the South did not establish wayfarers' lodges.[3]

Although providing decent, temporary shelter for the destitute was an important impetus behind the wayfarers' lodge movement, the COS's main goal was to inculcate the work ethic in the homeless population. In light of the failure of stringent laws to solve the problem of vagrancy, Albert O. Wright, president of the National Conference of Charities and Correction, proposed in 1896 a "mixture of force and kindness" that would compel vagrants "to live by their own labors." This the wayfarers' lodge was designed to accomplish. The labor required of the residents was not supposed to be remunerative, much less training for outside employment. It was a "work test," designed to separate the sincere, unemployed working-man from the lazy vagabond. The wood yard or stone pile, Cleveland's charity officials argued, would "tell the true story of the man's willingness to help himself."[4]

Reformers believed the wayfarers' lodges would be most effective if combined with the closing of police-station facilities for the homeless. Progress was slow, but two decades of campaigning against the station-house lodgings eventually yielded results. In 1886 Philadelphia closed most station houses to the homeless; New York, Baltimore, and some other cities shut down their tramp rooms in the 1890s. In 1901, Chicago combined the opening of its Municipal Lodging House with new restrictions on overnight lodging in the station houses. By 1907 only a third of American cities still lodged the homeless in police stations, and most of the large urban centers had abolished the practice.[5]

Charity professionals claimed considerable success for their antitramp campaign. The lodges had achieved their purpose of aiding the unemployed, with no cost to the taxpayers and, in many cases, without charitable donations. By selling wood and stone, a number of the lodges were able to meet their expenses without any outside assistance. The Friendly Inn in Indianapolis even recorded a profit of $500 in 1885. The lodge superintendents readily totaled up, for public appraisal, the thousands of lodgings and meals they provided each year. But it was not the help given the needy, but the assistance denied the unworthy that gave the charity reformers the most satisfaction. Contrary to popular fears, they claimed, the closing of the police stations had not caused undue suffering for sincere, unemployed persons in search of work—only for the indolent, who deserved to suffer until they changed their ways. In 1885 the Philadelphia police recorded over 120,000 "lodgings" in station houses; the wayfarers' lodge, 31,492. In 1886–87, after most of the station houses were closed to the homeless, police lodgings fell to about 15,000, but the figure for the wayfarers' lodge increased only slightly, to 33,628. The conclusion was clear: most of the men who had used the police stations had been work-shy tramps. Furthermore, during the lodge's first year of operation, 163 of the 515 nonresidents who applied at the Society for Organizing Charity "left of their own accord" without accepting the offer of food, lodging—and work—at the lodge. These individuals, SOC officers stated, "include the larger part of the *real* tramps who have come under our care."[6]

Unfortunately, the data cited by the Philadelphia SOC can just as easily be used to indicate the failure rather than the success of the wayfarers' lodge. Perhaps the men who had previously used the police station-houses avoided the SOC facility not because they were lazy, but because they found the "work test" patently absurd and the general treatment they received humiliating. In 1895 one writer impersonated a homeless man to investigate the Boston wayfarers' lodge. His trenchant observations provide a useful counterpoint to the views of the charity reformers.

I entered the office of the "Lodge" after a hard, slippery tramp of more than a mile through a storm of alternate sleet and rain. As homeless men do not carry umbrellas, I was drenched to the skin. Yet I was quickly shoved into line to wait my turn with the night-clerk who was registering applicants. "What's your name? How old are you? Where were your [*sic*] born? Next!" was the form with each applicant. When my turn for answering came, I involuntarily leaned over the rail just a trifle in order to make myself heard. "Here, you bum, you, what do you think you're doing here? Get off that rail and stand up straight! Lively!" was bawled at me from behind the desk. . . . I held my tongue in submission, as every poor devil who comes here is forced to do, and was rewarded for my self-restraint with a red card bearing a number—my mark of identity for the remainder of my sojourn. In the basement hallway, where I was sent from the office, a tall, saturnine functionary was crying with the voice of a street-hawker: "Take your hat and shoes to bed. Leave nothing in your shoes. Leave your underclothes loose. Tie your other clothes together in a bundle. Wear your check around your neck." As soon as I had stripped and bundled my outer clothes I passed through a doorway, where I received a metal check in return for my red card and was relieved of all my possessions except my shoes and hat. Then came the compulsory bath, so very disagreeable an affair that the repugnance of the begging fraternity to it may charitably be attributed to something else than laziness and incorrigible love of dirt. The floor of the bath-room was sloppy and cold to bare feet. If the tubs themselves were really clean, they certainly did not look so. Soap was convenient for the bathers, if its use was not much enforced. I am not prepared to swear that successive squads of bathers used the same water. I certainly did not see the water changed while I remained in the bath-room. . . . As I left, a coarse, dingy-colored, but clean night-shirt was given to me, and I was directed to my room up two flights of stairs. My bed was one of a number of cots in a clean, steam-heated, ventilated room, without a trace of the familiar lodging-house odor, and so, in spite of the humiliating experiences with the night-clerk and the bath-tub, I was well content to crawl between the blankets with my metal check around my neck. The novelty of being checked for dreamland, as a trunk is checked for a journey, was, it is true, a little disturbing, but talking aloud was strictly forbidden, and the stillness was highly conducive to sleep. We were rapped up before light, and within two minutes the dormitory was emptied. Once again in the basement hallway, we waited for our numbers to be called in a perilous cold draught,—a quite unnecessary hardship, as we might as easily have been sent from the sleepingroom in small squads. The dressing was done amid much confusion, for the hallway was overcrowded and we were in no very good humor over our treatment. My under-clothes were still clammy from the steam-cleaning to which they had been subjected during the night, and my outer clothes were nearly as wet as when they were tied up. It was as dangerous as it was unpleas-ant to get into them. When I was dressed, an axe was given to me and I set at work in the yard. The breakfast, to which I was allowed to go after two hours of wood-splitting and -piling, was served at a well-scrubbed counter in a cheerless room. It consisted of a hard ship-biscuit, an enormous bowl of soup, and several "hunks" of bread. The soup was ridiculously thin, and so peppery that it nearly blis-tered my tongue. It did not satisfy my hunger and did create a raging thirst for drink,—a sorry turn to serve easily tempted men. No one of my companions ate more than a third of what was in his bowl. The instant I stopped eating, I was gruffly ordered off the premises, and, all things considered, I was not loath to go.

In light of these conditions, it should come as no surprise that many home-less men would prefer even the most decrepit private lodging house, if they could afford it, to the bureaucratic ordeal of a night in the COS facility.[7]

At the turn of the century a number of cities opened municipal lodging houses, and in some of these facilities officials began to deal with the home-less in a more sophisticated manner. The three- or four-day limit on use of the facilities, for example, which had been commonly enforced in the wayfarers' lodges, was eliminated in some public institutions. However, as Frances Kellor pointed out in her 1915 study of unemployment, *Out of Work*, not all cities had municipal facilities, and of those that did, many were no better than the wayfarers' lodges. Edwin Brown, who toured the country's homeless shelters during 1909–10 in the guise of an unemployed man, found little to praise in public or private institutions. In the Pueblo, Colorado, Municipal Lodging House "there were twenty canvas hammocks, all of unspeakable filthiness, hung one above the other, on iron frames. There was no pretense of bedding. The occupants covered themselves with their old ragged overcoats, if they happened to have any, and those who were not so fortunate, simply shivered in their rags." In many facilities the food was almost inedible. In Kansas City the "so-called breakfast" consisted of dry bread, stewed prunes, and "some liquid stuff called coffee, without milk or sugar. . . . While we ate we were supposed to refresh ourselves spiritually by reading the religious mottoes on the wall." In Louisville, the men received only "water soup, water coffee, and coarse bread" after an hour's work chopping wood. "I left the place embittered," said Brown. "I felt I had been robbed, as others did who were forced into it, but it was a shelter." The procedures of many lodging houses often resembled that of a penitentiary. Consider, for example, the rules laid down by the Washington, D.C., Municipal Lodging House, printed on the back of the identification card given each lodger:

RULES

1. The house will be opened from 6 A.M. until 10 P.M., except for those who have registered, who are required to return by 8 P.M.
2. Breakfast served at 7 A.M.; Dinner, from 5 to 6 P.M.
3. No person under the influence of *liquor* will be admitted.
4. *No drinking, smoking or swearing will be allowed.*
5. All applicants admitted will be required to saw one-eighth cord of wood for supper, bath, lodging and breakfast.
6. No person may remain longer than three days.
7. All persons having stayed one night, and wishing further accommodations are *required* to report not later than 2 P.M.
8. All meals for *Sunday*, must be worked for on a week day.
9. At the end of the *Gong* at 10 P.M., all talking will cease.
10. All *valuables* must be left at the office.
11. Any *violation* of these rules will debar a person from the house.[8]

The attitude of the COS toward the homeless contained a strong element of authoritarianism. "Tramps, vagrants or loafers," said Lowell, are "unhappy beings [who] should be forced into a decent existence or kept in close confinement." If tramps refused to work, argued another charity professional, there was "more reason why they should be kept under constraint than is the case of the insane person." A New York COS official looked forward to establishing "frankly repressive measures . . . having for their object the suppression and final elimination of mendicancy and trampdom." In 1905, Eugene T. Lies, a Chicago charity worker, outlined a "comprehensive plan" to achieve that goal. It entailed, among other features, cooperation between charities and the police; a propaganda campaign against almsgiving; "the creation of a squad of state police who shall join hands with railroad police and small town authorities" to apprehend vagrants; and the construction of "a state farm colony for the habitual 'never work.'"[9]

The idea of a special institution for tramps was first seriously proposed at the New York Conference of Charities in 1895, when participants urged New York City officials to purchase property for a "tramp and beggar farm." The vagabonds committed to this facility would not be released until they "ceased to be a burden on society," as a result of their "moral and physical regeneration." A bill establishing such an institution was defeated in the New York legislature in 1896, but this was only the opening gun in the battle. During the next 15 years social workers grew increasingly insistent about the need for state facilities for vagrants, and through the constant propagandizing of Orlando Lewis and the widespread publicity given Edmund Kelly's tract The Elimination of the Tramp (1908), they managed to gain substantial public support for their idea.[10] The purpose of the proposed labor colonies, unlike the hastily drawn "tramp acts" of the late 1870s, was not to chastise the vagabond by giving him a 30- or 60-day dose of hard labor. Nothing less than the transformation of the mind of the vagrant was required. To accomplish this, supporters advocated indeterminate sentences for vagrants. Chicagoan James Mullenbach advocated an institution where "the confirmed bum or vagrant" would remain until, as a result of "firm, well directed and prolonged discipline he should regain the habits of industry and regular living." As for "incorrigible vagrants," social worker Benjamin Marsh argued, "segregation for life" was the only answer.[11]

The proposed state institutions for vagrants represented the apotheosis of the rural ideal that was so important to a wide variety of charity professionals during the post–Civil War decades.[12] They wished to "convert" the idle, not merely to the work ethic, but to a Jeffersonian version of it. "Our end with every street rover," Charles Loring Brace stated, "is to get him on a farm . . . . And the community have been repaid a hundredfold, by the change of a city vagabond to an honest and industrious farmer." Brace's program was privately run, and it placed *child* vagabonds in individual homes in rural areas. The proposed state farms for vagrants were to be public institutions, for adults. Yet the goal remained the same. One proponent of the labor colonies in New York State argued that the inmates should "receive instruction in agriculture, horticulture and floriculture, so that they may follow such pursuits upon their release." A San Francisco charity official, speaking before the Industrial Relations Commission in 1914, agreed. If tramps at a state farm were "taught to use the pick and shovel, the pruning of trees, or some sort of agricultural work, . . . about 75 percent of them could be made respectable citizens and an addition to society."[13]

Even at the time, these statements seemed rather naive. As Frances Kellor pointed out, the theory that farm work was always available ignored "the seasonal and isolated nature of farm labor, the growth of manufacture, and the differences in wage rates," as well as the cost of transportation to farming areas. Such criticism did not deter charity professionals from pursuing their goal, however, and the recession of 1907–08, with its accompanying increase of vagrancy, buoyed their hopes that the public could be swayed to their side. By 1910 supporters in half a dozen states had introduced bills for the establishment of a special institution for tramps, but none were passed.[14] In New York a more concerted effort was initially successful. Lobbying by charity leaders resulted, in 1911, in the legislature's authorizing a farm colony for the "detention, humane discipline, instruction and reformation" of male vagrants. A 900-acre site in Dutchess County was acquired the following year at a cost of $60,000. In 1913, however, a special investigatory committee argued against building the institution because of the "enormous expense" that its upkeep would entail. Despite the pleadings of charity officials, the plan was dropped, and no "tramp farm" was ever built.[15]

Ironically, some reformers had used the same rationale—the excessive cost of keeping vagrants in local jails and almshouses—as a reason for building a state facility. The narrow argument over which method would save citizens the most money, however, masked a deeper philosophical division about how to deal with tramps and vagrants. Despite their gains in taking over municipal treatment of tramps since the 1880s, the forces of organized charity had to contend with a large number of people who rejected their approach to the homeless population.

"IF A FAMILY IS burned out," said the loquacious New York boss George Washington Plunkitt at the turn of the century, "I don't ask whether they are Republicans or Democrats, and I don't refer them to the Charity Organization Society, which would investigate their case in a month or two and decide they were worthy of help about the time they are dead from starvation. I just get quarters for them, buy clothes for them if their clothes were burned up, and fix them up till they get things runnin' again." Behind Plunkitt's humor one can discern an important truth: his policy for dealing with the homeless was good "philanthropy," but "mighty good politics," too, because there were many people whose conception of charity differed greatly from that of the COS. Earthquakes, floods, and other disasters also encouraged people from diverse backgrounds to identify with the destitute. When the Chicago fire of 1871 left thousands homeless, over 30 private organizations sprang up, providing immediate assistance without the kind of careful investigation demanded by the Chicago Relief and Aid Society, a predecessor of the COS. As Karen Sawislak has shown, these sometimes short-lived groups represented a much different type of charitable endeavor than that of "scientific philanthropy," and their personalized, nonbureaucratic methods were rooted in frequently overlapping class, religious, or ethnic identities.[16]

The poor themselves found little of value in the COS effort to distinguish the "worthy" unemployed from the potential vagrant. In the 1890s laborers criticized "the inquisitorial and repellant attitude" of many charity workers. Barred from representation on the relief committees by private organizations during 1893–94, workers sometimes set up their own poorly financed but communally responsive aid societies. It was the working class, and those public officials responsive to them, that stymied the COS drive to abolish outdoor relief. In 1899, for example, the poormaster in Buffalo opposed a move to completely eliminate such assistance. He noted that many of the men on relief were dockworkers, and the seasonal nature of their labor made it difficult for them to make it through the winter months. The city council voted to reduce the appropriation for outdoor relief, but refused to entirely eliminate it. When a local newspaper, siding with the COS, criticized the aldermen for disregarding "the unanimous voice of the friends of the poor," the poormaster replied sharply that organized charity, despite its pretensions, did not represent the entire community.[17]

During the late nineteenth and early twentieth centuries, staid middle-class newspapers such as the *New York Times* and the *New York Tribune*, and their counterparts in other cities, wholeheartedly supported the COS policy for dealing with the homeless. Joseph Pulitzer's *New York World* and the papers controlled by the flamboyant William Randolph Hearst were less willing to follow the lead of organized charity. Reflecting the values of their largely working-class and immigrant readership, these mass-based dailies often distributed relief in kind without any inquiry whatsoever into the backgrounds of the recipients. During the winter and spring of 1894, the *World* gave away an incredible one and a quarter million loaves of bread through its Bread Fund; the *Chicago Mail* also distributed large quantities of food. The *New York Herald* set up a Free Clothing Fund, and the *New York Evening Mail* raised money to aid families threatened with eviction for nonpayment of rent. Charity professionals criticized these "socialistic" practices and were sometimes able to win newspapers over to their side. The Chicago COS managed to discourage the *Chicago Tribune* in 1907 from providing free food and shelter for the homeless without any work test. Most of the papers remained unconvinced, however. The *World*, in setting up its Bread Fund, claimed that it was fighting the "red tape" of established agencies and that the fund was the "most direct, simple, and useful of charities."[18]

On a day-to-day level, opposition to COS policies was most clearly revealed in conflicting attitudes toward beggars. Mendicancy was more than a minor annoyance in Gilded Age America. In 1880 there were an estimated 2,250 street beggars in Philadelphia alone. The beggar was the bête noire of charity reformers because he (or she) symbolized the breakdown of community control and the complete denial of the work ethic. For decades charity officials would carry on a running battle against the beggars who seemed ever-present on the urban scene. Levi Barbour, head of the Detroit COS, blamed "kind-hearted, gushing people, easily imposed on," for allowing beggars to exist. Merely giving a quarter to a man so that he could get home, Edward T. Devine warned in 1898, might "ruin" the individual and set him on the path to a life of dependency. Far better if the conscientious citizen directed all such supplicants to the local wayfarers' lodge, where the worthy and unworthy could be separated by means of a work test.[19]

The COS mounted a heavy propaganda campaign against giving to beggars. Exposés of the ruses beggars used to attract sympathy filled the pages of magazines at the turn of the century. Especially popular were stories of "rich beggars" allegedly concealing a solid bank account behind a mask of poverty.[20] In several cities the COS worked closely with the police to fight street begging. In New York, they appointed a special mendicancy officer, James Forbes (a former tramp), to coordinate their efforts. In 1905 Forbes reported that sympathy for beggars had declined significantly. While the COS campaign made some inroads, however, this was a considerable over-statement. In New York and elsewhere the police would continue, during the next three decades, to sporadically crack down on mendicants, arresting hundreds during some years and all but ignoring the problem at other times.[21] Citizens often refused to testify against mendicants, and some magistrates, out of "sentimentality," balked at sending them to the workhouse. Many beggars remained undeterred by the police under any circumstances. As Alice Solenberger noted, they "regarded the possibility of arrest as one of the accepted risks of the business."[22]

Beggars have always had to judge the fears and expectations of the persons to whom they make their appeals. At the turn of the century, however, their task was rendered more difficult because of the complexities of the new urban, industrial order. For a beggar to be successful, he had to understand the differing perceptions and values of men and women, native-born and immigrants, as well as people from different class and occupational backgrounds. As sociologist Erving Goffman pointed out, the externality of role playing is particularly important in the urban environment, where anonymous individuals continually come into contact with each other. The beggar understood this and used it to his advantage. Observers repeatedly used theatrical metaphors to describe the methods of beggars. One tramp memoirist described begging as "at once creative and histrionic. You make your own play, stage it, and act it yourself." Another writer observed that some beggars create "as perfect an illusion as the best actor can secure with all the advantages of makeup and lighting." Often, the interaction between almsgiver and beggar evolved into a kind of small drama—each person playing a role, arguing and joking over the validity of the proposed exchange of money until, inevitably, the transaction occurred.[23]

In dealing with the middle class and elite, mendicants had to find ways of circumventing their natural reluctance to give alms on the street. Many substantial citizens had a latent sympathy for the homeless, but even if genuine, the simple appeal of poverty was not likely to move them. Thus, many beggars adjusted their "short stories" (as they called them) to match the clichés of melodramatic literature about poverty. In one "picturesque dodge" the beggar would place a crust of bread on the sidewalk and then, when a well dressed man or woman approached, pounce on it and devour it "as if it were the choicest morsel he had eaten in weeks." Invariably, this would bring forth a "liberal donation" from passersby. "'Poor fellow,' they think, 'there is no sham about him. Here is a case of real necessity.'" Jack London, in discussing his panhandling at back doors while on the road in 1894, noted that it helped to "kill off" one's parents or grandparents when making a request for food or money. "Heart disease was my favorite way of getting rid of my mother, though on occasion I did away with her by means of consumption, pneumonia, and typhoid fever." Ironically, the potential almsgiver might respond much more readily to a false, romanticized story of woe than he or she would to the truthful tale of hardship that often had been a part of the beggar's real past.[24]

Women and child beggars were particularly adept at using Victorian stereotypes. Playing on the new public awareness of charities to help the poor, some female mendicants would enter saloons impersonating charity workers, Salvation Army girls, even nuns and ask for money for various "causes." Ben Reitman recalled working as a child for a blind beggar who asked him only to escort him from place to place "and stand about as though I were his son. Whenever an opportunity came I was to call him 'papa' so that people could hear me. For this I got fifty cents a day which was more than I could earn from selling papers and it was much more interesting." The elderly and the maimed also elicited greater sympathy from the public. The latter category included a variety of fake ailments or deformities, to which beggars themselves gave such names as "throw-out" (fake paralytic), "fit thrower" (fake epileptic), and "high heel" (a woman who wore one shoe with a five-inch heel to give the appearance of a deformed leg). The deaf-and-dumb trick was especially useful for avoiding questions by the police.[25]

The most calculated ruses that beggars used on the middle class, however, were designed to appeal to the bourgeoisie's heartfelt empathy for the down-and-out member of their own class. This was indeed a subtle fraud, for it presented the beggar as a "worthy" poor person who was trying manfully to recover from a series of setbacks. Some beggars employed the "shabby genteel" trick, in which the mendicant "tells a tale of reduced circumstances and hard luck, and bemoans the fate that drove him to beggary." Any beggar who could present an "air of having seen better days," one observer noted, "quickly excites sympathy." A variant of this trick was what might be called the "reluctant beggar" routine. One man was approached by a beggar who looked normal in appearance, except that "he wore no overcoat, though the day was cold. He had pawned his greatcoat, was the thought. Well, he got his fifty cents." Another frequently used scheme, *Literary Digest* reported in 1914, was "that of the guileless country boy" pretending to be lost in the city. Other beggars assuaged middle-class concerns about the work ethic by "selling" pencils, shoe laces, or other inconsequential items.[26]

In dealing with the working class, beggars had less need for such subterfuges; they could usually depend on class solidarity. In 1869 one reporter noted that there was one type of beggar "who is only seen in the vicinity of some workshop, factory or office, where he once had employment, and who only begs of old companions, or of those whom he knows, and who, as a rule, fairly and honestly states the purpose to which he intends to apply the money." To avoid the feeling of dependency, perhaps, the unemployed worker "never 'begs'; his request is always for a loan," even though the giver was quite aware that he would never be repaid. Other beggars appealed to union men by claiming to have been injured by strikebreakers, and it was not unusual for older mendicants to carry reference letters from a union to which they had once belonged. C. G. Truesdale admitted that the poor were "much more charitable and liberal than the rich, and often share their loaf with those poorer than themselves." Other observers agreed. "[I]t is the people of small means who are the most frequent givers to these street mendicants. They themselves are only a trifle removed from poverty, and have the close knowledge of what that means." Almost every tramp memoirist reinforced this fact. The poor, said London, "never turn away the hungry." F. C. Mills, who tramped through California in 1914, recorded a typical experience in his diary: "Asked a sad-faced woman who came to the door for work to do [to earn] breakfast. She said there was no work, but that I could have something to eat." Such attitudes on the part of the working class made tramping possible and allowed beggars to survive, despite campaigns against them.[27]

Among the new immigrant groups that began arriving in the 1880s and '90s, a sympathetic attitude toward beggars was rooted as much in religious or ethnic values as it was in a sense of working-class unity with the unemployed. In New York City, the attitude toward beggars among the Eastern European Jews of the Lower East Side was much different from that of "uptown" New Yorkers, whether Jew or Gentile. The professional beggar, or *schnorrer*, was in his way an accepted member of the community. Later to become the butt of numerous jokes, the schnorrer at the turn of the century was more often a pathetic than a humorous figure. As Hutchins Hapgood indicated in his 1902 study, *The Spirit of the Ghetto*, there were many Talmudic scholars or students of Hebrew literature who suffered a sharp decline in status after emigrating to the United States. "A ragged man, who looks like a peddler or a beggar," said Hapgood, "picking his way through the crowded misery of Hester Street, ... may be a great Hebrew scholar." The schnorrer could also be a person of artistic temperament, "a man so visionary and so averse to the practical that he will forfeit the esteem of everybody" by living as a mendicant. In 1901 one reporter insightfully noted that the schnorrers "do not actually beg, they may be selling matches or rather questionable fruit, but the warmhearted East Side sees through the poor devices of pride and buys and overpays with the tactful generosity which is one of its most admirable characteristics."[28]

Few outsiders had such a sensitive understanding of these Jewish mendicants. Less sympathetic observers spoke of "hardened offenders" who collected coins from sweatshop workers. Articles about beggars in the *New York Times* focused upon individuals discovered to have money on their person. One 98-year-old beggar with "a long orthodox beard" was arrested for vagrancy after he was seen "going from store to store, supposedly appealing for aid." A search of his clothing yielded almost $30 in coins, including 1,271 pennies. Two other elderly mendicants were found to have a total of $1,727 concealed in their ragged clothing. But the fact that such beggars "had money" and were "not starving" did not mean that the community which supported them viewed them as frauds. The *Times* may have shared the COS attitude toward beggars, but the denizens of Hester Street did not. It was estimated in 1905 that at least one hundred schnorrers made their living on the Lower East Side.[29]

A similar attitude toward mendicancy prevailed among South Italian immigrants. Indigent Italians who had the misfortune to be familyless members of an ethnic group that stressed family cohesion above all else did not usually turn to either public or private welfare institutions. They became beggars or organ grinders. "Begging is a well-nigh universal practice seemingly attended by no disgrace," said one observer of one poverty-stricken Sicilian neighborhood in Chicago. To a greater degree than Jewish schnorrers, Italian beggars operated outside of their own ethnic neighborhoods; as a result, they more often earned the enmity of charity reformers. The attempts by the COS to outlaw organ grinders and street musicians, however, ran up against public indifference and strong criticism from Catholic charities, which refused to cooperate with the COS in their antibegging crusades.[30]

"Mendicancy 'pays' in a certain sense," said one charity professional in disgust.[31] Despite repeated efforts to rid the streets of them, beggars continued to exist and even thrive. Partly this was a result of Victorian sentimentalism, but more often it was rooted in the harsh realities of industrializing America. Beggars might fake ailments and broken bones, but millions of workers knew the threat of such injuries were real enough. The well-dressed man shivering in the cold on a street corner probably wasn't really a down-and-out middle-class professional, but who could tell for sure? In the rough-and-tumble world of unregulated capitalism, anyone could lose all overnight, and it was not so uncommon for clerical workers and professionals to find themselves on the street as a result of circumstances beyond their control. In taking part in the small "urban dramas" of giving alms to beggars, the public was acknowledging—perhaps unconsciously in many cases—the dangers inherent in the insecure, unpredictable economic world of turn-of-the-century America. Against such anxieties the campaigns of organized charity had minimal effect.

Of course, not all elements of society were equally acquainted with the uncertainties of living without unemployment insurance, workmen's compensation, or a pension to help them through their old age. The new immigrants, the Chinese, and newly freed African Americans understood these realities best. Perhaps for that reason, these outcast groups were reputed to be the most generous in giving to the homeless. One vagabond related to John McCook that blacks in the South readily gave food to tramps of both races. Despite their poverty, "they will generally divide with you when asked." Josiah Flynt reported that black cooks in hotels could also usually be counted on to give food to beggars. In Chinatown, too, one tramp explained, there was "always a bite to eat for the asking—no Chinaman refuses to feed a hungry man."[32]

A mixture of religious values, class solidarity, and middle-class fears of "falling from grace" undoubtedly also motivated the many groups and private individuals who, especially during depressions, continued the practice of setting up soup kitchens or distributing food or clothing on a first-come, first-served basis.[33] Each day before opening for business, it was common for bakers to give away day-old bread to the homeless. In Philadelphia, the quaintly named Sunday Breakfast Association, established in 1878, regularly provided free meals (along with religious services) for the destitute. In Chicago, many restaurants dispensed free food, and a number of churches set up temporary sleeping quarters for the homeless. One Philadelphia organization, the Central Soup House, operated a fairly large facility throughout the 1890s. They offered free soup and bread during the winter months to anyone willing to stand in line and provided free baths during the summer. The officials "winked" at the people who disobeyed the rules by going through the line twice, because "they did not want anyone to go away hungry."[34]

The strong religious motivations behind many institutions like the Central Soup House put charity reformers on the defensive because they presented an alternative vision of how to assist the destitute. In a lengthy letter to the *New York Tribune* in 1880, one citizen expressed his concerns on this issue. While praising organized charity for helping to suppress mendicancy by ferreting out the "vagabond Good-for-Nothing," he nevertheless feared that COS policies might inadvertently destroy "the spirit of true charity among us." While it was "a good thing to defend ourselves against imposture," the Bible demanded "the duty of personal alms-giving."[35]

During the next decades, charity reformers worked hard to convince such skeptics, and among the Protestant middle class they were often successful. Their appeal was received most favorably by the old-line Protestant churches (Episcopal, Congregational, and Presbyterian) and by the Quakers. Among the denominations whose membership was predominantly working-class, however, there was considerable hostility to the methods of the new philanthropists. "Despite pressure from the Charity Organization Society," notes one historian in discussing Buffalo in the 1890s, "many Baptist, Methodist, and Lutheran churches insisted on dispensing aid to the poor in the old unscientific manner." It was the Methodists and the Baptists who supported missions in the most poverty-stricken areas, offering "classes, food, and sometimes rooms, together with large doses of religion." The Catholic Church, too, distributed food and clothing to the needy without coordinating their activities with the COS. Especially during the winter of 1893–94, many questioned whether it was necessary to investigate the destitute before feeding them.[36]

Among those who reached out to the growing number of homeless people in urban America, however, it was the new evangelicals—the fundamentalist "urban missionaries," the Salvation Army, and the Army's offshoot, the Volunteers of America—whose values and methods clashed most severely with those of the COS. Although they have received little attention from historians, these groups were far from insignificant.[37] The Water Street Mission in New York, founded in 1872 by a reformed drunkard and criminal, Jerry McAuley, was the first of numerous "rescue missions" that would spring up in the skid rows and slums of American cities during the next several decades. In its first year of operation, McAuley's mission provided 26,000 meals and 5,000 lodgings to the needy. The Salvation Army opened its first shelter for the poor in the lower West Side of New York in 1891, and by 1900 was operating 69 shelters and 23 restaurants and food depots for the poor and homeless across the country. In 1884, Albert B. Simpson left the Presbyterian Church to found what came to be known as the Christian and Missionary Alliance; by 1906 the Alliance had organized approximately 150 branches in the United States. These organizations usually established their own facilities for the homeless, although sometimes, as in San Francisco, the Salvation Army would take over the operation of a soup kitchen that had previously been set up by an ad hoc group.[38]

Although the evangelicals occasionally expressed the fear of "pauperizing" the poor, this was not their central concern. Salvation Army officials refused to make any distinction between the "worthy" and the "unworthy" poor. Believing literally the doctrine that Christ had died for the salvation of all, they did not feel it was appropriate to sort out humanity according to character traits. The poor suffered enough as it was, said Commander Frederick Booth-Tucker of the Army, and ought not, in addition, be nailed "to a cross of shame." The vast majority of the gospel missions did not use work tests or make inquiries into the backgrounds of the men. Some of the missions offered only coffee and a brief respite from inclement weather; others dispensed soup or more substantial food. By 1900, many of the Army missions provided free baths and reading rooms, along with lodging. One requirement enforced by almost all the missions was mandatory attendance at a sermon or lecture. Yet as S. H. Hadley, McAuley's successor at the Water Street Mission, emphasized, there was no attempt to force any religious commitment on the homeless man. "He is not lectured on his past. He is not exhorted. . . . Neither Bible nor tract is forced upon him."[39]

Ironically, while the evangelicals believed "the care of the body is of infinitely less importance than the fate of the soul and the spirit," they were often more successful in providing for the physical needs of the homeless than were the COS lodges or even the municipal lodging houses. The Salvation Army and Volunteers of America took pride in the quality of their shelters, which were more likely to provide accommodations for both men and women—and sometimes children—than were other institutions. The first Army homes for women and girls were set up in New York, Boston, and Cleveland in 1892. By 1920 the group had established 30 rescue and maternity homes. In New York, the Army also established day nurseries for working women and provided free breakfasts daily to 2,000 schoolchildren, "mainly the offspring of the very poor foreign element of the East Side." One woman who investigated an Army canteen for girls in New York was pleased that it placed no time limit on a girl's stay. "This is important in its psychological effect, for the unspoken, well-meant message to 'Move On' is disquieting when there is no place to move on to. The charity you receive here is unobtrusive, tactful, and not as difficult to accept as some." Emma Whittemore, a wealthy New Yorker, embarked on similar work among girls when she set up the Door of Hope rescue mission in 1890. Through her lecturing and writing, Whittemore inspired others to establish similar institutions, and by 1903 there were 61 Door of Hope homes across the country, caring for 3,800 young women.[40]

The urban missionaries did not adopt the "bureaucratic mode of thought" popular with some reformers of the Progressive era. More so than the Salvation Army, the small size of the gospel missions allowed a personalized approach to the homeless. "They lay no claim to efficiency," said sociologist Nels Anderson; "they avoid statistics and reports, [and] . . . they never lose patience with you." Theodore Dreiser, investigating a Bowery mission in 1904, found that the "whole spirit of the place is one of helpfulness." Coming from a writer who was hardly uncritical of American institutions, this was high praise indeed.[41] It is impossible, of course, to say to what extent the men and women who used the missions and Army's lodges were affected by the religious indoctrination they received. Most were probably more interested in getting "coffee-and" or a clean bed than they were in getting religion. Skid-row denizens tended to be cynical about the "mission stiffs" who claimed to have been converted to the true faith after hearing an evangelical sermon.[42] Still, there can be little doubt that conversions did regularly occur, since numerous men and women rose from the underclass to become officers of the organizations that rescued them.[43]

COS leaders, naturally, saw little validity in the program of the evangelical charity workers. Josephine Shaw Lowell feared the Salvation Army was "tempting many weak and weary men and women to relinquish the hard struggle to provide for themselves and to accept the dreadful alternative of a life of dependence." Others berated the evangelicals for failing to adopt a work test, and the leading social work magazine, *Survey*, even suggested that Salvationists soliciting on the street should be arrested under the antibegging ordinance![44]

Despite the attacks of the COS and some social workers, however, the evangelicals continued to expand their activities on behalf of the homeless, doing what one Salvation Army officer called "the dirty work of Christianity and civilization." Beginning in 1897, the Salvation Army moved beyond the traditional idea of the work test by establishing "industrial missions," in which the homeless, in addition to receiving food and lodging, were paid a small wage for collecting discarded paper, furniture, clothing, and other articles that could be salvaged and resold. By 1904 the Army was operating seven retail stores in Chicago alone, and some gospel missions combined shelter with labor in a similar manner. Although the Army's industrial missions sheltered most men for short time periods, some of those who stayed longer gained useful skills as drivers, cooks, or furniture repairmen. In addition, most of the larger missions operated employment bureaus; their activities in this area, like that of the Jewish and Catholic welfare agencies, often antedated that of the COS or public agencies.[45]

Salvation Army facilities, however, were never designed solely for the most destitute members of society. The Army also offered beds at seven to ten cents a night to migrant laborers and the working poor who needed temporary shelter until they could improve their circumstances. Only those unable to pay even those small sums were sent to the industrial missions. Cheap accommodations and meals prevented many from falling into the ranks of the homeless, while at the same time helping to keep the entire social service function of the organization financially viable. By providing such inexpensive lodgings, the Salvation Army recognized what many mainstream charity reformers refused to acknowledge—that there was no clear dividing line between the "honest" workman and the tramp.[46]

In 1889 Edward Lee, a New York missionary, presented an early environmental interpretation of homelessness that directly rebuked the COS emphasis on character traits and laziness. The men who sought help in the missions, he said, were not necessarily "bad or evil." Many were "driven there by hard fortune, by failure to obtain work, by sickness, by accidents, by any of the thousand evils which beset the pathway of the poor of great cities." Recognizing (as did Lee) the diverse causes of homelessness, the working class was less willing than the advocates of organized charity to censure the homeless. Although there were some wealthy backers who contributed to the missions, it was apparently the working class that gave them the most support. In 1899 it was reported that the Christian and Missionary Alliance in New Castle, Pennsylvania, was supported entirely by "poor working-men and women, and a few washer-women." In 1901 a Salvation Army official stated that "many of our Rescue Homes are now practically supported by the work and contributions of the women who have gone through them." A Chicago survey in the 1920s found that even unskilled workers set aside some money in their budget for charitable contributions. Mission workers were often astonished at the financial sacrifices that many working-class men and women were willing to make to aid their philanthropic enterprises. Workers did not need to have the usefulness of the rescue missions explained to them in annual reports—they understood it as a result of their own experience with unemployment. Nor were the retail stores and workshops of the Salvation Army inconsequential to the poor. To some degree they should be understood as examples of working-class self-help.[47]

IF THE GOAL of the COS and like-minded groups was to gain complete control over the homeless population, they failed. Yet their influence over municipal officials, the mainstream press, and the middle class was substantial, and their views would continue, until the 1930s, to dominate public debate on this issue. Until the early 1900s, there was near unanimity on this subject among welfare professionals. Stanford professor Amos G. Warner presented the standard view in his widely read *American Charities* (1894), which argued that "indiscriminate giving" was a more important cause of homelessness than unemployment.[48]

Among a minority of younger social welfare specialists, however, a different attitude toward the homeless was beginning to emerge. The professionalization of social work helped lessen hostility toward tramps and vagrants. The young men and women entering the newly emergent profession at the beginning of the century took a more prosaic view of their social role than had their predecessors who founded the COS movement. Accepting the inevitability of urban, industrial society and the fragmentation of social roles that it produced, they no longer felt the need to preserve Victorian values by punishing those who seemed to deviate most from them. This did not mean that all social workers became sympathetic to the homeless; stereotypes about this group continued to crop up in social work journals for decades. But the tramp increasingly became a problem to be solved rather than a demon to be exorcized.

At the beginning of the century, however, even those most critical of the traditional view seldom broke completely with it. Jeffrey Brackett, speaking in 1903 before the National Conference of Charities and Correction, strongly criticized the work test and argued for a less punitive approach to the homeless. Social workers, he said, should talk to the homeless, "to see how they can be restored to their homes and families if they have any, to try to get work for them . . . to find out all about their problem." This view was an advanced one for the time, yet Brackett tempered his remarks by admonishing the public against giving to beggars and urged the railroads to crack down harder on illegal train-riding.[49]

Another participant at the same convention mused: was the vagrant a "social parasite or social product"? The following year, in his hard-hitting exposé entitled *Poverty*, Robert Hunter argued forcefully for the latter theory. Homelessness, said Hunter, "follows unemployment more often than it precedes it." Hunter was no different than other commentators in condemning the lifestyle of the vagrants he had encountered, but his analysis of this group was far more subtle than that of any previous observer. Unlike Warner, he divided vagrants into a number of categories, including the indigent and infirm and those who were intermittently employed at low-wage jobs. His most important contribution was to acknowledge the large class of "accidental vagrants" who had become homeless through "force of circumstances alone." It was important, Hunter concluded, to "battle with the social and economic forces which are continuously producing recruits to that class."[50]

Shortly after the publication of *Poverty*, Hunter left social work permanently to take up a career as a muckraking author and lecturer. Perhaps for this reason, his seminal work received little attention from his former colleagues.[51] Raymond Robins, a young Chicagoan who shared some of Hunter's ideas, was more important than Hunter in influencing the social work profession about homelessness. Robins had himself participated in the world of tramps and hobos, working during the 1890s as an itinerant fruit-picker, coal miner, and day laborer. He thus brought considerable personal experience to his work at the Chicago Municipal Lodging House, where he served as director from 1902 to 1906. Robins spoke out against the unfair working conditions that, he argued, helped produce vagrancy, and he was one of the first to emphasize the stunting effects of child labor in leading adolescents into a life of vagabondage: "Exhaust the child. You may have to feed the adult. Exploit the boy laborer. The man tramp may exploit you." Soon others were taking up this theme.[52]

It was during Robins's tenure as director that Alice Solenberger began to gather information on the men who used the facility, research that resulted in the posthumous publication of her landmark study, *One Thousand Homeless Men*, in 1911. No previous observer had collected so much data on the homeless or analyzed the causes and consequences of homelessness so dispassionately as Solenberger. Instead of simplistically dividing the homeless into those who would and those who would not work, or the sick and the able-bodied, she carefully separated this group into such categories as "the crippled and the maimed," those injured by industrial accidents, the insane, feebleminded, and epileptic, the aged (a group totally ignored previously), seasonal and casual laborers, "chronic beggars," "confirmed wanderers or 'tramps,'" and homeless boys. She compiled data on the homeless by age, nativity, conjugal condition, and amount of education, and inquired into their state of health or physical condition. The book concluded with the description of cheap lodging houses and their effect on homeless men.[53]

On the very first page Solenberger set a new tone by stating that her purpose was not to find a way to "eliminate the tramp," but to alleviate the problem of homelessness as much as possible. She argued that the homeless man was a perennial problem that would always exist to some extent. This was a less apocalyptic view than that held by the advocates of repressive measures and was more in keeping with the bureaucratic phase of the Progressive mind. Despite her complex analysis of the causes and types of homelessness, Solenberger did not directly indict the industrial system as Hunter did, nor did she break free entirely from older attitudes. Solenberger occasionally mentioned "licentiousness" as a cause of vagrancy and supported the concept of labor colonies. Above all, however, she argued for recognition of the diverse causes and treatment of homelessness. She made an enlightened plea for evaluating each homeless man "on the basis of his individual merits and needs as those shall be discovered through intelligent, thorough, and sympathetic investigation of his history."[54]

One Thousand Homeless Men immediately became a required treatise in the field of social work. In briefly discussing the homeless in her classic *Social Diagnosis* (1917), Mary E. Richmond simply referred case workers to Solenberger's book. Subsequent students of homelessness all stressed the diversity of the group that had formerly been lumped together as "tramps." "It is not fair to assume that all homeless men are vagrants," said New York social worker Roy Gates in 1921. "There are many unfortunate and good men among them." Stuart Rice, who served as superintendent of the New York Municipal Lodging House during 1916–18, readily accepted Solenberger's classification of the homeless and emphasized the need for effective casework to help them. In discussing the causes of vagrancy, Rice focused on "the disintegrating tendencies of [the] environment," but he also gave considerable credit to some of the homeless for resisting this downward pull.[55]

Frank Laubach's *Why There Are Vagrants* (1916), an intensive study of one hundred men at the New York Municipal Lodging House, and Nels Anderson's *The Hobo: The Sociology of the Homeless Man* (1923), which concentrated on Chicago, carried a similar message. These researchers focused to a greater extent than had previous investigators upon the casual or migratory workers who frequented the skid row areas and utilized the municipal and private lodging houses. Both refined and extended Solenberger's typology and, by examining a smaller number of cases, were better able to present an in-depth examination of the lifestyle and motivations of the men who became homeless. Only a "multiple explanation" of vagrancy made sense, according to Anderson. While both he and Laubach recognized the importance of unemployment in augmenting the homeless population, they also stressed the rebellious quality of many young vagabonds, whose behavior partly reflected a rejection of stagnating small-town life or the monotony of industrial work.[56]

The moralistic approach to the homeless was too strong a tradition to disappear overnight. The distinction between the "worthy" and "unworthy" sometimes resurfaced, now dressed up in the more scientific language of personality disorder. Nevertheless, by the 1920s the dominant social work view of the homeless had undergone considerable change. The homeless were no longer described as deviant or assumed to be a threat to society, and some theorists now acknowledged that they shared many traits with the average citizen.

As is often the case, however, practice did not always keep pace with theory. By 1920, most municipal lodging houses had eliminated the three- or four-day limit on use of the shelters. Across the country, however, wide variation in these procedures continued to exist. Until 1931, New York's municipal shelter allowed only five nights per month stay for city residents and one night per month for nonresidents. Cleveland and Oklahoma City still enforced a limit of two consecutive days at the public shelter; St. Louis, three days. Some cities, in addition, regularly closed the municipal lodging house from May to October, with the expectation that homeless men could fend for themselves during the warm weather. On the eve of the Great Depression, Philadelphia and most southern cities still had no municipal shelter at all. In many smaller cities, police station-houses remained the only public facilities available to the homeless. Abandonment of the work test also proceeded at a halting pace. In 1916 Frank Laubach severely criticized the wood yard and stone pile as atavistic anachronisms in the context of modern society. Many other young social workers agreed, and in a number of cities in the 1920s they were able to eliminate the work test. Cities that set up facilities for the homeless for the first time in that decade usually did not require it of the lodgers. The traditional work test hardly disappeared, however. Cleveland, Philadelphia, Louisville, and other cities still operated a wood yard, and in Oklahoma City, Rochester, and elsewhere officials modified the test by requiring lodgers to do work keeping the parks clean or similar jobs.[57]

Overall, improvements in municipal care for the homeless after World War I were relatively modest. In most large cities, the municipal shelter was preferable to the wayfarers' lodge. In both types of institutions, however, the quality of the food was usually poor, and the common practice of forcing the men to leave the facility after breakfast at 5 or 6 a.m., regardless of the weather, underscored the continuing inflexibility of some of the rules under which municipal shelters operated. The views of liberal, young social work graduates of Columbia, Bryn Mawr, and the University of Chicago did not always impress older colleagues or the mayors and city councils responsible for funding municipal lodging houses. Finally, although it was no longer their main concern, some social work professionals continued to be excessively preoccupied with rooting out fraud among the homeless, as evidenced by a series of antibegging campaigns carried out in the 1920s.

More clearly positive in its effect was the increasing use of public relief by municipalities in the early twentieth century. Though not designed specifically for the homeless, relief expenditures by local government benefited that group and helped to prevent others from falling into it. The rising crescendo of middle-class opposition to outdoor relief in the late nineteenth century had led many city governments to curtail its distribution and, in a few instances, eliminate it altogether. The economic shocks of 1907, 1911, and 1914, however, created a growing public demand for a return to more liberal relief policy, and local politicians responded. In Chicago, for example, the total amount of outdoor relief distributed during 1906–07 was only $86,000, but during the following year this sum more than doubled. The return of prosperity in 1909 did not lead to any substantial reduction in the amount of relief distributed, and following the economic downturns of 1911 and 1914, expenditures continued to grow. Boston and other cities also sharply increased spending for relief. The relative prosperity of the 1920s did nothing to halt this trend, and during that decade appropriations for municipal relief reached an all-time high.[58]

Charity reformers could not prevent the distribution of relief, but by involving themselves in the administration of these funds they were able to retain some control over the process. Beginning in the 1890s, city governments began to turn to the COS for exactly that purpose. Charity officials had little choice but to accept, since the alternative entailed handing all relief monies over to ward bosses like Plunkitt. Whenever possible, the COS tried to replace the "dole" of money, food, or fuel with "work relief." In most cities, this meant taking part in such make-work jobs as street cleaning or street repair, but some communities inaugurated public works projects of the type that would later be duplicated on a much grander scale by the New Deal. If the nature of public relief was altered by the charity reformers' involvement, however, so too was the COS and its relationship to the poor. During depressions, Charles Henderson noted despairingly in 1908, "it is difficult . . . to distinguish between tramps and those unemployed who are really eager to work." Periodic downturns in the economy found charity officials abandoning their fine moral distinctions between the deserving poor and the undeserving idler in favor of a more practical policy of keeping the unemployed from starving. By the 1920s, younger social workers no longer questioned the beneficent effect of public relief in ameliorating poverty and preventing homelessness.[59]

Increasingly, welfare professionals spoke of the value of cooperation between public relief officials and private charities. While some social workers continued to attack the gospel missions for "indiscriminate giving," the Salvation Army gradually gained acceptance as a legitimate partner in working with the homeless. The perception of the organization was not hurt by the fact that it applied sound business principles to its charitable endeavors. As the economic side of maintaining a large organization grew in significance, the Army came to routinely judge the viability of their industrial homes and inexpensive hotels by whether or not they were paying enterprises.[60] Sales at Salvation Army stores began to rival salvage operations in importance, and by 1929 they provided about half the annual budget of all operations east of the Mississippi. The Army could not rely on wealthy benefactors, so they had little choice but to finance their organization largely through their own operations. The organization's leaders continued to maintain that their primary motivation was religious, but with the passage of time this aspect became less conspicuous. As the Army grew in size and influence, it lost much of its earlier evangelical fervor and became more bureaucratized.[61]

The Salvation Army's changing public image, as much as its remarkable achievements, made the organization more acceptable to mainstream social workers and public officials. Cognizant of the organization's success in reaching out to the urban poor, Stuart Rice was among the first social work professionals to acknowledge that "religious instincts may prove an effective starting point for rehabilitation" of the homeless. During the depression of 1921–22, New York City for the first time provided municipal funds to the Army to open and operate three shelters for the transient unemployed. One social worker, summarizing the prevailing view, stated that "the old arguments for or against public outdoor relief" were now meaningless, since "private and public relief are both present in one form or another in a large proportion of our cities," and both would continue to exist in the future.[62]

The growth of evangelical urban charities, the increased involvement of municipal government in sheltering the homeless, and the expansion of public relief during periods of depression all benefited the homeless to some extent. As the huge number of beggars thronging the streets in the early twentieth century attested, however, there were many destitute city dwellers who remained largely untouched by these activities. Whether on the road or in the cities, the homeless often had to find ways of surviving without relying on welfare institutions of any kind.

WHO WERE THE TRAMPS AND BEGGARS whose presence created such apprehension among charity workers and municipal officials? Limitations inherent in the available sources make it infeasible to calculate the size of the homeless population with any exactitude. It is possible, however, to trace relative changes in the number of homeless persons and to learn a good deal about their background and characteristics.[1] At the state and local level, statistics on arrests and incarcerations for vagrancy, lodgings in police stations and way-farers' lodges, and relief of vagrants in almshouses all provide insights into the nature of homelessness in the late nineteenth and early twen-tieth centuries.

Chapter 6.

Who Were the

Homeless?

As early as the 1850s, the level of homelessness fluctuated inversely in relation to the general state of the economy. But the depression of 1873–78, the most severe economic collapse up to that time, reinforced this pattern dramatically. As the numbers of homeless surged, controlling them suddenly became a much more important police activity. In Philadelphia, arrests for vagrancy increased from less than 2 percent of all arrests in 1872 to close to 12 percent by 1877, and the total number of vagrants detained by the police skyrocketed from less than 1,000 to over 5,000 (see graphs 6.1 and 6.2).[2]

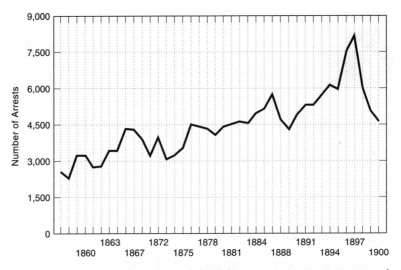

GRAPH 6.1. Total Vagrancy Arrests, Philadelphia, 1858–1900. *Source*: Reports of the Chief of Police, Annual Message of the Mayor of Philadelphia, 1856–1900. *Note*: Years 1865, 1868, and 1871 omitted; data unavailable.

Data on the number of lodgings in police station-houses in Philadelphia in the late nineteenth century confirm the importance of the depression of the 1870s, and subsequent economic downturns during the mid–1880s and 1890s, in generating homelessness (see graph 6.3). Statewide data for Pennsylvania and Massachusetts on the relief of vagrants in almshouses reveal a similar trend. Yet these figures also help dispel the myth that homelessness was a problem associated exclusively with hard times. Except for a brief period in the late 1880s, the homeless population never declined after a depression to its previous level, so that over the last three decades of the century the number of homeless remained fairly high even during prosperous years.[3] The end of the depression of 1893–97 brought a modest falling off in homelessness that lasted about 10 years, but between 1908 and 1915 the numbers of homeless men (measured by lodgings in the New York Municipal Lodging House) reached new highs. After declining sharply during and after World War I, the homeless population again rose during the depression of 1921–22. Railroad workers at the time reported that "never within their recollection has there been such a raft of tramps jumping trains as there are today." The return of prosperity (a condition that obviously did not apply to everyone) in 1923 did nothing to diminish the problem, and in 1927 the size of the homeless population again began to climb sharply. The growing demand for shelter in the New York Municipal Lodging House during

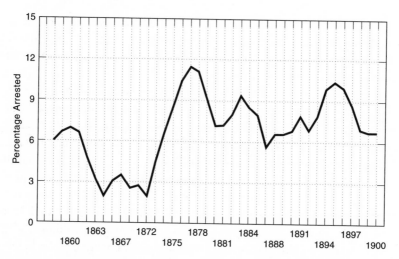

GRAPH 6.2. Percentage of All Arrests Who Were Vagrants, Philadelphia, 1858–1900. *Source*: Reports of the Chief of Police, Annual Message of the Mayor of Philadelphia. *Note*: Years 1865, 1868, and 1871 omitted; data unavailable.

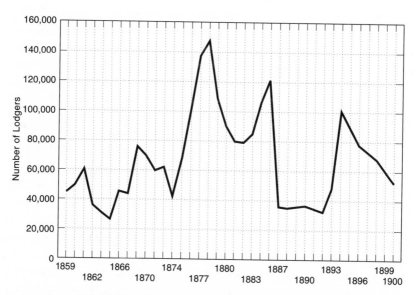

GRAPH 6.3. Philadelphia Police Station Lodgers, 1859–1900. *Note*: Data for 1887–1900 projected, based on the number of police station houses open to the homeless each year. *Source*: Reports of the Chief of Police, Annual Message of the Mayor of Philadelphia, 1859–1900.

1927–29 was a little-noticed prelude to the enormous expansion of the homeless population that began in 1930 (see graph 6.4).[4] Long before the crisis of the Great Depression, homelessness had become a permanent aspect of urban industrial society.

Homelessness was not limited to periods of economic decline. For many wage earners unemployment was irregular regardless of the general health of the economy. As David Montgomery notes, "the urgent need of heavily capitalized corporations to operate only at full capacity made job tenure increasingly sporadic for many workers." Seasonal labor, automation, the introduction of child labor, or simple overproduction all created unemployment that could, under certain circumstances, lead to homelessness. In 1900 about one-fifth of all workers in the United States were out of work from one to twelve months. Even if workers had been completely willing to adapt themselves to changing industrial conditions, a certain number would have become tramps because of the surplus of labor created by those conditions. The "accidental vagrants," as Robert Hunter called them, "are the floating element of 'the reserve of labor' or, in other words, of the unemployed classes. They are waiting to be used by the employers. Their waiting consists of a restless, agonizing search for employment."[5]

Being thrown out of work on a few hours' notice, or replaced by a machine that could do the work of 10 or 20 men, certainly led to an increase in the number of tramps. There is a sense, however, in which the homeless of the industrial era are best described not as unemployed so much as *underemployed* or *sporadically employed*. Low-wage agricultural work was often irregular in nature. Hobos who harvested grain in the Midwest, picked fruit in the South or Southwest, or cut timber in Michigan or Minnesota could usually count on an established pattern of seasonal employment, but if a man lost his job unexpectedly, was injured on the job, or squandered his "stake" in a card game, he might easily become destitute and wind up begging on the street. In the colder months, many hobos, as well as the nonmigratory homeless, had to rely upon "odd jobs" in the city. Part-time employment in construction, maintenance work, snow removal, dock work, and gardening, however, thrust the worker into a world where a paycheck was as uncertain as it was likely to be inadequate.[6]

Walter Wyckoff, a Princeton theology professor who tramped through the East and Midwest in the 1890s in the guise of an unemployed workman, learned firsthand what it was like to attempt to live by odd jobs, with little or no money to carry himself through from one day to the next. In Chicago, Wyckoff and another unemployed worker wandered among the warehouses and shops of South Water Street looking for work. Potential employers,

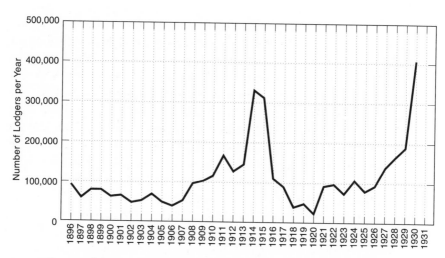

GRAPH 6.4. Lodgings per Year, New York Municipal Lodging House, 1896–1931. *Note*: Data for 1896 estimated, based on monthly average. *Source*: Department of Public Welfare, City of New York, *Annual Report, 1931* (New York, 1932), p. 86.

they gradually learned, held their general physical appearance against them, marking them as unemployable "bums" or "lousy hobos." Hungry and cold, the pair finally managed to earn fifty cents apiece loading oranges onto a truck. As Wyckoff noted, there was a "double strain, both on your strength and on your sensibilities," in the tedious process of searching for work all day. While many young, vigorous workers were able to take odd labor jobs and reenter the world of steady employment later on, this was harder for older men who had passed their peak period of efficiency.[7]

Although rarely acknowledged in the popular press, work-related accidents were another important cause of homelessness. Given the number of individuals who suffered from job-related disabilities at the turn of the century, what is surprising is not how many became tramps or beggars but how many were able to avoid that fate. In 1913, a statistician estimated that 25,000 workers were killed each year in industrial accidents and another 700,000 were disabled for four weeks or longer. Compensation for these accidents was often woefully inadequate. At the turn of the century, some large corporations began to treat injured workmen more generously, and after 1910 many states adopted workmen's compensation laws. Yet the payments provided to the victims of industrial accidents seldom came close to meeting the long-term losses suffered by the workers and their families.[8]

Contemporary studies indicated that anywhere between a fifth and a third of all homeless men were either temporarily or permanently disqualified for work. Almost a quarter of the vagrants arrested in New York at the turn of the century were physically handicapped in some way. The most common industrial accident suffered by men who became vagrants was the loss of an eye. While there were many charities to aid the totally blind, however, there was neither public nor private assistance for the person who had lost a single eye. Frank Laubach gave examples of homeless men who had suffered other disabling injuries. "J. K. is a powerful man, who has worked in a meat market for twenty years. A quarter of beef fell on his leg, permanently disabling him for all heavy work. He is too ignorant for anything else." Another man "was thrown from a truck and has been so injured that he can do no hard work." Yet another "had his right hand cut off by a thresher." Such cases were all too common.[9]

Not all of the vagrants' disabilities, of course, were caused by industrial accidents. Many of the illnesses they suffered from were the result of exposure and malnutrition, the consequence of having lived an uncertain existence for a period of months or years. Some vagrants were hurt in accidents outside the workplace, including many injured while riding the railroad. Regardless of the cause of the disability, however, most employers would not consider a handicapped person for a regular position, although they might hire him as a casual laborer. Cast off and forgotten, the maimed and the disfigured found it easy to drift into a life of vagabondage and begging.

WHAT CHARACTERISTICS DEFINED this growing class of impoverished individuals? Late nineteenth-century commentators portrayed the typical tramp as a poorly educated immigrant, without skills or talent, an "outsider" who moved from one community to another. In reality, however, the homeless were a much more variegated group than this image implied.

A valuable source for understanding the social and economic characteristics of the "down-and-out" in the late nineteenth century is the Vagrancy Dockets of the Philadelphia House of Correction for 1874–75, which provides an incredible range of information on individuals convicted of vagrancy. A diligent record keeper noted the age, sex, nativity, occupation, marital status, number of children, level of literacy, number of convictions, previous place of residence, time in the city before arrest, length of term sentenced, and length of term served by each of the inmates. In addition, for 1875, the record listed the religion of each convict as well. A sample of 614 men and 147 women was obtained from the Vagrancy Dockets.[10]

There was considerable diversity among the men convicted of vagrancy. Most vagrants were unmarried (63 percent) or widowed or divorced (13.8 percent). Almost seven out of ten of the men were literate, and another 14 percent could "read or write imperfectly." Their average age was 34.6 years, but the ages of the men varied widely, with 42 percent under 30 years old, 43 percent between 30 and 50, and 15 percent over 50. The nativity and occupations of these individuals were equally varied. Almost 60 percent had been born in the United States, and over half of these were natives of Philadelphia.[11] Among foreigners, the Irish predominated, making up 23 percent of all vagrants, though at the time Irish immigrants made up only 13 percent of the city's population.[12] The homeless men were drawn from a surprisingly wide range of skilled, semiskilled and unskilled occupations, together with a smaller number of farmers and peddlers and a few small businessmen (see Appendix, table A.1). Less than 4 percent were white-collar workers of any kind; most of these were clerks. At a time when clerical workers made up only about 7 percent of the urban work force, however, this figure was not insignificant.[13] Unskilled laborers (about 38 percent) were moderately overrepresented compared to the city's male work force at the time.

Most of the American-born vagrants were either permanent residents of Philadelphia or had migrated from other urban areas, especially New York City or small cities in Maryland, Delaware, New Jersey, or elsewhere in Pennsylvania. Nearby rural areas sent 21.8 percent of the total, and more distant farming communities accounted for only 8.7 percent. It is not possible to trace the origins of all of the vagrants, since some listed their last previous residence as the Philadelphia House of Corrections—a sad commentary on the lives of some of the inmates.

The depression of the 1870s drew an increasingly heterogeneous and mobile group of homeless men to the metropolis. The number of homeless who were Irish immigrants or unskilled workers was higher than the citywide percentage at the time, but the overall profile that emerges from the sample is that of a group whose educational, occupational, and ethnic background was not strikingly dissimilar from that of the city as a whole. One genuinely distinctive feature of the homeless group was their urban origins. At a time when scarcely more than three Americans in ten lived in cities, over two-thirds of the men convicted of vagrancy had been raised in urban centers. Well acquainted with city life, many homeless men probably traveled up and down the eastern seaboard states in search of work; Philadelphia was undoubtedly only one stop along the way. A smaller group of younger men journeyed much longer distances.

It is likely that, for most of the men convicted of vagrancy in the 1870s, homelessness was a new experience. Three-quarters of them had not been previously incarcerated for that crime; another 17 percent had been convicted only once before. About 4 percent, however, were serving their third term, and for another 4 percent it was their fourth, fifth, sixth, or—in one case—seventh conviction. Edward Callahan, a 25-year-old native Philadelphian who listed his former occupation as blacksmith's apprentice, had been convicted of vagrancy six times previously. Not surprisingly, he was sentenced to the longest term—24 months—of any of the men in the sample.[14] Men like Callahan who had received multiple convictions were likely to be on the way to becoming a permanent part of the homeless class. They were people who apparently drifted into a life of vagrancy or tramping and were unable to return to a more settled existence.

Were "confirmed tramps" (to use the parlance of the time) like Callahan different from those who had only recently fallen into the homeless class? Did the more "hardened" vagrants match the stereotype? The expectation that those who had been convicted a number of times for vagrancy were drawn from a group of unskilled, illiterate workers was not borne out by the data. The illiteracy rate of those convicted three or more times (21 percent) was only slightly higher than average, and the occupational range of the repeaters did not differ greatly from those serving their first term for vagrancy (see appendix, table A.1).

Evidence concerning the nationality and religious identity of those serving multiple terms for vagrancy also challenges the contemporary image of the tramp. Considerably more of those serving their first term in the House of Correction (42 percent) were foreign-born than were natives of Philadelphia (29 percent). Of the men convicted more than three times, however, the figures were reversed: only three in ten were born abroad, while native Philadelphians made up 44 percent of the total. Catholics were a slight majority of all vagrants, but Methodists and Episcopalians had a higher percentage of "repeaters," and overall there was no clear relationship between religion and multiple convictions for vagrancy (see appendix, table A.2). Native-born Protestant Americans, even those in the skilled trades, were just as likely to fall into a pattern of extended (or intermittent) homelessness as were unskilled immigrants still struggling to adapt to American society. The long-term homeless no more matched the tramp stereotype of the day than did the average homeless man.

Two subgroups among the homeless in the 1870s, however, were distinctive: African Americans and women. At a time when they comprised about 4 percent of the city's total population, blacks made up only 3.3 percent of the male vagrants convicted during 1874–75.[15] While conclusions drawn from this small sample must be viewed cautiously, there is little doubt that African American vagrants were an unusual group. Blacks were generally younger than average, with a quarter under 20 years of age. They were somewhat less likely to be married than whites, and almost all were Methodists or Baptists. Over half of the African Americans were illiterate (compared with only 15 percent of the whites), and their occupational pattern also deviated from that of other vagrants. The most striking difference was the complete lack of skilled artisans and the large proportion of servants, amounting to almost a quarter of the total.

Most black vagrants were probably former slaves who had migrated north after emancipation. They were much more likely to have been born outside Pennsylvania than other vagrants; over 60 percent came from other eastern seaboard states, with a large contingent from Maryland. But while they had been born in the South, most blacks were not recent arrivals in Philadelphia. Typical was John Lewis, a 25-year-old illiterate laborer from Virginia who was arrested for vagrancy in June 1875. At that time, Lewis had already lived in the city for six years.[16] None of the African Americans for whom such data is available had come to the city less than a week prior to their arrest (as was the case with one-fourth of the white vagrants), and a far larger proportion than average had lived in the city at least two years. Almost four out of ten had resided in Philadelphia 10 years or more. Yet while they had been in the city longer than most white vagrants, the blacks were less prone to be long-term vagrants. Only one African American had been convicted twice, and none had been convicted more than twice.

During 1874–75, 18.6 percent of the vagrants sent to the House of Correction in Philadelphia were women, a figure slightly higher than the proportion of females among the homeless who used the city's police stations for overnight lodging in the 1870s. Like the African Americans, women vagrants did not fit the pattern of white male vagrants. A far larger proportion of the homeless women (63 percent) were immigrants, with the Irish accounting for one-half of the entire group. The educational level of women vagrants was much lower than that of the men; almost a quarter were illiterate and another one-third were only able to "read and write imperfectly." The women's marital status was equally distinctive: women were twice as likely as the men to be married or widowed. Although the vast majority of vagrants of both sexes were white, the proportion of blacks among the women (7.5 percent) was considerably larger than among the men.

The overrepresentation of black and, especially, Irish women among the homeless population undoubtedly reflected their difficult economic circumstances, which was particularly harsh for married women with children. If the husband died or deserted the family—neither was an uncommon occurrence among the Irish poor—the wife would be left to fend for herself with few marketable skills, since the meager wages for sewing or domestic work were not adequate to support a family.[17] The resulting destitution, especially during economic depressions, forced some women into prostitution. Women who engaged in the illegal sex trade were not necessarily homeless, but they easily could become so. As Nels Anderson later noted, brothels "were filled with women who were homeless when not plying their trade," and these women were likely to become permanently homeless later in life. Homeless women were probably more likely to be foreign-born than were prostitutes, but the difference between the two groups was not great. Women in both categories often had suffered a devastating blow from the death of a male breadwinner. Just as many men moved in and out of the tramp class, many women alternated between prostitution and legitimate, if poorly paid, occupations.[18] The close parallel between fluctuations in the number of streetwalkers and vagrants in the late nineteenth century indicates that similar causes lay behind both unfortunate conditions (see graphs 6.5 and 6.6).

Exchanging sex for money was one alternative for the destitute woman. Another was to seek refuge in an almshouse or even in an insane asylum, or to simply drift into the hand-to-mouth existence of the street beggar. One can only wonder at the hard experience that brought one Irish immigrant, Mary Carlin, age 60, to the door of the Philadelphia House of Correction on June 9, 1874. Illiterate and widowed, she was described as having grey hair and grey eyes, with her "right ear torn out [along] with [the] ear ring" and one hand "drawn up with rheumatism." Perhaps it was her pathetic condition that prompted the prison manager to release her the same day she was brought to the institution, even though Carlin had been sentenced to the standard three-month term for a first offense. How she fared thereafter is not known.[19] Carlin's case was not unusual. Of those serving terms in the House of Correction for vagrancy, 58 percent of Irish women, compared with only 43 percent of all women, were 40 years of age or older. Homeless Irish women admitted to the Philadelphia Almshouse at this time were even older.[20]

The occupations of women vagrants mirrored the limited opportunities of female workers in general in the nineteenth century. Almost two-thirds of the women listed their occupation as "h.w.," an abbreviation that probably meant "housewife," although this designation did not preclude part-time employment at jobs such as sewing or laundry work that could be done at home. Almost all of the married women and most of the widows were

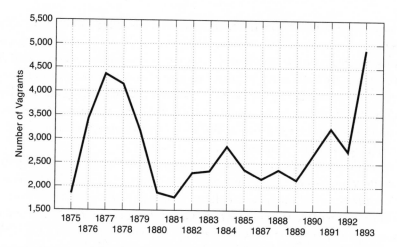

GRAPH 6.5. House of Corrections, Number of Vagrants, Philadelphia, 1875–1893. *Source*: Reports of the Chief of Police, Annual Message of the Mayor of Philadelphia, 1875–1893.

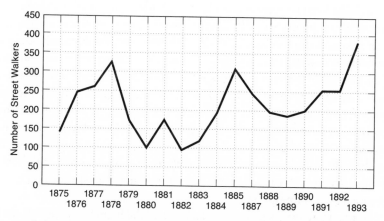

GRAPH 6.6. House of Corrections, Number of Street Walkers, Philadelphia, 1875–1893. *Source*: Reports of the Chief of Police, Annual Message of the Mayor of Philadelphia, 1875–1893.

categorized in this manner. Some kinds of semiskilled workers, notably seamstresses and factory workers, were fairly well represented among the women arrested for vagrancy, and there were a few waitresses and unskilled laborers as well as a nurse and one "saleslady." Another important characteristic of the female vagrants was their relative lack of geographic mobility. More than four out of five women vagrants in the House of Correction listed their regular residence as Philadelphia, and almost 40 percent had lived there 10 years or longer.

At a time when concern about the "tramp menace" was widespread, public opinion failed to even acknowledge the existence of homeless women. This is ironic since, compared to the men, a far higher proportion of homeless women were long-standing residents of the community. To all but the police, however, they remained largely invisible. Perhaps one reason for this was the identification of the "moral" problem of work with masculine duty during the Victorian era. The emerging feminine ideal did not—at least after marriage—include the necessity of paid labor. In fact, the domestic ideology of the day denigrated such work for women, especially if done outside the home. It was difficult, then, to criticize the unemployed homeless woman for moral failings, especially if her husband had died or deserted the family. When criticism was leveled at homeless women, it was not because of their laziness but because of their failure to care for their family. In 1882, one homeless woman in Philadelphia was sentenced to the maximum term of 24 months in the House of Correction because she was "a professional 'bum' and vagrant" who neglected her children and spent "what money she could obtain for rum." As time passed, the number of homeless women declined, as an increasing number of charities came to view women as a dependent class needing special assistance. Despite a growing concern for the plight of destitute women, however, the economic roots of female homelessness, which was often closely tied to the fate of husbands or fathers, remained largely unexamined.[21]

For the white men who comprised most of the homeless population, the popular image of tramps as a group of aggressively restless wanderers, traveling from place to place, had considerable validity. The Philadelphia data demonstrates that there was a large, mobile element among the homeless that had only recently arrived in the city. Almost six out of ten had been in the city less than a year, a third less than a month, 16 percent less than a week, and 8 percent actually had been arrested on the same day they had arrived! However, there also was a substantial number of homeless men who had lived in the community for many years, and almost one in five had resided in Philadelphia their entire life. Already, by the 1870s, there existed in embryonic form the two elements that would define the homeless population for the next half-century: a stable element that would remain within a single community for the most part, often living in the skid-row area; and a much more volatile, fluctuating group that traveled about the country via the freight car. The two groups were not entirely distinct, but the twin experiences of being "down and out" or "on the road" would largely define the lifestyle of the homeless as they emerged as a permanent element of American industrial society.

THE HOMELESS POPULATION underwent a number of changes in the decades following the depression of the 1870s. One of the most important of these was along gender lines. Since the late eighteenth century, a sizeable fraction of the homeless population had been female, and during the Civil War the number of homeless women (as measured by police-station lodgers) exceeded 40 percent of the total. After the war, however, the number of homeless women who lodged in the station houses gradually declined, to 10 percent by 1885 and to a minuscule 2 percent of all lodgers by the 1890s (see

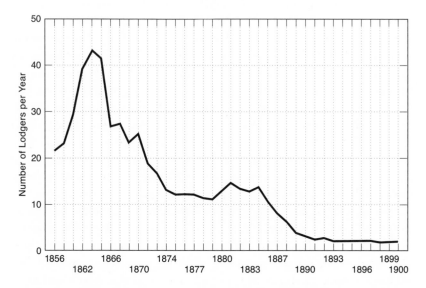

GRAPH 6.7. Philadelphia Police Station Lodgers, 1859–1900. Percentage of Female Lodgers. *Source*: Reports of the Chief of Police, Annual Message of the Mayor of Philadelphia, 1859–1900.

graph 6.7).[22] The data for station-house lodgers is probably less accurate as a barometer of homelessness for women than for men, because of the opening of other municipal or charitable facilities that women preferred to the crude accommodations of the station houses. Other measurements reveal modestly higher levels of homelessness among women. At the turn of the century, women made up 4 to 8 percent of those who used the wayfarers' lodges in the city. In New York, the number using the municipal lodging house was usually under 15 percent, and between 10 and 20 percent of the "non-resident poor" assisted by the Philadelphia Society for Organizing Charity (PSOC) were female.[23]

However measured, the female homeless population did not keep pace with the rapid expansion in the numbers of homeless men. During the decades between the Civil War and the Great Depression the world of the homeless became more exclusively masculine in nature than at any time before or since. In the aftermath of the Chicago fire of 1871, organized charities "remained particularly attuned to the needs of widows and their families, and the sick, aged and infirm of both sexes." Everyone, that is, but able-bodied men. This mentality reflected Victorian ideas about gender roles that would continue to influence the treatment of the homeless for decades to come. Indirectly or directly, of course, many of the same societal forces that promoted tramping among men could lead to female homelessness as well. Indigent women were helped to some degree, however, by the greater willingness of children to care for them than for fathers. A more important factor retarding female homelessness was the growth of charitable endeavors to assist impoverished women. Especially after the Civil War, institutions to aid women in difficult circumstances were far more numerous, as well as more liberal in their practices, than those available for men. Because of this, many charities dealing with the homeless did not feel the need to expend much energy on destitute women. During its first two decades, the Philadelphia wayfarers' lodge had accommodations for only 16 women. The supervisor explained in 1901 that it was unnecessary to "shelter many women, as other [private] shelters under good management" already took care of them.[24]

When public agencies did concern themselves with homeless women, they usually received better care than men. In Boston in the 1870s, homeless men were routinely sent to the police station-houses, but women were directed to the Chardon Street Home, which not only took them in but their children as well. They also tried to find jobs for women who could work. The Cleveland Associated Charities built a special facility for women that housed and fed over one thousand persons in 1886. The director noted that "not unfrequently, and at any hour of the night, some poor homeless woman is brought to the Home for temporary shelter." The organization did not set a time limit for staying at the shelter, and charity workers helped them find employment as domestics. Except for certain housekeeping tasks such as "cleaning the dormitories and bed-making," women usually did not have to do any work to earn their stay at homeless shelters. Only a few organizations set up sewing rooms to provide training for homeless women. It was assumed that a woman's true "work," after all, was being a wife and mother. In contrast, wayfarers' lodges for men required a work test, and they were much more likely to limit men's stays at a shelter to a few days at a time. Organized charities seldom provided employment services for men, since they assumed, as one charity reformer put it, that men were "*natural* wage-earners" who understood how to search for employment.[25]

The enormous growth of orphanages and other child-care institutions in the late nineteenth century also indirectly helped women avoid homelessness. In New York, the Children's Aid Society alone, by 1890, cared for 4,000 boys and girls. In nine out of ten cases, such children came from homes where the male breadwinner had died, so their placement in an orphanage helped some widows to survive financially, especially if the women were young enough to take up domestic service employment.[26] After 1910, the rapid spread of "mother's pensions" further reduced homelessness among women, inaugurating a policy of state support for impoverished widows (or deserted women) with dependent children that had no counterpart for indigent men.[27]

Throughout the industrial era, the homeless population remained overwhelmingly white (see graph 6.8). During and briefly after the Civil War, African Americans in Philadelphia made up between 7 and 13 percent of the lodgers using the police station-houses—two to four times their proportion of the city's population at that time. Beginning in the 1870s, however, the number of blacks who sought shelter in the station houses moved inexorably lower, falling to under 3 percent by 1894.

By the end of the decade, this situation had begun to change. The number of African Americans using the police station-houses had crept up to 5 percent, and they now comprised 7.6 percent of the nonresident poor aided by the PSOC. During the first decade of the twentieth century, the percentage of blacks who secured temporary lodging at the society's wayfarers' lodges rose higher, fluctuating between 8 and 11 percent, at a time when African Americans made up 5 to 6 percent of the city's population.[28] Other sources also suggest that homeless African Americans increased significantly after 1900. This development was undoubtedly related to shifting employment opportunities for black men. Black migration northward began a modest

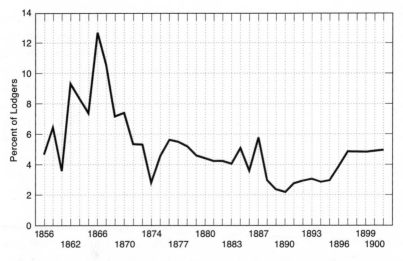

GRAPH 6.8. Philadelphia Police Station Lodgers, 1859–1900. Percentage of Black Lodgers. *Source*: Reports of the Chief of Police, Annual Message of the Mayor of Philadelphia, 1859–1900.

expansion in the 1890s that continued until 1916, when the wartime need for industrial workers led to a massive exodus of blacks from the South. These pre–World War I migrants, however, came north at a time of declining options for black laborers. Racism had always barred blacks from many jobs, yet in the late nineteenth century their unemployment levels were actually lower than that of white workers. The cause of this seeming contradiction, historian Alexander Keyssar has explained, lay in the overrepresentation of African Americans in service work, which despite poor pay provided more reliable employment than did industrial jobs.[29] Beginning in the 1890s, however, newly arrived immigrants began to crowd black men out of even some of the low-paying service jobs they had previously held, and black skilled workers and small businessmen suffered increasing discrimination.[30] The resulting rise in unemployment and occupational instability undoubtedly pushed more African Americans into the ranks of the homeless.

Perhaps because African Americans were a relatively insignificant part of the northern urban population at the time, observers took no notice of the increase in black homelessness. Instead, they focused their attention—and ire—on immigrants. Initially, the stereotype that tramps were predominantly foreign-born had some basis in fact. During the 1860s, immigrants made up about two-thirds of the police-station lodgers (see graph 6.9), and

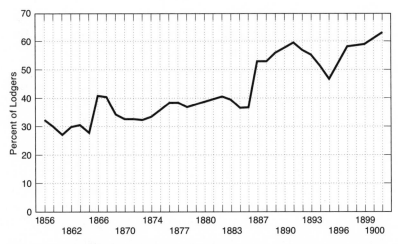

GRAPH 6.9. Philadelphia Police Station Lodgers, 1859–1900. Percentage of United States-Born Lodgers. *Source:* Reports of the Chief of Police, Annual Message of the Mayor of Philadelphia, 1859–1900.

slightly over half of all lodgers were Irish. During the depression of the 1870s, however, this began to change. By the 1890s, about 60 percent of homeless men in Philadelphia and Baltimore were born in the United States, and the Irish-born tramps, once the dominant group among the city's homeless population, had declined to less than a quarter of the total. These figures closely paralleled those of John J. McCook, who gathered information on police-station lodgers in 14 cities in 1891–92.[31]

The massive influx of immigrants from southern and eastern Europe after 1890 did nothing to halt the Americanization of the homeless population. By 1906, 70 percent of the men who sought lodging at the Philadelphia wayfarers' lodges were native-born. Of the one thousand homeless men Alice Solenberger studied in Chicago in the early 1900s, 625 were born in the United States, and most of the parents of these men were also native-born. At this time, 85 percent of the vagrants arrested in Chicago were American citizens, and only a handful were "new immigrants." Even in New York, the homeless population became predominantly American. By the mid-1920s, close to 70 percent of adult males using the city's municipal shelter had been born in the United States. In a city in which Russian Jews and Italians made up a substantial part of the city's population, their near absence from the rolls of the municipal lodging house was remarkable. As one observer noted in 1921, among New York's homeless, "the Slav, [the] Hebrew and [the] Latin are rare." It is clear that, even before World War I, the homeless population was mostly composed of a combination of "old stock" and second-generation Americans.[32]

The native-born were especially numerous among the railroad-riding tramps. Alice Solenberger found that three-quarters of this group were born in the United States. Men who wrote about their experiences on the road were adamant that those who tramped for long periods of time were overwhelmingly native-born Americans who often came from old-stock families. "You hardly ever see any foreigners with this class," one tramp told McCook, although "once in a while a London or a Liverpool bum" might be found riding in the boxcars. While Irish and English immigrants were usually represented among the tramp "fraternity," Italians and Jews were rare, despite an occasional well-publicized figure like Ben Reitman.[33]

When investigators began collecting data on the underclass of homeless men, they were incredulous at the relatively large size of the American-born component. One writer who surveyed police reports from 70 cities in 1886 discovered that in half the cases, "fifty per cent or more are Americans,—a proposition, if correct, as alarming as it certainly is most unlooked for." In 1891, *New York Tribune* editorialists scoffed at this idea, since it was well known that "tramps are recruited chiefly from among indigent foreigners . . . who drift naturally into the lowest employment of the depraved indolent." McCook, disturbed by his own results about the nativity of vagrants and wishing to allay the fears of his readers, went on to hypothesize that "a considerable number, possibly a majority of the American section [of the homeless], are of foreign, chiefly Irish parentage," although he whimsically concluded that "I have no statistical basis for this statement, but think it to be probably correct." A more objective appraisal was offered by Josiah Flynt, who, while agreeing that many tramps were children of immigrants, believed also that there were "thousands whose families have been settled here for several generations."[34]

The American-born component grew more slowly among the women who used the municipal lodging houses. Irish women continued to use these institutions in numbers far out of proportion to their percentage of the population. In 1906 in New York City, for example, almost half of the women who used the Municipal Lodging House were born in Ireland. Only 25 Russians (most of whom were probably Jews) and 7 Italians were among the 5,559 females who stayed at the municipal facility that year. Like their male counterparts, the native-born segment of the female homeless population would gradually increase. This demographic shift, however, lagged at least

30 years behind that of homeless men, and did not reach 50 percent until the onset of the Great Depression.[35]

Other characteristics of the homeless unemployed underwent less change during the early twentieth century. It seems likely that among the homeless, single males continued to outnumber married men by a large margin. Unmarried rates of over 90 percent recorded by McCook and Solenberger are undoubtedly too high, however, since one can assume that some married homeless men wanted to conceal their marital status from investigators.[36]

There is no reason to suspect, however, that tramps would lie about their age. Data from four cities for different time periods between 1874 and 1930 reveal a gradual aging of the homeless population. By the 1910s, younger men who had recently entered the ranks of the homeless now comprised only about half of the group, and the number of those over 40 years of age had increased. This trend intensified in the 1920s (see table 6.1).[37] By the onset of the Great Depression 60 percent of men living on the Bowery were over 40 and almost three in ten were over 50, while the number of younger homeless men had declined sharply. This trend was not uniform across the entire homeless population, however. Homeless men in Minneapolis in 1910 were younger than in other cities because the logging industry attracted more young workers. In general, the more mobile element among the tramps continued to be youthful. About 43 percent of those who Solenberger identified as "confirmed wanderers" or tramps were under the age of 30, compared with 35 percent of all of the men she surveyed. Other contemporary sources indicate that, if anything, Solenberger's data underestimated the youthfulness of this element of the homeless population. Almost half of a group of 400 men on the road surveyed by Nels Anderson in 1921 were

TABLE 6.1. Ages of Homeless Men, 1874–1930 (Percent)

	Under 30	30–39	40–49	50 +
Philadelphia 1874–75	41.9	27.3	15.1	15.4
Chicago 1902	27.7	20.9	24.0	27.4
Philadelphia 1911	28.7	24.4	21.6	25.3
New York City 1930	15.3	26.0	30.7	28.0

Source: Unpublished Vagrancy Dockets of Philadelphia House of Correction, 1874–75, Philadelphia City Archives; Chicago Municipal Lodging House data for 1902, Raymond Robins Papers, State Historical Society of Wisconsin; *Annual Message of the Mayor of Philadelphia, 1912* (Philadelphia, 1912), vol. 1, pp. 330–32; U.S. Census Bureau, Special Census of the Bowery, 1930, cited in *Literary Digest* 107 (November 29, 1930), pp. 20–21.

under 30. Since the 1870s there had apparently been little change in the age structure of this part of the homeless population.[38]

Throughout the entire period between the Civil War and the 1930s, urban origins predominated among the vagrant class. Of the 100 men in Laubach's sample, 63 had been raised in cities, and most of the remainder had grown up in towns, not farming communities. A study of the transient unemployed in the 1930s found that four out of five came from urban areas.[39] At the same time, however, an increasing proportion of the vagrant population was losing its volatile quality and becoming either permanent or long-term residents of a particular city. Especially after World War I, there was a sharp decline in the number of homeless who had recently come to the city and a corresponding increase in those who were natives of the community. Even in the 1870s, of course, a sizeable part of the underclass had lived in the city for many years. By the 1920s, however, this group now constituted a clear majority of the homeless (see Appendix, table A.3).

Widely differing and sometimes arbitrary occupational classification systems used by contemporary students of the homeless make it difficult to trace changes in the level of skill and types of work of these men. Nevertheless, some tentative conclusions are possible. Fewer than four of every ten vagrants arrested in Philadelphia in the 1870s were unskilled laborers, but over one-fourth were skilled artisans. During the next half century, a lack of skills became more common among the homeless. An investigation of men using the wayfarers' lodge in Baltimore at the beginning of the 1890s found 47 percent to be common laborers, and a decade later over half of the men who stayed at similar facilities in Philadelphia were unskilled. At the same time, the proportion of homeless men who were skilled manual workers declined somewhat. Solenberger's careful survey found that 21 percent had formerly been skilled artisans, and skilled workers made up between 14 and 19 percent of those who stayed at the wayfarers' lodges in Philadelphia.[40]

Several qualifications are in order, however, in assessing occupational change among homeless men. First, as Solenberger stressed, the last occupation listed by some homeless men may well have been an "end-of-the-line" job that did not reflect their true skill levels.[41] Also, as early as 1893–94, and certainly after the turn of the century, white collar workers were becoming more noticeable among the homeless. Solenberger was surprised to find that a tenth of the homeless men she studied were former clerks or salesmen and that 6 percent had been professionals at one time. Laubach discovered that 7 percent were former clerical workers.[42]

A comparison of statistics for men convicted of vagrancy in Philadelphia in 1874–75 and 1911 (chosen because it also was a depression year) allows a

TABLE 6.2. Occupations of Male Vagrants, Philadelphia House of Correction, 1874–75 and 1911.

Occupation	1874–75	1911
Professional	0.3	0.7
Small Proprietor	2.0	1.0
Farmer	2.5	3.2
Low White-Collar	3.8	2.8
Skilled	26.6	23.7
Semiskilled	22.2	12.1
Unskilled	38.0	54.2
Service	4.0	2.3

Source: Vagrancy Dockets, Philadelphia House of Correction, 1874–75, Philadelphia City Archives; *Annual Message of the Mayor of Philadelphia, 1912* (Philadelphia, 1912), vol. 1, pp. 330–32.

more detailed analysis of trends during the industrial era based on uniform definitions of skill levels (see table 6.2). The data confirm the contemporary impression that unskilled laborers became a more important element among the homeless by the eve of World War I. However, workers in a wide variety of skilled and semiskilled occupations could easily slip into the ranks of the homeless. Skilled artisans, in particular, still remained at risk. This was much less true of white-collar workers.[43] Nevertheless, the 97 clerks who served time for vagrancy in Philadelphia in 1911 were clear evidence that this occupational group was not completely immune to the ravages of unemployment. In general, a higher level of formal education was no longer a guarantee against homelessness. Literacy levels and rates of attendance at high school among homeless men differed little from the rest of society. Almost 93 percent of Philadelphia vagrants in 1911 were literate, and Solenberger and Laubach found that some had even attended college or business school.[44] Robert Hunter recalled the case of one homeless man in Chicago who once had been an editor "with a large and first-class publishing house. The books of some of the best American writers received his approval before they were published. To-day [1904] he is a pitiable wreck." The number of well-educated vagrants was increasing at the turn of the century, and even an occasional lawyer or teacher was no longer unknown.[45]

THE HARSH AND simplistic stereotype of the tramp popular in the late nineteenth century was greatly at odds with the complex reality of the growing underclass of homeless, unemployed men and—to a lesser extent—women.

Despite the diatribes of nativists, the increase in tramps and vagrants was not the result of immigration. Far from reducing vagrancy, Americanization actually contributed to the problem. The new homeless population was an indigenous and integral aspect of the growth of the United States as an urban, industrial nation, and it reveals much about that transformation.

Urban, industrial conditions promoted homelessness, but not equally among all segments of the population. Native-born white Americans had *always* made up a sizable part of the homeless unemployed. After 1900, however, they were an increasing majority of the down-and-out. This conclusion contradicts stereotypes of the Gilded Age and Progressive Era, as well as conventional historical wisdom, which has stressed the substantial benefits that accrued to native whites—at the expense of immigrants and blacks—as a result of their mobility into the new white-collar and professional jobs of the post-1890 period. Native-white dominance of these occupations was real enough, but social mobility theorists have overemphasized its significance by failing to take into account downward movement into the ranks of tramps and beggars. In his classic mobility study, *The Other Bostonians*, Stephen Thernstrom concluded that the most common change in status at the time was "from rags to respectability, and there was much less complementary movement from respectability to rags."[46] But when we study those who actually were "in rags" (something quite different from being an unskilled, but employed, worker), we discover that in fact the decline from "respectability" into the vagrant class was not so unusual, and that furthermore it often occurred in the very group supposedly most upwardly mobile in the social system of industrializing America.

Why were native-born white males more likely to become tramps or vagrants? Not because of forced unemployment alone. During the 1870–1920 period, differences in the levels of involuntary idleness between native-born whites and immigrants were not great.[47] Rather, the American-born were clearly less able or, perhaps, less willing to adapt to patterns of economic change that created periodic unemployment and rendered many occupations obsolete. Ideally, the smaller nuclear family and greater investment in the education of children emphasized by many white Protestants at the turn of the century promoted upward mobility. There were many factors, however, that could prevent the realization of that ideal; and when they struck, the native-white family was much less able to adjust than were many immigrants, despite the newcomers' impoverished circumstances. As a result of the use of birth control, native-white families were smaller than those of most immigrant groups,[48] and native-born whites were prone to keep their children in school longer. For manual workers in occupations that could lead to disabling injury, deskilling, or unexpected layoffs, this "stake" in the children's future through investment in formal education may have been a risky venture that could lead to severe family crisis and eventual homelessness. The characteristic that more than any other set almshouse residents apart from others in the nineteenth century was their small number of children. As Michael Katz has pointed out, "many people entered poorhouses simply because they had no one to give them a home." This also was why many ended up on the street, arrested for vagrancy.[49]

In contrast, the "family economy" practiced by many immigrant groups sacrificed the future mobility of children, but it also made it more likely that unemployed or injured family members would be provided for.[50] And even when it failed to do so, ethnic community cohesion provided a partially protected environment for those forced into the ranks of the homeless. An in-depth study of unemployed workers in the 1930s found that communal bonds were "an important source of intrafamily stability," especially among Jewish and Italian families.[51]

No group, however, was immune from falling into the homeless class, because no one was completely safe from the uncertainties of a largely unregulated capitalist economy. Whether black or white, immigrant or native-born, the homeless were drawn from a wide range of socioeconomic backgrounds and occupations. Given the right combination of unfortunate circumstances, homelessness was a condition that could happen to almost anyone.

ENFORCED IDLENESS MADE MEN TAKE TO THE road; depressions doubled and trebled the number of homeless; industrial accidents could turn workers into street beggars. During the Gilded Age and Progressive Era, many middle-class commentators failed to understand these facts of economic life. "The labor union 'recognizes' the tramp as 'the victim of our present economical [*sic*] system,'" the *New York Times* proclaimed pompously in 1886, "instead of recognizing in him, as other people do, the victim of a violent dislike to [*sic*] labor and a violent thirst for rum."

Chapter 7.

On the Road

To those who viewed the new homelessness of the post–Civil War decades in this manner, the issue was simple: there were some people who simply did not want to work. By the 1890s some critics were beginning to acknowledge a relationship between depressions and the increase in the number of vagrants. The main point, however, John J. McCook argued, was that tramps were drunkards and poor workmen—that was why they were the first to be let go during a depression.[1]

Labor unionists, reformers, and socialists strenuously objected to these arguments. Henry George and Terrence Powderly, speaking from their own bitter personal experience, viewed tramping as a harsh necessity forced upon unwilling workers. Labor journals periodically printed stories about tramps, portraying them sympathetically as men compelled to live in destitution as a result of factory shutdowns or other causes over which they had no control. As the data in the preceding chapter demonstrate, however, the tramps of the post–Civil War era were not always "the poorest of the mobile unemployed, . . . the flotsam of the new industrial order."[2] Certainly poverty and involuntary unemployment were key causes of much homelessness. They were not, however, the only causes, and even when they were powerful determinants they operated in a broad context that included many other factors. To understand this requires a careful assessment of both the men who traveled on the trains and the lifestyle they developed.

However biased the conservatives' point of view was, there is something to be learned from it. To view the tramp phenomenon as a simple product of forced unemployment is too simplistic. It mechanistically presents the homeless unemployed as an undifferentiated mass and fails to give due credit to workers as an active force in relation to their search for suitable employment. Carpenters and cigar makers had a long tradition of itinerary, but there were many industrial workers who were "compulsively restless" and voluntarily left their jobs, especially in the newer mechanized industries.[3] Almost 90 percent of a group of 118 tramps studied by one social worker in 1904 had voluntarily left their jobs at least once during the previous six months, and half of the employers who could be located described these men as "good, expert workmen." Much to the dismay of industrial managers, notes David Montgomery, "workers both stayed off work and quit their jobs with alarming frequency." They did so partly because they sought higher wages, but also because they were resisting the demands of the new industrial system, with its pattern of deskilling, long hours, and increased managerial control.[4]

Some of these men stayed within their communities, but others went on the road for varying periods of time. William Aspinwall, a tramp who corresponded frequently with McCook, traveled throughout the North in the 1890s, working as a repairman, as a woolen-mill operative, and at other jobs. Conservative commentators and industrial managers were wrong to label such individuals as "lazy." Despite the publicity given to tramps who lived solely by begging, most homeless men did not object to labor per se. From one point of view, however, they *were* poor workmen—if by this was meant workers who declined to adapt quietly to the demands of the new factory production system, or who viewed life on the road as preferable to starvation wages in a dead-end job. Middle-class moralists may have been correct in some cases when they accused tramps, as the Illinois Charities Board did in 1876, of "apparent indifference to offers of employment," when the employment offered was underpaid or involved dangerous working conditions. Many tramps may have taken on a series of jobs in succession in a quest to find suitable work, or to tide them over until they could find such work.[5]

Although 83 percent of those interviewed in McCook's "tramp census" of 1891–92 attributed their condition to being "out of work," inquiries of this kind tell us nothing at all about the motivations of these men, who were asked a series of matter-of-fact questions by police officers before they were allowed to enter the rooms in the station houses set aside for the homeless.[6] Careful studies of homeless men by social workers and sociologists, as well as numerous memoirs by men who spent part of their life on the road, give some insight into the values and background of those who became tramps during the industrial era. They reveal a close relationship between the thrust for managerial efficiency and mechanization of factory production, unemployment, and the reaction of the working class to these circumstances.

"Ah! That is a thing worth knowing," said one tramp in describing his first trip on the road. "To know that you can escape any disagreeable situation by donning overalls, cutting down your standard of living, and battering [begging] your meals if you want to." Many of these "disagreeable situations" were related to industrial employment. Frank Laubach found that "temperamental disqualifications for work and thrift" affected more than half of the 100 homeless men he investigated in 1916. One man spent his days "wandering from one part of the country to another, working on railroads when he can get a job, and never staying in one place more than a month or two. When asked his reasons for living this way, he said he liked the variety." Another told Laubach that he "had gone to work in a factory but found the work less enjoyable than scouting, so he decided to go on the road. . . . He says he is enjoying life a whole lot better than 'fellows who stand by a machine all day.'" Some men came to prefer part-time work, even if it meant relying on charity some of the time, because it allowed them to shape their lives around a preindustrial pattern of intermittent work and leisure. One gardener "hibernate[d] in the city" during the winter, "depending upon free lunches and charitable sources of food supply." A man who rebelled against being "cooped up in a factory" found intervals of vagabondage made work more acceptable.[7]

On closer examination, the "laziness" of some tramps was really a predilection for a lifestyle that allowed the worker to avoid some of the rigors of the industrial order. Laubach talked with one man, "a good tanner," who by choice worked only six months a year. Another, an ironworker, labored only in the winter. "[I]n the summer it gets too exhausting, and he starts out to tramp the country until cold weather comes again." The man explained that "there are thousands of men in the [iron] business who do the same thing, and that the iron foundries can never find enough men during the summer." One contemporary hobo song expressed this idea quite well:

> I met a man the other day,
>   I had never met before.
> He asked me if I wanted a job
>   A-shovelin' iron ore.
> I asked him what the wages was,
>   And he says, "Two bits a ton."
> I says, "Old man, go chase yourself,
>   I'd rather be a bum!"[8]

Many of the migratory laborers who engaged in seasonal work probably shared these views. Transient laborers played an essential role in railroad construction until the 1890s and in harvesting and timber cutting until the 1920s, when mechanization began to reduce the need for such workers. Each July and August, between 100,000 and 250,000 hobos took part in wheat harvesting alone. Most were unskilled workers, joined sometimes by unemployed mechanics or clerks. By the World War I era, some college students also took on this work to help pay for the next year's tuition.[9]

A contemporary study of migratory workers found "striking differences" in their life stories. One group drifted "from job to job and locality to locality as chance forces impel them," while others had established "a definite cycle of seasonal occupations from which they seldom depart." In the winter many returned to skid-row areas of cities, where they did intermittent menial jobs until warmer weather brought renewed opportunity in construction or farming. This work pattern represented a considerable deviation from that of most factory laborers. "The American hobo," said Anderson, "is a critical selector of his jobs; his independence is often mistaken for laziness." The inconsistent work habits of these able-bodied workers annoyed even the most objective observers of homeless men. "After a few years of seasonal employment," said Alice Solenberger with barely concealed exasperation, "they reach a point where they will not work continuously, even if they could. They really do not believe in doing so, nor will many of them admit any necessity for saving more than enough to carry them from one season to the next."[10]

Solenberger also discovered "a number of homeless men who were very fair workmen but who found it impossible to work in factories or in other places where they felt themselves driven and under pressure." One example was a young, frequently unemployed immigrant who

> was given a position of some responsibility at the Municipal Lodging House one winter and surprised all who knew him by filling it remarkably well. When removed from it and placed in regular work outside of the institution he failed within a fortnight and was again upon the streets. The superintendent of the lodging house asked him why it was that he worked so well in the one place and so poorly in the other, and he gave this reply: "You let me do my work my own way. You do not say "Hurry up, there, hurry up"! I cannot hurry—it makes me sick, so I leave. But I like to work here—can I come back?

It was a telling commentary on some aspects of the emerging industrial system that this man, who "worked rapidly and required little or no supervision," was nevertheless "in danger of becoming a vagrant in spite of his proved possibilities for usefulness." Ironically, it was the "initiative, originality and adventurous spirit" of some men that led them into a life of vagabondage.[11]

More stolid opposition to industrialism was evident among workers who, in the words of economist W. H. Beveridge, found "their hard won skill superfluous in a new world" but would not give up their obsolescent trades. Laubach noted three cases of men whose occupations had entailed working with horses (a coachman, a blacksmith, and a stableman). Each claimed that increasing use of the automobile had made it difficult for them to find employment, yet because of what Laubach called "individual idiosy[n]crasies," all found it easier to drift into a life of intermittent panhandling than to retrain themselves. A sailmaker staying at the Municipal Lodging House preferred to work less often and live a semivagabond existence rather than give up his craft.[12]

"Without doubt," Laubach concluded, "many men begin the wandering life in revolt against the monotony of modern industry." The memoirs of men who took up the tramping life voluntarily shows that this factor was indeed important at the beginning, although many such individuals eventually became disillusioned with life on the road.[13]

Harry Kemp, who grew up in the 1890s in the steel town of Mornington, Ohio, reacted against the narrowness of both the town's environment and that of his own home. After spending hours one summer day listening to one vagabond's "stories of the pleasures and adventures of tramp-life," he decided to set out on the road himself. Jim Tully's general assessment of tramp life was far less positive than Kemp's. "At times," he admitted, "I cursed the wanderlust that held me in its grip." Yet, he quickly added, "while cursing, I loved it. For it gave me freedom undreamed of in factories." Tully, like Kemp, grew up in an Ohio factory town. He dropped out of school and went to work for $3 a week heating steel links for a chain maker. The morning whistle of the factory, he later recounted, "always grated on my nerves like glass." Realizing that "I darn near have to pay the factory to work here," Tully boarded a freight that took him to Muncie, Indiana, and from there into a life of vagabondage that lasted several years.[14]

Another tramp memoirist, William Edge, opened his narrative with a description of his life as a factory worker in Cleveland in 1918:

> In the morning, when the alarm went off, it was dark; dark when I had finished breakfast in the hash house; dark when I punched the time clock of this damn' stove factory. The factory was always gloomy. Even the corners which were lighted by dazzling glass bulbs, were dirty, sordid, cobwebby. And at quitting time, when I went up toward 55th Street, chased by a biting wind, it was dark.

Edge and a friend decided to take up the "hobo life" as a means of escaping these conditions, and they began a 10-month tour of the East, working at a variety of jobs. He vividly described the lifestyle of workers in rapid turn-over jobs, men who moved about not necessarily because they were laid off but because they disliked the nature of the work or sought higher pay or shorter hours elsewhere. John Worby was such a person. Worby described how he had drifted into tramp life not because he could not find work but because the work he could find bored him. He took to the road and soon found that he had become "addicted" to "professional hoboing."[15]

Perhaps it was the anonymous "jack-roller" named Stanley, however, whose descent into the underclass of tramps and beggars most clearly revealed an antagonism to modern society. In reaction to the confining routines of work and institutions, Stanley escaped repeatedly by taking to the road. In his autobiographical memoir, the words "discipline," "monotonous," and "dull" recur with depressing regularity, becoming a kind of litany of protest. Stanley's rebellion began earlier than for most. Orphaned at age eight, he was sent to Parental School, "a hole of discipline and drabness." Reunited with his stepmother, he "began to feel like going a million miles away, just to keep out of her reach." Sent to a reform school, he found "everything was regular and had a fixed routine and [was] monotonous."

After being paroled, Stanley started fifth grade at a public school, but he "bummed from school" and learned to exist by begging, a pattern that he would repeat numerous times in the future.[16]

Stanley's aversion to the discipline of routine labor was equally strong. At one point he got a job in an electrical equipment factory, assembling parts for thirty-three cents an hour, but soon quit and rejoined his delinquent friends. Later Stanley obtained a position at a wholesale grocery, labeling boxes of cheese, but he found this "humdrum and monotonous" and left. He held down a job as a dishwasher for over a month, but soon gave up and returned to the road.[17]

Like Stanley, a number of the men who later wrote about their tramping experiences actually rode the trains for the first time while still boys. Ben Reitman claimed that "by the time I was six I could hold on to a freight car pretty well. . . . Before I was ten I was familiar with all the territory between Chicago and Elkhart, Indiana." It is unlikely that very many tramps began their explorations as early as did Reitman or Stanley, but teenage vagabonds were not unusual. Among the 220 men Solenberger identified as tramps or "confirmed wanderers," almost 19 percent were 19 or under. She did not record the ages at which these individuals first became homeless, but if the men who left memoirs of their experiences can be taken as typical, a majority initially entered the tramp world before the age of 22.[18]

Youthful tramps often exhibited an aversion to parental discipline as well as to the institutional controls of schools or reformatories and to inhumane working conditions. These factors can seldom be neatly separated: they operated together, reinforcing each other. Laubach discovered that one out of every four of the vagrants he studied complained that their fathers had been "harsh or unjust." The death or desertion of a parent was another common theme. Six out of ten of the men had come from broken homes, and they frequently cited ill-treatment by stepparents as a reason for originally running away. Another tramp, who first set out on the road at age 14, had endured several years of being a "hand-me-down" child, passed from one relative to another after his parents had divorced. Occasionally, as in the case of Josiah Flynt, rebellion against a harshly rigid religious upbringing also played a role.[19]

The desire to escape difficult family circumstances, however, was only part of a more general reaction of these adolescents against their total environment, which in every way hedged in their lives with stultifying limitations. For many, poverty was an ever-present specter. As a child Stanley learned to steal food by breaking into boxcars parked on railroad sidings. Reitman gathered coal from nearby tracks where stray pieces had fallen from passing freights. Not surprisingly, many of the boys who became vagrants had to go to work at an early age. Settlement workers in Chicago, much closer to the problem than most, realized that the dead-end jobs to which the children of the slums were consigned gave them only "a dull distaste for work" that was an underlying cause of much child vagrancy. "Grinding poverty and hard work beyond the years of the lad; blows and curses for breakfast, dinner, and supper; all these are recruiting agents for the homeless army," said journalist Jacob Riis.[20]

The work routines enforced on young delinquents in reformatories also promoted vagrancy. Reformatories accomplished little, one critic argued in 1871, because the managers' claim that the children would learn some useful trade there was a sham. Typically, the child in such an institution was "taught only to perform some simple mechanized process, and this not that he may be better able to support himself when he grows up, but in order that certain work for which the institution gets pay may be accomplished." "In practice," says one historian, "many of the reformatories were nothing less than a boys' or girls' prison." No wonder boys like Stanley found the tramp world a tempting alternative. While a teenager, Josiah Flynt had himself escaped from a Pennsylvania reform school and lived eight months on the road.[21]

Young vagrants who claimed they were "seized with a desire to roam," then, were not simply suffering vaguely from "wanderlust," as some commentators claimed. They were reacting to the social conditions of their lives, much of it either directly or indirectly a product of industrialism. A writer who interviewed New York boys who built hobo camps along the Hudson River summed up their view of the world: they "prefer a life of aimless adventure, despite its many privations and hardships, to the humdrum existence of an ordinary, workaday mortal."[22]

Not all of the individuals on the road, of course, were so self-consciously rebellious. Many migrant workers in the Midwest, one Wobbly recalled, "were compelled by poverty to steal rides on freight cars." There were many other workers who probably looked upon the "side-door pullman" as little more than a convenience. Some of these men were unemployed; others may have had jobs waiting for them. "When the iron works in Cleveland closed down," an unemployed worker told Wyckoff, "that laid me off. I couldn't get no job there, so I beat my way here." In 1906 the *New York Times* commented on workers who, "to save a few dollars," "beat" their way from town to town in search of work; "according to good authority, this sort of travel is very heavy." Radical labor organizer William Z. Foster hoboed across the South and Far West while holding down a variety of jobs. His experience was not unusual.[23]

Workers were not the only ones who utilized the railroads in this manner. Criminals of various kinds found the boxcar to be a convenient means of escape. The "yegg," or criminal tramp, noted one observer, "robs his store or house, or cracks his safe, then flies on, taking the blinds or decking on top of a 'flyer' [express train]." Despite their reputation for lawlessness, Josiah Flynt indicated, tramps would seldom "steal anything more valuable than fruit from freight-cars and metal from idle engines." To throw suspicion off themselves, however, some robbers would "become tramps for a time," temporarily donning the ragged garb of men on the road.[24] With the decline of tramp violence in the 1890s, others began to use the railroads without paying. In 1898 the young Sherwood Anderson thought nothing of "beat-[ing] my way homeward on a freight train," and by 1915 poor college students' habit of traveling by boxcar was familiar enough for Ernest Poole to include such a scene in his popular novel *The Harbor*. In the mid-1920s, future novelist James Michener escaped the confining atmosphere of a small town in Pennsylvania to roam the country as a tramp. This would become even more common in the 1930s.[25]

Those who rode the freights for convenience or simply to save money were not genuinely homeless, but to some degree their behavior reflected the same motivations of tramps who stayed on the road for much longer periods of time. Even for those hobos who could afford the fare, a historian of migratory labor has noted, it was "a custom or a passion to steal rides on the railways, to beat railway companies," and Bertha Thompson found that many men "enjoyed beating their way about the country from job to job, making good money and spending it fast. It was just a principle of theirs to get their transportation free." She encountered college students, too, who "got a big kick out of bumming their way," even though they had money and were able to pay for their own meals. In both cases, riding the railroads without paying constituted a symbolic protest of sorts.[26]

THE REASONS FOR tramping were as various as the individuals who comprised the new class of mobile, homeless men. Making too sharp a distinction between "involuntary" and "voluntary" causes of this phenomenon obscures the complex social reality that often lay behind an individual's going on the road. Even the most poverty-stricken often had some choice about whether to remain in, or leave, their community. As Barrington Moore pointed out in his book *Injustice*, desperation is not an objective condition but a subjective judgment, and what one person views as an acceptable—though disagreeable—situation, another may find intolerable.[27] The extent to which tramping was voluntary, then, is problematical. What is not in doubt is that there was a close relationship between the growth of industrial society and the increase in the number of tramps and vagrants. Whether they took part in it for a few days or for several years, the homeless who traveled shared similar experiences. Life on the road was arduous and, at times, dangerous. Nevertheless, it represented a respite from—and often a reaction against—many of the trends that were transforming the American social and economic system in the decades after Reconstruction: the increasing power of technology, the quest for economic efficiency, and the growth of organizations and bureaucratic thinking.[28]

Especially for the young able to withstand its rigors, tramp life offered a temporary escape from the demands and disciplines of urban, industrial society. One of the most common feelings expressed by those who left memoirs of their tramping experiences was the sense of freedom and release from constraints. Upon leaving the employ of a steel company in the company town of Johnstown, Pennsylvania, William Edge stated he "felt relieved" after he "got on the train, Pittsburgh bound. . . . The shadow of paternalism had gone. I felt like a free agent again." "I not only saw fresh faces every day, but I also saw 'fresh country,'" recalled John Worby in describing his early tramping experiences. "I was glad that I had learnt [sic] to hold my own so soon." "The beggar and the tramp dislike being hemmed in by laws and conventions," said one writer, "and there are many men on the road to-day purely and simply to escape obedience to civilized customs." It was for this reason, said Bertha Thompson, that tramps preferred not to use charity organizations unless necessary: they interfered with one's sense of independence. "And they want your whole life history," she said contemptuously. "I'd rather steal or beg on the street."[29]

Tramps, Allen Pinkerton admitted, had a "genuine love for the outdoor world." This quality made life on the road similar in some respects to the brutalizing yet energizing experience of the frontier shared by a previous generation. The hobo "jungles"—even the term has connotations of being outside civilization—were often described in a manner that brings to mind the frontier environment. Stanley described one such scene: "[N]othing appeals to my imagination any stronger than an evening in the 'jungle'—after a good supper, to lean back and smoke and tell stories of adventure and to be free, out in the open spaces." No cowboy on the open range could have expressed it better.[30]

A strong appeal of life on the road was its color and variety. "In Hobo Land," said Jack London, "the face of life is protean—an ever changing phantasmagora, where the impossible happens and the unexpected jumps out of the bushes at every turn." Tramp life embodied a reaction against the planning ideal that was a key element of the new social order. This was as true of the skid-row derelict and urban odd-jobber as it was of the vigorous young men who rode the freights. "They possess no foresight," said Robert Hunter; "they are rarely retrospective. . . . Tomorrow must take care of itself." For the homeless man on the road, uncertainty was sometimes frightening, sometimes exciting, but always a reality. "Always something comes along to catch my attention," Ben Reitman said of his own tramping excursions, "and I follow caring not what went before nor what will come after." Again it was the anonymous "jack-roller," Stanley, who provided the most emphatic statement: "My life was always uncertain. I never knew what was going to happen to me. No plan did I ever have. Circumstances were the only plans I ever had."[31]

The tramp, Nels Anderson astutely observed, "never carries a watch." Men on the road were not time-conscious the way most Americans increasingly were, an aspect of tramp memoirs that often makes it difficult to pin down the time period of the author's experiences. While many transients who were looking for work had specific destinations in mind, there were others who had no particular goal in their travels. "If you ask a tramp where he is going," said one observer, "he will probably answer vaguely, 'Oh, down South, I guess,' or 'Out West,' or some other equally indefinite place. If you urge him still further he may mention some State, but that will be as much as he can tell."[32]

Because vagabonds lived from day to day, the gratification of immediate needs played a large role in their lives. The pleasure of smoking and, especially, of eating are lovingly described in hobo songs and in the reminiscences of men who wrote about life on the road. In books about tramping, liberal "handouts" are always portrayed in almost excessive detail:

> It was indeed [recounted one tramp memoirist] an enormous parcel she gave me. I opened it when I was a safe distance up the street and found a pint bottle filled with coffee, meat sandwiches, raisin cakes, bread and jelly, doughnuts, and an apple. Frisco [another tramp], whom I had met at the end of my walk, had fared equally well. He had fried egg sandwiches, currant pie, bread and jam, cold baked potatoes, and two bananas. We walked out along a country road, and, spreading our feast beneath a tree in the midst of the meadow, made a hearty meal.[33]

It may have been true, as Hunter noted, that tramps' "habits of living rob them of systematic memory," but the passion for anonymity among the denizens of the road could also be quite deliberate. Between 10 and 15 per-cent of the men who applied for assistance at the Philadelphia Society for Organizing Charity in the late nineteenth century declined to provide per-sonal information to charity officials. Three of every ten men who applied for assistance at the Chicago COS told stories that could not be verified or were found to be manifestly false. The men who rode the rails seldom used their real names. When questioned by investigators like McCook, tramps usually made up patently false names like "John Brown." While on the road, they adopted "monikers," described quaintly by Jack London as "the *nom-de-rails* that hoboes assume or accept when thrust upon them by their fel-lows." Such names, further illustrating a love of concrete expression, were usually a combination of an obvious physical characteristic with the city or area of the country from which the man had come: "Frisco Wingey" (a one-armed tramp), "Chicago Red," or "Boston Slim" would be typical. Less fre-quently, personality traits (such as "Bullhead" or "Silent Jack") or habits ("Corncob" or "Dopey") would be used.[34]

The moniker served as a first barrier to protect the privacy of men on the road. Those who tried to pry behind it were sometimes abruptly cut off in mid-sentence. Carl Schockman, a young man who went tramping with his brother in the 1930s, recalled one such conversation with a teen-aged vagabond:

"Where is your home" [asked Schockman].
"I ain't got any."
"Don't you have a mother or father or anyone who—"
"Quit your askin' questions," he almost shouted. "I git enough of that from the lousy dicks [railroad police]."

As Flynt noted, "A man's ancestry, like his own personal private history, is a tabooed [*sic*] subject among box-car travelers, even when a little child starts the inquiry." John J. McCook learned the same thing when he conducted a series of interviews with homeless men in 1894. Perhaps most of the men on the road had nothing to hide, but the culture of the road, in this instance, acted as a defense for the most vulnerable members of the group. The use of a special argot further separated these men from a potentially hostile outside world. A tramp might *drill* (walk), *flop* (sleep) outside, *batter privates* (beg at homes) to get a *lump* (parcel of food). A man without *jack* (money) in his *kick* (hip pocket) would at least not have to invent a *ghost story* (fanciful tale used in begging) to get some *mulligan* in the *jungle*. Significantly, symbols of authority, whether persons or institutions, were usually given ironic or derisive names: policemen were *bulls* who carried *saps* (clubs); train conductors were *cons*; jails were *cans*; employment agents were *sharks*; a village policeman was a *town clown* who might send you to the *pogie* (workhouse). Men on the road also developed nicknames for important cities that were rail centers. Pittsburgh was known as *Cinders*; Kalamazoo as *the Zoo*; Minneapolis as *Minnie*; Washington as *the Cap*; less endearing was *Louse Town* (Columbus, Ohio) and *Death Valley* (Cincinnati). Significantly, Chicago was called *the Village*, indicating, perhaps, that every wanderer could feel at home there.[35]

Although men often traveled in groups, acquaintanceships made on the road were usually short-lived. "[O]wing to the uncertainty of circumstance," Jim Tully noted, "the most expert of drifters find it impossible to travel together."[36] As life in the "jungles" revealed, however, the individualism of men on the road was not usually competitive, and men on the road were usually willing to contribute to common needs, recognizing that such communalism would be quite temporary.

In his travels as an itinerant worker in California, F. C. Mills described the jungle as "the unsung center of hobo life, its kitchen, bedroom, bathroom, its public forum, library and bureau of information." Except in California and some parts of the South, the jungles, like the railroads, were seldom used by tramps or hobos during the winter months. From April to November, however, they were continuously occupied by a population whose composition shifted not only from one day to another, but sometimes from hour to hour. The ideal jungle, said Nels Anderson, should be "convenient to the railroad but inaccessible to the highway." It was usually hidden from view by trees or shrubbery. Preferably, it was not more than one or two miles from a town— close enough to be able to walk to, but far enough away so that the local constabulary would usually consider it off-limits to his jurisdiction. The larger camps were usually located near a stream or some other source of water, a necessity for both cooking and for washing one's clothes. Contrary to popular myth, most men on the road washed their clothes whenever they had the opportunity to do so. Most descriptions of hobo camps mentioned lines stretched across trees to hang washing out to dry.[37]

In the clearing at the center of the camp there were places to build fires and a number of makeshift benches. On the periphery of the more frequently used jungles there were shelters of various kinds, made from discarded wood, tarpaper, or tin. By the 1920s some of the camps had taken on a semipermanent appearance. One tramp described "a pearl" of a jungle on the West Coast in which a "kitchen had been built like an outsize sideboard from wood and flattened kerosene tins." He found "other comforts" as well: "old chairs, a dilapidated couch, the rear seat, complete with the torn hood, of a motor-car, and an iron bedstead with a grass filled mattress." Another writer found "huts of all descriptions" in one jungle. "Some were about the size of dog kennels and were made of brick or stone. Others were built of brush or tin, and a few were constructed in such a fashion that they looked like scrap heaps with holes bored into them. The huts were lined with paper, rags, grass and straw."[38]

Certain unwritten rules of conduct and cooperation were required of everyone who entered the camp. Each newcomer had to bring or procure firewood or something to eat for the others. "Here you share and share alike in true fraternal style. . . . Staple foods are always left behind for the common supply." Some men would go to town on "begging expeditions," and they often could get food either free or at cut-rate prices from sympathetic shopkeepers. The men were expected to share any cooking utensils they might have with them and to assist in washing them afterward; they were also supposed to help keep the camp clean, to the degree that this was possible. These "regulations" were evident in the camps as early as the 1870s. "While you remain," said Pinkerton in describing a "settlement of tramps" near Philadelphia, "you may have as good as they have, providing you show yourself willing to assist to the extent of your ability." If not, "you must take to the road again of your own accord to avoid a broken head and summary ejection."[39]

The contingents of Coxey's Army in 1894 were more organized than the men staying in the jungles. The quasi-military facade of the "industrial armies" required reveille at 7 A.M., followed by washing up and the distribution of the day's rations. Otherwise, the Coxeyites had much in common with "ordinary" tramps. Like other men on the road, they were able to depend from time to time on the largesse of local citizens. The "officers" had no advance plan about where to stop along the way to Washington, and participants in the march joined or left their group at will.[40]

The communal nature of the hobo camp did not exclude violence any more than did the temporary communalism of the frontier. Especially when too much liquor had been flowing, fistfights could easily erupt and sometimes turn into general melees. As Tully laconically noted, "A hobo camp is not a YMCA when trouble starts. Some great pugilists have been developed on the road." Criminals did occasionally prey on tramps, but such incidents usually occurred in boxcars when groups of robbers waylaid individuals who were traveling alone. Seasonal workers returning to the cities after receiving their wages were particularly vulnerable to such attacks.[41] Violence between tramps, however, was not a major theme of those who wrote about their experiences on the road. In the absence of official law enforcement a kind of tyranny of the majority acted as a check upon much antisocial behavior. Anyone caught stealing from a sleeping man would receive summary justice—often a whipping, a forced monetary "contribution" to the jungle, and ejection from the camp. And although most of the men who used the camps had begged for money or food at some point, such behavior was viewed as inappropriate to the communal spirit of the jungles. Men who begged from other tramps were ostracized as "jungle buzzards." The irony was that tramps, viewed as dangerous by many people, were actually "more than usually companionable among themselves."[42]

Tramps and hobos were hardly political in the usual sense of that term. Most could not even vote because they failed to meet residency requirements of their winter locales.[43] Their lifestyle on the road, however, had much in common with what Richard Oestreicher has referred to as workers' "subculture of opposition" to increasing corporate domination during the post–Civil War period. With the collapse of the Knights of Labor in the late 1880s and '90s, this subculture fragmented. Despite a lack of industrial unions, however, strikes and walkouts continued and even increased, and an oppositional culture was evident in rent strikes, riots over food prices, and the persistence of preindustrial work habits among some laborers, often rooted in ethnic or religious values.[44]

The behavior of tramps and hobos represented, in some ways, a variant of this oppositional working-class culture. Although they operated within industrial society, their pattern of intermittent work and leisure, as well as the social organization of the hobo jungles, reflected a commitment to preindustrial values. In contrast to immigrant workers, however, few of the men on the road had come from a peasant background. By 1900 most tramps were native-born Americans who had grown up in cities, and their opposition to industrialism was often highly individualistic in nature. The attraction of hobos to the radical Industrial Workers of the World (IWW) may have had as much to do with that organization's decentralized, almost anarchistic structure as it did with the IWW's outspoken hostility to the established economic order. Many IWW members, recalled one ex-wobbly, "just couldn't 'stay put'" because of "their antipathy for factories and smokestacks."[45]

The informal rules of conduct in the jungles sound very much like the distant descendants of the rudimentary, democratic organization of the semi-criminal and outcast elements of eighteenth-century London. "The London proletariat," Peter Linebaugh has explained, "was not incapable of self-government; yet because it needed to be mobile in order to find work and was scattered throughout the city, it could not, at least in this period, develop broader or more durable instruments of self-rule." Transient laborers often expressed their anger over "wage slavery" and the power of big business, but their oppositional mentality was more likely to find expression in symbolic terms.[46] Tramps sometimes destroyed railroad property "in retaliation for the inhuman abuse of the homeless, working wage-earner," and the "kangaroo court," a popular hobo tradition, allowed homeless men to satirize legitimate legal proceedings for their own amusement (a custom that also had its roots in eighteenth-century England, if not earlier).[47] Despite their egalitarian and anticapitalist impulses, however, the transient workers' need for mobility and paramount belief in "liberty" above all else placed severe limitations on their ability—or desire—to organize.[48]

The tramps' identification of freedom with mobility made their lifestyle especially attractive to African Americans. Almost all the authors who described their tramping experiences mentioned black vagabonds. A fundamental difference, however, was evident in the relationship of the two racial groups to the industrial economy. Since African Americans participated little in the emerging industrial/bureaucratic order prior to World War I, they seldom took to the road in response to the constraints or uncertainties of that system. Their participation instead should be seen as an aspect of African Americans' response to growing economic and political repression in the South.

One could make the case that the first black "tramps" were the slaves who, during the Civil War, ran away from the plantations at the earliest rumors of the approach of Union armies. In the immediate aftermath of slavery, freedom of movement per se seemed especially important to a race that had been denied geographic mobility during the long years of bondage. As Peter Kolchin has pointed out, at that time some black migrants had specific economic goals, but many moved simply "to affirm their freedom, because free movement was one of the obvious earmarks of their new status." By the end of the century, with the return of white supremacy and the reenactment of stringent vagrancy codes, freedom of movement again became crucial to African Americans in the South.[49]

Beginning in the 1870s, young black men began to take part seasonally in railroad construction, logging, and sawmill work, and it is probable that they often traveled illegally on the trains to get to their jobs. One contemporary noted that black sawmill workers were "not inclined to stay long in one location." The logging camps were isolated, and most workers were homeless men with few if any possessions. Jacqueline Jones notes that, while whites often outnumbered blacks in the lumber camps, "black men performed the heaviest labor." Nevertheless, the work offered young African Americans an alternative to the boredom and oppression of sharecropping, while traveling by freight car undoubtedly broadened their perspective and awakened some to the idea of escaping from the South entirely. Manual laborers were not the only African Americans who used the trains. Thomas Dorsey's uncle, a musician, "wandered about—mostly as a hobo on freight trains" at this time. At the outset of the depression of 1893, William Aspinwall found "thousands of Negroes," as well as many whites, on the road in the South. Clyde V. Kiser plausibly estimated that 5 percent of black migrants at the turn of the century were "chronic ramblers," but a considerably larger number may have participated intermittently in life on the road. Some of these were escapees from the racist justice system of the South. Jim Tully encountered a black tramp from Georgia who had run away after having been sentenced to six months labor on a plantation.[50]

African Americans had another reason for being attracted to life on the road. At a time when American society was becoming increasingly segregated along racial lines, the underclass of tramps and vagrants usually accepted blacks on a fairly equal basis. This is not to say that no problems between blacks and whites occurred, but given the close contact, general poverty, and rough lifestyle of many men on the road, the amount of racial conflict was surprisingly low. Coxey's Army, notes a historian of the movement, "remained remarkably open to all comers," and there was little friction between black and white participants. In one case a Polish immigrant and an African American, who might in another setting have been bitter enemies competing for unskilled labor positions, found it possible to travel together on the road without animosity. Racial intermingling was common on the road. Josiah Flynt, for example, casually noted at one point that he "rode from Syracuse to Rochester with a [white] kid and two colored tramps." As a young man in the 1930s, the writer Louis L'Amour had a similar experience. However, another memoirist of that time, while emphasizing that African Americans "were largely accepted by the other hobos I knew," noted that sometimes in the South "black men were not allowed to ride in the same boxcar with whites." Such attitudes may have incited the incident at Scottsboro, Alabama, in 1931, in which a brawl between black and white tramps led to accusations that the blacks had raped two white girls riding on the same train. Although such incidents do not seem to have been common, it is probable that some degree of informal segregation did take place in the hobo jungles or on the trains in the South.[51]

The "new" European immigrants seldom rode the freights, and Asian immigrants never did. With these exceptions, the hobo jungles were racially and ethnically very diverse. F. C. Mills noted that on any given day in the hobo camps in California "there may be 20 men of all ages, colors, and

nationalities (usually very few or no Greeks, Italians, and Southern Europeans generally), cooking and boiling up [their clothes], sleeping." African
Americans usually would be welcomed as readily as whites and invited to
partake of whatever food or liquor was available. In the rare instance when
they were not, blacks defended their unwritten "rights" to access. When
white tramps attempted to exclude blacks from entering a hobo camp in New
Jersey, black tramps did so anyway, leading to a violent confrontation in
which one man was killed. In 1885 the *New York Tribune* described a tramp
colony of a dozen men in Westchester County; its cook was a black man who
reportedly always carried a revolver with him. Perhaps it was this propensity of blacks to defend themselves that made them acceptable to most white
tramps; in 1903 it was two black tramps who wounded a Pennsylvania Railroad detective renowned for his "tramp catching" raids.[52]

The egalitarian nature of the culture of the road, however, was probably the most important cause of racial tolerance among tramps. Harry
Kemp described one scene in a Texas railway station waiting room where
wanderers of both races gathered around a coal stove and exchanged useful
information, with no apparent sign of racial antagonism. Carl Schockman
depicted a similar situation in a jungle in the same state, with blacks, whites,
and Mexicans sharing food around a campfire. There were numerous other
examples of tramps and hobos aiding each other on the road, with no
regard to racial differences. African American tramps even took part—
undoubtedly with pleasure—in the theatrical "kangaroo courts" that
mocked the impartial justice of the American legal system. "The Negro on
the road," concluded sociologist Theodore Caplow in the 1930s, "enjoys
relatively greater status than he can expect elsewhere," and the level of
racial prejudice there was "markedly low." The hobo jungle was seemingly
one of the most racially integrated institutions in America.[53]

Compared to African Americans, women were seen only occasionally in
the boxcars or jungles. Bertha Thompson, recalling the early days of her own
tramping experience just before World War I, noted that the arrival of a
woman in a hobo camp "caused a little stir." Given the gender restrictions
prevalent at that time, and the path of rebellion that tramping symbolized, it
is not surprising that few women rode the rails. The women who did go on
the road became, of necessity, hardened by the experience. Having broken so
completely with the Victorian code of appropriate female behavior, they
may have felt no reason to maintain a "ladylike" demeanor. Women "on
tramp," a male vagabond told McCook, were "a bad lot." One middle-class
commentator claimed that such women were "much more irreclaimable than
the men [on the road]. They have less true politeness, less sense of honor, and

if dishonest are much more subtle." In 1903, the superintendent of a girls' reformatory worried that female vagabonds were "easily led" and frequently became "the victims of designing persons." Such hostile or patronizing views were typical of outside observers, who were appalled that women or girls would even consider partaking of such a rough, "male" activity.[54]

Although Thompson claimed that the women she had known on the road before World War I were "almost always alone," the scattered accounts of female tramps reported in the press indicate that this was not necessarily the case. Women sometimes traveled with men, usually singly but sometimes in groups. One observer wrote in 1879 that he had even seen three girls in upstate New York who "had been tramping all summer as leaders of a band of tramping boys." Some women on the road were prostitutes who, as McCook put it, supported themselves through "solicitation at extremely low rates." There is no evidence, however, that most female vagabonds were involved in the illegal sex trade. If they traveled with a man, they did so for companionship or protection. Perhaps because many tramps had taken to the road to escape entangling or oppressive family relationships, they sometimes viewed men and women riding the rails together with contempt. "I have seen several women on tramp," Aspinwall told McCook, "but [they are] low-down creatures. The men call them bags, old Bag. A man along with a Bag don't stand very high in [our esteem]."[55] There is no evidence of violence being used against such couples, however, or of any attempt to exclude them from the jungles.

The number of female vagabonds may have been slightly underestimated because of the propensity of some women to masquerade as men. In 1880 the *Railroad Gazette* reported that one tramp captured by railroad police in New Jersey "turned out to be a woman in man's clothing." From time to time similar incidents of cross-dressing were noted in the press. Such a disguise helped women traveling alone to avoid the inevitable sexual advances that would have occurred had their real identity been known. For others, however, taking on a masculine identity may have constituted a more serious rejection of the confining female roles of that era. In 1902 one "Jimmie McDougall," the leader of a "large and dreaded band of marauders and tramps who have long been the terror of Monroe County [New York] farmers," was discovered to be a woman after her arrest. She revealed herself as Teresa McDougall, a former actress (appropriately) who had run away from her husband.[56]

In light of the rough-hewn male camaraderie that tramps and hobos shared, it is not surprising that homosexuals also, to some extent, were attracted to life on the road. The term used by many tramps to refer to a newcomer to the road—"gay-cat"—became popular in the 1890s, a time when the word "gay" was increasingly being applied to prostitutes and the demimonde of urban red-light districts.[57] It is probable that most gay-cats were not homosexuals, much less male prostitutes. Nevertheless, the incorporation of this term as part of tramp argot acknowledged the participation of homosexuals in life on the road. After 1900, tales of the seduction of well-bred boys between the ages of 10 and 15 by adult tramps became a staple of tramp memoirs, and some writers tried to use such stories of "boy slaves" to counteract growing public sympathy for homeless men.[58] The abuse of young boys (known as "prushuns" or "punks" in tramp lingo) by adults made for sensational copy but was undoubtedly highly exaggerated. Very few tramps started out so young. Of 400 tramps interviewed by Anderson in 1921, 8 percent left home before age 17 and only 4 percent before 16. In any case, youngsters running away from difficult family relationships or a bad work environment hardly needed to be seduced.[59]

There is much evidence, however, that sexual relationships did develop on the road between older teenagers and adults (often called "jockers" or "wolves"), as well as between adult men. Jim Tully stated that he was often approached by men on the road for purposes of sex. William Aspinwall provided some unusually frank observations on homosexuality among tramps, albeit in language (perhaps to please McCook) that left little doubt that he found such practices repugnant. In punctuationless prose, Aspinwall related witnessing tramps engaging in sodomy. "I have seen them at it in the Box Cars . . . I have seen others have had them . . . [part of manuscript missing] they taste each others Person in their mouths [however] you will only see one in a great while that will do this." One homosexual tramp (identified only as "W. B. P.") interviewed by Anderson in 1921 stated that he had "learned to submit to the wolves almost immediately upon leaving home," and believed such relationships were common among tramps and hobos. Others maintained just as strongly that they were untypical. Anderson—the most knowledgeable expert on the homeless during the interwar years—thought same-sex contacts were "very prevalent among the tramp population." He reminded readers, however, that many boys on the road sought to avoid such relationships and would not "travel in company with men because of their fear of being suspected of having improper relations with them."[60]

The contemporary usage of "boy" to include young men up to age 21 and even older misrepresents one aspect of this phenomenon.[61] Many of the jocker/prushun relationships were clearly between adults. W. B. P. said that it was not obvious whether, in his own case or others, "boys on the road [become homosexual] because they have been introduced [earlier] to the practice, or if they learn it on the road and become tolerant of it." It is probable that punks who submitted to an older man did so for a variety of reasons, including the need for protection or money, and sometimes because of their own sexual inclinations. As George Chauncy has emphasized, in the particular "bachelor subculture" in which tramps and hobos moved, some men engaged in same-sex relations without necessarily regarding themselves as homosexual. Some prushuns could be decidedly effeminate. For example, one young man W. B. P. traveled with for a while "stood in every position that one would expect [of] a girl" and "handled his hands as a girl would." As Chauncy notes, however, in many cases the prushun or punk was not himself interested in homosexuality, but nevertheless "was sometimes equated with women because of his youth and his subordination to the older man."[62]

Part of the sexual behavior of tramps and hobos was dictated by the context of life on the road, in which women were seldom available. For the more impoverished homeless man, this remained true even in the city, because as W. B. P. explained, "Women don't want to have anything to do with a dirty tramp, and the tramp knows it." On the other hand, the freedom of the hobo jungles undoubtedly acted as a lure to men who were already interested in same-sex relations but were constrained from expressing themselves because of community mores or family considerations. Sexual behavior of all kinds was more likely to be tolerated and openly expressed in the hobo jungles than elsewhere. "I watched a young [heterosexual] couple carry on in the most brazen way," said John Worby, "and talk of things without the least restraint." Aspinwall noted as well that masturbation "is practiced to some extent, . . . and among Hobos I have frequently caught them in the act."[63] Life on the road, then, allowed a variety of sexual practices to flourish that normally would have been condemned by the larger society.

REGARDLESS OF TRAMPS' race, gender, or sexual orientation, going on the road presented an opportunity to escape from confining disciplines, structures, and roles. Yet the cost of freedom was sometimes high. For however vivid the experiences it offered the traveler, however genuine its fraternal aspects could be, the world of the tramp and the hobo was a dangerous one.

Even if one was not accosted by trainmen or railroad detectives, riding the rails was at best uncomfortable. It was inherently hazardous and, for the unwary or unlucky, could lead to serious injury or even death. Tramps were sometimes able to stow themselves away in boxcars or coal cars while the train was taking on fuel, but to avoid detection by the yard crews or railroad police who inspected the cars, they often preferred to board the train while it was already in motion but had not yet picked up much speed. This method, known in the parlance of the road as "decking" a freight, was described as exciting by writers like Jack London, who depicted the ability to "hold down" a train in heroic terms in his book *The Road*.[64]

For most men on the road, however, the hazards of boarding and riding a train were simply a necessary evil. Decking a train was especially dangerous for novices. Edwin Brown portrayed a ride in a coal car in terms more terrifying than exhilarating: "I finally reached a point where I was hanging on to the corner of the car by my fingers and feeling every moment that I would be dashed to the earth . . . . Then we began to slow down." Riding on top of a freight car or on the bumpers (ledges between the cars), unsheltered from the elements, was often painful. Conversely, a sealed freight car could be sweltering during the summer months. Traveling at night was advantageous because trains made fewer stops and detection was less likely. "There were many," said Tully, "who had made trips from Kansas City and Omaha [to Chicago] under the friendly shield of darkness most of the way." Riding at night, however, was much more perilous than daytime travel. "Men had frozen to death going over the Rockies, even in summer," one tramp memoirist remembered. Even under the best of conditions, riding at night was only for the more experienced or daring. *Waiting for Nothing*, Tom Kromer's realistic novel of tramping in the 1930s, vividly describes the experience of "decking" a train at night:

> It is so dark you can hardly see your hand in front of you. . . . You can judge how fast a drag [train] is coming by listening to the puff. This one is picking up fast. . . . I start running along this track. I hold my hand up to the side of these cars. They brush my fingers as they fly by. I feel this step hit my fingers, and dive. I slam against the side of the car. I think my arms will be jerked out of their sockets. My ribs feel like they are mashed, they ache so much. I am bruised and sore, but I made it.[65]

Contrary to the popular image of tramping, it was not always easy to find an open box car, day or night. A favorite alternative was riding the blinds—the space between the locomotive tender and the "blind" end of a baggage car (called such because the forward door of the car was locked) that was generally inaccessible to trainmen. As a precaution while riding the blinds or on top, some men attached themselves to a handrail with their trouser belt.[66]

Finally, for the more adventurous, there was "riding the rods." Beneath each boxcar were two steel gunnels, about 18 inches below the floor and only a few inches above the tracks. The rider could lie against one rod and grasp the other or lean against the battery box. To ride the rods (or "trucks") of a passenger car required a small piece of wood about ten inches long, referred to humorously as the "universal ticket." The wood was grooved so that it could be clamped onto the small lateral rod between the cross-section and the axle and truck of the passenger coach. In this manner the rider improvised a precarious seat for himself.[67]

Riding the rods was an excellent means of avoiding detection. Trainmen seldom checked beneath every car, and it was easy to get on and off the train. Because of the small, confining space, a man riding the trucks was not likely to be accidentally thrown from a swaying train. There were other hazards, however. The rider was only a few inches from the dust and cinders of the road bed. Riding the rods with a friend, Flynt "suffered almost beyond description. The gravel and dust flew about our faces until the exasperation and pain were fearful." At least Flynt had no problem keeping mentally alert during his ride. The monotonous sound of the wheels on the rails could all too easily lull a man to sleep; and falling asleep could mean falling to one's death. No wonder most of the tramps who traveled this way did so in pairs.[68]

Anyone who tramped for any length of time was bound to suffer some kind of injury, if not from falling from a train then as a result of exposure, bad food, or malnutrition. As many as a thousand men each year lost their lives while riding the rails.[69] There was a reason that two well-known hobo ballads were entitled "The Dying Hobo" and "The Hobo's Last Ride." Railroad journals and newspapers regularly reported cases such as that of a man who, while riding the rods in 1884, caught his clothing in the planks of a road-crossing. He was pulled under the car and "the wheels caught him and cut him in two at the waist." Such occurrences were common enough that towns along well-used rail lines regularly disputed which municipality was responsible for providing coffins for homeless men found dead along the tracks. Most railroads established private graveyards for bodies that were "often disposed of without inquest or report." The death of a tramp could be as anonymous as his life.[70]

Whatever psychological benefits it provided, the lifestyle of the man on the road was punishing and, in the long run, enervating. Tramping made Tully, for one, "old and wearily wise at twenty." Laubach found only a quarter of the homeless men he studied were "physically sound." Seven percent were tubercular; 13 percent suffered from malnutrition; 17 percent from exposure. Unless he found a way of reentering regular employment, a few years on the road could turn the strong, independent young wanderer into the maimed or prematurely aged denizen of skid row, consigned to a life of begging or the hand-to-mouth existence of the odd-jobber. The successful vagabond, Harry Kemp noted, needed "all the knockabout resourcefulness and impudence" he could muster. The truth was that he needed something else as well: luck.[71]

Clearly, however, there were many for whom the benefits of tramping outweighed the dangers. The moralistic repudiation of life on the road by individuals who exchanged it for a more stable existence often rang hollow. One vagabond who after many years decided to settle down, "convinced that the road is a snare and a delusion," urged youngsters to "stay at home." He himself had not taken such advice from his own parents, however. In 1907 Ben Reitman lectured in a Bowery mission, urging young vagrants to give up tramping. Reitman seemed more than a little hypocritical, however, since he had intermittently been a vagabond "for many years" and had been arrested 43 times for vagrancy. Others were more sincere in admitting that the adventure of life on the road made the hardship more acceptable. "Yes," one tramp told writer Floyd Dell, "I went hungry sometimes, and I took my life in my hands every time I hopped a freight; but I didn't mind that. I was free."[72] Such "freedom" had considerable limitations built into it, but it was a powerful lure for many of the men who took to the road during the years between the Civil War and the 1930s.

THE EXPERIENCE OF BEING "ON THE ROAD" represented only one side of the world of the homeless. Equally important was the urban dimension. The increase in the number of homeless men (and, to a much lesser extent, women) in cities in the decades before World War I created a growing need for housing for such individuals. Like African Americans and other racial minorities, the homeless became increasingly segregated, residentially, within urban areas.

Chapter 8.

In the City

The first well-known centers of homeless men developed in Bangor, Seattle, and other logging centers. However, the emergence of "skid rows" (a term that probably originated in Seattle) in these cities to accommodate the influx of seasonal laborers was not typical of the evolution of homeless districts in urban America.[1] In most mid-nineteenth-century cities the homeless were not concentrated in a single area. Much like the early immigrant groups, transient or unemployed persons clustered in several sections of the city but were not highly segregated within those areas.[2] Until the 1870s or '80s, the homeless of both sexes usually lived in neighborhoods known primarily for their poverty and vice activities, rather than for homelessness per se. In Philadelphia, for example, the Southwark/Moyamensing section south of Lombard and east of Ninth Street was already, prior to the Civil War, a center of poverty, prostitution, and homelessness and would remain so until the 1880s.

The city's first wayfarers' lodge, set up in 1885, would be located only a few blocks from the Southwark slum. Vagabonds and beggars also lived in other parts of the city, however, including the nascent skid-row area between Chestnut and Arch Streets.[3]

The first centers of homelessness had several distinctive features: a lack of large buildings for housing transients; the existence of destitute families as well as single men and women; and a degree of racial intermingling that would be much less common by the turn of the century. Low-grade lodging houses were usually nothing more than converted private homes in which patrons, for perhaps ten cents a night, were allowed to sleep on the floor side by side. A report by the Philadelphia Society for Organizing Charity (PSOC) in 1882 described "these lodging houses filled with men and women, in the very lowest stage of degradation, sleeping eight and ten in one room, color and sex mixed promiscuously." Except for the lack of rules about coming and going, these accommodations differed little from that of the police station-house facilities that had been available to the homeless since the 1850s. Despite the low fee charged for staying overnight, such housing could be quite profitable. In 1883, the PSOC reported on one house where 30 men and women slept nightly in a 16-by-30 foot cellar. The owner reputedly earned $1,000 a year from renting out this space, although the structure itself was not worth more than $500.[4]

In the 1880s, Southwark/Moyamensing and other similar areas began to decline as centers of the homeless population, and the nascent skid-row area began to develop to the north. By 1895, over 80 percent of the vagrancy arrests in Philadelphia took place in three wards located mostly in the area north of Market between Twelfth Street and the Delaware River. This area, abutting the city's red-light district and near to both its emerging China-town and furnished-room section, would remain as Philadelphia's skid row until the 1970s, when it was demolished. Unlike the older, more heterogeneous areas like Southwark, skid row housed few women or families, and the men who lived there now resided mostly in large, multistory lodging houses. In 1895, when the police raided a lodging house at Eighth and Race Streets, they discovered that almost 80 men and boys were paying ten or fifteen cents a night to sleep there. In one way, the development of districts dominated by such lodging houses reflected the growth of more specialized land use practices in the maturing industrial metropolis. Like red-light districts, skid rows originated in marginal urban areas already experiencing residential and commercial decline. As John C. Schneider has shown in his study of nineteenth-century Detroit, this isolation of the homeless within specific part(s) of the city was not entirely inadvertent. It was abetted by the actions of newly professionalized police forces intent on reinforcing class boundaries by keeping vagrants, prostitutes, and beggars out of respectable neighborhoods.[5]

The historical evolution of homeless areas in Philadelphia had much in common with that of other major cities. In pre–Civil War Detroit, the Woodbridge-Atwater section, known early on as a center of vice and poverty, attracted the bulk of the city's homeless population. As in Philadelphia, however, beginning in the 1880s Detroit's nascent skid-row area developed elsewhere: initially in the Potomac Quarter on the lower East Side, then shifting to Michigan Avenue on the West Side after 1915 as the expansion of the central business district and the emerging black ghetto displaced the older lodging-house area. In Chicago, neighborhoods along North Clark Street and West Madison Street from the Chicago River to Halstead Street evolved into one of the nation's largest skid rows. Because of its importance as a rail center, by the 1890s Chicago was already considered the "hobo capital" of the United States. In addition to a large number of local unemployed or casual laborers, Alice Solenberger noted, it attracted "deck hands from the lake boats, railway construction laborers, men from the lumber camps of the North, and men from all over the Central West who are employed in seasonal trades of many sorts." Prior to the 1920s, the population of the West Madison section averaged about 60,000, with considerable fluctuation depending on seasonal demands for labor and the state of the economy. Two other important rail hubs, Omaha and Minneapolis, also developed extensive skid rows at this time, while San Francisco's South of Market area emerged as the most important center of transient and casual labor on the West Coast.[6]

The most famous of such districts was New York's Bowery, which by the turn of the century had become synonymous with homelessness. Like other skid-row areas, the Bowery had evolved over many decades. Prior to the Civil War, the Five Points area had a reputation for vice and homelessness, but the nearby Bowery was known as a colorful shopping and entertainment district, where the working class went to relax and audacious "Bowery b'hoys" and "g'hals" promenaded in their finery. Even during the 1850s, however, the Bowery, nearby Chatham Street, and the area below City Hall were distinguished by a style of rooming house life that was seldom found in other parts of New York. In the late 1860s reporters described the growth of cheap restaurants and the emergence of "filthy" and "cheerless" lodging houses along the thoroughfare. By 1868 Battery and City Hall Parks were already known as gathering places for the homeless. In his guidebooks *Lights and Shadows of New York Life* (1872) and *New York by Sunlight and*

Gaslight (1882), James McCabe described the Bowery in increasingly critical terms, extolling its raucous variety and evening gaiety while warning visitors of increasing numbers of beggars, prostitutes, and vagrants, who were now able to find temporary quarters in "the cheap lodging houses and hotels [that] never seem to close."[7]

As Kenneth Jackson has pointed out, an important turning point in the history of the Bowery was the construction of an elevated railroad line on the street in 1878, which "transformed the street below into an urban underworld" and helped drive away retail businesses. This event, and politicians' protection of vice and prostitution on the street, accelerated the decline of the Bowery into a skid row area.[8] In the 1880s and '90s the number of ten- and twenty-five-cent lodging houses, pawnshops, and cheap clothing stores on the Bowery and adjoining streets increased dramatically, and the image of the area began to change. By 1908, although the Bowery was still to some extent an immigrant and working-class shopping district, outsiders now identified the area as "the place for the homeless, for the out-of-kilter, for the rudderless wrecks who drift." When a sociological study of the area appeared the following year, its author thought it appropriate to title it *The Wretches of Povertyville.*[9]

The most serious negative feature of skid-row areas was also their raison d'etre: the need to house large numbers of men in structures originally designed for far fewer tenants. In 1877, one reporter described a typical lodging house for tramps at 153 Chatham Street. Although the men slept in rows on canvas cots, the managers nevertheless provided bathing facilities, free coffee and newspapers in the morning, and writing paper and pens for the residents. Prices ranged from five to fourteen cents, depending on the level of privacy of the sleeping accommodations. Within a decade, anyone wishing these kind of personal services would have to pay higher prices to get them. Most of the new lodging houses included few amenities, as landlords strived to reduce costs and to house the largest number of tenants in the smallest available space. By 1890 perhaps 13,000 individuals in New York roomed nightly in 345 lodging houses. Two decades later, urban missionary Dave Ranney estimated the number had risen to 50,000. "To be profitable," he added, "a hotel must have at least 250 guests; most far exceed that." In Minneapolis's Gateway area, landlords tripled their rent by remodeling "[e]very type of building, from theaters and stores to warehouses." Beginning in the late 1880s, large lodging houses were also built in Chicago, San Francisco and other major cities, and by 1900 the trend had spread to smaller communities as well.[10]

Jacob Riis and others writing for a middle-class audience often focused sensationalistically on the most disreputable housing in skid-row areas. In reality, however, there was a wide range of available accommodations for homeless or transient workers. The most expensive were the YMCA, followed by the Mills or Dawes hotels, described as "semi-charitable institution[s] for the poor" catering mostly to older workers "who are down on their luck but not yet bums or hobos." These lodging houses, Robert Hunter noted, accommodated, "with fair comfort, a class of clerks and other workmen who get a reduced rate as continuous lodgers," often renting rooms by the week as well as by the night. Cramped quarters were the rule for all skid-row housing, but at the turn of the century the difference between a fifty, twenty-five, or ten-cent lodging house was still enormous. A 10-foot-square room, rented for forty cents a night, was exceptionally large. William Edge described a twenty-five-cent "doss house" that was a more typical example of the "better sort" of accommodations available to homeless men: "There was only one narrow bed to a room. Each was a pigeonhole, with electric light, a window, a chair, and a cot. The room fitted the cot so exactly that a narrow strip of concrete floor, two feet wide, was the only clear space in the room." More common than lodging houses with separate rooms of this type were the "cage" hotels, usually multistory buildings that were divided into 5-by-7-foot cubicles, sometimes more than one hundred per floor; one cage hotel in Chicago housed a thousand men a night. Hunter described the "cages," which rented for anywhere from fifteen to twenty-five cents, as "little more than small boxes made by partitions." There was only a clothesline for the lodger to hang his garments on, and a wire screen covered the top of the cubicle "to prevent a pillaging neighbor from 'lifting' a suit of clothes in the night."[11]

Cages often had no furniture whatsoever. At best a single, small lightbulb provided illumination. The main ventilation came from windows at the end of long corridors. These allowed minimal circulation of air in the summer and none at all in the winter, when lodgers shut them tight to retain what little warmth was generated by an often inadequate heating system. In New York, the law required a minimum of one toilet for every 15 beds and one wash basin for every 10 beds, but payoffs to the authorities allowed many landlords to ignore such rules. In Chicago the cheap lodging houses were completely unregulated; on average, there was only one toilet for every 40 occupants. The cage hotels usually had no bathing facilities or hot water, even on a communal basis. Often the bedding and floors were dirty, and bedbugs and lice were common. These conditions changed little during the next half century.[12]

Alice Solenberger found the cage hotels to be confining, squalid places, as well as potential fire traps. She acknowledged, however, that they were "more generally popular with the men" than the dormitory-style lodging houses, where overnight lodging at the turn of the century cost anywhere from seven to twenty cents. Despite their small size and often decrepit condition, the "cubicles" allowed some minimal level of privacy.

This was not true of the cheaper "flophouses." In 1869 a New York reporter provided a revealing glimpse of a prototype of the dormitory lodging house:

> In a basement, dimly lighted by a kerosene lamp, are twelve beds
> ranged around the wall, each with a number at its foot, and the guests,
> like those in public institutions, lose their personal identity, and
> become figures of arithmetic upon entering. The walls are damp and
> green with moisture, and the odor is almost unendurable.

Dormitory lodging houses increased significantly in size in the 1880s and '90s, although their overall capacity seldom matched that of the new cage hotels. Most of the flophouses were constructed from already existing older housing by converting the floors above a retail store or saloon into sleeping quarters. Sometimes the saloon itself, after closing hours, doubled as a place to sleep. The best of the dormitories had rows of narrow cots, or sometimes bunk beds stacked two or three high. The seven-cent "flops" provided tenants with only "a strip of canvas, strung between rough timbers, without covering of any kind." The hammocks were sometimes stacked atop each other, which "was not the most secure perch in the world," as Jacob Riis put it. In 1908, a writer for *McClure's* described one of the largest flophouses of this type, the Bismarck, located on Mulberry Street in the Bowery. The narrow alley leading to the hotel's entrance was "indescribably filthy," and the covering of the ten-cent canvas "bed" was changed only on a monthly basis. "The Bismarck never had a bath, nor a wash-basin." The windows of a second floor "sitting room," unfurnished except for benches along the walls, "were covered most of the time with cobwebs and dirt, and the floor was littered with rubbish." In the 1920s, a British visitor left a similar impression of a flophouse in Buffalo, where a putrid odor "permeated the place and filled head and lungs like an unclean curse."[13]

For those without a dime to their name, it was possible to get a place to stay in the lowest-grade lodging house for two to five cents a night. Some low-grade flophouses had no beds at all; others provided dilapidated mattresses or rags for patrons to sleep on. Robert Hunter vividly depicted one such establishment that he visited in Chicago. "On the first floor there were certainly a hundred men sleeping on the floor itself, without mattresses or bedclothes" and only newspaper to lie on. Lodgers paid three cents for these accommodations. On the second and third floors, the men paid five cents a night to sleep on beds "covered with rags and dirty, ill-smelling quilts." Almost any unused building space could be converted into sleeping quarters. In the 1920s, notes architectural historian Paul Groth, even movie theater owners sometimes took advantage of the demand for such housing by permitting "people to sleep all night for 5 cents in an uncomfortable wooden seat in a room that was at least dark and dry, if not well ventilated."[14]

At the bottom of the lodging-house world were the "stale-beer dives," usually located in the damp, windowless cellars of tenements. Traveling with the police when they raided one such establishment on Mulberry Street, Riis encountered dozens of ragged men and women seated around a keg, drinking "[d]octored, unlicensed beer" from tomato cans. Four dingy rooms "that might once have been clean" held 75 homeless persons. "The privilege to sit all night on a chair, or sleep on a table, or in a barrel" went with the purchase of two cents worth of beer. As Walter Wyckoff discovered when he visited a stale-beer dive in Chicago, tramps who came to talk but not drink were summarily asked to leave.[15]

The down-and-out using Salvation Army shelters, wayfarers' lodges, and municipal lodging houses increased over time, but in big cities these institutions never housed more than a fraction of the homeless population. Riis and McCabe claimed that the police station-houses were the place of last resort for the homeless. In the warmer months, however, most penniless tramps preferred to "sleep under trucks and wagons, and [in] the darkest corners of blind alleys, and on benches in the public parks, until driven away by the police." Others sought shelter in the subways or even in unused tunnels beneath the subways. Despite its risks, some of the homeless always preferred to sleep outdoors, while others were forced to do so because of rules requiring lodgers to arrive before a certain hour.[16]

THERE IS LITTLE DOUBT that the tired streets of skid row were places of poverty, degradation and—for the uninitiated—danger. The freedom to "live in relative obscurity and with minimum of interference from the police" attracted a variety of con artists, small-time gangsters, and "jack rollers" to these urban areas.[17] For denizens acquainted with the surroundings and aware of its hazards, however, skid row was not a threatening environment. Given the crowded, dilapidated tenements of immigrant and black neighborhoods at the turn of the century, housing conditions in skid row, though deplorable, were not truly exceptional. What primarily set this area apart from the rest of the city was its population base, which was disproportionately transient and, by the early twentieth century, overwhelmingly male. Much of the skid-row environment reflected these demographic realities.[18]

The development of skid row was part of a larger urban trend of the late nineteenth century that saw increasing numbers of men and women, alone or as childless couples, living in apartments or furnished rooms.[19] Skid row was a special variation of this lifestyle, one built around the needs of a predominantly single male population, many of whom lived in the city only part of the year and most of whom drifted in and out of jobs frequently. Even "permanent" residents of skid row moved about almost continuously. In San Francisco's South of Market area in the late nineteenth century, no more than one in five residents remained at the same location during any five-year time period.[20] The domination of cheap lodging houses in the housing stock of the skid-row area reflected the status of residents who could not make long-term rental commitments. However decrepit, such housing was a necessity for many familyless transient or casual laborers.

So, too, were the employment agencies that existed in every skid row area. A few municipal lodging houses provided a job service for homeless men, but the vast majority of workers continued to rely on private agencies to learn about available work. Operating with a minimum of bookkeeping, most employment agencies put up colorful signs at strategic locations to announce jobs. In 1915 one reformer criticized the typical employment agency as "one of the worst factors [facing the transient worker]. It is very often in league with the bosses at the camps, and it divides with them its profits." The agencies had no concern for the suitability of the worker to the job. Their sole interest was to fill positions as quickly as possible and to collect their fee. Homeless men contemptuously referred to the locales where the employment agencies were located as "slave markets," even while recognizing that they needed them.[21]

For quite different reasons, other skid-row institutions were just as essential. The most important of these were the taverns and cheap restaurants that proliferated as rapidly as did the cheap lodging houses in the late nineteenth century. In the mid-1920s, sociologist Harvey Zorbaugh counted 44 restaurants or lunchrooms along Chicago's North Clark Street between the river and Chicago Avenue. These establishments were "dark and not over[ly] clean, and the windows [were] uniformly opaque with steam and dust." The food served there, however, was simple, plentiful, and, most important, inexpensive. A decent meal could be had for ten cents or even less in many skid-row restaurants. There were small lunch counters at the back of bars in San Francisco, "Jack Black" related, where one "could buy for a nickel a big plate of something that looked like stew, and a hunk of stale bread," and in Philadelphia in the late nineteenth century "function shops" ingeniously resold food that had been collected by beggars.[22]

At least as important as the cheap restaurant was the tradition of the "free lunch," which saloons used to entice customers. In his memoir, *Old Bowery Days*, Alvin Harlow recalled that in the 1880s the free lunch, if not always of high quality, was always ample in variety. The "meats, salt and pickled fish, [sauer]kraut, cheeses, pickles, [and] rye bread" available to anyone who bought a drink could sustain a man for most of the day. The free lunch was popular in bars catering to all classes, but it was particularly important to the homeless man with little money to spare. Some tramp memoirists claimed that for periods of time they virtually lived off the free food in bars. Taverns advertising hot sausages, stews, and bread did not always live up to their promises. One ex-Wobbly recalled that some free lunches tasted more like "wooden crackers and sliced laundry soap." In most cases, however, for the price of a five-cent glass of beer a man would get enough food to at least keep him from starving.[23]

Regardless of whether they came for the free lunch, homeless and transient workers retreated to the taverns to socialize, to meet friends, and of course to drink. As one observer noted, "[t]he universal recreation, and with many a necessity, is liquor," and saloon owners easily recouped the price of the free lunch from those who bought more than the required one drink. Some saloons also doubled as employment centers. The tavern owner allowed contractors to place advertisements for jobs on the mirror behind the bar, and runners would periodically come to pick up any men who wanted work. In some cases, when the job was outside of town, the runner would bring the men back to the same saloon to sleep at night, then pay them each day in brass checks cashable only at that saloon! In such circumstances, the skid-row tavern became an all-purpose institution, providing room, board, and transportation to work, bringing together impoverished local workmen, migratory laborers, tramps, and casual laborers, who shared a culture defined by their outsider status and lack of fixed abode. In the skid-row tavern they each could find camaraderie and a degree of acceptance denied them by the larger society.[24]

A variety of other enterprises lined the streets of lodging-house districts. Pawnshops, dealing in "relics of misfortune," did a brisk business wherever homeless men were concentrated. In San Francisco, the pawnshop district was heavily concentrated in the lodging-house area South of Market. The

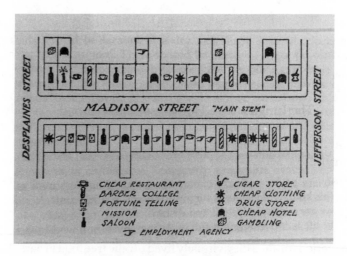

FIGURE 8.1. This 1923 map shows the types of businesses catering to the homeless in Chicago's "main stem" section. *Source*: Nels Anderson, *The Hobo* (Chicago: University of Chicago Press, 1923).

most common article pawned was clothing, which netted, on average, only $1.73 for the owner. Such a sum was sufficient, nevertheless, to tide a man over for a few days until he could get a job.[25] As areas like the Bowery developed in the late nineteenth century, pawnshops replaced banks, and cheap men's clothing stores drove out the millinery shops that once catered to a more mixed-class clientele of both sexes. Zorbaugh noted the large number of "clothing exchanges, resale shops, and second-hand stores" that lined North Clark Street. San Francisco's skid row had 51 used clothing stores. In 1908, secondhand shirts sold for three to ten cents, trousers for ten to fifty cents, and overcoats for anywhere from twenty-five cents to a dollar. Street hawkers peddled shoestrings, buttons, combs, and other small items.[26] Five-cent barber shops were also common on skid row, often two or three on a block, and the homeless benefited from the existence of student "barber academies" that cut men's hair for free.[27]

Also interspersed among the lodging houses and saloons were storage rental businesses, the popular billiard rooms, and an occasional bookstore, whose wares consisted largely of "blood-and-thunder stories of robbers, detectives, wars, pirates, and the outlaws of the West," along with "lewd pictures, which are sold in packages and exhibited on the walls of saloons and bawdy houses." Most bookstores, appealing to the radical streak in many hobos, also carried socialist and anarchist literature. For those looking for more conventional reading matter, or merely trying to escape temporarily from inclement weather, the reading room of the local public library or YMCA could always be counted on as a place to rest up for a couple of hours.[28]

It is not surprising that "men going nowhere and in no hurry to get there" also sought out the bawdier forms of entertainment available in big cities, including gambling, risqué shows, or illicit sex. Burlesque theaters, vulgar side shows, and five-cent "museums" featuring "highly colored pictures" of women in tantalizing poses gave some streets of the homeless district a honky-tonk quality. Some streetwalkers continued to ply their trade in the lodging-house districts, but by World War I most of the brothels had disappeared from these sections or at least moved to their outskirts. Nevertheless, in many cities the red-light district developed adjacent to the area of cheap lodging houses, so homeless men still had easy access to prostitutes if they wanted it. So-called Bohemian areas (such as Towertown in Chicago), home to poor artists, writers, and musicians, often developed near skid row as well. Living in fairly close proximity to each other, the denizens of the rooming-house and Bohemian districts often patronized some of the same businesses and restaurants as did the skid-row residents. Perhaps for that reason, by the 1920s some writers began to refer to skid row, or its main thoroughfare, as "hobohemia."[29]

Unlike the bordellos, illegal gambling houses continued to operate on skid row. In Chicago, West Madison Street was honeycombed with such establishments, most located on the second floor of taverns, shoe stores, or furniture stores. Newly arrived from a stint in the wheat fields, many hobos lost their "stake" in these gaming houses, where professional gamblers took advantage of the naive. The gambling-hall operators and card sharks, observed Nels Anderson, counted on the fact that many men on skid row "didn't seem to be much worried about the future." On his way out of Lynch's, a popular Chicago gambling hall, one casual laborer told Anderson that he had lost everything he came in with—twelve dollars. But "if he had any wish," Anderson noted, "it was for money to get back into the game."[30]

BECAUSE THEY SEEMED to lack the picturesque quality of men on the road, the urban homeless attracted far less attention in the middle-class print media than did the railroad-riding tramps. When writers did turn their gaze to skid row, they tended to focus on the most deplorable living conditions and irreclaimable personality types. This pattern had been set early by Jacob Riis in his vividly written, but highly moralistic study of New York's poor neighborhoods, *How the Other Half Lives*, which lashed out at tramps as the dregs of society. Emphasis on the most negative aspects of the skid-row population, however, was even true of those commentators who were fundamentally sympathetic to the plight of the homeless. Theodore Dreiser described the Bowery residents as "dismal wanderers, living largely in doubt and despair," and Harvey Zorbaugh, whose 1929 sociological study of Chicago's Near North Side was in some ways so insightful, claimed that hobos and casual laborers exhibited "a high degree of personal and social disorganization." Skid row, said Zorbaugh, was "a jungle of human wreckage . . . filled with derelicts, all manner of the queer and unadjusted."[31]

Like the criticism of railroad tramps as "outcasts," there was a good deal of truth in the statement that the men on skid row didn't "fit in." In the early twentieth century, the cheap lodging-house district was one of a number of fairly well demarcated areas defined as economically or culturally marginal by the larger society. Other marginalized areas included the red-light district, Chinatown, and the emerging black ghetto. Despite its decrepitude, however, skid row played a significant role in industrial society by providing a base for the fluctuating migrant labor force and casual laborers who, though frequently denigrated, were necessary to the functioning of the new urban order.

A visitor to skid row might easily conclude that the men wandering the streets to "pick over refuse barrels and boxes and drink the leavings in beer kegs" were representative of that section of the city. It was true that in the summer and early fall, when the hobos left for the farms and other jobs, the derelicts became more noticeable in the lodging-house districts. Alcoholic bums, however, were far from typical skid-row types—if such a type existed at all. Prior to World War I, during the winter months, migratory or transient workers probably comprised a majority of the residents of skid row. The hobos often followed a regular pattern that included logging work in the early spring, large-scale construction jobs and railroad work (laying or repairing track) in the spring and summer, and harvesting wheat, fruit, or vegetables in the summer and fall. Some also worked as loggers in the winter, but most returned to the city at that time, where they either lived off their earnings or resorted to temporary "inside" work. Most hobos were young and unmarried. As Anderson discovered in his interview of a 58-year-old lumberjack, however, if a man remained robust, he could continue such a work pattern for decades. In addition to the hobos, the lodging-house population was also drawn from "homeguard" casual laborers (men who never left the city), regularly employed but impoverished workers, petty criminals, retirees, runaway boys, and "professional" beggars. An investigator for University of Chicago sociologist Ernest W. Burgess discovered the variety of ways in which skid-row residents survived. There were "some who work—bill collectors, window washers, laborers, odd job laborers, as well as men with steady jobs." Panhandling and "petty rackets" supported others, and "remittance men" made do as best they could on the modest sums they regularly received from relatives. Small pensioners, unable to afford housing elsewhere, lived there too.[32]

There were also, Burgess's investigator reported, the pathetic "old timers," who "crawl out of their cage [room] about noon, . . . go down with their nickel and get a coffee an', then look up some of their friends and try to get the price of a bet." After several hours of panhandling, "if they are fortunate, they will have the price of a bottle, their night's lodging and a meal." These elderly men represented, perhaps, the saddest spectacle on skid row. In 1908 one investigator noted that aged Bowery residents often lived in the same lodging house for years, "but they paid each night as they entered, for they expected each night to be their last. Old customers looked into each other's faces at evening with a glance which meant: 'Hello! back again?'" Solenberger found that 85 of the 132 homeless old men she studied had, in the past, been "self-respecting and fully self-supporting members of society." A variety of circumstances had brought them to destitution: inadequate wages, lack of children to support them, "loss of savings through bank failures," unpredictable business reverses, poor health, or "crippling accidents." Although most had worked for years for a single firm, few of the companies would help them. Only about one in ten was able to obtain a meager pension of $4–5 per week from the Charity Organization Society. "Dread and uncertainty of the future," said Solenberger, "cause the greatest suffering to the homeless aged." Solenberger also found that about 5 percent of the homeless men were suffering from various degrees of insanity. A much higher number were handicapped. The hand-to-mouth existence that could easily result from such conditions was common among residents of the lodging-house districts. It represented, however, only one type of skid-row lifestyle. At the other end were workers with regular jobs who, for financial or other reasons, chose to live in the partially subsidized twenty-five- to fifty-cent hotels such as the Dawes Hotel or the Mills House. In between these two extremes there was a wide spectrum of individuals.[33]

"All who live on West Madison Street are somewhat sensitive about the fact that they do," Burgess's investigator reported. "They are conscious that they are classed [classified] as bums by the public." The men knew, from personal experience, that this view was biased. The average lodging-house tenant saw his surroundings as a community. He might travel away from it temporarily, but with each return trip it would gain in familiarity. Despite its obvious drawbacks, the lodging-house district was in its way a protective environment for those who sought refuge there. Part of the attraction was the sense of security the street conferred on the down-and-out. The anonymous jack-roller, Stanley, felt safe there from the judgmental eye of the respectable citizen: "I mingled with bums and derelicts like myself, and people did not stare at my misery." The term, "skid row," with its connotations of failure and decline, was never used by those who actually lived there. The standard name tramps and hoboes gave to the community of homeless men was "the main stem." This phrase simply signified that the district's primary thoroughfare was usually an offshoot of the main street of the city's central business district. Whether consciously intended or not, however, the appellation also had overtones of vitality.[34]

The defining period of the main stem as an urban community was the two decades prior to World War I. In the 1920s, the area began to lose some of its volatile quality. Nevertheless, throughout that decade and the 1930s, the main stem continued to serve as a haven for single, unemployed or sporadically employed men (and, to some extent, women) who would have found little acceptance elsewhere. Even those who, as a result of some unforeseen improvement in their lives, were able to leave the main stem found it difficult to do so. This was partly a matter of economics. "I can live here cheaper than I could anywhere else," said one resident of West Madison Street. "Meals here only cost me 15 or 20 cents, but if I went out of this neighborhood, I would have to pay 30 or 40 cents for a meal and then get nothing to eat" (a comment on the smaller portions served there). He then added, however, that it was also the ambiance of the street—the same street that to outsiders looked so dirty, even dangerous—that held him there. "[W]ho the hell wants to stay out in a furnished room by himself?" he said. "I'd die of lonesomeness [sic]." "This seems to be the biggest attraction of the street—it's [sic] lodging houses and hotels," said Burgess's investigator. "Here the men find companionship and here one can make acquaintances, and through the grapevine one always hears of new jobs, new rackets and the latest developments in how to get by." The lodging house was often the center of a network of communication among homeless men. "Every 'flop-house,' every sally [Salvation Army center] is an information bureau," one migratory worker reported in 1933. "It doesn't matter where you are going, you can find out how the bumming is, how the flops treat you, are they clean, how they feed [you]. You can find out whether the Bulls are hard [hostile], what [rail]roads run through there."[35]

Although the word "independent" might sound strange when applied to a group of men and women often living a precarious existence, that is exactly how many of the residents of skid row thought of themselves. Even Riis admitted that it was "their greater promise of freedom" that attracted teenage tramps to the Bowery lodging houses. "There are no troublesome rules to obey there," he explained, "no hours to keep, and very little to pay." Such motivations explain the fierce resistance of some of the homeless to staying in institutions, even if only for a day or two. Responding to such sentiments, the philanthropic Dawes Hotels went out of their way to assure potential lodgers "that so long as they are orderly and deport themselves in our hotels, their independence will not be interfered with, [n]or will they be affronted by unasked advice or interference in their private affairs." Nels Anderson believed that this was a prime motivation of many elderly men living on skid row. No longer able to work, they nevertheless were "too independent to go to the almshouse." Typical of the aged, homeless men interviewed by Anderson in the 1920s was a 72-year-old, "very beat and gray," who "ran away from the poor house two years ago and has managed to live. He seldom gets more than a block or two from his lodging. . . . He is a good beggar and manages from fifty cents to a dollar a day from the 'boys' on the 'stem.'" The elderly who lacked family support, said Frank Laubach, "had to choose between living in some Old Folks' Home" and the penurious "freedom of vagrancy." Given the decrepit state of most almshouses, and the restraints on behavior they imposed on inmates, many apparently preferred a destitute existence on skid row with a modicum of independence to the terrors of institutionalization.[36]

Despite severe constraints on their lives, the homeless attempted to exercise some freedom of action and influence over circumstances. This was true even of the casual laborer's interaction with the exploitative skid-row employment agencies. The experienced job seeker, William Edge stated, "never accepts a job lightly. One walks about, reads every board, discusses the probabilities with other job-hunters. Much information is thus passed along." Saloons and barbershops also provided homeless men with the opportunity to share useful information—not only about jobs and lodging houses, but about more mundane topics: what streetcorner provided the best opportunities for successful panhandling; which burlesque houses had the most stimulating entertainment; even which saloon offered the most generous free lunch.[37]

The desire of the homeless or transient worker to widen the boundaries of his world was expressed in a unique way through participation in the "hobo college," an institution founded by millionaire James Eads How. Appalled at the treatment of hobos and the lack of educational institutions for the homeless, How helped organize the Brotherhood Welfare Association, which in

1907 set up the first of six hobo colleges in cities around the country. These varied in size; Bertha Thompson described a typical smaller college as a single "large room with maps and pamphlets and pictures of Carl [*sic*] Marx and Lenin, Jack London and J. Eads How." These institutions offered free lectures by sympathetic academics and well-known streetcorner orators, as well as tramp authors like Jim Tully. How himself lectured frequently, urging establishment of an eight-hour day, old age pensions, and a national labor bureau that would serve as a clearinghouse for the unemployed. Under How's protege, Ben Reitman, the hobo college in Chicago developed an especially broad panoply of activities. "Night after night during the winter months," notes historian Roger Bruns, "grizzled itinerants gathered at the college to hear Ben and other lecturers speak on such academic subjects as philosophy, literature, and religion and on such practical concerns as vagrancy laws and venereal disease." In Chicago and New York the colleges went further, offering courses in sociology, law, and labor relations. Chicago's hobo college had an auditorium for amateur theatrical productions, musicals, and debates. Especially popular were the kangaroo court burlesques of the legal system and other institutions. Many of the colleges also provided reading rooms and sometimes free food and coffee.[38]

At first, critics tended to poke fun at the idea that the homeless could have any interest in serious intellectual matters. In time, however, most came to change their views when they witnessed the untutored enthusiasm of the audiences that packed the lecture halls to hear featured speakers.[39] The tramp who came merely to find a place to sleep sitting up for a few hours was "looked upon as a pest" and expelled. Spirited discussions followed the lectures, which frequently took a critical view of social and economic relations. "Needless to say," said How, "the kind of education we want him [the transient or casual laborer] to get is not the kind the Chambers of Commerce or the Bankers' Association are interested in. We want to educate him to labor's interests." How's intent that the hobo colleges would become "a rendezvous" where the homeless could "feel safe" was largely realized. Skid-row residents very much viewed the colleges as community meeting places as well as educational centers. In addition to public lectures, many hobo colleges also provided the homeless with practical advice. Before she made her first tramping expedition, Bertha Thompson went to the hobo college in Los Angeles to get information about train riding and the cities she would be visiting. "Every type of wandering person," she said, "came in and out of its doors, men and women."[40]

The hobo college, Thompson noted, gave homeless workers a forum "where they could express themselves." In a less organized way, this was also true of the soapbox orators who, in mild weather, held sway almost nightly on the street corners of the main stem. In Chicago, Washington Square on the Near North Side, known to all as "Bughouse Square," was the primary locus of such activity. The square was a hangout for tramps, who provided an audience on a regular basis for all kinds of radicals and free-thinkers. The square doubled as a place to meet and socialize and as a recreation center providing free intellectual entertainment: "By day its benches are filled with men reading newspapers, talking, or just sitting in the sun. But at night, crowded along its curbstones, are gathered groups of men, often as many as a hundred in a group, listening to the impassioned pleas of the soap-box orator, the propagandist, and the agitator." When the IWW set up a local branch in Chicago in 1916, organizers drew on Pete Stone and other local "characters" who had become famous speaking at Bughouse Square. In other cities the IWW also could usually count on local orators from the lodging-house districts.[41]

NOT ALL OF those who lectured from soapboxes (or orange crates) were men. Rebelling against her Presbyterian upbringing in a small Indiana town, Martha Biegler came to Chicago, found a job with the *Chicago Daily Social-ist*, and took up public speaking. She quickly became the most popular woman speaker on Bughouse Square. In the 1920s and '30s Biegler became well known as the manager of one of the few charitable lodging houses caring for homeless women. Lucy Parsons, the widow of one of the Haymarket martyrs, also lectured to enthusiastic audiences, who usually approved of her anarchist philosophy.[42]

Except for the soap-box orators, however, women participated very little in the public life of skid row. Unless they were prostitutes, they rarely entered saloons on the main stem, and billiard halls and burlesque theaters were off limits to them. In limited numbers women did live in skid-row areas, however. In 1905, 3 of the 63 cheap lodging houses in the Bowery were exclusively for women, and a few "cage" hotels rented rooms to both men and women. Waitresses, scrubwomen, laundresses, and others who could afford to live nowhere else roomed there, eking out as narrow an existence as did their male counterparts. Riis and others found the sexes to be most intermingled among the most destitute class of skid-row residents. The "stale beer dives" attracted both sexes and sometimes were even run by women. Women beggars often lived together in "the worst class of lodging houses in the city," but apparently under more communal arrangements than that of homeless men. In 1898, one reporter described houses where a dozen or more women beggars shared one or two basement rooms rented by other elderly women, who charged each occupant ten cents a night, "or 5 cents, if they can beg enough food to help supply the larder from which all the guests are fed." "Warm-hearted servant girls" also helped such impoverished women by supplying them with food pilfered from their well-to-do employers. In the summer, when the Bowery's male population temporarily declined with the exodus of migratory workers, homeless women became more visible among the rows of "sitters" who huddled together in the outer hallways of Bowery tenements.[43]

Although women were a relatively small segment of the skid-row population, their higher illiteracy rate and lack of skills probably forced more of them into absolute destitution than was true of the men. Yet their plight occasioned little public comment or concern. "God help the women hoboes," said one observer during the depression of 1914–15. "No one speaks for them. Not old hags, but some pretty young girls, no jobs, no homes, so thin you can see through 'em." Women at the other end of the age spectrum often fared no better. In the 1920s, many older derelict women on the Bowery could be found sleeping overnight in the cheap restaurants that were among the few skid-row institutions that welcomed both sexes. "There at the tables they collapse and sleep till dawn," reported one investigator. The women, he found, fell easily into "talk of what was once their homes, of lost husbands, lost children. They are the lost old women of New York."[44]

Homeless African Americans were far less accepted in urban America than they were on the road. Throughout most of the nineteenth century, the more heterogeneous homeless/slum areas of the urban North often contained impoverished people of both races, but the number of black vagrants was relatively small. Between about 1890 and 1915, the black homeless population expanded in size and at the same time became more segregated. This growing separation along racial lines partly reflected a general pattern of increasing institutional segregation in northern cities at the turn of the century, a trend that accelerated after World War I.[45] Municipal lodging houses generally accepted individuals of both races without segregating them. Only occasionally was this policy not followed, as, for example, in 1931 in Philadelphia when officials set up a temporary homeless shelter and separated blacks from whites in the dormitories. The situation in private charities, however, was more complicated. The gospel missions drew no color line. In Philadelphia at the turn of the century the Gospel Help Mission, the Samaritan Shelter, and similar evangelical institutions explicitly admitted all, regardless of "color, race, or creed." Larger private charities more often either segregated the races in separate facilities or simply excluded blacks altogether. In 1912, civil rights activist Ida Wells-Barnett lashed out at the white social service agencies in Chicago for their racially biased policies, especially those dealing with the homeless. "Even the Women's Model Lodging House," said Wells-Barnett, "announces that it will give all women accommodations who need a place to sleep except drunkards, immoral women and negro [*sic*] women. What, then, is the negro to do?"

To a greater degree than most charities of the day, the Salvation Army was sympathetic to blacks, yet the agency's evolving racial policies were ambiguous. The Salvationists' millennial beliefs taught them that all souls could be saved, and the Army early reached out to African Americans as well as poor whites. Salvationists denounced lynching, and the Army's founder, General William Booth, even preached at a black church in Mobile, Alabama, when he visited the country in 1903. In their writings and lectures, however, Salvation Army leaders often accepted racial stereotypes. This may have been one reason that relatively few African Americans were attracted to the organization, but the evangelical nature of many black churches was probably a more significant factor. To its credit, the organization from the beginning had a policy of caring for the homeless of both races. With rare exceptions, however, by the 1920s it had established separate lodging facilities (and rescue homes for women) for blacks and whites. This policy, which was as true of army centers in the North as in the South, would remain in effect until after World War II.[46]

Segregation of homeless African Americans was also evident in residential patterns. By 1920, the areas normally referred to as skid row or the main stem had become all-white communities. Homeless African Americans rarely frequented the bars on skid row. The lodging houses catering to the homeless were everywhere drawing the color line, forcing blacks to seek lodging elsewhere. Yet, from a variety of statistical sources it is clear that their numbers had increased. Where, then, did homeless blacks go? Like the vast majority of African Americans, they now lived within the highly circumscribed black ghetto that emerged after (and, sometimes, before) World War I. The black residential area was stratified along class lines, with the middle-class section a kind of vanguard area that slowly expanded, leaving behind neighborhoods into which poorer blacks moved.[47] The oldest, most dilapidated area of the ghetto often developed into a district of vice and prostitution, attracting clients of both races. Parts of this area also came to be known as a district of cheap lodging houses, low-class saloons, and stores specializing in secondhand merchandise—much like that of the white skid-row districts. In Chicago, this area was originally located on the upper part of South State Street and adjoining streets, between 22nd and 30th Street, with relatively easy access to the railroad yards to the south and southwest.

In Cleveland, the black lodging-house district was identified with lower Central and Scovill Avenues on the near East Side. The housing stock in these neighborhoods was usually among the oldest in the city, but the rents also were among the cheapest, partly because these districts were often near the dirt and noise of industrial areas, railroads, or elevated lines.[48]

Black casual or transient laborers who lived in these areas shared much of the lifestyle of their white counterparts. The number of saloons, billiard halls, and lodging houses there far exceeded the city average. There were several aspects of the black lodging-house districts, however, that distinguished them from the white main stem. First, the black lodging-house areas remained centers of vice and prostitution; indeed, in some cities such illegal activities expanded greatly in the early twentieth century.[49] Additionally, the housing stock of black areas did not consist overwhelmingly of large lodging houses. Single houses—though usually in bad condition and often broken up into kitchenette apartments or single rooms—continued to exist in these neighborhoods. It is likely that a substantial number of transient black laborers did not live in large lodging houses but stayed with individual black families as lodgers. In 1930 in the urban North over 30 percent of all black families took in at least one lodger, compared to only about 10 percent of white families.[50]

In some ways, the areas that housed homeless or transient African Americans retained the mixed character that destitute persons of both races had shared prior to 1890. In addition, because of their relative poverty and crowded housing conditions, the average black family's lifestyle had much more in common with that of the transient laborer than was true of most white families. In 1929 in Chicago, an astonishing 88 percent of African American families on the South Side lived in a single room, a figure double that of South Side whites.[51] Although now as ghettoized as the rest of the black population, the black casual or homeless laborer remained part of a more broad-based, if impoverished, community that included churches, dance halls, and other institutions that both genders used.

By the 1920s, the population of white skid-row areas was shrinking. The number of transient workers declined as mechanization of farming lessened the need for harvesters. At the same time, the proportion of skid-row residents who were white-collar workers or impoverished elderly people expanded. The number of better educated homeless men was already increasing on the eve of World War I. At that time Laubach found that "[e]ducated vagrants form a distinct class" among the men using New York's Municipal Lodging House, and Owen Kildare commented that the well-educated "genteel has-been" made up "a substantial portion of the

Bowery population."[52] The increase in the proportion of derelicts, coupled with a sharp decline in the number of young migrant workers, significantly increased the average age of skid-row denizens. By the end of the 1920s this trend had sapped some of the vitality from skid-row institutions and businesses. Despite demographic change, the population of skid row remained quite variegated, but to outsiders the men who lived there appeared increasingly sedentary, more pathetic than dangerous. This shift in perception of skid row would be only one of a number of factors contributing to the changing image of the homeless in the first decades of the twentieth century.

AS THE HOMELESS BECAME AN ESTABLISHED feature of American society in the early twentieth century, the image of this outcast group underwent a dramatic transformation.[1] In middle-class literature and periodicals the view of the tramp as a dangerous, criminal agitator all but disappeared. No single stereotype replaced it; rather there emerged a number of overlapping—and frequently competing—images. Aspects of the traditional view that were not discarded were sometimes transformed in a way that would have astounded the moralists of the 1870s. What was once regarded as a defect in the moral sensibilities of the vagabond—such as his irresponsible desire to avoid work—sometimes became little more than a quaint idiosyncracy, if not actually a trait to be admired. The figure of the

Chapter 9.
A Changing Image:
The Homeless in
Popular Culture,
1890–1930

tramp also was significant in vaudeville, popular music, and early motion pictures. Reflecting the concerns and sentiments of a working-class or mixed-class audience, these popular entertainment forms often employed the symbol of the homeless man to criticize the inequities of the new industrial order. While the image of the tramp changed and became more complex, its function as a mirror for the society's divisions and anxieties remained unaltered. Emblematic of the conflict between work and idleness, charity and justice, organization and freedom, the figure of the homeless man continued to touch deep emotional chords.

The influential *Atlantic* editor William Dean Howells played a key role in introducing the middle class to a new perspective on the homeless.[2] During the 1880s and '90s, Howells repeatedly employed the evocative symbol of the tramp to express his anger over the injustices of the American economic system. In *The Undiscovered Country* (1880) and at greater length in *The Minister's Charge* (1887), Howells presented his readers with case studies of the descent of innocent people into the homeless class. In *The Undiscovered Country*, Egeria Bynton and her father misplace their belongings on a train and are forced to get off at a small village as dusk approaches. Wandering the streets of the town in the twilight, they find they are mistaken for traveling beggars and receive no aid. The irony was sharp: people would not readily believe a *real* tale of misfortune, if it involved something so mundane as lost luggage on a railroad car. After their "painful experience" is over, the elder Boynton reflects that "it's well for once, no doubt, to find ourselves in the position in which we have often contemplated others." No doubt, too, that was exactly the moral that Howells hoped his readers would draw from this vignette.[3]

What was a minor episode in *The Undiscovered Country* became a major theme in *The Minister's Charge*. "Lem" Barker, a naive country lad who comes to Boston with excessively high hopes of becoming a poet, loses his money to a couple of confidence men. His pride too strong to return to David Sewell, the minister who originally befriended him, he winds up on a park bench one night and at the wayfarers' lodge the next. Through the eyes of a young vagabond whom Lem meets at the shelter, Howells provides a startling description of a lodging house from the point of view of the homeless men who used it. The novelist reinforces the tramp's anonymity by never revealing his name. For all the administrators of the institution cared, the tramp might as well have been nameless. The pair receive numbered cards, and for every procedure at the lodging house, they are required to use these identifying numbers.[4]

The Minister's Charge also shows how absurd, from the tramp's perspective, is the "work test" that charity reformers took so seriously. When Lem asks his friend if he intends to return in the afternoon to saw wood and earn a free dinner, the tramp replies, mockingly, "No, sir, I can't spare the time. . . . I don't mind the work, but I hate to waste the time." Howells drives home the inequities of the treatment of the homeless by contrasting Lem's struggling existence with the pleasant lifestyle of Reverend Sewell, but he saves the final irony for later, when Sewell discovers that Lem is staying at the wayfarers' lodge. The minister fears that his charge might have become "so far corrupted by [the lodge's] comfort as to be unwilling to leave the Refuge. He had often seen the subtly disastrous effect of bounty [on the impoverished], and it was one of the things he trembled for in considering the question of public aid to the poor." In Howells's most famous novel, *A Hazard of New Fortunes* (1890), an encounter of a wealthy couple with a street beggar provided an opportunity to further criticize the bourgeoisie's fear of aiding the "undeserving poor." "Oh, I don't say he was an imposter," Basil March tells his wife afterward. "Perhaps he really was hungry; but if he wasn't, what do you think of a civilization that makes the opportunity of such a fraud? That gives us all a bad conscience for the need which is that we weaken to the need that isn't?"[5]

For Howells, the massive increase in homelessness during the mid-1890s symbolized an approaching crisis of American civilization, brought on by the inequities of industrial capitalism.[6] America's wealth, the novelist wrote in 1894, "is like witch's gold in its malign and mocking effects. . . . The tramps walk the land like the squalid spectres of the laborers who once tilled it." In his utopian novel, *A Traveler from Altruria* (1894), Howells pursued this theme by satirizing the inequities of work and leisure among different classes. The story takes place at a summer resort, an institution (the narrator states) of growing importance as a haven "for our weary toilers." The "toilers" in question, however, turn out to be entirely from the middle and upper class. One vacationer finally admits that manual laborers "have no leisure to spend." "Except when they go out on a strike," adds another guest with grim humor. The "vile and loathsome-looking tramp" who suddenly appears midway through the novel is a sharp reminder that not everyone is so lucky as these vacationers. *A Traveler from Altruria* raised a disturbing question: were substantial citizens really so "deserving" themselves? If not, ought they to pass judgment so harshly on the tramp and the beggar? In an 1896 essay, Howells stated that there were "hundreds and even thousands of people who are insufficiently fed and clad in New York," and if some of them ask for alms, "one must not be too cocksure it is a sin to give to him."[7]

Stephen Crane shared much of Howells's perspective on the homeless unemployed, but his vision was more intense and fatalistic. In February 1894, at the suggestion of fellow writer Hamlin Garland, Crane posed as a tramp and wrote about his experiences. His brilliant essays, "The Men in the Storm" and "An Experiment in Misery," presented readers with a window on the lives of the down-and-out in New York City. The latter article, published in the *New York Press*, brought Crane a measure of popularity he had not previously attained.[8]

In vibrant naturalistic prose, "The Men in the Storm" portrayed the homeless queuing up before a charity lodging house in midwinter. In "An Experiment," Crane allowed readers to view their world through the eyes of a young tramp wandering the city's streets. Both essays present the homeless as defeated and pathetic. At the time, the idea of the conspiratorial tramp was making a brief comeback as a result of Coxey's Army and the railroad strike of 1894. "We have, in fact," the *Nation* intoned darkly, "come dangerously near the condition of things at the time of the French Revolution." Crane, however, mocked the notion that "the men in the storm" could be dangerous. Concerned only where they could get their next bowl of soup, the huddled wanderers "swore, not like dark assassins, but in a sort of American fashion, grimly and desperately."[9]

Crane's portrait of the tramps themselves was more radically subversive of middle-class stereotypes than was that of Howells, who despite his sympathy for homeless men often presented them as frightening figures with "sodden" faces, "at once fierce and timid."[10] Crane juxtaposed typical citizens hurrying home to "hot dinners" with the tired men lined up before the lodging house and found the two types had much in common. Many of the tramps, he wrote,

> were men of undoubted patience, industry and temperance, who in time of ill-fortune, do not habitually turn to rail at the state of society, snarling at the arrogance of the rich and bemoaning the cowardice of the poor, but who at these times are apt to wear a sudden and singular meekness, as if they saw the world's progress marching from them and were trying to perceive where they had failed, what they had lacked, to be thus vanquished in the race.

The reader could hardly miss the point: most tramps were neither political subversives nor incurable "bums," and with a bad turn of circumstances almost anyone could find himself "in the storm."[11]

The perspective of Howells and Crane was not typical at the time, but their writings did introduce new ways of viewing tramps and vagrants, and in the long run they helped to break down the stereotypes that had first emerged in the 1870s. Those stereotypes did not disappear quickly. In 1894 the *North American Review* published an article on vagrants that was as hostile as anything that appeared two decades before. "The relation of the vagrant to the criminal class," said the author, "is of the closest character; it is hard to say where the one begins and the other ends." Since they lived "a miserable, vicious, and wicked life," tramps deserved to be "severely punished, and by force exterminated—that is to say converted into working members of the community by being set to some employment more or less profitable." Here, still intact, was the old image of the criminal, lazy, incorrigible vagrant.[12]

Such hostile commentary enjoyed a brief resurgence during 1894–95, but by the turn of the century it would be fairly unusual. Most writers who commented upon vagrants now did so with less rancor. In his novel *With the Procession* (1895), for example, Henry B. Fuller used the appearance of "tramps and beggars and peddlers" to illustrate the deteriorating character of one Chicago neighborhood. But the story's middle-class protagonists feared the petty thievery of this "disconcerting phalanx," not their potential for violence or revolution. In the 1890s, a note of ambiguity, even outright contradiction, crept into magazine and newspaper articles about tramps, with sympathetic pieces placed side by side with essays that recapitulated the negative stereotype.[13]

No one better illustrated the increasingly ambiguous attitude of the middle class toward tramps in the 1890s better than Josiah Flynt Willard, whose essays on vagabonds were gathered together in 1899 in his popular book *Tramping with Tramps*. Flynt (who dropped his last name as a writer) was the soul of inconsistency, and virtually every image of the vagrant that had ever appeared could be found in *Tramping with Tramps*. Because he had himself tramped intermittently, Flynt was able to provide a wealth of personal insights into life "on the road." Flynt often felt the need to end discussions of interesting or attractive aspects of tramping by tacking on a moralistic disclaimer, and he urged the railroads to crack down hard on illegal train-riding. Despite these incongruities, Flynt's writings helped promote a less negative image of the tramp. Flynt de-emphasized the capacity of vagabonds for murder and mayhem, and he explicitly denied that they were engaged in any type of political conspiracy. Most importantly, Flynt was able to impart a view of the tramp world that was based upon something more than conjecture or paranoia. *Tramping with Tramps* aroused public interest because the author's experiences were authentic. As one reviewer noted approvingly, "he did not conceal a pocketful of money and send a trunkful of good clothes from place to place ahead, so that he might be a gentleman on the sly."[14]

Soon others were donning overalls and temporarily joining the ranks of the homeless to enlighten a middle-class audience.[15] The most important of these was Walter Wyckoff, who described his experiences as an unemployed laborer in a two-volume memoir entitled *The Workers: A Study in Reality* (1897, 1899). Like Flynt, Wyckoff was unable to break free entirely from older preconceptions of the homeless. At one point he casually mentions that the "professionally idle" formed "a large percentage" of the urban vagrants.[16] For the most part, however, Wyckoff realistically described both the positive and negative features of vagabond life. He discussed the camaraderie of manual laborers, as well as the hardships of their existence. Few readers could have come away from Wyckoff's volumes without feeling an increased sympathy for the down-and-out. Wyckoff communicated what it was like "to look for work and fail to find it; to renew the search under the spur of hunger and cold" until one accepted "any employment, no matter how low in the scale of work, that would yield food and shelter." More than physical deprivation accompanied such a fall, however; Wyckoff found the entire experience alienating. At one point, while walking down a road with a gang of day laborers, he passed "some young women in smart dog-carts." He recognized one of them, but "she did not see us, or rather saw through us, as through something transparent." Stephen Crane had a similar experience while researching the lifestyle of tramps. From the perspective of the middle class, these authors implied, to be homeless and unemployed was to be almost nonexistent.[17]

An early fictional exploration of this motif was Robert Cowdrey's 1891 novel, *A Tramp in Society*. The story's main character, Edgar Bartlett, is a well-to-do merchant until he suffers a severe financial setback as the result of economic depression and the embezzlement of funds by an employee. A disastrous fire completes the rout of his fortune, and as time passes he falls lower and lower on the social scale, eventually taking up begging. "Now I want to ask you a question," says Bartlett to a wealthy man who befriends him. "Was I at fault, or was it the conditions under which we live?" His friend emphatically agrees that "it was not your fault. The crushing weight would have drowned the best of men."[18]

In 1891 this theme was still quite unusual, and Cowdrey's novel (which turns into a tract for Henry George's single tax scheme) did not reach a very large audience. In the wake of the depression of 1893–97, however, more influential writers began to take up this topic.

The most important of these from a literary standpoint was Theodore Dreiser. Dreiser's novel *Sister Carrie* (1900) describes the slow and excruciating fall of one leading character, George Hurstwood, into penury, beggary, and eventual suicide, at the same time that a young migrant to the city, Carrie Meeber, is rising to prominence in the theater. As a child, Dreiser endured severe poverty, and at one point while writing *Sister Carrie* he was almost penniless, so he had a very realistic appreciation of Hurstwood's decline.[19] Hurstwood is described early in the novel as "a very successful and well-known man about town," the manager of a "sumptuous" Chicago saloon frequented by the rich and the prominent. He is a Horatio Alger type who "had risen by perseverance and industry, through long years of service" to his present position. By the end of the story this "picture of fastidious comfort" has been reduced to living in fifteen-cent Bowery lodging houses. The once substantial citizen soon finds himself so weakened physically that he has little alternative but to turn to panhandling. Drifting lower and lower, Hurstwood finally takes his own life. His "nameless body" is buried in the Potter's Field.[20]

Dreiser later explained that he had conceived of the Hurstwood character one day while, unemployed and down on his luck, he found himself sharing a park bench with some tramps in City Hall Park. It was Hurstwood's immoral conduct (theft and deserting his family for another woman) that made *Sister Carrie* controversial and led Frank Doubleday to suppress the distribution of the book that he himself had published.[21] Many middle-class readers, however, must have found Hurstwood's precipitous slide from respectability to rags equally shocking. Neither in *Sister Carrie* nor elsewhere did Dreiser use the theme of homelessness to criticize the economic system, but his message to his middle-class audience was still clear: This could happen to you, too.[22]

For some readers, Hurstwood's immorality may have partially justified his decline into the vagrant class. The popular writer Elizabeth Stuart Phelps eliminated all such ambiguities in her story "Unemployed," published in *Harper's Monthly* in 1906. When nineteenth-century moralists spoke of the "race of life," they assumed that tramps and vagrants were the contestants who came in last. Phelps repudiated such a view in "Unemployed" and inserted a rather obvious symbolic touch by calling her protagonist John Racer. Racer, a middle-aged music teacher, loses his position and embarks on a frightening and unsuccessful search for employment. The lifestyle of his family slowly deteriorates, and they are forced to move into a tenement and sell their silverware to make ends meet. Racer finds that his age and training render him unqualified for manual labor jobs. "Every man's hand is at the other man's throat now," says an acquaintance who has fallen into similar circumstances. "You earn your living at the bayonet's point." Racer reluctantly takes up begging, but unlike Hurstwood, he is saved from thoughts of suicide by the unexpected appearance of an old friend who helps him get a job. To the white-collar employees who read this tale, however, this melodramatic ending offered scant consolation. The essential moral of the story was that a diligent, decent person could still be reduced to a state of beggary by forces outside his control. "He had tried, like a man, to do a man's work," the narrator interjects at one point. "The merciless modern world had none to offer him."[23]

"Imagine yourself a beggar," exhorted social worker Stuart Rice in 1916 in advocating more sympathetic treatment of the homeless. As time passed, more of the middle class were willing to do that, partly as a result of their own experience with unemployment, or even with homelessness, and partly because writers like Howells and Phelps furnished them with new insights. In 1922, the *New York Times* published the story of a woman whose husband had gone through a series of setbacks similar to those depicted by Phelps. As debts mounted, the wife tried to keep up a proper "front," even though it often meant cutting back on the most basic of necessities. The self-proclaimed "matron bum" stated that she now felt a kinship with the Central Park "loungers" and "gentlemen bums" and wished them well.[24]

The view of the tramp as a product of forces beyond his control was often accompanied by an implied—and sometimes quite explicit—censure of the new industrial system that was coming into being. Henry George's *Progress and Poverty*, published in 1879, was the earliest signficant statement of this theme. To George, the simultaneous appearance of tramps and millionaires signaled the incipient breakdown of the type of society that the "free labor" doctrine had glorified—a nation of farmers, prosperous shopkeepers, and independent artisans—and its replacement by something resembling the dreaded European system of sharply defined classes. George accepted much of the negative stereotype of the tramp that had arisen during the 1870s. Yet he introduced a new note by claiming that this "poisonous pariah" was actually "avenging on society the wrong that he keenly, but vaguely, feels has been done him by society."[25]

In an 1887 editorial entitled "Tramps and Millionaires," the *New York Tribune* disputed George's contention that both of these social types were the result of unequal distribution of land. The two were, instead, the product of "character, temperament and capacity," which the tramp lacked because he was "born lazy" and was only interested in indulging "his animal appetite."[26] As time passed, this conservative view commanded less allegiance, as bloated fortunes, conspicuous leisure by the elite, and behind-the-scenes machinations by various "trusts" damaged the reputation of the American businessman.[27] Comparisons between the tramp and the millionaire became increasingly common, but it was the "idle rich," not the wealthy per se, whom writers most often equated with tramps. Such sentiments were not limited to the middle class. Dime novels such as Frederick Whittaker's *Nemo, King of the Tramps*, aimed mainly at mechanics, also took up this theme.[28] As early as the late eighteenth century, Americans had identified idleness with European luxury and "decadence."[29] Some of the most popular writers drew upon this tradition in criticizing the "vagabond rich." Mark Twain's *A Connecticut Yankee in King Arthur's Court* (1889) compared the monopolists with "protected" industries to the English aristocracy, which fattened off the labor of peasants; one of Dan Beard's illustrations portrayed the king with his scepter and a ragged tramp as "two of a kind." "The aristocracy of Europe," said the popular writer Josiah Strong, "has always furnished many professional idlers." Now, he feared, the "growth of great corporations and trusts" had allowed a similar class to develop in America.[30]

The appropriation of the "tramps and millionaires" theme by Theodore Roosevelt in 1908 was proof of its growing popularity. "I do not envy the idler," the advocate of the "strenuous life" told a group of farmers in upstate New York, "neither the idle son of a multimillionaire nor the hobo." Roosevelt adopted a type of rhetoric that had already been put to more radical uses by others. The Populist Party platform of 1892 had proclaimed that injustice bred both paupers and millionaires. In 1899, Toledo mayor Samuel M. ("Golden Rule") Jones stated that charities could at best be only a palliative for growing inequality, for if "we are to continue a system of industry and trade that makes millionaires and billionaires on the one hand, we must have paupers and tramps on the other." Robert Hunter also took up this theme. Further to the left, the anarchist and self-styled "hobo philosopher" Roger Payne used the same logic to argue for a radical leveling of the economic system.[31]

Regardless of the political convictions of those who used the tramps-and-millionaires theme, the image of the vagabond that they presented was largely negative. The idle rich and the idle poor, said one labor unionist, constituted "two types of wasted lives."[32] At the turn of the century, however, a new image of the tramp was emerging, one that often resonated with positive connotations. Sometimes picturing the man on the road as heroic, more often as picturesque or merely humorous, the new image did not always conflict with the perception of the tramp as a casualty of forces beyond his control. Yet even among those who continued to include an element of victimization in their portrayal of the homeless man, negative aspects received much less attention than previously. If the theme of tramp-as-victim raised doubts about the fairness of the new economic order, the new image of the vagabond as a heroic or picturesque figure revealed a latent hostility to the nature of work itself under the industrial/bureaucratic regime. Interestingly, the qualities ascribed to the tramp that would later be romanticized were first used by conservative commentators, who incorporated them into their derogatory image of the vagrant. "He is composed of

Bedouin and bandit," the *New York Tribune* editorialized in 1885, and was in revolt against "conventional restraints, and the decencies of civilized life." John J. McCook claimed that the tramp was a person who had discovered that he could abandon work and regular routine "and yet live,—nay, grow fat, perhaps, and vigorous and strong." Perhaps, McCook mused, this was the result of his being "free from worry and responsibility." This image, meant to be repulsive, in fact betrayed considerable envy for the tramp class. Another writer claimed that beggars, because they lived in the open air, were "much healthier than the pent-up factory hand or shop-girl. . . . They have little care or anxiety, except the fun of dodging the policeman." There was something appealing, charity reformer Francis Peabody admitted, "about a man who in the midst of a world of work can be perfectly free from the trammels of industry."[33] To be sure, rebellion against the industrial system was a significant aspect of vagabond life. To present tramps as healthy, robust, and carefree, however, was a considerable misrepresentation. This was more a middle-class dream of what it would be like to escape from the "American nervousness" caused by the impact of technology and incipient bureaucracy than an accurate description of tramps and their mode of existence.[34]

Behavior that seemed irresponsible to some was soon being touted by others as a virtue. Admiration for the courage and endurance of men on the road was evident throughout *Tramping with Tramps*, however often the author slipped into bourgeois moralizing about tramps as "failed criminals" trying to avoid work. Flynt was at pains to correct the impression that the vagabond had an easy time of it. While riding the rails, "he encounters numerous dangers and hardships, and it is months before he knows how to meet them heroically."[35]

No wonder Jack London much preferred the writings of Flynt to those of Wyckoff.[36] In London's *The Road*, serialized in *Cosmopolitan* magazine prior to its publication as a book in 1907, all ambivalence about tramps is discarded in favor of a hearty affirmation of a life lived totally outside the rules of "normal" society. Drawing upon his own experiences tramping across the country in 1894, London had no sense of guilt about his behavior. *The Road* contains some useful insights into the lifestyle of the men on the road, but they are often expressed in exaggerated form, and the trials and tribulations of life in the boxcars and hobo jungles acquire almost a mythic aura at times. London effectively integrated the figure of the tramp into the primitivist genre, a literary form that he himself helped establish. Instead of struggling against nature, however, as the heroes of *The Call of the Wild*, *White Fang*, and *The Sea Wolf* do, London's larger-than-life tramp pits himself against that most prominent symbol of modernity, organization, and capitalism: the railroad. The chapter "Holding Her Down" is a breath-taking description of London's successful effort to evade capture by a determined train crew. He uses superior knowledge of railroading, plus brute endurance, to outwit his rivals. It is a fast-paced tale of tramp against train, of a man who would adapt technology to his own unauthorized uses against the paid agents of one of the nation's largest enterprises. "The overland," exulted the author, "had stopped twice for me—for me, a poor hobo on the bum. I alone have stopped the overland with its many passengers and coaches, its government mail, and its two thousand steam horses straining in the engine."[37]

The Road appealed strongly to those who feared that, with the passing of the frontier and the growth of a more sedentary lifestyle, American civilization was drifting into soft middle age. There was a repeated emphasis in the book on youthfulness, with all the rugged strength that London associated with that term. London claimed that "only a young and vigorous tramp is able to deck a passenger train." London spoke favorably of the masterful individuals who lived outside the rules and morality that governed the average person—"the aggressive men, the primordial noblemen, the *blond beasts* so beloved of Nietzsche," and he contrasted the frontier West with "the effete East."[38]

At the end of the chapter "Holding Her Down," London slipped in an aside. "Of course, I have selected a fortunate night out of my experiences, and said nothing of the nights—and many of them—when I was tripped up by accident and ditched." A comparison of London's 1894 diary with *The Road* indicates that the latter was indeed far from being an objective account. To a growing number of readers, however, the more mundane aspects of tramping were no longer very interesting. London astutely recognized that the more Americans became ensnared in the disciplines and order of technological society, the more they needed to believe that there still were individuals who embodied the nineteenth-century ideal of freedom in its most primitive form. Some critics complained that *The Road* "glorified the morally disintegrating influence of tramp life" and was "far from the best kind of reading for American youth." Others, however, found the book attractive for that very reason—its lack of sympathy for the placid, bourgeois life—and hailed it as a "hobo epic."[39]

Most of the significant books about vagabond life published during the 1920s and '30s were too realistic to present the tramp as a heroic figure. It became almost de riguer, however, to include vignettes of tramp endurance or hardship and to invidiously compare this mode of life with what one writer called "the soft security and comfort of a dull-spaced city existence."

Writing under the pen name of "Tramp A-No. 1" (a.k.a. "the Famous Tramp"), Leon Ray Livingston produced a series of 25-cent "adventure stories" for boys that often utilized themes from *The Road*, although Livingston's purple prose and stilted admonitions against "wanderlust" found no parallel in London's book.[40]

During the Progressive Era, a dramatic increase in walking or hiking long distances may have made the image of the tramp articulated by London more acceptable. This type of activity, sometimes known as pedestrianism, also tended to glorify feats of endurance. In 1909 the *New York Times* followed the hike across the country undertaken by Edward Payson Weston (dubbed "The Leather Man") on a week-by-week basis, and in 1910 the editors gave page-one treatment to the story of a 59-year-old doctor who walked from Newark to Philadelphia in 24 hours.[41] Because "tramps" like Weston never used the railroads and were considered to be engaged in a kind of sport or diversion, they were immune to the hostility leveled at common vagabonds; this was true even though they sometimes accepted free food and lodging along the way. The line separating the two types, however, could be quite narrow. Charles F. Lumis called his book, *A Tramp Across the Continent*, "the diary of a man who got outside the fences of civilization and was glad of it." In discussing his motivations, Lumis sounded much like Jack London: "I was after neither time nor money, but life . . . life in the truer, broader, sweeter sense, the exhilarant joy of living outside the sorry fences of society."[42]

The heroic tramp was too sharp a break with the traditional view to completely replace it as the dominant image of the vagabond. Furthermore, the "walking" literature, as well as stories by London and his imitators, had an elitist premise that limited their effectiveness. They were, after all, tales of exceptional people. London considered himself to be a part of "the aristocracy of the Road," and Lumis had nothing but disdain for the "two cheap tramps of the ordinary sort" whom he encountered at one point in his travels. More pervasive ultimately than the heroic image was the view of the tramp as a picturesque figure.[43]

If Jack London's "hobo epic" appealed to people who feared that an urbanizing America was undermining the nation's frontier virtues, the image of the vagabond as a quaint "character" was attractive to those disturbed by the homogenizing sameness that modernization seemed to entail in a democratic society. Both images were spawned by a nebulous anxiety about the effects of industrialism and technology. Yet there was a major difference between the two cultural symbols. London's aristocrat of the road was a skilled "professional" who, paradoxically, labored strenuously to escape the tedium of normal employment. The picturesque vagabond, on the other hand, did not work very hard at avoiding work. Not terribly disturbed by his lot in life, he seemed to drift about aimlessly. In a bizarre way the figure of the heroic tramp reaffirmed the work ethic by glorifying the struggle of the freestanding individual. The rival image of the picturesque tramp, however, seemed to raise doubts about the beneficence of that ethic. In the years just prior to World War I, articles began to appear suggesting that laziness could be both "positive and negative" or asking, "Is Hard Work Healthful?" By the mid-1920s *Harper's* and the *Saturday Evening Post* were admonishing readers about "tapering off on work" and "our need for wasting more time." Stripped of his criminal and subversive qualities, perhaps the "lazy" vagabond had lessons to offer Americans after all.[44]

At the height of the scare over Coxey's Army in 1894, the *New York Times* published an editorial that attempted to distinguish the Coxeyites from "genuine" tramps. The true tramp, although he cherished some animosity toward society, found the company of the Coxeyites "boring." "The Coxeyites resemble him in nothing but in aversion to toil and soap. In the romantic and picturesque elements of his character, which give him, in spite of his disrepute, some claim upon the kindly, they do not resemble him at all." The tramp, in other words, warranted sympathy only if he remained utterly apolitical. The Coxeyites, demanding employment from the government, were not picturesque enough. The idealized vagabond had no aims of his own. He was a quaint figure who existed solely for the benefit of others—a charming antidote to the perceived dullness of American life, a colorful reminder that the work ethic had its limitations, that America as a civilization had become "frightfully industrious."[45]

Increasingly in the early twentieth century, articles in newspapers and magazines designed for a middle-class audience focused on the endearing or idiosyncratic traits that allegedly set the vagabond population apart from the average citizen. Some of these characteristics had some basis in fact; others were close to being complete fabrications. A good example of the latter was the emphasis the press placed upon the choosing of a hobo or tramp "king." As early as 1892, various well-known vagabonds vied for this honorific and humorously incongruous title. There can be little doubt, however, that such "coronations" were nothing more than public-relations stunts. In the case of the Britt, Iowa, "hobo convention" of 1900, the crowning of a hobo king—like every other aspect of the "convention"— was the idea of a group of local businessmen casting about for promotional gimmicks that would make their town better known. Most of those who attended this event were actually middle-class individuals on a lark, and at the end of the festivities the organizers politely but firmly told the small number of genuine tramps to leave town at once.[46]

Another aspect of tramp life that fascinated many people was the alleged use of signs or markings by the homeless. In the 1870s, some commentators regarded tramp messages left in "code" as evidence of conspiratorial designs, but by 1900 they were prone to view such markings merely as a quaint form of communication. As the years passed the legend of hobo signs grew apace, until by the mid-1920s they had become so elaborate that the vagabond would have needed a handbook to decipher them.[47] In reality, it is probable that when such markings existed at all, they were quite rudimentary. One former vagabond writing in 1884 stated that a "crude and meagre system of wayside signs for the initiated" existed, and William Aspinwall told McCook that tramps "will make some sign on . . . the sides of doors or someplace where their friends may see it." Flynt, however, stated that such signs were "a fabrication so far as the majority of roadsters is concerned," and Nels Anderson said he had "never seen such signs" and doubted their existence altogether.[48]

The middle class were equally fascinated by the language of men on the road, another picturesque trait that became exaggerated. A favorable review of Glen Mullin's *Adventures of a Scholar Tramp* (1925) commented on "the rich vein of hobo vernacular which is reproduced here—cusses and all—in the picturesque drollery of the original." William Edge told of a vagabond who "had fared well with a group of well-to-do Bohemians who lived vicariously his adventurous life, and who were delighted with his flair for picturesque speech." Many men on the road did, of course, use a special jargon, although probably not as many terms as some writers imagined. In their quest for the quaint and the curious, however, some people went one step further and expected the wanderer at their back door to speak in a special dialect. "There is no such thing as a tramp dialect," one vagabond said flatly, "but nevertheless, almost any honest tramp will talk one for you, if he sees a chance for profits ahead."[49]

Harry Kemp, Floyd Dell, and other "vagabond" intellectuals lifted such themes to a more middle-brow level of culture, self-consciously identifying the picturesque or bohemian qualities of the tramp world with an artistic sensibility that, they argued, was all too often lacking in the lives of ordinary Americans. Kemp became trapped in his own literary persona, forced to play the role of the "tramp poet" by exaggerating or overdramatizing his real-life tramping experiences.[50] At the hands of some authors, the homeless man became romanticized almost beyond recognition. Only a confirmed workaholic would have objected to the carefree vagabonds who tripped gaily through Henry Knibbs's "Ballad of the Bos" (1914): "Knights of the tie and rail we are, / Lightly meandering everywhere." The apotheosis of this literature was reached in an article in *Forum* in 1925, in which the author stated that tramps preferred to travel at night because they "find a delicious mysticism in plunging through the darkness on the top of a swaying train." The same year another writer treated the sophisticated readers of *American Mercury* to a discourse on "The Art of Bumming a Meal." The essay was virtually an invitation to join the happy-go-lucky world of tramps and beggars. "Say what you will, it's a healthy life," said one reporter after an investigation of tramping that lasted all of two days.[51]

Stories that romanticized the tramp helped to crowd out traditional stereotypes of the dangerous or subversive tramp. The new, innocuous caricature, however, continued to emphasize the inherent laziness of the homeless. Furthermore, by excluding any negative content from the description of tramp life, the picturesque image provided a rationalization for neglecting the real problems of the homeless man. One might wonder whether Norman Rockwell's friendly, smiling, storytelling tramp, replete with straw hat and homemade pipe, had any problems at all. The Rockwell painting, which graced a *Saturday Evening Post* cover in 1924, fit in comfortably with other Rockwell motifs that glorified the passing of small-town life in the wake of the urban/industrial juggernaut. It emptied the image of the tramp of any element of class conflict or resistance. It is likely that this nostalgic, nonthreatening image was especially attractive to the rising middle- and upper-middle-class professional/managerial group that was now expanding and diversifying its patterns of consumption. Most of the articles portraying the tramp as a picturesque figure appeared in the kind of mass-circulation magazines that appealed strongly to this growing social-economic stratum.[52]

IT IS DOUBTFUL that Rockwell's homespun, nostalgic tramp touched the emotions of the average manual laborer or file clerk. In an era of declining union membership, continuing labor surplus, and probusiness government, real-life homelessness was a nagging reminder of class inequities to a broad spectrum of workers.[53] Beyond the purview of the middle-class magazines, however, in cartoons, vaudeville, music, and especially in early motion pictures, an alternative image of the tramp emerged that was more satisfying to the working class. On one level, this image and that of the romanticized vagabond had a good deal in common. The costume and manner of speech of both types of tramp characters was often intentionally humorous. The depictions of the homeless that appealed to working-class audiences, however, were more likely to include themes of class oppression and resistance, and even when the tramp figure was comical, the humor was often tinged with pathos.

This "oppositional" image emerged at the same time that Howells, Crane, and London were using tramp characters to criticize the social system, but its origins lay not in novels or magazine articles but in alternative media that (initially, at least) appealed mostly to blue-collar workers. The colorful folk-music tradition of the working class often reflected an abiding sense of class inequities under capitalism. Hobo songs, which sometimes evolved with many variations, frequently contrasted the idle rich with the unfortunate homeless man. As one Wobbly song put it:

> The bum on the rods is hunted down
> As the enemy of mankind
> The other is driven round to his club
> Is feted, wined and dined . . .
>
> The bum on the rods is a load so light
> That his weight we scarcely feel,
> But it takes the labor of dozens of men
> To furnish the other a meal.
>
> As long as you sanction the bum on the plush
> The other will always be there,
> But rid yourself of the bum on the plush
> And the other will disappear.

Only a few hobo songs like the IWW "anthem," "Halleluia, I'm a Bum," became widely known among the general population, but in less fiercely political form such sentiments found their way into many popular ballads in the early twentieth century. Songs that sympathetically described the lives (and sometimes, as in "The Dying Hobo," the deaths) of men who rode the rails were common. Other ballads used the motif of catching a freight train to tell stories of poverty, escape, or painful separation from loved ones. The nostalgic or comic tramp favored in middle-class magazines separated the audience from its subject, turning the homeless man into a symbolic "other." For the working class, however, the depiction of men on the road in folk music was more often rooted in a realistic understanding of the possible consequences of homelessness. Despite its melodramatic tone, the immensely popular ballad "Where Is My Wand'ring Boy Tonight?" related an experience that rang true for many workers and their families:

O, where is my wand'ring boy tonight,
The joy of his mother's pride?
He's treading the ties with his bed on his back,
Or else he's bumming a ride. . . .
He's on the head-end of an overland train,
That's where your boy is tonight.[54]

The themes of being on the road, with all the dangers and opportunities it entailed, was particularly strong in the African American musical tradition of the blues, a musical form whose rise coincided with the growth of tramping. Most bluesmen had themselves ridden the rails at one time, and when they came north during the Great Migration, many did so by hopping a freight. The idea of escaping the South that way was appealing to blacks who were contemplating leaving but lacked the money for a railroad ticket:

Green Diamond's blowin' her whistle, trains coming round the trail
Can't ride the pullman, guess I'll ride the rail.

In addressing the theme of homelessness, however, the bluesmen's experience with racism gave their music a harsher edge than that of most white songwriters.

Dreamed last night that the whole world was mine,
Woke up this morning, didn't have one lousy dime.
So I'm leaving here tonight if I have to ride the blinds.
Catch a freight train, special—engineer lose no time.

The motif of escape could take on a different meaning with some women blues singers. "I've got the blues, I've got boxcars on my mind," sang Ida Cox in a 1925 recording that must have touched the experience of many black women in the South. "I hate that train they call the M and O;/ It took my baby away, and he ain't comin' back to me no more."[55]

If the image of the homeless man in popular song was realistic, even harshly so at times, a less serious tramp character made its appearance in cartoons and vaudeville. Several tramp characters, including "Weary Willy" and "Tired Tim," appeared regularly in American newspapers. Both were comical, eternally stumbling through life's trials, usually the object rather than the initiator of humorous situations. The "weary" and "tired" prefixes did not denote laziness so much as fatigue and an inability or lack of desire to improve their lot in life. The best known tramp cartoon figure was probably Happy Hooligan, who surfaced later in other entertainment media, including several plays about the comic strip, a popular song, and even an early movie serial. The song "Happy Hooligan" (1902), by Victor Vogel and Bryan Stillman, expressed well the contradictions between Hooligan's personality and the predicaments into which he stumbled:

> Happy Hooligan is a very funny man,
> Misfortune seems to follow him about. . . .
> He means to do good, but is misunderstood.
> He must have been born on a friday!
> Though chuck full of pluck, he plays on hard luck;
> His face and his clothes are untidy.
> So drink to this man, with glass or with *can*
> Poor Hooligan, lowly in station.
> In appearance a sight, his heart seems all right.
> He's the happiest man in the nation.[56]

The numerous tramp acts that appeared in vaudeville and, occasionally, in musicals in the early twentieth century had much in common with the Happy Hooligan character. Tramp comics like Paul Barnes, Lew Bloom, Nat Wills, and the young W. C. Fields were extremely popular. Their routines, and those of many lesser known performers, had many variations and could include pantomine, slapstick, dancing, cycling, and even (in the case of Fields) juggling. Despite the stage tramp's poverty and poor treatment at the hands of others, however, like Happy Hooligan he steadfastly maintained a genial outlook. In contrast to many of the working-class songs about men on the road, the tramp routines of vaudeville only occasionally contained material critical of the social system. Some pseudo-hobo ballads popular with vaudeville comedians, however, effectively used self-parody to question the stereotype of the "lazy" homeless man. "Who Said I Was a Bum?" begins by repeating the traditional middle-class view of the tramp, then shifts to a dissenting perspective that working-class members of the audience must have found particularly amusing:

> There's just two things that I despise,
>   Two things I always shirk:
> The first thing is a cake of soap,
>   The other one is work.

My life to me is just a spree
  I'm always on a lark.
Somebody said, "You're just a bum,"
  And I don't like that remark.

CHORUS:
  Who said I was a bum?
  Who said I was a bum?
  I haven't worked in twenty years,
  I guess I'm not so dumb.

  And as I tramp along the road
  The people hear me hum,
  "I know I'm a hobo, but
  Who said I was a bum?"

Dressed in shabby but quaint outfits, both the cartoon tramp and his vaude-ville counterpart appeared innocuous. Nevertheless, their antics encour-aged contradictory emotions in the audience. On the one hand, they ren-dered the homeless man comical, the victim of other characters' mischief or cruelty. They also, however, inspired a degree of sympathy, leaving the audience with the vague feeling that the homeless man was not necessarily a "bum" and deserved a better fate.[57]

Like vaudeville and the cartoons, the new art form of the cinema initially drew its audience primarily from the working and lower middle class.[58] Poor children were especially attracted to the small Nickelodeon theaters that grew in number at a staggering rate after 1905. Some early films, which prior to 1915 were quite short, explicitly dealt with issues of class relations and poverty. One of the most hard-hitting of these, *From the Submerged* (1912), brilliantly demonstrated growing class inequalities by contrasting homeless men, struggling to survive, with scenes of high-society types who go slum-ming in poor neighborhoods. In most cases, however, issues of class were dealt with more indirectly in the early cinema, especially in comedies that made fun of bosses, the police, or other authority figures.[59]

Some early tramp characters in the movies reinforced the traditionally hostile attitude toward the homeless man. An early short film, *The Tramp and the Bather* (1897), is a comedy in which a tramp steals a bather's clothes. Another short film, *The Fake Beggar* (produced by Thomas Edison in 1898), exposes a fraudulent street beggar pretending to be blind and legless. In longer films produced in 1905, Edison portrays tramps as burglers or train wreckers, and an early William Paley movie, *Tramp on the Farm* (1904) depicts a homeless man "who happily wallows in a pigsty, sleeps in a dog-house, and finally ends up sharing a drink with the dog." Other early films, however, such as the *Happy Hooligan* series (1900–1901), *Weary Willy Takes His Annual Bath* (1900), and *An Awful Skate; Or, The Hobo on Rollers* (1907), emphasized pathos and humor.[60]

Two films produced by Siegmund Lubin initiated a much different approach to this subject. In his fascinating film *The Tramp's Dream* (1899), a tramp sleeping on the grass dreams that he is received by two well-dressed, respectable couples and an unattached young woman; the group lunches together, and the woman finds the tramp appealing. The tramp then wakes up and sadly realizes that he had only been dreaming. In *The Tramp's Revenge* (1905), two tramps successively appear at the door of a home begging for food. Both receive handouts from the owner, Mrs. Brown. When a third tramp comes to the door, the woman lets her dog out to drive the man away. The tramp subverts her intention by capturing the dog, however, and disappears with the animal. In contrast to other early tramp films of this period, Lubin's movies exhibit a marked sympathy for the homeless man. In *The Tramp's Dream*, the fact that the tramp appears to be as dishevelled in his dream as in reality reinforces the depressing conclusion that such a person can never be accepted in "normal" society. *The Tramp's Revenge* implies that, within limits, aiding homeless men is an acceptable practice, and the comic element in this little drama is at the expense of the homeowner, not the tramp.

Charlie Chaplin's famous screen persona of the "little tramp," first introduced in 1914, has often been described as a universal symbol of the average person, buffeted by the winds of fate, struggling to survive through the mechanism of humor. At one level this is quite accurate and helps to explain Chaplin's enduring popularity.[61] The description, however, ignores the specific historical context in which Chaplin's tramp character emerged. In 1914–15, the United States was in the grips of a sharp economic decline, and the number of homeless men applying for lodging at city shelters was at an all-time high. Whether or not—as he later claimed—Chaplin's idea for the tramp character derived from his encounter with a real hobo in San Francisco, a wide range of images of homeless men, positive and negative, were available to Chaplin, and at one time or another he drew on all of them. The comedian did not always depict the tramp in a positive light. Stylized violence was standard in Chaplin's burlesques, and the little tramp is frequently portrayed as a thief. Perhaps recalling his own impoverished upbringing, however, Chaplin would primarily use the tramp character as a foil to criticize aspects of the dominant social/economic order.[62] This tendency was masked so well behind a facade of slapstick humor that even conservative critics who noted it were usually forgiving. A case in point was *Variety*'s appraisal of *Work* (1915), which the reviewer found "disgusting at many points, but since the audience will laugh there is no real cause for complaint."[63]

Chaplin's little tramp, Charlie, has much in common with real homeless men. At different times he is shown living in a patchwork dwelling (*A Dog's Life* [1918]), sleeping in a homeless shelter (*Police!* [1916], *Triple Trouble* [1918], and *The Kid* [1921]), emerging from the undercarriage of a train (*The Idle Class* [1921]), and on many occasions pilfering food to survive. Like many men on the road, Charlie has been frequently arrested; in a half dozen films he plays the part of an escaped convict. Although often scripted as an "idler" living an aimless existence, the Chaplin character is just as likely to be an unemployed worker looking for a job. Like many homeless men at that time, he is willing to accept any type of work, but his choices are limited. At different times, Charlie is an artist, a film extra, an amateur nurse, a paper-hanger's assistant, a janitor, a fireman, an odd-job man, a bricklayer, a waiter, a porter, a handyman, a carpenter's assistant, a circus extra, and even, in *Laughing Gas* (1914), a dental assistant. The positions he holds as an "assistant" are hardly stepping stones to permanent skilled jobs, and most of the other jobs in the list require no prior training. They are, in other words, exactly the kind of short-term, low-paying jobs that real homeless men would most likely have to accept.[64]

In other ways, too, Chaplin's tramp comedies were rooted in a reality that working-class audiences could understand. Film historian Charles Musser has shown how Chaplin, in such early short films as *Making a Living* (1914), *The Tramp* (1915), and *The Pawnshop* (1915), repeatedly contradicts or makes fun of the work ethic by having Charlie ingeniously avoid tasks, shift duties to others, or sabotage the authority figure who oversees the work process. In *Work* (1915) and *His New Job* (1915) Chaplin carries out a more concerted assault on the world of work, savagely satirizing a system that forces an "assistant" (Charlie) to do all the labor while the boss sits idly by.[65] Although in Chaplin's films the little tramp is almost never an industrial worker, a number of "bosses" stand in as the equivalent of factory foremen or supervisors. Significantly, in *Work*, the family who hires the paperhanger and Charlie is called the Fords—a fairly obvious connection to the new assembly-line process of production that had just been introduced by Henry Ford a year before.

Chaplin readily incorporated the "tramps and millionaires" theme into his films, but in a more imaginative way than social critics who used it merely to denounce growing class inequalities. In Charlie's world, million-aires and foppish aristocrats (with names like Lord Helpus and Count de He-Ha) are exposed as stupid, lazy, and incompetent—the same traits tradi-tionally ascribed to homeless men—at the same time that the little tramp, though a chronic bumbler, is amazingly inventive in overcoming the obsta-cles placed in his path. In his very first film, *Making a Living*, Chaplin plays a lord who is later exposed as a penniless impostor. This becomes a common theme in Chaplin comedies, as Charlie ridicules the pretensions of the upper class by showing how easy it is to impersonate them.[66]

The use of this theme helped broaden the appeal of Chaplin's films at a time when movies were in transition from a predominantly working-class entertainment form to one in which the middle class also participated.[67] Many small businessmen and white-collar workers, as well as skilled arti-sans, connected the growing chasm between rich and poor to threats to their own status. The middle class, no less than the working class, attended Chaplin's films in droves. Chaplin's genius was to create a character who yielded a separate meaning for the working class without alienating the middle class. Chaplin's ability to humanize the homeless man without incurring criticism reached its appogee in *The Kid*, in which Charlie finds and raises an abandoned child (Jackie Coogan), both of them living a homeless, if happy, existence until the boy's mother learns of his where-abouts and attempts to reclaim him. Emptied of its comedic content, the film veered dangerously close to the older man/young boy sexual relation-ship that many writers disparaged in describing life on the road. But the comedy in Chaplin's first full-length feature film was acknowledged by all as brilliant, and no one made the connection.[68] Instead, at a time of intense cultural and political backlash, Chaplin became the first screen artist to present the homeless man as a believable father figure, making him more acceptable to a wider audience than ever before. In spite of their subversive qualities, however, Chaplin's films never suggested—even satirically— that collective action against corporations or the government might be a solution to problems of class oppression. Symbolically, at the end of each movie (at least until *Modern Times* in 1935), Charlie always walks off down the road alone. Like many real-life homeless men, the little tramp could be rowdy and rebellious, but in most respects he remained the quintessential individualist.

Homelessness did not disappear in the 1920s, but its harsher aspects were obscured from view as old stereotypes of the lazy vagabond reemerged in tamer, more nostalgic form. After *The Kid*, even Chaplin turned away from using the tramp as a subversive figure. *The Gold Rush* (1925) and *The Circus* (1928), though further examples of Chaplin's genius, contained no hint of social criticism. The dominance of the nostalgic image would be short-lived, however. The economic collapse of the 1930s would lead to a sea change in attitudes toward the homeless, as well as in the policies for dealing with them.

THE GREAT DEPRESSION BROUGHT THE ISSUE of homelessness back to the forefront of public consciousness and debate, injecting a note of realism into a topic that had largely become a battle of cultural symbols. Illegal train-riding, which had declined in the 1920s, again became commonplace as an army of unemployed wanderers took to the road in search of work. Shantytowns built by the homeless sprang up in cities across the nation, and social workers and municipal officials struggled to deal with increasing numbers of the destitute crowding into private and public shelters. By 1932, the "starvation army" of men (and, to some extent, women and children) on the

Chapter 10.

From Tramp to

Transient: The

Great Depression

road had become the clearest evidence of a nation in the midst of a deepening economic crisis. Out of these circumstances would come the first—and only—federal program in American history designed to deal directly with the problem of the homeless unemployed. The Federal Transient Service, a neglected aspect of the New Deal's Hundred Days legislation, broke new ground in providing humane treatment for this outcast group.

For the homeless, the transition from the 1920s to the 1930s was not as dramatic as it later seemed. Although no one noticed it at the time, one of the earliest signals of weakness in the booming economy of the 1920s was the rise, beginning in 1927, in the number of homeless men using municipal shelters. The onset of the Depression in the fall of 1929 accelerated a trend already underway. By 1932, New York's municipal shelter was turning away men because of overcrowding. Other cities had similar experiences. In 1931, the number of homeless using shelters increased 280 percent over the previous year in St. Louis, 421 percent in Minneapolis, and an astonishing 700–750 percent in Detroit and Cleveland. When Philadelphia's new homeless facility reached capacity in October 1932, destitute men were forced to seek shelter in two police stations that still had "tramp rooms." So many arrived there nightly that some men slept on the stairs or in the lavatory. Even smaller industrial centers like Chester, Pennsylvania, and Charlotte, North Carolina, were inundated with huge numbers of new homeless. By January 1933 the problem had reached crisis proportions. Nels Anderson told a Senate subcommittee that by his "conservative" estimate, based on a three-day census taken at that time, there were at least 1.5 million homeless people in the United States.[1]

Not since the 1890s had Americans seen so many men riding the freights. Southern Pacific trains entering the rail center of San Antonio sometimes carried "as many as two hundred and fifty [illegal passengers] on big nights," and on a typical month in 1932, 2,000 hobos came through Birmingham, Alabama, on the trains. Railroad authorities were soon overwhelmed by this problem. Some trainmen were sympathetic to the homeless, of course, but even railroad detectives hired specifically to remove hobos found their task impossible. It would, one observer noted, "require an army to enforce the regulations and keep the freights free of trespassers."[2]

No part of the nation was spared the onslaught of homelessness in the 1930s. Although California, Florida, and Arizona received higher than average numbers of transients, wanderers came from—and traveled to—every part of the country. A transient census of September 30, 1934, documented over 20,000 interstate transients in California, but at the same time 8,438 California residents had traveled to other states. Industrial states like Massachusetts, Michigan, and Pennsylvania had many more out-migrants than in-migrants, but Ohio and New York attracted more homeless persons than they sent to other states. A good deal of transiency occurred either within states or involved movement to nearby states. Complaints about hordes of vagabonds descending on Florida ignored the fact that 28 percent of the transients there were residents of the state.[3]

The initial response of social agencies to this growing crisis was halting and uncertain. To some extent, officials remained hampered by settlement laws, often dating to the colonial era, which mandated the return of potential public charges to their state of legal residence. The number of "removals" for such reasons actually increased in the 1930s, and states sometimes fought court battles over which jurisdiction was legally responsible for destitute persons. In the early 1930s, however, such constitutional quarrels affected relatively few people. There were so many homeless that background checks were not feasible, and men could, with impunity, lie about their residency when they sought entrance to a municipal facility. Even if they were denied assistance under the rules, most of the homeless had no intention of returning to their previous domicile. As Bertha McCall of the Traveler's Aid Society noted, transients "dislike to hear [about their] 'legal residence,' for they know full well there is nothing there for them. They would rather roam on and on."[4]

Everywhere, the financial exigencies of the Depression placed new limitations on communities' ability to respond to the crisis. Responses to a 1933 U.S. Senate questionnaire asking municipal officials, "How are you meeting the problem of the transient unemployed in need of relief?" revealed the near collapse of public assistance for this group in many smaller communities. Typical answers were "One night's lodging, two meals, and insist they move on" (Selma, Alabama); "Price of meal and overnight shelter" (New London, Connecticut); "Night's lodging and breakfast" (Gettysburg, Pennsylvania). Many towns provided only lodging; others only a meal. A quarter indicated they had no plan at all or no funds to carry one out. A number of respondents plaintively related, "can't take care of our [own] citizens," let alone provide for outsiders.[5]

In big cities the number of homeless persons seeking assistance was proportionately greater than in smaller communities, partly because unemployed wanderers hoped they could find work there, but also because many of the new homeless could not even afford the 10 or 25 cents per night needed for an overnight stay in a skid-row flophouse. Putting aside former differences, public agencies and prominent private charities in most cities readily joined forces, setting up ad hoc committees to deal with the crisis. Local branches of the Traveler's Aid Society, which only on rare occasions provided shelter for the homeless, often assisted by referring cases to other agencies. The immediate need was for additional shelter space. Almost all cities expanded old facilities or opened new ones during 1930–31. Chicago, where distress was greater than in most communities, set up seven new shelters in the fall of 1930.

In some ways, the Depression accelerated the adoption of the more humane treatment of the homeless that younger social workers had begun to institute after World War I. In most urban centers, emergency committees established central registration bureaus to screen individuals before they were sent to a homeless shelter. In Kansas City, two social workers "devoted much of their time to the personal interests of the men, trying to help them solve their problems with an intelligent understanding of their needs, or securing work for them." Services for the homeless were expanded in a number of cities. In Chicago, the municipal shelter now provided free barber services, clothing pressing, and shoe repair. Shelter administrators often relaxed residency requirements at their facilities and, where it still existed, modified or eliminated the traditional work test. In Cleveland, for example, the homeless were now allowed to stay on "as long as was necessary, regardless of place of residence." To social workers in Pittsburgh, a work test "for men made homeless by inability to find work seemed unnecessary, if not unfair," and it was quietly abandoned, as it was in Louisville and some other cities.[6]

These new policies were far from universal, however, and in many respects care of the homeless remained disgracefully inadequate. Muckraking author Matthew Josephson, surveying what he called "the other nation" in 1933, noted that "watery oatmeal and black coffee" was still standard breakfast fare in most municipal shelters. Homeless men especially disliked being forced to leave the facility at 6 A.M. daily. Since even casual labor jobs were scarce, the men complained that during the fall and winter they would often spend much of the day just trying to keep warm, later returning to "wait for hours at a time to get a dish full of that slop they throw at you." Social welfare administrators in Seattle, Kansas City, Cleveland, and a few other cities instituted much-needed medical services for the homeless, but in most communities such treatment was either nonexistent or reserved for local residents.[7]

The plight of homeless African Americans was often ignored. Regardless of size, most communities in the Deep South had no municipal shelters at all, and where such facilities did exist, they excluded blacks. In the North, municipal facilities usually admitted both races, but the location of these shelters was often inconvenient for African Americans. In 1933, the only lodging house in Harlem was the Colored Branch of the Salvation Army. African Americans preferred it to the municipal shelter on E. 25th Street not only because of its location, but because the Colored Branch was cleaner and offered better food. The army's shelter, however, had only 166 beds. In Chicago, municipal authorities responded more effectively to the needs of African Americans by opening a temporary shelter, run by the Urban League, in the city's South Side black belt.[8]

Two of the nation's largest cities lagged behind in adopting new policies toward the homeless. At the onset of the Depression, Philadelphia still had no municipal lodging house. Homeless men who were unable to pay for lodging on skid row were forced to go to the privately run wayfarers' lodge or to one of the religious missions. An investigation discovered "between 500 and 600 men sleeping each night on bare concrete floors in the cellars of the police stations." The city did not acquire space for a shelter until November 1930, when the Baldwin Locomotive Works made a vacant warehouse available, rent free. Once the new shelter was set up, however, it quickly became known as one of the most advanced facilities in the country, with social workers, a doctor, and trained nurse on duty full-time and a whole floor of the eight-story structure devoted to recreational activities for the men.[9]

New York, in contrast to Philadelphia, had been one of the first cities to establish a municipal lodging house, but as the number seeking shelter there increased in the late 1920s and early '30s, officials refused to modify the archaic policy of limiting stays at the facility to five days each month. In January 1931, a group of one thousand homeless and unemployed persons, with the support of the Communist Party, demonstrated to end this practice. The marchers claimed the lodging house was overcrowded, criticized the lack of clean bedding, and demanded free clothing, laundry facilities, and "three nourishing meals a day" for shelter residents. The superintendent of the shelter, J. A. Mannix, responded with a snide remark that some homeless men avoided the municipal facility because they "object to taking a bath" and denied there were any significant problems at the institution. The demonstrations did, however, lead to more flexible rules for stays at the shelter, as well as to some improvements in other areas. When he visited the facility in 1934, Mayor Fiorello LaGuardia found both the food and sleeping quarters acceptable; the only change he ordered was to refurbish the "dingy and poorly lighted" washrooms.[10]

The Depression also brought about changes in the practices of private agencies dealing with the homeless. By the 1920s, the Salvation Army had become a regular part of skid-row life in major urban areas and the most important agency for care of the homeless in many smaller communities. As the number of men seeking assistance rose, however, the army was forced to curtail the traditional approach of its industrial homes, in which food and lodging were provided in return for their help in the "salvage" operations of collecting paper or repairing used clothing and furniture. As one historian of the army notes, "the sheer number of applicants made this increasingly difficult anywhere." In October 1930, "overwhelmed with applicants, with employees working double shifts," the agency opened eight "free food stations" in Manhattan; within a year they were serving almost 50,000 meals a day. A new 2,000-bed shelter, opened in 1932, was soon filled to capacity. In other cities as well the agency turned its attention to the immediate task of helping the homeless survive. By 1932 the army was faced with a growing budgetary crisis, as families "discarded fewer items, wore clothes longer, and did not replace the icebox with a refrigerator quite yet." The agency managed to curtail expenses by retrenching some of its paid staff, but the real solution would not come until mid-1933, when the New Deal program for transients began to contract out some of their new service centers to private charities.[11]

DESPITE AN EMERGING consensus among welfare professionals, the policies of municipal officials and organized charity toward the homeless was not accepted by all elements of the population. As in past depressions, disputes quickly arose between social workers and locally based groups who favored more traditional methods of assisting the poor. By 1932, a growing class division in attitudes toward the homeless was evident, and the perspective of many local politicians and social workers was increasingly at odds with that of the ordinary citizen.

The first indication of this was the renewal of the age-old controversy over soup kitchens. In most large cities, local charities had been running soup kitchens during the winter months for decades. They now expanded their operations, joined by numerous ad hoc groups that sprang up in response to the emergency. In 1930, in Philadelphia, one-time boxer Eddie Palmer set up a soup kitchen and free breakfast program for children in his South Philadelphia neighborhood, with local grocers contributing free food to the effort. It would be only one of many such operations in the city. In early 1931, one New York social worker reported the existence of 82 breadlines in the city, each serving an average of a thousand meals a day "to any and all comers." In black communities, Baptist and African Methodist Episcopal churches were especially active in aiding the homeless. In Harlem, the Abyssinian Baptist Church provided food, fuel, clothing, and shoes for the destitute, ran a small shelter, and fed 2,000 persons a day at a soup kitchen. Oklahoma City became renowned for its two large soup kitchens, one of which was designed specifically for unemployed veterans. The Salvation Army and local Community Chest roundly criticized the "mass feeding" conducted at these facilities because there was no effort "to determine residence or to discover whether people were already receiving aid from other agencies."[12]

Much to the consternation of professional social workers, local groups serving the poor in this manner usually refused to place themselves under the aegis of citywide organizations whose goal was to rationalize the distribution of aid and prevent fraud. In Seattle, for example, the Central Registry of leading charitable organizations imposed a work requirement on homeless men receiving food and shelter, but its policies were subverted when a local newspaper "catering to working men" established a breadline during the winter of 1930–31 serving an estimated 2,200 persons daily, "no questions asked." Organized charity remained frustrated by the fact that "nine of ten smaller organizations giving service to homeless men continued to act independently." A 1931 survey of 80 such groups by a Philadelphia social worker revealed much about the causes of this conflict. Twenty of the organizations refused to even participate in the survey. Of the remaining sixty, only four made any effort to inquire into the background of those they assisted, and few had "any effective system of accounting." The investigator also found considerable duplication of services among the small organizations. He concluded condescendingly that only a handful met criteria that would justify their continued existence. These small charities were blithely unconcerned about the "fraud" of homeless men who, some social workers complained, got more than their share of free food by going from one soup line to another.[13]

The emergence of local groups during 1930–32 reenergized a pattern of resistance to the modernization of charity. These small-scale charities brought a perspective to the task of benevolence that was miles removed from that of most social workers—even those who, in response to the crisis, eliminated the work test and attempted to expand individual treatment for the homeless. Many "soup societies" were rooted in working-class consciousness and neighborhood loyalties. Welfare professionals, however sympathetic to the downtrodden, were prone to filter their views through the lens of bureaucracy and social work theory.

In addition to breadlines and soup kitchens, social workers were disturbed by the increase of beggars during the Depression. By the 1920s, most welfare professionals recognized the complex causes of homelessness and no longer stressed the old dichotomy between the worthy and the unworthy poor. There was no softening, however, of their attitude toward urban mendicants. Beginning in the late 1920s, charity workers, public officials, and the police joined forces in cities across the country to reduce street begging and to reform—if possible—the beggars themselves. Such arrangements gave unusual authority to caseworkers to control the disposition of persons convicted of street begging. In St. Louis, for example, beggars were paroled only if they were "willing to accept the treatment" recommended by the caseworker. If they failed to follow the prescribed plan to reform their behavior, however, they would be returned to jail. In Cleveland, mendicants were jailed for 20 days, then "given the opportunity to work at the Wayfarers' Lodge." Those who refused this "opportunity," however, would be "rearrested and returned to the workhouse."[14]

The rapid increase in street beggars induced panic in some social workers. "Immediate action is necessary," warned a New York welfare official in January 1932, "if New York is not to revert to creating and maintaining a pauper class." The antibegging campaigns of the early Depression years were usually accompanied by an attempt to educate the public about the presumed negative effects of giving money or food to mendicants. Officials again promoted the substitution of tickets that beggars could exchange for free food and lodging. These efforts to eradicate begging, however, were no more successful than similar past crusades had been. In 1931, Cleveland officials echoed the complaints of social workers elsewhere when they conceded that panhandling "still continued in the city in spite of the [antibegging] plan" instituted a year before. As the number of destitute or unemployed persons increased, devoting energy to controlling vagrancy or combating begging began to seem misguided. In New York, a witness told a congressional committee in 1933, judges were finding it difficult "to differentiate between the so-called hobo and vagrant and the temporarily unemployed" and hesitated to convict someone "who has not actually done anything very seriously wrong." No one, an observer in Philadelphia noted the following year, was "so cold-hearted" that they would enforce antibegging ordinances at a time when "the self-dependent and industrious worker is forced, through no fault of his own, to beg for enough to keep going."[15]

Declining income levels did not necessarily lead people to turn away from street beggars. As one Illinois relief worker noted in 1933, "the public is still susceptible to 'panhandling' and the tales of woe of strangers who meet them upon the street." He reached this conclusion after asking one 40-year-old man receiving aid to impersonate a beggar. In less than three hours, the man

> made 27 contacts, was given aid totaling $1.37 (in amounts from 5c to 25c) by 10 [individuals], was taken into a restaurant 4 times and fed, was offered whiskey 6 times, was told by young women [beggars] not to solicit in their territory (he named the streets!), was invited to meet one of the men next day to be given a shirt, was given 4 lectures on the consequences of being a bum, and received 9 polite refusals.

If this was typical of what beggars could expect from the public, it is no wonder that antibegging campaigns failed.[16]

"In Philadelphia, as in most cities," one commentator noted in 1932, "the poor are taking care of the poor." A contemporary sociological study found "very few families who at one time or another did not share material possessions with other friends among the workers and with no apparent feeling on the part of either party that [their] independence had been destroyed." Some people continued to shun the homeless, of course, but many identified with their plight enough to extend traditional neighborhood charity to destitute strangers. "[W]ithout the patience and generosity of the general population," wrote one man who rode the freights in the 1930s, "a hobo could not have survived on the road." As a teenager growing up in California, Richard Nixon later recalled—with considerable distaste—that his grandmother "was always taking care of every tramp that came along the road, just like my mother, too." Nixon worried that feeding the homeless would weaken their work ethic, but for many citizens this view now seemed irrelevant.[17]

A common assumption about the first years of the Depression is that most Americans tended to blame themselves for the unemployment and poverty that befell them. The public's response to the homeless, however, casts doubt on this idea. According to traditional conservative doctrine, no group's moral character was more suspect than the homeless, who seemed the embodiment of failure in a society geared to individual achievement. Yet people gave money to beggars, fed homeless men at the back door, and set up soup kitchens in record numbers—all indications of a degree of identification with the most destitute of the unemployed. In 1930, Mayor Harry Mackey of Philadelphia spoke sympathetically about the homeless forced to sleep in police station cellars, explaining that these men were impoverished "through no fault of their own" and should not be lumped together with "the 'down and outer' as we know him in normal conditions." It was important, Jane Addams said, to "guard against the tendency to call a man a failure because he is out of work." The huge increase in unemployment led some to question the morality of vagrancy laws. "To punish the homeless under such circumstances," one law professor argued, was "not only futile but cruel."[18]

The proliferation of shantytowns—sometimes called "Hoovervilles" in ironic reference to President Herbert Hoover—in cities across the country further increased public sympathy for the homeless. "They are everywhere," said John Dos Passos in an essay on Detroit's new homeless, "living in shacks and shelters along the waterfront, in the back rooms of unoccupied houses, the others just sleeping any place. In one back lot they have burrowed out rooms in a huge abandoned sandpile." An estimated thousand people lived in St. Louis's Hooverville, located on the banks of the

Mississippi near the city dump. In New York, noted one observer in 1931, hobos were "homing into the city in larger numbers than ever before and have set up a 'jungle' for themselves in the heart of the East Side" on vacant lots owned by the city. Although obviously in violation of city building and fire codes, the people who lived there were seldom troubled by the authorities, and in many cases they received assistance from local residents and "friendly" speakeasies. In Pittsburgh, sympathizers "piled in provisions" to two shantytowns, where men and families lived in shacks created out of tar paper, tin, and other scrap materials. "Hoovervilles are in a separate nation, with separate codes," said one investigator. As in the hobo jungles, denizens of the shantytowns often engaged in bartering for clothing or shoes. At night some would go to the produce market, returning with "discarded onions, apples, carrots, a bit spoiled" but still edible, to be shared or traded. And like the jungles, the Hoovervilles welcomed African Americans as well as whites. In cities where sharply drawn racial lines were commonplace in many aspects of life, patterns of segregated housing did not extend to the ramshackle collection of structures that sheltered the homeless.[19]

The homeless were central to three key images that came to symbolize the breakdown of the American economic system in the 1930s. The first was the long, snaking lines of people hoping to receive enough food to get them through another day. The second was the shantytowns. The third was a group of World War I veterans, the Bonus Army, who in 1932 traveled to Washington to demand that Congress pay them the bonus they were not scheduled to receive until 1945. After encamping in Anacostia Flats for several months to lobby Congress, they were driven from the capital at bayonet point by troops commanded by Gen. Douglas MacArthur.[20] The use of the military against the Bonus marchers reinforced Hoover's image as insensitive to the sufferings of the poor and contributed to his resounding defeat in the 1932 election. The Bonus Army and the public response to it, however, also demonstrated the extent to which the condition of homelessness had become a defining element of the American experience. Traveling to the District of Columbia mostly by boxcar, the veterans often received assistance along the way from sympathetic townspeople and railroad workers. At Anacostia, they created a large-scale shantytown that grew in size until it was a small, self-governing city of over 20,000. Drawn from a wide variety of occupational groups, its population included women and children as well as men, blacks as well as whites. The integration of African Americans into all aspects of camp life, including governance, was a particularly striking feature in segregated Washington.[21]

The Bonus Army was very much representative of the population as a whole. Perhaps for that reason, as well as because most of the men were veterans, the public reacted strongly against MacArthur's unnecessary brutality. Despite the hostility of some local authorities and state police, the veterans fleeing the capital often received assistance from townspeople in nearby states. In Johnstown, Pennsylvania, the plea of leaders of the Bonus marchers that the Bonus Army was "composed of folks just like themselves" struck a responsive chord in a steel community where unemployment was running particularly high. Mayor Edward McClosky allowed a large remnant of the group to temporarily encamp there before they, too, dispersed and "melted away into the sea of joblessness."[22]

THE HOOVER ADMINISTRATION could expel the Bonus Army from Washington, but it could not obliterate the larger social significance of this episode. By the summer of 1932, riding the freights illegally had become more commonplace than at any time in American history. With the rise of mass transiency, the image of the homeless man underwent yet another transformation. The humorous or picturesque caricature popularized in middle-class magazines in the 1920s faded from view. In its place there emerged a much more realistic portrait that, if anything, now overemphasized the degrading aspects of homelessness. When Matthew Josephson referred to the men at the New York Municipal Lodging House as "robots with baggy trousers and disheveled coats," he reflected a common literary perspective of the 1930s. Novels like Edward Dahlberg's *Bottom Dogs* (1930), Tom Kromer's *Waiting for Nothing* (1935), and Nelson Algren's *Somebody in Boots* (1935) presented the men on the road as defeated and dejected—in Algren's words, "a ragged parade of dull grey faces, begging, thieving, hawking, selling and whoring. Faces haggard, and hungry, and cold, and afraid." In the hands of these writers, the homeless came to symbolize the brutality of an unjust system but lacked any individuality or sense of common purpose.[23]

The struggle to survive was unquestionably an important aspect of homelessness, but it was disingenuous to portray transients merely as passive victims of class oppression. If they had really been so apathetic in the face of Depression conditions, they would not have gone on the road in the first place. Writers on the left were correct, of course, in ascribing a lack of clear political goals to the transients. The Industrial Workers of the World had long ceased to be active among hobos; and despite the participation of a small contingent of Communists, even the Bonus marchers had no coherent political agenda beyond the quest for the bonus itself. The very act of riding trains without paying, however, exemplified the spirit of "rebellious discontent" that would become increasingly prevalent among workers as the Depression wore on. Only occasionally did workers justify riding the rails in ideological terms, as for example the Socialist party organizer who bluntly told Bertha Thompson, "The railroads rob the workers. Shouldn't we rob the railroads?" As in the past, most who engaged in tramping simply took for granted that they would ride for free if they could get away with it. The difference in the 1930s was that far more people were on the road, and they were drawn from a wider range of backgrounds than ever before.[24]

In some ways, the demographic profile of the mobile element of the homeless population in the 1930s continued to develop along lines already established before World War I. Data gathered in 1934–35 revealed that a disproportionate number of unattached male transients came from urban areas and that eight out of ten were unmarried. About 95 percent were native-born Americans, and most of these had parents who also had been born in the United States. As was traditionally the case, the transients tended to be much younger than the resident homeless who did not migrate, with two-thirds of the former under 35 years of age.[25]

Some aspects of the transient population, however, underwent significant change. The age spectrum of the transient group in the 1930s broadened to a degree at both ends. John C. Webb's study of transients in 13 cities found that about 12 to 16 percent of the men were over age 44, and a survey of Pennsylvania's homeless unemployed revealed that 10 to 14 percent were actually 55 years or older. These figures were surprising, because older homeless men usually did not migrate in search of work. Much of this was probably attributable to businesses economizing by laying off middle-aged workers. Already a problem in the 1920s, this trend intensified during the Depression when many employers, compelled to reduce their workforce, fired older workers and retained cheaper, more physically robust younger laborers.[26]

What attracted far more attention than the hardships of older workers were the numbers of boys and young men riding the rails. About 40 percent of unattached transients in 1934 were under age 25, with 20 percent 19 years old or younger. The numbers were higher in the South, which attracted youngsters in the fall and winter because of its milder climate. The unemployment crisis was an underlying cause of most youth transiency. At a time when young men would normally be entering the workforce for the first time, few new jobs were available. "We had hoped the depression would soon end," two teenage vagabonds later related, "but in time our hopes began to wane, for the factories continued laying off men instead of hiring them." More than the inability to find a job lay behind youth transiency, however. Thomas Minehan, who spent two years studying children on the road, found that even before the Depression hit, "many homes of the boy tramps were extremely tenuous. Death had taken a father, divorce the mother; separation divided the family and many never had a home at all." George Outland's more scientific study of over 3,000 transient boys in Los Angeles led to similar conclusions. Over half of the youngsters came from broken homes, including 25 percent who lived with stepparents and 14 percent who had been raised by relatives, friends, or in orphanages; almost a third of the main breadwinners were on relief at the time the child ran away. Many more boys on the road came from skilled workers' homes than was true of older transients, perhaps indicating that the loss of income in such families created more stressful family conditions.[27]

In July 1933, Illinois relief workers seeking to fill positions for a conservation project interviewed 52 homeless men aged 18 to 25. A few representative case studies provide insight into the lives of transients in the 1930s, and help clarify the complex and often frightening circumstances that contributed to a young person's decision to leave home.

Case No. 9: "Oscar" comes from Texas — is 19 years old — 8th grade only — left home six months ago — has been transient all over the West including California — sleeping in Missions and box cars — bumming his food at Missions and back-doors — had a letter from his sister 2 months ago — says [she] received Red Cross flour.

Case No. 33: "Reginald" is a truck driver — unemployed since November, 1931, 19 years old — 2 sisters living at home — left 2 weeks ago hunting work, been on the road off and on for 2 years travelling by freight — communicates with family regularly — family on relief — 8 [people] living at home altogether including grandparents.

Case No. 42: "Peter" is experienced as a hotel clerk — no work in 2 years — comes from Butte, Montana — has one brother — been away two years looking for work — for 4 years he has been supporting his widow[ed] mother with odd jobs — one year ago he couldn't get enough work to continue [his] responsibility — sent his mother to married sister who's husband works in mines — he gets about 7 days work in a month — odd jobs have been enough to get him by lately — hitch hikes on road — wrote home 10 days ago.

Twenty-eight of the 52 men interviewed mentioned some family tragedy or disruption that contributed to their leaving home. Behind the quest for employment often lay a great deal of suffering. Yet despite problems at home, many of the men expressed the desire to help family members or to keep in touch with those who remained behind.[28]

Women became a noticeable part of the homeless population on the road for the first time in the 1930s. Part of this was due to the increase in homeless families, whose antecedents can be traced to the 1920s. Relatively cheap automobiles and an expanding highway system made it possible for poor families to travel around the country, living off odd jobs. In the mid-1920s, local authorities in the Midwest and West were already becoming annoyed by the "hobo tourist" who moved from one autocamp to another, "always begging and remaining in one city until ordered to move on." As unemployment grew at the end of the decade, social workers in St. Louis complained of the increasing number of "auto tramp" families, "skilled at getting by," who sabotaged their casework treatment by refusing to sell their cars and settle down. "They get gasoline from some other source—usually generous individuals—and continue their journey to the next city." The number of such families moving from place to place, accepting temporary jobs or panhandling to survive, expanded greatly in the early 1930s. Although at mid-decade they made up only 20 percent of all transients, this was a huge increase over previous decades.[29]

Most women or girls on the road were members of families traveling together in this manner. In 1934–35 females made up only about 3 percent of the unattached transients, although in Chicago and some other cities the figure may at times have been double that. While the absolute numbers were small, they were still dramatically higher than in the past; Nels Anderson estimated that there had been at least a tenfold increase in the number of women hobos during the first years of the Depression.[30]

The lives of homeless women could be even more difficult than those of men. "Homeless, friendless women are much troubled with their belongings," one investigator perceptively noted. "They cannot trudge the streets and look for work if they are burdened by their bundles and suitcases." Some simply abandoned their possessions, moving "late at night from the rooms for which they cannot pay, leaving everything they own in default of money." At the same time, reported another observer, women "hate the idea of charity" even more than men. "They half starve themselves. But they do not go to bread lines, nor do they eat at soup kitchens."[31]

Especially when they were on the road, women faced the constant threat of sexual harassment. Some avoided this problem by traveling with a male companion, with the pair posing as a married couple when dealing with authorities or begging for food. It is likely that most such relationships were formed on the road and, given the nature of transient life, that many did not last very long. Young women traveling alone, dressed in overalls and with their hair cut short, sometimes dodged potential difficulties because they "looked just like boys." As one "lady hobo" explained, women "wear pants so they won't be molested and pass [themselves] off for men in getting on and off trains." This tactic did not always work, however, and she herself acknowledged that she had "been raped on several occasions and [had] given in on several more." The fact that some prostitutes traveled on trains, going from one jungle to another, caused additional problems for single women on the road. Women who refused an offer of money for sex might find themselves in danger of assault. Unless they knew the person, women simply avoided conversation with men or boys on the road. Hobo memoirist Maury Graham recalled that women transients in the 1930s protected themselves by being "tough and hard as nails." Another young man told of a woman hobo he encountered who went a step further. "[A]rmed with a 38 caliber pistol," he explained, "she permitted no one to come near her."[32]

It is significant that women transients were generally younger than males, with twice as many females likely to be under age 20. That some younger women were now willing to abandon long-held gender roles by riding in boxcars or hitching rides reflected the impact of changing social and cultural patterns of the postwar era. One woman transient articulated the combination of factors behind her decision: "that her savings were gone, that she could live cheaper on the road, that she wanted to travel, never having seen much of the country," and that she wanted to "be free of her lover." Bertha Thompson concluded that, among the unmarried women transients she had spoken with, economic motives could not be easily separated from the influence of new cultural values that challenged traditional constraints on women's behavior. "Their stories," said Thompson, "are very much the same—no work, a whole family on relief, no prospects for marriage, the need for a lark, the need for freedom of sex and living, and the great urge to know what other women were doing."[33]

Economic factors probably played a greater direct role in the lives of transient women who were married or widowed. During 1929–33, the unemployment rate of women workers actually exceeded that of males. Layoffs during these years affected married women as much as single women—if not more so in many cases where the families had become dependent on their income to make ends meet. Homeless women were much more likely than homeless men to be married or separated. Only about four of ten unattached transient women were single, a rate less than half that of men on the road. Among women who were heads of transient families, only 22 percent were married but 70 percent were separated, widowed, or divorced.[34]

Another distinctive element of the homeless population in the 1930s, African Americans, increased much more rapidly than did the female homeless. African Americans comprised about 10 percent of the U.S. population in 1930 but by 1935 made up over 12 percent of the population of Federal Transient Service shelters. Surprisingly, the proportion of the homeless population that was black was considerably higher in the North than the South, although most blacks still lived in southern states. African Americans averaged only 7 or 8 percent of the population of major northern cities in 1930, yet in 1931 they made up between 15 and 27 percent of the homeless staying in municipal shelters there.[35]

The sharp growth of black homelessness was a product of both racial and structural economic forces. The movement of blacks into industrial jobs in the North after 1916 provided African American men with steady work preferable to unskilled labor, but ironically it also made black workers more vulnerable to downturns in the economy. As early as 1928 in Chicago, Cleveland, and elsewhere in the North, blacks were the first to be laid off when industries like steel, autos, and meatpacking began to cut back on production. By the time the economy as a whole went into a tailspin in late 1929, some blacks had already been unemployed for over a year. The Depression also undercut black women's jobs. In the past, domestic service jobs for either sex were less likely to be eliminated during recessions, but the severity of the Great Depression changed this pattern. "As white housewives balanced the budget," St. Clair Drake and Horace Cayton noted, "their Negro servants were often the first casualties." Even during good times, black women had often found it necessary to work to help the family make ends meet. The upsurge of unemployment among both industrial and service workers thus struck particularly hard at African Americans in the North. The result was not only a higher level of homelessness in general among blacks, but a much greater tendency for black women, compared to whites, to become homeless.[36]

For blacks as well as whites, the Depression reversed the trend that had led to a greater preponderance of unskilled workers among the down-and-out. Although still the largest single category in 1934, unskilled labor (31 percent of all male transients) was no longer predominant. Skilled workers (17 percent) declined in number somewhat from earlier decades, but factory operatives (23 percent) increased sharply, and domestic service work (11 percent) was no longer invulnerable. While small businessmen and managers (4 percent) seldom became homeless, this was no longer true of other white-collar workers. Lower-level white-collar workers (11 percent) and professionals (3 percent), though still underrepresented, suffered much more than in previous decades.[37]

To the middle class, it was the sudden increase of clerks and professionals in breadlines that was most shocking. In 1934, a University of Chicago researcher reported that a "pathetic class of old white-collared men" had taken up residence on West Madison Street, attempting to survive on a $1.50 a day by addressing envelopes. "This work is unsteady," he noted, "but these addressers strive very hard to keep up their appearance." Many of these men had formerly been bookkeepers or accountants. Responding to this situation, welfare officials in Chicago and New York opened special shelters for homeless white-collar workers—a break with the tradition that all homeless received the same treatment regardless of class background. Most cities, however, did not have the funds or manpower to provide such specialized facilities. For the most part, the homeless clerical worker or store manager could not avoid rubbing shoulders with other, less educated down-and-out citizens. As one writer commented in *The New Republic* in 1931, "misery has amalgamated these hitherto separate elements. A man who hangs out at one of these skid row dumps [cheap restaurants], even though his collar is or once was white, stamps himself as out of a job."[38]

THE 1930S witnessed a noticeable shift in public opinion about the homeless. Unlike the 1870s, the huge increase in the number of people standing in soup lines or riding the freights during the Great Depression did not generate a hostile backlash. Only occasionally—such as Douglas MacArthur, in stating that the Bonus Marchers were potential revolutionaries—did anyone suggest that homeless men were subversives.[39] The long-standing image of the lazy homeless person appeared less often, and the humorous tone of many newspaper stories about beggars and lodging-house residents was replaced, for the most part, by more prosaic factual accounts. The word "tramp" itself virtually disappeared from print. After 1930, "hobo" or the blandly neutral "transient" would be the most commonly used terms for the homeless. During the Depression many people continued to view panhandlers as a nuisance, but few had any real fear of them, and (in behavior that a later generation of Americans would undoubtedly find incomprehensible) housewives willingly opened their back doors to strangers asking to be fed.

Public perceptions of the homeless nevertheless retained an element of ambiguity. City dwellers were well aware of the new segregated patterns of urban life, and with some justification they continued to associate skid row and its denizens with slum conditions, cheap saloons, and prostitution. The plight of the individual destitute person (or family) invoked sympathy. Massed in one place, the homeless were a different matter. It was perhaps for that reason that the construction of new homeless facilities outside of skid-row areas was strongly opposed in many instances. People did not object to the spending of public money for shelters, but they feared that if temporary institutions became permanent they would damage community life and property values. In reality, the line between the new (temporary) homeless and the old (permanent) homeless was a porous one, but people drew it anyway. Empathy for the beggar, the panhandler, and men and women riding the freights, then, did not necessarily extend to the skid-row derelict.[40]

This ambivalence would allow the return of older, negative stereotypes after 1935, when New Deal relief programs began to lift some of the working class out of desperate economic circumstances. At the beginning of the decade, however, hostile views of the homeless were largely absent from public debate as local relief agencies and charities struggled to deal with an unprecedented number of people asking for shelter. As early as 1930, reformers began to push for federal assistance, pointing to the lack of uniform treatment of the nonresident poor at the state and municipal level. The Hoover administration steadfastly refused to support federal relief legislation of any kind, however, and between December 1929 and March 1933 a variety of bills designed to aid nonresidents failed to pass Congress.[41]

After several false starts, leading welfare organizations came together in 1932 under the auspices of the National Council of Social Work to create the National Committee on Care of Transient and Homeless (NCCTH). During 1932–33, the NCCTH coordinated activities of organizations and, to demonstrate the magnitude of the problem facing the nation, conducted two censuses of the homeless population. Most importantly for the future, it developed plans for aiding transients that would strongly influence the Roosevelt administration when it took over. "I see no answer but a federal answer," Nels Anderson, referring to the transient problem, bluntly told a Senate committee in January 1933. In May the new Democratic Congress, as part of the Federal Emergency Relief Act (FERA), finally took up this call and authorized the funding for "needy persons who have no settlement in any one State or community." Harry Hopkins, appointed by Roosevelt to head FERA, set aside an initial $15 million for the Federal Transient Service (FTS), the first federal agency in American history designed to aid the homeless unemployed.[42]

In establishing the Transient Service, Hopkins relied heavily on assistance from the NCCTH and its chairperson, Ellen Potter. In an April 1933 policy statement, the organization had argued for coordination of federal, state, and local authorities in dealing with the homeless, for minimum standards for all shelter accommodations, and for adequate medical treatment for transients. The 1933 policy statement firmly rejected the traditional focus on making homeless men work for their meals and shelter. "Any work that is offered," the committee stated, "should not be considered in any sense as a compulsory work test." Acknowledging the difficulty of placing the men in outside employment, the committee stated that some of the residents would be employed at the facility itself, including "cleaning and guarding the premises, guarding the property during the day and at night, or [assisting] in [the] laundry or kitchen." With purposeful vagueness, they added that "ingenuity will need to be shown in finding work for the other men." These recommendations would significantly influence the transient program as it evolved.[43]

Participation in the federal program required states to develop a transient relief plan and apply for funding. To circumvent widely varying state settlement laws, Hopkins defined a "federal transient" as anyone who had lived less than one year in a particular state. Care for such individuals would be entirely reimbursed by FERA funds. Care of "state transients" (those who had resided for more than one year in the state) and local homeless would be paid for on a matching basis, with the federal government providing most of the money. A 1934 survey found that transient bureaus in 6 of 13 major cities accepted locally resident homeless in addition to nonresidents. By December 1933, 40 states had established transient relief programs; eventually only one state—Vermont—declined to participate.[44]

Transient centers were technically under the control of state relief agencies, but in most cases the need for FERA approval of monthly budget requests led state administrators to look to Washington for instruction in running transient programs. Throughout most of its two-plus years of existence, the Federal Transient Service was administered by Elizabeth Wickenden, who began as assistant director of the Transient Service in 1933 and was appointed acting director the following year. Only 24 at the time, she brought energy, enthusiasm, and dedication to the task of organizing a network of transient facilities across the country. Eventually the FTS established 300 transient centers in cities and towns and over 300 camps in rural areas. In many smaller cities, the FTS contracted with restaurants, lodging houses, and private agencies (usually the Salvation Army or religious missions) to feed and house transients, reimbursing the agencies on a per capita or per diem basis. Cities of over 200,000 population usually had state-run transient centers with facilities for much larger numbers of homeless. Most of the centers were housed in rented buildings, refurbished if necessary for use as homeless shelters. In some cases, the FTS virtually took over private shelters, hiring already existing personnel and supplementing them, if necessary, with additional employees.[45] At its high point in August 1934, 400,000 unattached individuals and over 50,000 persons in families were registered with the FTS. This number declined steadily during the next six months, then rose again to over 350,000 in August 1935, just before the agency began to phase out its operations.[46]

Conditions within the federal transient centers varied widely. The most serious deficiencies occurred in the smaller facilities contracted out to the Salvation Army or, occasionally, to religious missions. A diary left by two young transients, James Carlone and Bob O'Hara, indicated some of the conditions they found in such shelters in New Jersey. Sleeping accommodations were adequate, and they were generally pleased with the relatively high level of personal freedom compared with the regimentation of municipal lodging houses. Carlone and O'Hare complained repeatedly, however, of the poor quality of the food and the bare-bones "recreational rooms" of the privately run shelters. In smaller transient facilities generally, little was done for the homeless beyond providing basic necessities, and most transients viewed them simply as places to stay for a few days, then move on— perhaps to another transient shelter.[47]

Though fairly numerous, the small transient centers probably cared for only a fraction of the total homeless population under government supervision. In Pennsylvania, for example, the seven centers with capacities of under 100 housed only 441 persons, while the five with capacities over 100 lodged almost 6,000—including 4,200 in the main Philadelphia center alone, one of the largest centers in the country. Conditions were often much different in the medium-sized and large transient centers, run mostly by state-appointed personnel. After their experience at a string of small New Jersey shelters, Carlone and O'Hare were pleasantly surprised by the treatment they received at the Allentown, Pennsylvania, transient center. As in most transient centers run directly by government personnel, the beds were iron cots with sheets and woolen blankets—surplus materials acquired by Wickenden from the U.S. Army. The men were particularly impressed by the recreational facilities. The two rooms for that purpose were airy and well-lighted, one "a library with large easy chairs and a very good collection of books" and newspapers, the other "well furnished with card tables and a large ping pong table and a few easy chairs." They described the food as "incomparable as shelter's [*sic*] go. It's clean and wholesome." Furthermore, unlike the Salvation Army–run FTS centers they had visited, "you don't have to get a ticket for a meal[,] just go in and sit down in a place that is given you on arrival." Carlone and O'Hare's excitement over the simple pleasures of a good meal and a clean bed were shared by other transients, who viewed the federal shelters as much superior to many private charitable facilities or cheap lodging houses.[48]

Not all of the larger transient centers earned such accolades. State files of the FTS contain folders detailing complaints against various transient centers, especially overcrowding and inadequate recreation facilities. A June 1934 evaluation of the program by Ellery Reed summarized some of these problems. Showers and toilets usually met a "fairly good standard of cleanliness" but were often too few in number. Sleeping quarters were usually in large dormitories, and bedding and pillows were always adequate. Filled to near capacity, however, the sleeping areas frequently failed to meet the suggested minimum air space of 500 square feet per person. Recreation rooms always existed, but—echoing complaints of many of the men—Reed found them "usually poorly equipped."[49]

Acknowledging these limitations, Reed still concluded that most transient centers were fairly successful in carrying out their basic responsibilities toward the people under their care. Some aspects warranted special praise. The centers provided free clothing for the men and often maintained clothes-mending facilities. In most cases the food served in the centers was far superior "both in quality and quantity" to that of private or municipal lodging houses. The FTS represented a tremendous improvement in the level of health care afforded America's homeless. Transient centers were required to have a physician in attendance at least part of the day and an orderly or nurse on duty during the night. Medical treatment was paid for by FERA, but hospitalization, if necessary, was supposed to be the responsibility of local public welfare programs. Stretching the rules, however, allowed transient camps in Arizona and New Mexico to become "low cost tuberculosis hospitals," and in Baltimore Dr. Frank Furstenberg established a center to treat men who, as a result of heavy labor, had developed hernias. Not to be underestimated, as well, was the impact of free dental care at the transient centers. "Many an old timer," one observer noted, "wandering about the land with bad teeth or none at all, has for the first time in his life received proper dental attention."[50]

Other positive features of the transient program were less tangible but no less significant. One was the program's clear break with the traditional policy of limiting stays at homeless shelters to a few days. By allowing transients to remain as long as they wished, the FTS removed an element of insecurity from their lives that in the past had hampered even the most sympathetic policy makers. From the beginning, progressive social workers had hoped that the federal program would not only allow transients to survive but help rehabilitate them. With that in mind, the FTS jettisoned the "work test," substituting in its place the ideal of reeducation or training for long-term employment. For a number of reasons, it was an ideal that was difficult to realize. Shelter residents were technically required to do 30 hours of work a week, but in reality many men did much less. In addition to room and board, most men received only one dollar per week, although skilled workers sometimes received more; men at the rural camps could make up to three dollars a week. Finding outside work was not easy, however, especially in industrial areas. Local residents feared competition for scarce jobs, and early New Deal relief programs like the Civil Works Administration specifically excluded nonresidents. As a result, many shelter residents wound up doing work around the facility. Except for a very small number of white collar workers, most of those who worked on the outside obtained only temporary jobs, usually at unskilled labor.[51]

Potentially more important than outside work was the training that transients received from educational programs and jobs in the shelters. Shelter administrators in large urban areas tried to provide both formal classes and on-the-job training for residents. The "practical" educational program for transients age 18–25 staying on board the U.S.S. Mercy, a converted Navy vessel that served as a congregate shelter in Philadelphia, offered training in carpentry, clothing repair, cooking, machine shop, painting, plumbing, and electrical work, as well as "leisure time" classes in math, bookkeeping, and languages. In conjunction with an agricultural project, some of the men on the Mercy were also able to take extension courses at Penn State University in horticulture, animal husbandry, and other related subjects.[52]

Educational opportunities at the main Philadelphia center, at 18th and Hamilton Street, were even greater. In addition to training in English, math, and a variety of skilled trades, by 1935 the center offered classes in barbering, photography, tailoring, office practice, art and design, shorthand and typing, French, and Spanish. In a number of large cities, courses in music and drama provided both training and an opportunity for transients to present performances. In Texas, centers without libraries of their own developed arrangements with public libraries, and transients were able to enroll at the University of Texas on a cooperative plan. Everywhere, transients turned out weekly or biweekly mimeographed newspapers that served as the unofficial organs of their centers or camps. About 250 in number, with titles like *Nomad*, *Highway Citizen*, or (more prosaically) the *Quaker City Trumpet*, these papers informed residents about activities in the centers while providing some measure of journalistic training for the men who produced them.[53]

In the large urban facilities, educational and recreational programs expanded steadily in scope, as administrators responded to the needs of the sizeable number of men who stayed for an extended period of time at one shelter. Even in the large transient centers, however, many transients' stays were too brief to allow participation in formal training or other organized activities. In contrast, the transient camps built in rural areas had much less turnover. That, and the isolation of most camps from urban areas, promoted a more cohesive community life. The camps were modest in size (usually under 200 capacity), operated independently of the large centers, and employed relatively few social workers. Consequently, their organizational structure was less bureaucratic, and camp supervisors did not necessarily feel the need to apply casework methods to the men staying there.[54]

Unused Army barracks were sometimes converted into FTS camps, but for the most part these rural facilities were built from the ground up by homeless men who then became the camp's first residents. Unlike the residents of urban centers, most of the men in the camps regularly worked 30 hours a week, primarily at farming, conservation, or small-scale public works projects.[55] They also had a more significant role in running the camps. Many FTS camps were surprisingly self-sufficient. Camp McMahon, in New Jersey, had its own power station and water system. A 1934 FTS report indicated that supervisors played little role in day-to-day operations of the facility. "Every responsibility for the smooth operation of the camp" lay with the men, "who draw their cooks, kitchen police, mess steward, quartermaster, hospital aides and other details from their own number." Camp Green Haven, a larger camp north of New York City, drew upon more specialized trades among the residents, including "tailors, shoemakers, plumbers, painters, blacksmiths, electricians, store-room and canteen clerks and other personnel necessary to run a camp with 200 men." One California camp went further, setting up furniture-making and machine and auto repair shops as part of its "self-help and rehabilitation scheme," and everywhere the rural camps maintained vegetable gardens to supplement purchased food.[56]

WITH THEIR EMPHASIS on self-help, camaraderie, and shared responsibilities, the organization of the camps echoed aspects of the communal culture of the Bonus Army and the hobo jungles. This was less true of the urban centers, but there, too, homeless men trained as barbers, tailors, and carpenters found employment in the shelters, and most FTS facilities were policed by unarmed guards selected from the transients.[57]

Both types of transient facilities brought together men from a wide variety of occupational backgrounds. As the program evolved, however, white-collar workers and professionals occasionally received special treatment in centers like New York City's Hartford House, a facility designed to rehabilitate better-educated homeless men. Although the men in the program were allowed to live in small groups in rooming houses, in other ways their activities differed little from that of transients in other centers. They even helped to renovate the building, aided by an interior decorator among the transients. Separating a group out by occupation did enable the center's administrators to focus more on the men's specific reeducation and training needs. The resulting job placement rate of 50 percent was much higher than that of most regular transient centers. Facilities for the white-collar homeless were rare, however. For the most part, the FTS centers and camps brought people of different classes together rather than separating them.[58]

This leveling tendency was less evident when it came to race. Most of the FTS camps were open to all racial groups. For example, Camp Frontier in upstate New York was 11 percent black. Apparently many of the smaller, subsidized transient centers also admitted African Americans, perhaps because the number of men they housed was not large enough to make separate facilities economically feasible. In the larger urban centers, however, racial segregation was much more common. In the South, the FTS set up separate shelters for blacks, which Reed sheepishly admitted were often "not quite equal to those provided for the whites." In the North and West, including border states, there was usually some separation of blacks and whites in the dining room and the sleeping quarters. In Philadelphia, and probably elsewhere in the North, the races were also segregated in infirmaries. Black staff members were often hired to interview black transients at local FTS registration bureaus; undoubtedly one of their jobs was to explain the unwritten rules of racial etiquette in the transient facilities.[59]

Only in the rural camps, then, did anything approaching genuine racial equality prevail. There is no evidence, however, that the pattern of modified segregation typical of the large urban facilities impeded African Americans or other racial minorities from taking part in the programs offered to transients. Nor, apparently, did housing the races in close quarters lead to any significant racial violence; no race riots broke out in any of the shelters. This may have been simply another example of the general decline in racial violence that occurred during the 1930s, when people temporarily put aside racial differences in the common struggle to survive hard times. It also, however, reflected the egalitarian traditions of men on the road—traditions that for decades had allowed them to coexist without duplicating the racial divisions of the larger society. Even in the South, segregated camps were preferable to exclusion of blacks or the absence of homeless shelters altogether.

The FTS made a sharper distinction along gender lines. Women transients, whether unattached or members of families, were not housed in congregate shelters. As Wickenden explained to Harry Hopkins, the Transient Service placed single women in "boarding houses, the YWCA or similar organizations on a contract basis," while homeless families were "given light housekeeping rooms, an apartment or a house, depending on available facilities," and issued food and clothing as needed. Both groups received far more individualized attention from caseworkers than did unattached homeless men. Such special treatment, which cost substantially more than housing and feeding people in shelters, was possible only because women made up a relatively small proportion of the total transient population. The FTS program for transient women was more humane than congregate care—or the complete lack of facilities for homeless women in some cities. It also, however, reinforced some age-old stereotypes about both sexes. The NCCTH's 1933 policy statement argued strongly that "mass shelter facilities are not desirable for women." As one social worker later explained, privacy was "essential to a woman," because women had always been protected and were unaccustomed to "the easy give and take with any type of human being which men learn at an early age." This implied that huge shelters were good enough for men, who unlike women could largely fend for themselves. In contrast to their "comprehensive program" of individual care for women, the FTS approach to homeless men focused on job training and group activities. The FTS program for men was more extensive than that of any other private or public agency, but it ignored the fact that not all of the causes of homelessness among men were employment related. The Transient Service did little to enlighten the public that not only homeless women, but many homeless men as well needed a "comprehensive program" to restore them as functioning members of society.[60]

While the federal transient program was in operation, the number of homeless persons on the road and living in shantytowns declined sharply. The pressure on municipal and private lodging houses eased, and in some cities (like Washington, D.C.) local municipal shelters or private agencies even closed down. In 1934, the young hobos Jim Carlone and Bob O'Hare reported that they had "not seen one young fellow of our age on the road. That alone speaks very good [sic] of the Transient Camps of New Jersey."

Harry Hopkins claimed that the transient program "pulled men and women by the hundreds of thousands from the despair of aimless wandering, misery, and the complete neglect of health, back to self-respect and their place in the world of working people." There was much truth in this assessment, but the last phrase was an exaggeration at best. As historian Joan Crouse noted in evaluating the impact of the FTS in New York State, despite its many positive features the program had relatively limited success in helping the homeless to get permanent jobs.[61]

An estimated one million persons passed through the New Deal's transient program during its short existence. How many benefited in the long run from the educational programs and on-the-job training of the transient service is impossible to say. Surely tens of thousands owed their survival to its existence, not only because of the food and shelter the program provided but because of the hope it inspired in destitute citizens. In light of FTS's obvious usefulness and good administrative record, many social workers assumed that the program would continue to be funded. They were wrong. In June 1935, FERA suddenly announced that state transient bureaus should close some centers and reduce their overall budgets substantially. After two months of uncertainty about the fate of the program, Hopkins abruptly ordered that the entire program be phased out beginning on September 20.[62]

The abandonment of FTS was only a small part of the Roosevelt administration's shift from direct relief to large-scale public works projects and Social Security during 1935–36.[63] The very success of the transient program made it easier for New Deal policy makers to eliminate it. By substantially reducing transiency, the FTS lessened public awareness of homelessness and convinced many that the problem had been solved. By the summer of 1935, shantytowns and ragged men (and boys) riding the freights were no longer the symbols of a nation in economic crisis, though ironically, the number of transients enrolled in federal centers or camps was nearly at its high point by September. Beginning on September 20 no new transients were accepted into the program, and supervisors of shelters and camps began the painful process of reducing the number of homeless persons under their care.

Initially, the FTS attempted to return persons under their care to their place of origin. In most cases, however, this action was as futile as it had been in the past. Hopkins and other New Deal administrators had assumed that most transients would find jobs through the new Works Projects Administration, especially since many of the rural FTS camps would be taken over by the WPA. Only a fraction of the men were able to do so, however. As Wickenden noted, because "there were never enough jobs for all the eligible people it was virtually impossible to get even a proportionate share of Work[s] Projects Administration jobs for nonresident people." A year after the phaseout was initiated, a national survey found that 21 percent of the men had obtained jobs on WPA projects; 14 percent had found other employment, and 12 percent were on general relief. The largest number of men, however, 43 percent, had simply left of their own accord, their whereabouts unknown.[64]

Despite difficulties finding work for shelter residents, the dismantling of FTS centers proceeded apace.[65] Between September and December, 1935, the population of most federal facilities fell by 50 to 75 percent. With winter approaching, many of those who had found temporary refuge in transient shelters were again being forced onto the street. Philadelphia exemplified the national situation on a small scale. In October, the city's huge transient center on Hamilton Street was turning away 50 to 100 men a day, and private agencies in the city were "filled to overflowing." The only suggestion the head of the city's transient bureau, Lena Roberts, could make was that the homeless voluntarily commit themselves to the House of Corrections as vagrants. By the beginning of 1936, the center sheltered only 692 "unemployables"—men judged "unfit for work of any kind," while in the streets outside the shelter hundreds of "employable" (but unemployed) men were "sleeping in stables or vacant houses and, when these could not be found, in snow-covered doorways or drafty subway stations." In a sign of things to come, Mayor S. Davis Wilson used his influence to get 200 men admitted, but for two days only. When the federal facility closed in April, the city temporarily assumed responsibility for the remaining 300 shelter tenants, moving them to a much smaller building. The following January, over the protests of shelter superintendent George Wilkins, the city ordered these men sent to the county Home for the Indigent or, if they were not Philadelphians, returned to their original place of residence. The city then opened a small municipal lodging house, with a philosophy much different from that of the federal transient centers. "It will be a clearing house," said Mayor Wilson, "where men in need will get overnight shelter and care, and breakfast in the morning."[66]

In the South and some border states, the end of the FTS was particularly devastating. In Memphis, New Orleans, Jacksonville (Florida), and elsewhere the homeless either had to turn to begging or rely exclusively on private charities. In Charleston, South Carolina, the only public lodgings available were prison cells with space for 16 persons. In Houston, even the local Salvation Army and religious missions were judged "badly substandard." Conditions in the North and West were better, but there, too, the sudden withdrawal of federal involvement left the homeless dependent on financially strapped city agencies, private charities, or the generosity of the public. The closing of the local federal shelter in Muncie, Indiana, led to an "epidemic" of beggars and caused a crisis for the Muncie Mission, which suddenly was inundated with homeless men. Larger communities also struggled with the upsurge of homelessness. In New York, there was a sharp increase in the number of men sleeping in parks and subways, and by 1937 even the city's playgrounds were "overrun by vagrants at night." Investigators who visited five Midwestern cities in 1936 found that accommodations for the homeless were often "temporary or makeshift" and public support inadequate. The best that "able-bodied, unattached men" could now expect was "a meal or two and perhaps one or two night's lodging."[67]

The Federal Transient Service had done much to alleviate the suffering of the homeless for a period of time, but unlike the Wagner Act or Social Security it did not change underlying structural conditions to permanently benefit the group being assisted. Social Security itself did nothing for transient workers, who, like domestic servants, were excluded from its program.[68] While it existed, the Transient Service was a shining example of what a truly national program could do for transient or homeless persons. But it left no legacy, set no precedent for later federal action on behalf of this neglected group of citizens. The end of the federal program turned back the clock to what one FTS administrator called "the old 'overnight flop and morning coffee' system of the archaic past." The New Deal had always been reluctant to challenge the entrenched power of state governments, but the transient program was in a weaker position than most federal programs because it had no real political constituency. After 1935, the homeless would again become a problem exclusively for the states and for local communities, neither of which had the resources or the will to effectively improve transients' lives.[69]

THE RELEASE OF CLOSE TO 400,000 persons from the federal transient centers in late 1935 taxed local welfare institutions to the limit. "In most cases," one reporter said of New York City's homeless, "the best that can be offered these strays is the municipal lodging house at night—and the public streets by day." Some of the homeless responded to this situation by taking to the road. The hobo jungles, little used while the Federal Transient Service was in operation, experienced a dramatic revival. During the winter of 1935–36, Florida and California instituted border patrols in an attempt to bar indigent persons from entering their states. The effect of this action was limited at best and failed to discourage a new wave of transiency during the "Roosevelt recession" of

Chapter 11.

The Forgotten

Men, 1935–1975

1937–38. The blockades, however, did symbolize the return of a hostile, punitive attitude toward homeless wanderers, an attitude best illustrated by the title of a 1938 *Commonweal* article on the treatment of transients: "Move On, You!"[1]

While the FTS was in operation, police had often broken up the urban shantytowns. When, during 1935–36, some of the homeless attempted to rebuild them, local authorities moved quickly to prevent it. In Denver, one welfare official reported that when shantytowns were started they were "immediately broken up by the police, railway agents, or section gangs." In New York under Mayor LaGuardia, the large colony of homeless men living in ramshackle housing in the Hunts Point section of the Bronx was allowed to remain far longer than in most cities, but in January 1937, the 75 shacks were torn down—ironically, by WPA workers. The city made no provision for alternative housing for the 200 men evicted, beyond offering to provide one free night's lodging for those who were penniless.[2]

This reaction on the part of many states and localities led Ellen Potter, Elizabeth Wickenden, and others to agitate during 1936–38 for a restoration of some version of the federal transient program. With the exception of California Congressman Jerry Voorhis and a few other staunch liberals, however, this call inspired little interest in Congress and none at all in the Roosevelt administration, which had turned its attention to other matters. The problem of homelessness had not gone away, in fact it had increased, but with the apparent decline in boy transiency the public had lost interest in the issue. A three-part series of articles in the *Saturday Evening Post* in 1936 brought back many of the old stereotypes about the homeless while criticizing the New Deal for becoming involved with transients in the first place. In "Rest for Weary Willy," John Benton, a former transient center administrator, referred to the Transient Service as an "Alice-in-Wonderland venture" that provided a soft life for men who often did not deserve such good treatment. "At eight o'clock," said Benton of the camp procedures, "in a leisurely and gentlemanly fashion, work begins." On the other hand, "meals were on time, and you ate regardless of your sins." Benton's description of the camp residents was designed to appeal to the snobbery of the middle class: "Mostly they come, I'm afraid, from the lower strata. Your chances of becoming the client of a Transient Bureau will be much enhanced if you are gorgeously tattooed, take food with your knife and use the double negative." Using selective interviews with four transient camp supervisors, Benton managed to convey the strong impression that most of the men were lazy drunkards or young men on a lark who used the camps as stopovers while they traveled about. He closed with a description of one of the interracial transient camps, informing his readers that "the Negroes work only half a day" and spent much of their time playing horseshoes.[3]

In 1939, the publication of Carey McWilliams's exposé of California agriculture, *Factories in the Field*, and John Steinbeck's powerful novel *The Grapes of Wrath* temporarily renewed public concern for the grim situation facing transient laborers. Steinbeck's deep personal knowledge of the migrants who made the trek from "dust bowl" Kansas and Oklahoma to California, often carrying all their possessions strapped to the top of an old jalopy, gave a ring of authenticity to his story of the fictitious Joad family. The enormous popularity of Steinbeck's novel, the 1940 John Ford film adaptation of it, and Woodie Guthrie's *Dust Bowl Ballads*, led to much hand-wringing and many public pronouncements about the need to aid the Okies. The only significant governmental action that followed, however, was the establishment in April 1940 of a congressional Committee to Investigate the Interstate Migration of Destitute Citizens. During 1940–41 the committee, headed by California Congressman John Tolan, traveled to eight states and heard the testimony of 500 witnesses. The several thousand pages of facts and opinions about migrant farm workers and transients in general constitute an important source of information about a group that previously had received little attention, but it led to no changes in public policy of any significance. By the time the committee finished its inquiry, some of the people they studied were already being drawn into war preparedness work. Symbolizing the shift in national priorities, in March 1941 the Tolan committee was renamed the Committee Investigating National Defense Migration. By the spring of 1942, the booming war industries of southern California would be attracting a new wave of migrants under circumstances radically different from those experienced by the destitute newcomers who had arrived only a few years before.[4]

As a historian of the dust bowl migration notes, part of the empathy for the Joads was rooted in race, "because the nation found intolerable for white Americans conditions it considered normal for California Mexicans or Negroes." Equally significant, however, was the fact that the Okies were *native-born*, dispossessed farmers, and, perhaps most important, traveled as families. This combination of characteristics touched deep chords in the self-image of many Americans and may have resonated with particular power during 1938–41, when the reforms of the New Deal were largely over and the beginnings of a conservative political shift were underway. In reality, despite the growth of homeless families, most transients in the 1930s were still unattached men. These individuals were overwhelmingly drawn from urban areas, not farms; and the percentage of those who were black and, on the West Coast, Mexican was substantial. Steinbeck's novel revealed a great deal about class relations and oppressive labor conditions in California's burgeoning agribusiness, but it provided much less insight into the causes of most Depression-era transiency.[5]

Even more forgotten than the men and families on the road were the large number of homeless who seldom, if ever, left the communities they lived in. The population of America's skid rows fluctuated considerably during the Depression, increasing during the early 1930s, falling off during 1933–35 because of the federal program for transients, then rising after 1935 only to decline again as the economy began to pick up at the end of the decade. These variations, however, masked long-term trends that began before the 1930s and would continue after World War II. The most important of these was the rapid decline, beginning in the 1920s, of the hobo population that had traditionally returned to the main stem during the colder months of the year. Mechanization in wheat farming and logging operations decreased the need for these seasonal workers. By the late 1920s, many of the young men who in the past might have filled the cheap lodging houses during the winter months were now no longer living on skid row. To some extent during the Depression, unemployed people who had not previously been homeless replaced them, increasing the size of the skid row population for a while. World War II, however, drew many of these men into either the army or the booming war economy. In one two-month period in 1943, 100 Bowery residents joined the armed forces, while another 200 acquired jobs in hospitals, restaurants, or on the railroads. By 1944 manufacturing concerns in the Midwest were recruiting workers from skid-row flophouses. Postwar economic expansion, coupled with veterans' benefits like the G.I. Bill, continued to help many who had been temporarily homeless during the Depression, providing an impetus for them to successfully reenter the economy and leave skid row behind.[6]

Throughout all of these changes, a core group remained on skid row, an element of the homeless population that would become more significant in the postwar era. This group tended to be composed of older men, past the prime employment years, too frail to engage in the kind of unskilled labor they had undertaken when younger but usually able to do less physically demanding work. Writing in 1939, sociologist Theodore Caplow stated that such older men "tended to remain in one city, or within a fairly circumscribed neighborhood, either as retired tramps or as displaced individuals who have been driven by necessity to the mission and the flophouse." It is probable that many had no family to help them, or that their families had disowned them. Others suffered from debilitating injuries that limited or destroyed their ability to work. After World War I, ex-soldiers who were unable to readjust psychologically were another element on the main stem, and the mentally ill, though a relatively small element, also lodged there. Some former seasonal laborers, no longer needed to harvest crops in the Midwest, also gravitated to skid row and became casual laborers. By the 1930s, all of these types were fixtures on skid row, but to categorize them in this way presents something of a false impression, since in many cases the same person had several of these characteristics.[7]

While some of this "homeguard" group was able to benefit from war-industry work, many were not able to take advantage of postwar employment opportunities. They remained, while skid row and the surrounding society changed. In 1934 the resident homeless in major urban areas were already, on average, 15 years older than the typical transient. The aging of the skid-row population became more pronounced after World War II. By the end of the 1950s, most residents of skid row were middle-aged or elderly. About half of the skid-row populations of Philadelphia and Chicago were between the ages of 45 and 64, with another 17 percent 65 or older. In Minneapolis, half the men on skid row in 1958 were more than 60 years old, and 22 percent were over 70. Other cities displayed similar demographic patterns.[8]

The environment of skid row continued to deteriorate in the postwar period. The near elimination of dormitory-style lodging houses (except in the missions) did little to improve the quality of housing for the down-and-out. The cage hotel became the most common type of private housing used by the homeless. By 1960, 42 percent of skid rowers in Philadelphia and Minneapolis, and two-thirds of those in Chicago, lived in "single room occupancy" (SRO) hotels. Rental prices rose steadily throughout the postwar era but varied widely from city to city. In 1946 it was possible to rent cubicle rooms in Philadelphia for less than $2 a week. By 1960, rents there had more than doubled, and rooms averaged $3.35 a week in Minneapolis and $5 a week in Chicago. Housing costs were steeper in New York, where in 1964 SRO accommodations cost $9 to $15 per week or more. Increasingly, the cage hotels functioned not as temporary quarters for seasonal laborers but as semipermanent domiciles for relatively long-term tenants. Many older men now rented their rooms by the month, cramming their few possessions into a space no larger than a good-sized closet in an ordinary home. Few improvements had been made in the cage hotels since they had been converted to mass occupancy at the turn of the century, and by the 1950s many were in decrepit condition. In 1956, city inspectors in Philadelphia temporarily shut down over a third of the skid-row lodging houses because they were fire hazards, and in Chicago and elsewhere building code violations were common in this type of housing.[9]

Skid rows declined steadily in size during the postwar period. The population of Chicago's West Madison Street area, which during the 1930s probably housed at least 30,000 persons, declined to 21,000 by 1950 and to 13,000 by 1958. The Bowery, no longer the nation's largest skid row, shrank from an estimated 14,000 inhabitants in 1949 to less than 8,000 in 1964. Everywhere, skid row remained a male bastion. "There are almost no women on the Bowery," noted one investigator in 1964. "There are not even prostitutes or 'B' girls." He found no women in the lodging houses or missions, and 16 of 19 bars surveyed had no female customers. In Philadelphia, researchers estimated no more than half a dozen women lived in the Vine-Race Street skid row. Homeless women did exist, living in rooming houses located in rundown neighborhoods near skid row or in "Tenderloin" districts where gambling and prostitution flourished. They were far fewer in number than were homeless men, however. In New York, for example, the maximum number of homeless women housed by the Department of Welfare in 1963 was 47.[10]

The smaller size of skid rows had little effect on the number of bars, liquor stores, and cheap restaurants there, but other businesses catering to the needs of skid-row residents became scarcer. By 1950 there were fewer pawnshops, pool halls, and barbershops. As the number of secondhand stores declined, open-air "thieves markets," where men dealt in stolen goods, became more common. The hobo colleges disappeared, and (except for the bars) little of the once vibrant, if risqué, nightlife of the old "main stem" survived. By the early 1960s not a single movie house or burlesque theater remained on the Bowery. Chicago, with the nation's largest homeless population, offered more entertainment outlets for skid-row residents, but even there the most common recreational activities consisted of going to a bar or watching television, either in lodging-house lobbies or bars. Lacking much of the former context of surrounding stores and services, the SRO hotels increasingly became island outposts, providing inexpensive housing and, in the hotels' sparsely furnished lobbies, some opportunity for camaraderie among the lodgers. To those who understood its ways, skid row was not a particularly dangerous place, but it was increasingly isolated, largely cut off from the larger urban context.[11]

Although many of the men on skid row were now older, the contemporary image of skid rowers as unemployable derelicts presented a very false impression of the work patterns of the men who lived there. Investigators studying skid rows between 1957 and 1960 found that between 70 and 86 percent of the men living there had worked to some extent during the preceding year. About one quarter of skid-row residents held steady jobs, defined as working at least 48 weeks a year. In Philadelphia, over four in ten regularly employed men on skid row actually worked *more* than 40 hours per week. For most homeless men, however, employment was intermittent, with workers hired often for a few weeks, or even a few days, at a time. Service work, especially in restaurants, now made up as much as a third of skid-row employment, and an additional 30 to 50 percent of the homeless worked as unskilled laborers. Only 7 percent of skid-row residents did skilled work, and only 8–14 percent were factory operatives or other semi-skilled workers.[12]

An earlier generation of homeless men often relied on begging or petty thievery to supplement the meager wages earned from casual labor, but this was probably less true of the post–World War II period. A study of the homeless in Philadelphia carried out by a team of Temple University researchers in 1960 found that only 9 percent of the men on skid row earned any income from begging, stealing, or gambling. Even assuming that some men would not admit to such activities, there is little doubt that various forms of public aid were now much more important than begging as sources of income for the homeless. In both Philadelphia and Chicago, half of the men on skid row received some form of government aid or, much less frequently, income from a private pension. The most common form of aid was public assistance, followed by Social Security, veteran's pension, and unemployment insurance. The income derived from these benefits seldom was enough to live on, even on skid row. Veteran's pensions provided the most income; almost 60 percent of the veterans on skid row received over $750 per year and another 15 percent over $1,000 annually. Only 9 percent of Philadelphia's homeless, however, were eligible for such benefits. Only about one in ten homeless men was able to live entirely on income from government aid. For the homeless, Social Security largely failed to provide what its name promised. At a time when retired workers received an average yearly benefit of almost $1,000, two-thirds of Philadelphia's homeless men received less than $750 and 41 percent less than $500, undoubtedly because the uneven employment history of most homeless men reduced the level of their benefits. The increase in government transfer payments generally, a key factor in raising part of the working class out of poverty in the 1950s, benefited the men on skid row at a level best described as just above the survival line. The typical skid-row pensioner's budget of $75 per month was only $5 shy of his average monthly income, leading one investigator to conclude that only the slimmest of margins "separates the skid-row resident from destitution."[13]

Although they lived in extreme poverty, in other ways the homeless continued to have much in common with the working class as a whole. Many homeless men had higher levels of skill and education than one would expect, given their employment history. Almost half of those interviewed in the Temple University study stated that the longest steady job they had ever held involved skilled, semiskilled, or white-collar work. Only 18 percent were doing such work at the time. Studies in other cities found only modest differences in formal education between the homeless and the rest of the U.S. population. Almost all the homeless were literate, and their high school attendance rate was only slightly lower than the national average; 6 percent had even attended college. For the most part, the slide into homelessness was not due to inadequate training or ability but to debilitating life experiences. Many of the down-and-out had once held decent jobs, but for a variety of reasons—prolonged unemployment, exhaustion of savings, ill health or physical handicap, marital discord, or simply the need for inexpensive lodgings—they wound up on skid row.[14]

The aspirations of the men on skid row were not so different from those of other elements of the working class. Almost half of the men living on Chicago's West Madison Street told interviewers that they desired retraining in skilled occupations, and 16 percent hoped to become clerical workers, technicians, or professionals. In light of the receptivity of skid-row residents to learning new skills, sociologist Donald Bogue argued that a retraining program should be made a part of any plan for the rehabilitation of these men. Bogue was well aware, however, that city governments were unlikely to inaugurate such a New Deal–style retraining program. The most that city councils in Detroit, Chicago, and a few other cities were willing to do was establish employment offices and alcohol treatment centers in skid-row areas. Bogue estimated that in Chicago a minuscule 3 percent of all expenditures earmarked for skid row were designed to improve conditions or rehabilitate the men. Politicians and reformers, focusing on the negative features of the old lodging-house districts and the men who lived there, instead turned their attention to the task of containing—and finally demolishing— skid row itself.[15]

SKID ROW BECAME the focus of attention partly because the homeless population living there was now much less mobile. Fewer and fewer men rode the rails, and even within cities many of the homeless never left a fairly circumscribed geographic area. The era of widespread transiency seemed a part of the distant past, and Woodie Guthrie's folk songs about life on the road, radical in their intended identification with the poor, now sounded more like a swan song for the footloose vagabond. Transient and migrant laborers still existed, of course, but they no longer elicited the nostalgic concern the public had shown for an earlier generation of tramps. When Mexican agricultural workers were brought in to work the beet fields of Michigan, Ohio, and Minnesota, they were transported in uncovered trucks all the way from Texas. The grueling trips lasted four or five days, with unlicensed drivers evading police inspection by using back roads. When native-born, white transient workers traveled long distances, they now were much more likely to hitch rides or take a bus than travel by boxcar. In neither case did men on the road any longer seem a fit subject for romanticization.[16]

By default, the smaller, more isolated skid rows became *the* symbol of homelessness to Americans after World War II. Although usually expressed in milder terms, the image of the skid-row resident that emerged in the late 1940s and '50s performed a similar function to that of the "criminal, lazy tramp" popular in the 1870s and '80s. In both cases popular perceptions exaggerated some traits and invented others to create a kind of negative reference group for the dominant values of the era. The homeless man of the post–World War II era seemed the exact opposite of William H. Whyte's energetic, upwardly mobile "organization man," who worked in the city but lived in one of the new suburbs springing up everywhere on the outer edges of the metropolitan landscape.[17] The language of pathology and disease reemerged in both popular stories and scholarly works dealing with the homeless. The public came to associate skid row with alcoholism and to see the skid-row derelict—uneducated, unemployable, and lazy—as representative of the homeless population.

In 1946, a *Time* magazine reporter interviewed "Juke," a garrulous Chicago panhandler described as smelling of "vomit and cheap booze." Between shots of liquor at a local tavern, Juke complained of how difficult begging had become with the return of prosperity. People hesitated to give money to panhandlers, he claimed, because "there are too many jobs offered along Madison Avenue [in Chicago]." Juke informed the reporter that the railroads were offering good money for part-time work, but on skid row they "don't get any more men today than they did before the war," when wages were 50 percent lower. The figure of Juke, presented as a typical skid rower, was both repulsive and mildly humorous, and the *Time* article conveyed the impression that the homeless as a group were dirty, alcoholic, and uninterested in steady work. In 1949, the *Chicago Daily News* published a twelve-part exposé on the city's skid row and its "living dead," focusing on the most squalid saloons and cage hotels, with grim photos of derelicts sleeping in garbage-strewn alleys. The paper's readership increased by as much as 20,000 a day as a result of the series. During the next two decades, such stereotyped conceptions of skid row would become common.[18]

Increasingly, the media's focus shifted to the alleged psychological problems of the homeless, presenting them as maladjusted deviants. In 1952 a *Saturday Evening Post* article about Detroit's skid row identified *all* skid-row residents as alcoholic bums, uninterested in the steady jobs that were "going begging" in the city. "Money on skid row is for liquor; other things can be had without paying or be gone without," the author stated decisively. The homeless man, said another writer in 1956, "is what the psychiatrists label an 'infantile personality.'" Like children, the homeless "seek escape from almost everything through the alcoholic doorway to forgetfulness or fantasy." In his popular writings on the Bowery, journalist Elmer Bendiner recycled old stereotypes in modern psychological dress: "The Bowery Man cannot fail because he is not expected to succeed. He cannot be disappointed because he has no hope. He enjoys the childhood fantasy of attending his own funeral, savoring the grief of those who mourn him." The jobs available to men on skid row, Bendiner claimed in *The Bowery Man*, "offer a guarantee against responsibility, advancement, or success." As a result, the homeless have "no anxiety for the job."[19]

Academic studies of the homeless from the 1950s to the mid-1970s usually reinforced popular stereotypes, even when they presented data that could be read quite differently. Donald Bogue's authoritative study of skid rows emphasized the diversity of the homeless population, but Bogue spent so much time on their drinking habits that a reader might well conclude that alcoholism was the most important feature of skid-row life. While acknowledging that "almost all men on Skid Row under 65 years of age, even the heavy drinkers, are potential workers," Bogue devoted only one short chapter (out of 19) to the work experiences of the homeless. The titles of two prominent sociological studies of the homeless, Howard Bahr's *Disaffiliated Man* and Bahr's and Theodore Caplow's *Old Men Drunk and Sober*, said much about the dominant scholarship dealing with skid row. Scholars writing on the homeless usually presented factual information in an objective manner, but they often drew harsh conclusions from the data. Samuel Wallace, generally a sympathetic observer of the homeless, summed up his own study of skid row by focusing on the deviancy of those who lived there: "The skid rower does not bathe, eat regularly, dress respectfully, marry or raise children, attend school, vote, own property, or regularly live in the same place. He does little work of any kind. He does not even steal. The skid rower does nothing, he just is. He is everything that all the rest of us try not to be." To the "disaffiliation" theorists, notes anthropologist Kim Hopper, skid row was "an anti-community of exiles—the listless, aimless haunt of old men void of ambition or bonds, for whom the empty ritual of a shared bottle provided the only semblance of sociability."[20]

Contemporary studies that contradicted or qualified the standard interpretation of homelessness remained unpublished and were generally inaccessible.[21] In his 1964 survey of Bowery conditions, Columbia University researcher George Nash explained that, contrary to commonly held stereotypes, the appearance of many homeless men differed little from that of other poor workmen. The number of derelicts seemed greater than was actually the case, Nash argued, because they were the most visible people on skid row, often sprawled conspicuously in doorways or on sidewalks for hours at a time. Alcoholism was certainly more common on skid row than elsewhere, but even mainstream researchers acknowledged that the typical resident of these areas was not an alcoholic or "dependent" personality type. Most of the men on skid row either worked or had been workers in the past, and within a narrow framework they were just as much interested in living independent lives as were the millions who hoped to establish themselves in a small bungalow in Levittown or some other suburb. The isolation of SRO tenants in one of the lowest rent districts in the city was mostly the result of economic necessity. At a rudimentary level, the skid-row lodging house met the needs of its residents. In their 1986 study of SRO hotels in Chicago that had escaped the bulldozer, Charles Hoch and Robert Slayton found that residents appreciated the convenience, security, and affordability of this type of housing, even though many complained of the small size of the rooms and inadequate maintenance of the buildings. Such attitudes probably were true of skid rowers in the immediate postwar decades as well, although conditions in the cage hotels of the 1950s were in many ways inferior to the SRO hotels surveyed by Hoch and Slayton in the 1980s.[22]

The extent to which skid rows of the postwar era remained viable communities is difficult to assess, but clearly the perception of skid-row residents as totally bereft of family, friends, or connections to fellow workers misconstrued the nature of their lives. The image did contain a core element of truth in one respect: lack of family support continued to be an important cause of homelessness during the postwar era. In Philadelphia, half the men on skid row had no contact with close relatives at all and another quarter saw family members only once a year. To a significant degree, however, networks of friends substituted for low levels of family aid. The declining institutional infrastructure of skid row was to some extent counterbalanced by the growing demographic stability of its population. In contrast to the hobos and casual laborers of previous generations, pensioners were likely to remain at one address for extended periods of time, which undoubtedly made long-term friendships more likely. A third of the men interviewed in Philadelphia said that they had three or more close friends who would lend them money if they needed it, and another 25 percent had one or two friends whom they could count on. In his 1960 study of Minneapolis's Gateway district, Keith Lovald discovered that close friendships were common among men living in hotels and lodging houses. This was often the result of the men's former work experience. Many older men on skid row, Bogue stated, had shared experience with "production lines, itinerant work in agriculture, shops, trucks, strikes, bosses, unions, etc." He also suggested that skid-row pensioners, though living on the edge of destitution, might be more satisfied with their lifestyle than "many older men who live elsewhere in comfort but in semi-isolation and without companionship."[23]

Interpersonal relations on skid row were not all positive, of course. Bogue found that many men on West Madison Street disliked the excessive drinking of some residents and feared being robbed by "jackrollers," especially those who preyed on the elderly. On the whole, however, residents' feelings about skid row were far from completely negative. The most common favorable quality mentioned was the "congeniality" of those who lived in the area. Despite living in close quarters, most skid rowers were surprisingly tolerant of others. Michael Harrington witnessed little violence among the homeless he worked with on the Bowery in 1951–52, and a decade later urbanologist Jane Jacobs, in *The Death and Life of Great American Cities*, emphasized that the parks where the homeless congregated in some cities were not centers of criminal activity. The men who gathered there, she stated, "behave respectfully to one another and are courteous to interlopers too."[24]

This spirit of toleration did not always apply, unfortunately, across the color line. While remaining residentially segregated, African Americans and, to a lesser extent, Mexicans, Puerto Ricans, and Native Americans became a presence on skid row after World War II, especially in the cities of the Northeast and Pacific Coast that experienced heavy black in-migration from the South. Between 1950 and 1957, blacks increased from 1.4 to 9 percent of Chicago's skid-row population; in 1960 they made up 15 percent of the inhabitants of Philadelphia's skid row. As the population of the old lodging house districts declined, the expansion of black ghettos led to black encroachment on sections of what had once been all-white communities. In the early 1960s, two-thirds of black skid-row inhabitants in Chicago still lived in the predominantly black South State Street section, where three large lodging houses now catered to blacks, but a third had moved to West Madison Street, formerly an all-white area. African Americans in previously all-white skid-row districts generally lived in separate lodging houses and were excluded from most bars. In other ways, however, the movement of blacks and other minorities into or near skid-row areas seemed to promote a degree of acceptance across the racial divide. Bogue reported that in Chicago, in "restaurants, movies, and in public facilities such as the Reading Room, the missions, and the public welfare agencies, there is much more interracial contact now than in the past." Whites and racial minorities were now also more likely to get to know each other through working together on the same types of jobs.[25]

By focusing almost exclusively on the historic lodging-house sections of cities, scholars understated the size of the black homeless population in the 1950s and '60s. A substantial number of blacks with a lifestyle similar to that of skid rowers lived in other poor sections of the black community, much as they had done since the turn of the century. George Nash's 1964 survey of the homeless in New York City found, in addition to the Bowery, three less concentrated centers of homelessness in Manhattan. One of these was central Harlem. An estimated 4,500 homeless blacks lived there in rooming houses or basement rooms in apartment complexes, where men often worked as superintendent's helpers in exchange for free lodging. Nash's data indicates that 31 percent of the homeless in Manhattan (compared with only 16 percent on the Bowery alone) were African American. Philadelphia and other cities also had sections where black "skid-row like people" lived. Even with a broader definition of what constituted a homeless area, the homeless population at the time was still predominantly white. Blacks, however, represented a larger segment of the down-and-out population than was understood at the time. To an even greater degree than the whites on skid row, they were the hidden homeless of the postwar era.[26]

SKID ROW PERFORMED a necessary function for those who lived there, but to policy makers it was mainly a "problem" that fostered a negative image of cities. Responding to the exodus of population and jobs to the rapidly expanding suburbs, many major urban centers inaugurated "revitalization" programs designed to make central cities more attractive.[27] As one of the most glaring examples of the "blight" on the urban landscape, skid row and the men who lived there came under more scrutiny by the police after World War II than at any time since the turn of the century. When homeless men wandered from skid row into the central business district or middle-class residential areas, the police responded in force. Beginning in 1949, they stepped up patrols in the vicinity of Philadelphia's Independence Hall area, in an attempt to rid the historic district of homeless men who had drifted over from the skid-row area, located only a few blocks to the north. During the next decade the authorities carried out periodic raids in several other midcity parks when homeless men began to congregate there. At first this included Franklin Park, on the eastern edge of the skid-row area, but so many homeless men continued to use the park that eventually the authorities ceased trying to oust them. In other cities, also, certain squares became known as "skid-row parks." The police were more forceful in removing the homeless from the vicinity of prominent institutions. In 1964, in one Manhattan police precinct, arrests for disorderly conduct skyrocketed after officials from nearby New York University convinced the police to crack down on the number of homeless men wandering around the campus. Such actions helped to maintain class boundaries in the city and improve the image of downtown neighborhoods. Keeping the homeless out of sight as much as possible, officials hoped, would make central city areas more appealing to businessmen, shoppers, and tourists.[28]

Large-scale "roundups" of homeless men attracted media attention, but the impact of day-to-day policing within skid row was much more significant. Because of the growing challenge to the constitutionality of vagrancy statutes, almost all of the homeless picked up by patrolmen were charged with public drunkenness or disorderly conduct. Their real "crime" in most cases, however, was behavior that created a public nuisance: sitting in doorways or on the sidewalk, urinating in public, or ignoring traffic signals when crossing the street. In the postwar era, the pattern of arrest and conviction of homeless men on skid row evolved into a kind of ritual, one that occupied the police a great deal. In Minneapolis, for example, an astonishing 44 percent of all persons arrested in 1957 resided in the Gateway area of cheap lodging houses. "Maximum police power is exercised 24 hours a day, seven days a week," Lovald reported. In Chicago, police surveillance of the skid-row district on the near North Side cost at least $58,000 a month. Cities probably recouped a good deal of this expense through the system of fines ($15 in Minneapolis) assessed the men in lieu of 10 or 15 days of incarceration. Most alcoholic skid rowers repeatedly experienced the "revolving door" of arrest, conviction, payment of fine, overnight stay in the lock-up, and return to skid row. Many men had been convicted dozens of times. Police operations in skid row became so regularized that patrolmen routinely arrested more men toward the beginning of the month, when assistance checks arrived and most men would be able to pay their fine.[29]

In addition to routine arrests, from time to time cities embarked on more wide-ranging "cleanup" campaigns in skid-row districts. Noting that "private capital is beginning to plan large housing improvements on the Lower East Side," the New York Chamber of Commerce in 1946 established the Bowery Improvement Committee to lobby for more police action against "chronic drunkards" on the street. Anticipating future profits from a gentrified Bowery, the Committee's chairman, Wilfred Kirk, stated forthrightly that "we want to continue our efforts in attracting more capital so that slum conditions will be replaced with a wholesome environment—good for the family, for business and for city revenues." Later renamed the Committee to Abolish Bowery Conditions, this group pressured the municipal government throughout the 1950s and early '60s to take stronger action against vagrants and peddlers. The most concerted effort to rid the Bowery of loiterers and drunks took place in 1964, when New York City hosted the World's Fair. Discarding the traditional policy of short jail terms for disorderly conduct, judges meted out sentences ranging from one to six months. At one point, close to 20 percent of the Bowery's population was in jail. A punitive approach to the homeless, however, could never be anything more than a temporary expedient. "In cold truth," explained one observer in 1962, "neither the city nor the state has the physical equipment necessary to 'clean up the Bowery.'" Any attempt to do so, he added, "would not only wreck the already creaking penal and hospital system of the City of New York but also the entire budget of the Public Welfare Department."[30]

The arrests of men on skid row deterred the homeless from moving beyond well-defined boundaries. Like the failed campaigns against begging earlier in the century, however, homelessness was too complex a phenomenon to be banished by police roundups. Facing a seemingly intractable problem, reformers began to contemplate a more drastic solution—the abolition of skid row altogether. By the late 1950s, the groundwork for the physical destruction of skid row had already been laid. Authorities allowed skid rows to deteriorate by refusing to fix sidewalks or repair streets. The enforcement of building codes led to basic improvements in some lodging houses but promoted the abandonment of others. Many owners preferred to simply vacate old buildings rather than incur the expense of costly repairs. As a dilapidated area with a shrinking population and no significant economic function, skid row became ripe for urban renewal in many cities.[31]

The move to demolish skid rows was only one part of an extensive effort in the 1960s and '70s to renovate aging metropolises by replacing "blighted" areas of old housing and declining commercial value with new residential units or office towers. Much urban redevelopment was blatantly class-biased, with the goal of replacing older working-class neighborhoods with housing and businesses designed for the middle class and elite. In some cities, residents successfully prevented, or at least delayed, implementation of plans for the wholesale destruction of their neighborhoods. Such resistance was not possible for the inhabitants of skid row, however, who lacked political influence or the ability to organize on their own behalf.[32]

The poet W. H. Auden, who lived near New York's Bowery district, told a reporter in 1961 that he could not understand the need to bulldoze old neighborhoods that were still viable. "Leave the Bowery as it is!" said Auden. Few others, however, objected when the wrecking ball began to come down on the dilapidated structures of skid row. Beginning in 1958, when Minneapolis started leveling the Gateway district, one city after another demolished all or part of its primary lodging house area. In Philadelphia, the razing of the skid-row district to the north of Independence Mall began in 1965 and continued intermittently for the next decade. In 1976, the destruction of the remaining cage hotel, the Darien, forced out the last 300 residents of the district. In the 1960s, urban renewal projects also eliminated skid rows in Boston and Detroit, and much of the West Madison Street area in Chicago fell victim to the wrecking ball. During the following decade the trend intensified, and the number of SRO hotels in Cincinnati, Seattle, San Diego, and other cities declined precipitously. The process of change in the Bowery was more gradual. During the late 1960s and '70s, much of the legendary street was transformed through demolition or conversion of old buildings to modern uses, as builders attempted to cash in on the extraordinary rise in real estate values in Manhattan. By the 1990s, only a remnant of the homeless population continued to reside there.[33]

The redevelopment agencies that carried out the destruction of skid rows paid relatively little attention to the problem of finding new housing for the men forced to vacate the SRO hotels. In Minneapolis, each skid-row resident evicted received $5 along with free advice about housing from relocation staff. In Philadelphia, a Diagnostic and Relocation Center that had been set up in 1963 helped some skid-row residents find alternative housing in cheap hotels in working-class neighborhoods. Perhaps because they mistrusted the bureaucracy responsible for the demolition of their living quarters, however, many of the men simply left on their own, presumably seeking shelter elsewhere in the city. In Chicago, the report setting out the proposed urban renewal project promised that "relocation of the residents of the area will involve a carefully thought out program of residence change and social coordination." In the end, however, nothing was done to ease the transition of the evicted men, many of whom had lived for years in the same skid-row lodging house and knew nothing of other neighborhoods in the city. A rare exception to this pattern of neglect was San Francisco, where activists managed to force the local redevelopment agency to provide some replacement housing for skid-row residents evicted from their domiciles. In most cities, skid-row residents had to fend for themselves, not only in finding new housing but in adjusting to a new environment—a prospect that must have been particularly frightening to the elderly and the disabled.[34]

Although some SRO hotels managed to survive the juggernaut of urban renewal, by 1980 skid row was no longer a significant part of the urban landscape in the United States. As mayors and city councils soon learned to their dismay, however, the demolition of the lodging house districts did not end the problem of homelessness. In the last two decades of the twentieth century, the nation's cities would again have to contend with large numbers of ragged, displaced persons roaming the streets. The homeless, considered little more than a troublesome nuisance between 1945 and 1975, would once again emerge as a major social problem.

PUBLIC AWARENESS OF THE "NEW HOMELESS"
can be traced to the late 1970s, when beggars and
"street people" became increasingly noticeable in
the downtowns of many cities. During the recession
of the early 1980s, the homeless population continued to increase,
shocking many who had assumed that such visible signs of destitution had been eradicated from American society. Like the "tramp
problem" of the late nineteenth cen-
tury, the new homelessness was not
a temporary phenomenon. The economic recovery of 1983–84 failed to
halt the growth of the homeless

Chapter 12.
A New Homeless?

population. A widely cited 1984 Department of Housing and Urban
Development report estimated that there were 250,000 persons living
on the street or in shelters on any given night. By 1990, that figure
had doubled. A 1996 Urban Institute survey estimated that on an
average night 470,000 persons in the United States were sleeping in
shelters but that a much larger number, close to 2 million, had experienced homelessness at some point during the previous year. Regardless of how one measured the phenomenon, by the end of the twentieth century a much enlarged homeless population was apparently on
the way to becoming a permanent feature of postindustrial America.[1]

Most recent studies of homelessness stress the sharp differences
between the new homeless and the down-and-out of the skid-row
era. Both groups shared the experience of living on the edge of

survival, but the homeless of the post-1975 period are much more likely to sleep in public shelters or in abandoned buildings, parks, or alleyways. The destruction of the skid row lodging houses, along with a more general decline in affordable housing for the poor in the 1970s, forced many low-income persons into the emergency shelters that cities and private charities hurriedly set up at the end of the decade.[2] Although difficult to imagine, the financial resources of the new homeless were even more limited than those of many skid-row residents. In 1986, the average income of homeless persons in Chicago was only $168 per month—a figure only slightly higher than that earned by homeless men in the late 1950s. By 1996, average monthly income for a homeless person had risen to $267. Taking inflation into account, the real income of the homeless at the end of the century was still substantially less than that of their skid-row predecessors.[3]

Both market forces and governmental policies contributed to the creation of an enlarged, desperately poor homeless class. Deindustrialization and the shift to a high-tech and service economy eliminated many unskilled or semi-skilled jobs, with disastrous effects on factory workers and young people entering the labor force without adequate education. Appropriately, Dale Maharidge and Michael Williamson opened their 1985 photo-essay on homelessness, *Journey to Nowhere*, with evocative views of the rubble-strewn, abandoned steel mills of Youngstown, Ohio. Such environments were a breeding ground for homelessness, not only for laid-off older workers but for young people who had expected to follow in their fathers' footsteps. The new homeless were far less likely than their predecessors to engage in wage labor of any kind, and when they did get such work the minimum wage they earned was worth much less, in real dollars, than in 1970. These changed economic circumstances have forced the homeless to rely to a greater extent than previously on such public assistance as is available, supplemented by a meager income from "shadow work" like collecting junk, bottles, and even selling blood plasma. Perhaps a third of the new homeless found it necessary to beg for food or other necessities. Panhandling, which during the 1950s and '60s was largely limited to skid row and nearby neighborhoods, again became commonplace in center city areas in the 1980s.[4]

With the significant exception of Social Security pensions, the declining value of government assistance to the poor in the late twentieth century also increased the likelihood of individuals falling into homelessness. Beginning in the 1970s, the real value of Aid for Dependent Children, unemployment compensation, food stamps, and other public aid began to decline, and eligibility rules for benefits became more restrictive as a consequence of the conservative backlash against welfare.[5]

These developments hurt the poor in general, but they were particularly hard on women and children. Homeless women, a relatively rare phenomenon during the skid-row era, increased rapidly in number during the 1980s and '90s. In 1987, females made up 20 percent of the adult homeless population; by 1996, the figure had risen to 32 percent. Most striking was the growth rate of homeless families, almost always headed by women. Between 1982 and 1992 the number of homeless families in New York City alone increased 500 percent. Homeless families tended to be more common in the Northeast than the West or, especially, the South, but everywhere their numbers increased dramatically. A survey of 26 cities in 1993 found that 43 percent of persons seeking shelter and food at homeless facilities were women with children. For single mothers, the causes of homelessness were not limited to their inability to pay the rent and feed their children. Economics was often intertwined with deep family conflicts. Some homeless mothers were escaping from abusive husbands; others were forced onto the street as a result of conflicts with relatives with whom they had been sharing living quarters. The complexities of single parents' lives made their experience with homelessness particularly harrowing, as well as challenging to social service workers trying to help them.[6]

ALTHOUGH HOMELESSNESS affected all age and racial groups to some extent, the new homeless of the post-1975 period tended to be much younger than their skid-row predecessors, and they were far more likely to be Hispanic or, especially, African American than in the recent past. A 1996 national survey by the Urban Institute found that almost three-quarters of homeless adults were under 45 years of age and almost half under 35; only 2 percent were 65 or older. The almost complete disappearance of the elderly as an element of the homeless population can largely be ascribed to the 1972 Social Security reforms, which raised old-age pensions by 20 percent and tied benefits to changes in the cost of living. No single piece of legislation in American history, perhaps, did more to reduce poverty and prevent homelessness. When inflation rose sharply in the late 1970s, social security recipients were not affected. To a significant degree, the vulnerability of younger persons to homelessness was due to their lacking a similar social safety net.[7]

The typical skid-row resident in the 1950s or '60s had been a white male in his 50s. By the mid-1990s, blacks (41 percent) and Hispanics (11 percent) made up half of the homeless population in the United States, with much higher percentages in most large cities, and the homeless of all races were usually in their twenties or thirties. Often overlooked was the extraordinarily high level of homelessness among Native Americans (8 percent of all homeless in 1996), one sign of the extreme economic degradation of the small, urbanized Native American population. Minority males outnumbered minority females among the homeless, but the number of black women living on the street was still much higher than in the past.[8]

Why were racial minorities overrepresented among the homeless? Structural changes in the economy and the tightening of the housing market for the working poor had a more severe impact on African Americans than whites. The recession of the early 1980s hit blacks especially hard because they were more likely than whites to be employed in stagnating or declining industries. In Chicago, 71 percent of new applicants for general assistance between 1981 and 1984 were black. The lack of education among inner-city youth, at a time of transition to an economy demanding higher skill levels, added to the problem. African Americans also faced continuing racial discrimination in some occupations, especially the skilled trades. At the same time, the growing number of one-parent households in the black community undercut family income. Finally, since the 1960s the commitment of the federal government and unions to raising urban minorities out of poverty has too often been weak or inconsistent. President Lyndon Johnson's "War on Poverty" programs had some beneficial effects, but they were underfunded almost from the beginning as a result of the Vietnam War. The election of Richard Nixon in 1968 led to their further curtailment, a process that would continue under Jimmy Carter and Ronald Reagan. Equally important, as economist Helene Slessarev has pointed out, even in the 1960s there was a fundamental contradiction in the liberal approach to inner-city poverty, since the development of antipoverty programs "coincided with massive urban renewal projects that in many cases destroyed existing communities and created artificial new ones with little economic infrastructure." All of these changes made African Americans, especially those in their 20s and 30s, particularly vulnerable to homelessness.[9]

Regrettably, the public has generally failed to understand the complex causes and nature of the new homelessness. For example, although women and children now make up a larger proportion of the homeless than at any time since the Civil War era, the average citizen remains largely unaware of their existence, since almost all homeless families live in shelters. The media's focus on center-city street people also ignores the fact that, in 1996, 21 percent of the homeless were located in suburbs and another 9 percent in rural areas. Because many homeless do not act or look "normal," people readily jump to the conclusion that the homeless population is composed primarily of potential criminals, psychotics, or drug addicts. At best, these generalizations are gross exaggerations. Today, as in the past, the most common illegal activity engaged in by homeless persons is petty theft; despite a few sensational cases, the homeless rarely commit violent crimes. Estimates of mental illness among the homeless vary from 25 to 40 percent. Between a third and a half are substance abusers, with alcoholism more widespread than drug abuse. Though substance abuse is more common among the homeless than among the general population, and rates of mental illness far above average, neither of these pathologies is typical of the homeless population as a whole. Furthermore, it is important to recognize that substance abuse and psychiatric problems are more often an effect than a cause of homelessness. Given the sometimes hellish nature of life on the street, it should come as no surprise that many homeless persons become mentally disoriented or turn to alcohol or drugs. Substance abuse and mental disability are serious problems among the homeless, but they seldom operate alone. They are most often combined with other factors, such as unemployment, physical disability, or family conflict.[10]

THE TRANSITION from the "old" to the new homeless was not as abrupt as it appeared in the late 1970s. Aspects of the new homelessness were already evident as early as the mid-1950s. It was then that the first stage of deindustrialization began, accompanied by the movement of whites to the suburbs and the massive influx of poor black migrants into the cities. One result was a rise in black unemployment that quickly reached a level double that of white workers, where it has remained ever since. This trend coincided with the displacement of poor African Americans from some neighborhoods due to highway construction and urban renewal.[11] Together, these two catalysts virtually guaranteed an increase in black homelessness. Although few noticed at the time, at the beginning of the 1960s a new type of homeless person was becoming more common. In New York City, a third of the men seeking shelter in the municipal lodging house at that time were African Americans, and the Salvation Army also recorded a sharp increase in the number of young minority males seeking assistance. A similar trend was evident in Philadelphia, where, in 1960, 32 percent of the black men on skid row were under age 30, compared with only 13 percent of the whites.[12]

During 1965–73, this shift in the demography of the homeless population was temporarily interrupted. The participation of minority males in the Vietnam War and, to a lesser extent, in antipoverty programs removed many potentially homeless persons from the large urban centers. Only a few years after the end of the war, however, a new wave of homeless persons, mostly in their 20s and 30s and disproportionately black or Hispanic, began to appear on city street corners. Many were Vietnam veterans, unable to find work after being discharged. This time the media would take notice, as cover stories in magazines and newspapers announced the arrival of a disturbing type of poverty that, in reality, had been at least 20 years in the making.[13]

The educational levels of those who become homeless, relative to the rest of the population, represents an even stronger element of continuity between the new homeless and their skid-row predecessors. Since World War II, the educational attainments of the homeless have steadily risen, paralleling national trends. The amount of formal schooling completed by those who become homeless has consistently been only marginally below the national average. The common belief that the homeless are illiterate is even less valid today than it was a century ago. Matched against community-wide data, the proportion of the homeless who have attended college has varied little from that of the rest of the population, although the number of college graduates has always been much smaller than average. In 1996, 27 percent had some college education, up from 20 percent in 1987. To be sure, the number of homeless with less than 12th-grade education, 37 percent in 1996, is higher than average, and high unemployment levels among high school dropouts (especially among minorities) have contributed to the rise in homelessness. A high school diploma or even college education, however, is no longer a guarantee that a person will not end up on the street.[14]

Some characteristics of the new homeless are clearly distinctive, but there are also strong continuities, not only with the down-and-out of the skid-row era, but also with the homeless of earlier generations. The age, race, and gender composition of today's homeless population bear a striking resemblance to the urban vagrants and beggars of the early nineteenth century; and the 1996 survey, which reported that one quarter of the homeless suffered childhood abuse and a third had run away from home while they were children, sounds eerily similar to stories of childhood trauma reported by youthful tramps in the late nineteenth century. In their study of the homeless of Austin, Texas, in the 1980s, David Snow and Leon Anderson concluded that many were "on the street because they had never been associated with relatively stable and supportive family networks." Much the same, unfortunately, could have been said about the homeless at any point during the past two hundred years. In many respects, the homeless of the postindustrial era are better understood as a variation on a very old theme than as a genuinely new phenomenon.[15]

The same is true of the public response to the reemergence of the homeless as a social issue. The initial belief that the increase in street people would subside soon yielded to a more sober realization that homelessness was a growing national problem. After much foot-dragging, even the conservative Reagan administration was willing to provide increased funding for emergency food and shelter for the homeless. Under Reagan and his successor, George Bush, however, federal aid for the homeless continued to be outstripped by the increased numbers needing assistance. In 1994, the Clinton administration acknowledged the enormous extent of homelessness and requested more funds to deal with it, but a Republican-dominated Congress limited the increases sought, and state and local governments continued to have considerable control over how, and to what extent, federal funds for the homeless would be spent. Overall, the rise in governmental support for homeless programs after the mid-1980s was heartening, although there were wide variations in the type and level of assistance provided by different municipalities. This response was far more effective than the often punitive policies carried out by city governments and private charities before the Great Depression. Although much more humane than the earlier treatment of tramps, however, programs for the homeless in the 1980s and '90s remained focused on emergency provision of shelter and food, with some ancillary services. The traditional goal of making the lives of the homeless temporarily more bearable remained intact. The kind of structural reforms that would help lift people out of homelessness permanently—affordable housing, job training, less penurious welfare benefits, and a decent minimum wage—were clearly beyond any municipality to enact, and a fundamentally conservative federal government had no interest in supporting such changes. Indeed, the dominant ideological thrust of the post-1975 period argued that many of the poor, including the homeless, were undeserving of such assistance.[16]

The recent growth of social activism on behalf of the homeless marks a more important break with the past than the relatively modest expansion of government assistance. Indeed, much of the progress in aiding the homeless can be credited to the local organizations that have provided direct assistance to the homeless. Local associations, churches, and the Salvation Army have had a long tradition of assisting the homeless, but never before have so many citizens been willing to donate their time and money to help the destitute. The 1996 Urban Institute report estimated that 12,500 food distribution programs, 5,700 shelters, 4,400 transitional housing programs, and 3,300 outreach centers were in operation across the United States. Equally significant has been the emergence of advocacy groups, which have fought to maintain the legal rights of the homeless and to raise public consciousness about the complex nature of homelessness. It is only since the 1970s that legal advocacy groups working on behalf of the homeless and broad-based organizations like the National Coalition to End Homelessness (founded in

1980) have existed. Advocates have been most successful on the legal front, beginning with the victory in the 1979 landmark case of *Callahan v. Carrey*, which mandated that New York City provide shelter for all homeless men— a subsequent ruling extended this right to homeless women as well. Local support groups have also been successful in helping homeless persons obtain government benefits. Between 1987 and 1996, there was a marked increase in use of food stamps among the homeless and a corresponding rise in receipt of AFDC benefits among homeless families.[17]

Enlightening the public about homelessness has proven much more difficult. Since 1980, the traditional image of the "lazy bum" has been largely supplanted by a stereotype that exaggerates the drug addiction, mental illness, and alleged criminality of the homeless population. Occasionally, perceptive observers like Anna Quindlen and Peter Marin attempted to counteract this image by recounting the many diverse causes and consequences of contemporary homelessness. A more typical perspective, however, was that of one op-ed writer who said of the homeless: "What you see, if you stop and look, is craziness, drunkenness, dope, and danger." Such views, and the complaints of downtown merchants about bag ladies and beggars accosting their customers, helped undermine initial widespread empathy for the plight of the new homeless. By the end of the 1980s, however, a more important cause of shifting public opinion may have been simple psychic exhaustion of dealing on a daily basis with street people whose numbers, despite the generosity of the citizenry, never seemed to decline. By the early 1990s, compassion for the homeless was turning to apathy and even anger. One contemporary observer explained how, after a while, people once sympathetic to beggars had become frustrated: "Irritation took root. We had given and given, surely enough to expiate our blessings. Now could we have our streets back?"[18]

The 1990s witnessed the return of punitive tactics for dealing with the homeless. Led by New York Mayor Rudolph W. Giuliani, cities began to pass "quality-of-life" ordinances that allowed police to arrest homeless persons for trivial misdemeanors like sleeping or sitting on sidewalks. By the end of the decade, the National Law Center on Homelessness reported that three-quarters of 49 cities surveyed had such statutes on the books. Sacramento's city council went so far as to sue a private agency, Loaves and Fishes, for failing to obtain a permit to feed the homeless on Sundays. The more aggressive policies toward street people resembled police practices of the skid-row era, when "roundups" of the homeless were normal. The difference was that, by the 1990s, skid row no longer existed. The emerging compromise was to combine the "hard" policy of removing the homeless from the streets with the "soft" one of providing them with emergency food and shelter.[19]

The growing impatience of the average citizen with the existence of desperate people in rags demonstrated the difficulty of changing age-old attitudes toward the homeless. The passage of quality-of-life ordinances coincided with a period of unparalleled economic expansion in the 1990s. Like the tramps of the industrial age, the homeless of the postmodern era are an embarrassing reminder that economic growth has not benefited all. Few are willing to contemplate the idea that the homeless represent only the most extreme case of inequality in the United States, the growth of which has forced many of the working poor into circumstances only a few steps removed from homelessness. It is much easier to support policies that soothe the conscience of the middle class while keeping the homeless out of sight as much as possible.

THE TENDENCY throughout American history has been to view the homeless as outcasts or deviants, despite the fact that they have always had much in common with the rest of the population. Today, as in the past, many of the homeless have the ability to be productive members of society. Like the street corner men studied by anthropologist Elliott Liebow in the mid-1960s, they share the goals of the larger society but lack the personal resources, or sometimes the physical and mental capacity, to realize them. In light of the perception of the homeless as dependent on charity and government aid, it may surprise many to learn that most homeless persons want to live self-sustaining lives. Only the desire to retain some semblance of independence in their lives can explain why many homeless persons refuse, even on the coldest winter nights, to accept public shelter. Earlier generations of homeless exhibited this quest for independence by living in hobo jungles, building shantytowns, or sleeping in 5-by-7-foot "cages." Today's street people are more likely to sleep in alleyways, abandoned buildings, or even underground tunnels, where some men spend much of their day in near-total darkness.[20]

The compulsion to stereotype the homeless as dependent and deviant turns the poorest Americans into an abstract "other," separate and inferior from everyone else. Although their problems are more severe, however, destitute people living on the streets and in homeless shelters are not so different from the rest of us. They never have been. Any genuine effort to end homelessness must begin with a recognition of that essential truth.

Appendix

TABLE A.I. Occupations of Philadelphia Vagrants, 1874–75, by Number of Convictions (Males)

	All	2	3 or more
Professional	0.3	—	—
Proprietary or clerical	8.3	9.6	6.7
Skilled	26.6	25.5	31.1
Semiskilled	22.2	22.3	15.6
Unskilled	38.0	38.2	44.4
Service	4.0	4.2	—
(Number)	(603)	(95)	(43)

Source: Vagrancy Dockets, Philadelphia House of Correction, 1874–75, Philadelphia City Archives. Excluded from the table are men whose occupations were unknown or of indeterminate skill level.

TABLE A.2. Multiple Convictions for Vagrancy, Philadelphia, 1874–75, by Religion (Males, Percent)

	All Vagrants	2 Times	3 or More Times
Catholic	51.4	58.4	41.8
Baptist	3.6	—	7.0
Presbyterian	8.2	4.6	11.6
Methodist	16.8	13.9	23.3
Episcopal	10.9	15.4	16.3
Lutheran	5.4	6.2	—
Other	3.8	1.5	—
(Number)	(368)	(65)	(43)

Source: See Table 1. Note: "Other" includes 2 Jews, 8 members of other Protestant groups, 3 listed as "none" and one "infidel."

TABLE A.3. Homeless Population: Length of Time Resident in City (Percent), 1874–1931

	1874–75	1906	1922	1931
Men				
Less than 1 year	58.3	20.8	6.8	3.0
1–5 years	5.8	7.9	15.6	11.4
Over 5 years	16.3	38.9	34.3	59.2
Native of city	19.7	32.4	43.3	26.3
Women				
Less than 1 year	48.3	8.6	7.6	3.6
1–5 years	4.2	6.8	5.8	8.6
Over 5 years	31.6	61.3	43.2	58.3
Native of city	15.9	23.3	43.1	29.4

Source: Unpublished Vagrancy Dockets, Philadelphia House of Correction, 1874–75, Philadelphia City Archives; New York City Bureau of Public Welfare, *Annual Report, 1906* (New York, 1907), 315; idem, *Annual Report, 1922* (New York, 1923), p. 159; idem, *Annual Report, 1931* (New York, 1932), p. 84.

Notes

CHAPTER I

1. [Nels Anderson], Summary of Report on Homeless Census of January, 1933, [and] February 21, 1933, in Box 82, Traveller's Aid folder, New General Subject Series, Federal Emergency Relief Administration, Transient Division, Record Group 69, National Archives.

2. On problems of definition and counting, see Gregg Barak, *Gimme Shelter: A Social History of Homelessness in Contemporary America* (New York: Praeger, 1991), pp. 27–33; and Joel Blau, *The Visible Poor: Homelessness in the United States* (New York: Oxford University Press, 1992), pp. 18–24.

3. For a defense of a broad definition of homelessness, see Kim Hopper, "Homelessness Old and New: The Matter of Definition," *Housing Policy Debate* 2 (1991), 773–85.

4. For a discussion of the early police system, see Roger Lane, *Policing the City: Boston, 1822–1885* (Cambridge, Mass.: Harvard University Press, 1967), chs. 1–2; James F. Richardson, *The New York Police: Colonial Times to 1901* (New York: Oxford University Press, 1970), chs. 1–2.

5. Eric H. Monkkonen, *Police in Urban America, 1860–1920* (Cambridge, Eng.: Cambridge University Press, 1981), pp. 93–96.

6. Peter Rossi, *Down and Out in America: The Origins of Homelessness* (Berkeley: University of California Press, 1989), p. 9.

7. Significant exceptions include Paul T. Ringenbach, *Tramps and Reformers: The Discovery of Unemployment in New York City, 1873–1914* (Westport, Conn.: Greenwood Press, 1973); *Walking to Work: Tramps in America, 1790–1935*, ed. Eric Monkkonen (Lincoln: University of Nebraska Press, 1984); Joan Crouse, *The Homeless Transient in the Great Depression: New York State, 1929–1941* (Albany: State University of New York Press, 1986); and *On Being Homeless: Historical Perspectives*, ed. Rick Beard (New York: Museum of the City of New York, 1987). Useful popular histories include

Kenneth Allsop, *Hard Travellin': The Hobo and His History* (New York: New American Library, 1977); and Roger A. Bruns, *Knights of the Road: A Hobo History* (New York: Methuen, 1980).

8. For a survey of the literature on social mobility in the United States, see Howard Chudacoff, "Success and Security: The Meaning of Social Mobility in America," in *The Promise of American History: Progress and Prospects*, special issue of *Reviews in American History* 10 (1982), 101–12. Important exceptions among nineteeth-century community studies include Alan Dawley, *Class and Community: The Industrial Revolution in Lynn* (Cambridge, Mass.: Harvard University Press, 1976); Priscilla Ferguson Clement, *Welfare and the Poor in the Nineteenth-Century City: Philadelphia, 1800–1854* (Rutherford, N.J.: Farleigh Dickenson University Press, 1985); and Kenneth A. Scherzer, *The Unbounded Community: Neighborhood Life and Social Structure in New York City, 1830–1875* (Durham, N.C.: Duke University Press, 1992).

9. "Tramps," *New York Times*, May 5, 1875, p. 4.

10. On the strength of localism in mid-nineteenth-century America, see Thomas Bender, *Community and Social Change in America* (New Brunswick, N.J.: Rutgers University Press, 1978), pp. 86–108, and Robert Wiebe, *The Search for Order, 1877–1920* (New York: Hill and Wang, 1967), pp. 1–10.

11. For a general discussion of these trends, see Daniel T. Rodgers, *The Work Ethic in Industrial America, 1860–1920* (Chicago: University of Chicago Press, 1978); David Montgomery, *Workers' Control in America* (Cambridge, Eng.: Cambridge University Press, 1979); David Montgomery, *Fall of the House of Labor: The Workplace, the State, and American Labor Activism, 1865–1925* (Cambridge, Eng.: Cambridge University Press, 1991), chs. 3–6.

12. See, in particular, the seminal essays by E. P. Thompson, "Time, Work-Discipline, and Industrial Capitalism," *Past and Present* (1967), 56–97; and Herbert Gutman, "Work, Culture, and Society in Industrializing America, 1819–1914," in Gutman, *Work, Culture, and Society in Industrializing America* (New York: Vintage Books, 1976), pp. 3–78, which directly or indirectly spawned an enormous number of case studies.

13. David De Leon, *The American as Anarchist: Reflections on Indigenous Radicalism* (Baltimore: Johns Hopkins University Press, 1978).

14. Theda Skocpol, *Protecting Soldiers and Mothers: The Political Origins of Social Policy in the United States* (Cambridge, Mass.: Harvard University Press, 1992).

15. Judy Hilkey, *Character Is Capital: Success Manuals and Manhood in Gilded Age America* (Chapel Hill: University of North Carolina Press, 1997), ch. 7.

CHAPTER 2

1. Darrett B. Rutman, *Winthrop's Boston: A Portrait of a Puritan Town, 1630–1649* (Chapel Hill: University of North Carolina Press, 1965), p. 225; David M. Schneider, *History of Public Welfare in New York, 1609–1867* (Chicago: University of Chicago Press, 1938), p. 148.

2. See Peter Burke, *Popular Culture in Early Modern Europe* (New York: New York University Press, 1978), pp. 46–47. See also Peter Linebaugh, *The London Hanged:*

Crime and Civil Society in the Eighteenth Century (Cambridge, Eng.: Cambridge University Press, 1992), p. 151.

3. Abbot E. Smith, *Colonists in Bondage: White Servitude and Convict Labor in America, 1607–1776* (Chapel Hill: University of North Carolina Press, 1947), pp. 136–51; Carl Bridenbaugh, *Cities in the Wilderness: The First Century of Urban Life in America, 1625–1742* (New York: Oxford University Press, 1938), pp. 78 (quotation), 79–80, 82–83, 233; Marcus W. Jernegan, *The Laboring and Dependent Classes in Colonial America* (New York: Unger, 1960), pp. 199–200; Gary B. Nash, *The Urban Crucible: Social Change, Political Consciousness, and the Origins of the American Revolution* (Cambridge, Mass.: Harvard University Press, 1979), pp. 250–55.

4. Robert Cray, Jr., *Paupers and Poor Relief in New York City and Its Rural Environs, 1700–1830* (Philadelphia: Temple University Press, 1988), pp. 31–36 (quotation, p. 31); Raymond A. Mohl, *Poverty in New York, 1783–1825* (New York: Oxford University Press, 1971), 43–44 (quotation, p. 43).

5. Bridenbaugh, *Cities in the Wilderness,* pp. 231–32, 391–92, 394 (quotation), 395.

6. Rutman, *Winthrop's Boston,* p. 225; Jernegan, *Laboring and Dependent Classes,* pp. 196–97; Gary B. Nash, *The Urban Crucible*; Nash, *Red, White, and Black: The Peoples of Early America,* 2nd ed. (Englewood Cliffs, N.J.: Prentice Hall, 1984), pp. 216–17; John K. Alexander, *Render Them Submissive: Responses to Poverty in Philadelphia, 1760–1800* (Amherst: University of Massachusetts Press, 1980), pp. 11–25; Billie G. Smith, *The "Lower Sort": Philadelphia's Laboring People, 1750–1800* (Ithaca: Cornell University Press, 1990), pp. 150–75 (quotation, 165).

7. Sharon V. Salinger, *"To Serve Well and Faithfully": Labor and Indentured Servants in Pennsylvania, 1682–1900* (Cambridge, Eng.: Cambridge University Press, 1987), ch. 5; Susan E. Klepp and Billie G. Smith, eds., *The Infortunate: The Voyage and Adventures of William Moraley, an Indentured Servant* (University Park: Penn State University Press, 1992); Vagrancy Dockets of Philadelphia County Prison, 1790s, Philadelphia City Archives; Billie G. Smith, "Black Women Who Stole Themselves in Eighteenth-Century America," in Carla Gardina Pestana and Sharon V. Salinger, eds., *Inequality in Early America* (Hanover, N.H.: University of New England Press, 1999), pp. 146–52. The information on the slave Harry is included in the selection of Vagrancy Docket records reprinted in *Life in Early Philadelphia: Documents from the Revolutionary and Early National Periods,* ed. Billie G. Smith (University Park: Penn State University Press, 1995), pp. 79–80. For a similar pattern of slave runaways in New York, see Shane White, *Somewhat More Independent: The End of Slavery in New York City, 1770–1810* (Athens: University of Georgia Press, 1991), pp. 147–48. For the context of use of vagrancy laws against runaway servants, see David Montgomery, *Citizen Worker: The Experience of Workers in the United States with Democracy and the Free Market During the Nineteenth Century* (Cambridge, Eng.: Cambridge University Press, 1996), pp. 27–29.

8. David M. Schneider, *The History of Public Welfare in New York State, 1609–1866* (Chicago: University of Chicago Press, 1938), pp. 148–49 (quoting Duane), 150–51; Mohl, *Poverty in New York,* pp. 16–17 (quoting Varick).

9. Edmund Morgan, *American Slavery, American Freedom: The Ordeal of Colonial Virginia* (New York: Norton, 1975), pp. 168, 237–39, 383–84.

10. 2 Hening 298, 299 (1672). Morgan, *American Slavery, American Freedom*, pp. 213–92. Morgan neglects the second of these statutes, despite its obvious relevance to his thesis.

11. *The Laws of Virginia: Being a Supplement to Hening's The Statutes at Large* (Richmond: Virginia State Library, 1971), 253–55. See also 4 Hening 208 (1727). Barbara Bellows, *Benevolence Among Slaveholders: Assisting the Poor in Charleston, 1670–1860* (Baton Rouge: Louisiana State University, 1993), pp. 6–9; Peter Wood, *Black Majority: Negroes in Colonial South Carolina from 1670 through the Stono Rebellion* (New York: Norton, 1974), pp. 239–68.

12. See, for example, James T. Lemon, *The Best Poor Man's Country: A Geographical Study of Early Southeastern Pennsylvania* (Baltimore: Johns Hopkins University Press, 1972), pp. 94–96, 227; Darrett B. Rutman, "People in Process: The New Hampshire Towns of the Eighteenth Century," in *Family and Kin in Urban Communities, 1700–1930*, ed. Tamara Hareven (New York: New Viewpoints, 1977), pp. 16–37; Jeffrey G. Williamson and Peter H. Lindert, *American Inequality: A Macroeconomic History* (New York: Basic Books, 1980), pp. 3–30; Karl-Tilman Winkler, "Soziale Mobilitaet in Nordamerika, 1700–1800," *Scripta Mercaturae: Zeitschrift fur Wirtschafts- und Sozialgeschichte* 19 (1985), 80–87; James A. Henretta and Gregory H. Nobles, *Revolution and Evolution: American Society, 1600–1820* (Lexington, Mass.: D. C. Heath, 1987), pp. 231–33; Paul G. E. Clemens and Lucy Simler, "Rural Labor and the Farm Household in Chester County, Pennsylvania, 1750–1820," in Stephen Innes, ed., *Work and Labor in Early America* (Chapel Hill: University of North Carolina Press, 1988), pp. 126–43; R. Douglas Hurt, *The Ohio Frontier: Crucible of the Old Northwest, 1720–1830* (Bloomington: University of Indiana Press, 1996); Ronald Schultz, "A Class Society? The Nature of Inequality in Early America," in Carla Gardina Pestana and Sharon V. Salinger, eds., *Inequality in Early America* (Hanover, N.H.: University Press of New England, 1999), pp. 212–16.

13. Cray, *Paupers and Poor Relief*, 136–67, esp. 165–66; Richard B. Morris, *Government and Labor in Early America* (New York: Columbia University Press, 1946), p. 28; Richardson Wright, *Hawkers and Walkers in Early America: Strolling Peddlers, Preachers, Lawyers, Doctors, Players, and Others, from the Beginning to the Civil War* (New York: Ungar, 1965 [1927]); Lemon, *Best Poor Man's Country*, pp. 12–13; Gregory A. Stiverson, *Poverty in a Land of Plenty: Tenancy in Eighteenth-Century Maryland* (Baltimore: Johns Hopkins University Press, 1977), pp. 140–42; David Bensman, *The Practice of Solidarity: American Hat Finishers in the Nineteenth Century* (Urbana: University of Illinois Press, 1985), pp. 9–10; Douglas Lamar Jones, *Village and Seaport: Migration and Society in Eighteenth Century Massachusetts* (Hanover, N.H.: University Press of New England, 1981), pp. xv (quotation), 49–50; Robert Humphreys, *No Fixed Abode: A History of Response to the Roofless and the Rootless in Britain* (New York: St. Martin's, 1999), pp. 70–77; Alan Forrest, *The French Revolution and the Poor* (New York: St. Martin's, 1984), pp. 8–10 (quotation, 9). Jones's approach to migration in his book is much more balanced than in his article, "The Strolling Poor: Transiency in Eighteenth-Century Massachusetts," *Journal of Social History* 8 (1975), 28–54. This article and Allan Kulikoff's "The Progress of Inequality in Revolutionary Boston," *William and Mary Quarterly*, 3rd ser., 28 (1971), 375–411, overemphasize the number of poor people

involved in transiency because they use "warnings out" as a measure of the wandering poor. In the seventeenth and early eighteenth century this may have been fairly accurate, because the process of warning out was selective and apparently often involved actual banishment of persons whom the community feared would become public charges. At some point in the eighteenth century, however (varying from town to town), this often became a mere legal mechanism designed to save taxpayers from taking care of indigent newcomers. Such "warned out" people were often not removed, however, and many stayed in the town and even became substantial citizens. In 1791 the Massachusetts town of Milford, for example, warned out "all persons who have come to reside in said Town since the 10th of April, 1767." The town's historian noted that the process "soon became a mere bugbear formality, and nobody was deterred from moving in and staying through dread of its disgrace." Adin Ballou, *History of the Town of Milford, Worcester County, Massachusetts, from Its First Settlements to 1881* (Boston: Franklin Press, 1882), p. 96. For the manner in which warnings out actually operated, see Robert A. Gross, *The Minutemen and Their World* (New York: Hill and Wang, 1976), pp. 90–91 and, for a compendium of facts, Josiah Benton, *Warning Out in New England* (Boston: Clarke, 1911). See also Michael Zuckerman, *Peaceable Kingdoms* (New York: Norton, 1970), p. 113n, for some caveats on Benton. Kulikoff's own data shows substantial mobility among all classes.

14. Barbara H. Rosenwein and Lester K. Little, "Social Meaning in the Monastic and Mendicant Spiritualities," *Past and Present* 63 (1974), 4–32, esp. 27–28; Ray C. Petry, *Francis of Assisi: Apostle of Poverty* (Durham, N.C.: Duke University Press, 1941), pp. 45–49; Eric Doyle, *St. Francis and the Song of Brotherhood* (New York: Seabury Press, 1981).

15. Nash, *Red, White, and Black*, p. 69; Perkins quoted in Lewis A. Coser, "The Sociology of Poverty," *Social Problems* 13 (1965), 141; Margaret K. Rosenheim, "Vagrancy Concepts in Welfare Law," 54 *California Law Review*, 515–16n (1966); A. L. Beier, "Vagrancy and the Social Order in Elizabethan England," *Past and Present* 64 (1974), 3; A. L. Beier, *Masterless Men: The Vagrancy Problem in England 1560–1640* (London: Methuen, 1985), pp. 3–13; Humphreys, *No Fixed Abode*, ch. 3; Jernegan, *Laboring and Dependent Classes*, pp. 189–91; Linebaugh, *The London Hanged*, pp. 70–71.

16. Perry Miller, "The Puritan State and Puritan Society," in Perry Miller, *Errand Into the Wilderness* (Cambridge, Mass.: Harvard University Press, 1956), pp. 141–52; Jernegan, *Laboring and Dependent Classes*, p. 199; Frederick B. Tolles, *Meeting House and Counting House: The Quaker Merchants of Colonial Philadelphia* (Chapel Hill: University of North Carolina Press, 1948), pp. 53 (Penn quotation), 54 (Pemberton quotation), 57, 66; Charles Chauncey, *The Idle Poor Secluded from the Bread of Charity by the Christian Law. . . .* (Boston, 1752).

17. Jernegan, *Laboring and Dependent Classes*, pp. 193–94, 202; Edmund Morgan, *The Puritan Family: Religion and Domestic Relations in Seventeenth-Century New England* (New York: Harper and Row, 1966), pp. 143–46; Perry Miller, "The Marrow of Puritan Divinity," in Miller, *Errand*, pp. 89–92; Rutman, *Winthrop's Boston*, p. 217; Morris, *Government and Labor*, p. 12.

18. Morris, *Government and Labor*, pp. 5–6; Edward W. Capen, *The Historical Development of the Poor Law in Connecticut* (New York: Columbia University Press,

1910), pp. 59–60 (quotation); Jernegan, *Laboring and Dependent Classes*, pp. 200–01; Schneider, *History of Public Welfare in New York*, pp. 149–50.

19. Jernegan, *Laboring and Dependent Classes*, p. 201 (Smith quotation); Morris, *Government and Labor*, pp. 12–13; Alexander, *Render Them Submissive*, pp. 51–53.

20. *American Museum* 4 (1788), 57–78; Carol Smith Rosenberg, *Religion and the Rise of the American City: The New York City Mission Movement, 1812–1870* (Ithaca: Cornell University Press, 1971); Jonathan Ashley, *The Great Duty of Charity, considered and applied....* (Boston, 1742), pp. 7, 9, 10, 11.

21. Introduction, *Jonathan Edwards: Representative Selections*, ed. Clarence H. Faust and Thomas H. Johnson (New York: Hill and Wang, 1962), pp. lxxvii–lxxxvi; Joseph A. Conforti, "Samuel Hopkins and the New Divinity: Theology, Ethics, and Social Reform in Eighteenth-Century New England," *William and Mary Quarterly*, 3rd ser., 34 (1977), 572–89; Alan Heimert, *Religion and the American Mind from the Great Awakening to the Revolution* (Cambridge, Mass.: Harvard University Press, 1966).

22. See, for example, *The Beggar, and no beggar; or, every Man a King if he will. A parable....* (Philadelphia, 1749), pp. 9–13; Rosenberg, *Religion and the American City*, pp. 28–29.

23. For overviews of these changes, see Sam Bass Warner, *The Urban Wilderness* (New York: Harper and Row, 1972), pp. 55–84; Howard P. Chudacoff and Judith E. Smith, *The Evolution of American Urban Society*, 4th ed. (Englewood Cliffs, N.J.: Prentice Hall, 1994), pp. 45–70, 78–81; Edward K. Spann, *The New Metropolis: New York City, 1840–1857* (New York: Columbia University Press, 1981); Kenneth A. Scherzer, *The Unbounded Community: Neighborhood Life and Social Structure in New York City, 1830–1875* (Durham, N.C.: Duke University Press, 1992), pp. 67–86, 137–60. On the geography of prostitution, see Timothy J. Gilfoyle, *City of Eros: New York City, Prostitution, and the Commercialization of Sex, 1790–1920* (New York: Norton, 1992), pp. 29–54.

24. Bruce Laurie, *Working People of Philadelphia, 1800–1850* (Philadelphia: Temple University Press, 1980), ch. 1; Sean Wilentz, *Chants Democratic: New York City and the Rise of the American Working Class, 1788–1850* (New York: Oxford, 1984), ch. 3; Alan Dawley, *Class and Community: The Industrial Revolution in Lynn* (Cambridge, Mass.: Harvard University Press, 1976); Jonathan Prude, *The Coming of Industrial Order: Town and Factory Life in Rural Massachusetts, 1810–1860* (Cambridge, Eng.: Cambridge University Press, 1983), p. xi; Alfred Chandler, *The Visible Hand: The Managerial Revolution in American Business* (Cambridge, Mass.: Harvard University Press, 1977), 77 and 50–78 passim; Robert H. Wiebe, *The Opening of American Society: From the Revolution to the Eve of Disunion* (New York: Vintage Books, 1984), pp. 259–64.

25. See Edward Pessen, *Riches, Class, and Power Before the Civil War* (Lexington, Mass.: D. C. Heath, 1973), pp. 9–164; Williamson and Lindert, *American Inequality*, chs. 4–5; Donald Adams, Jr., "The Standard of Living During American Industrialization: Evidence from the Brandywine Region, 1800–1860," *Journal of Economic History* 42 (1982), 903–17.

26. Benjamin J. Klebaner, "Public Poor Relief in America, 1790–1860" (Ph.D. dissertation, Columbia University, 1951), pp. 225–28; Richard C. Wade, *The Urban Frontier* (Chicago: University of Chicago Press, 1964), pp. 167–73; Samuel Rezneck,

"The Depression of 1819–1822: A Social History," in Rezneck, *Business Depressions and Financial Panics: Essays in American Business and Economic History* (Westport, Conn.: Greenwood Press, 1968), p. 56; Mohl, *Poverty in New York*, pp. 14–34; Rosenberg, *Religion and the Rise of the City*, pp. 30–42; Priscilla Ferguson Clement, *Welfare and the Poor in the Nineteenth-Century City: Philadelphia, 1800–1854* (Rutherford, N.J.: Fairleigh Dickinson University Press, 1985), pp. 24–37; Lisa Wilson, *Life After Death: Widows in Pennsylvania, 1750–1850* (Philadelphia: Temple University Press, 1992), pp. 59–65.

27. Priscilla Ferguson Clement, "The Transformation of the Wandering Poor in Nineteenth-Century Philadelphia," in *Walking to Work: Tramps in America, 1790–1935* (Lincoln: University of Nebraska Press, 1984), pp. 66–67; Gary B. Nash, *Forging Freedom: The Formation of Philadelphia's Black Community, 1720–1840* (Cambridge, Mass.: Harvard University Press, 1988), pp. 213–17. On black economic status before the Civil War, see James and Lois Horton, *In Hope of Liberty: Culture, Community and Protest Among Northern Free Blacks, 1700–1860* (New York: Norton, 1997), pp. 101–24. See chapter 6 for data on ethnic composition of the homeless.

28. Mohl, *Poverty in New York*, pp. 31–32; Schneider, *History of Public Welfare*, pp. 151–55 (quotation, p. 155). On the development of vagrancy laws and judicial interpretation in New York, see James D. Schmidt, *Free to Work: Labor Law, Emancipation, and Reconstruction, 1815–1880* (Athens: University of Georgia Press, 1998), pp. 68–81.

29. Scherzer, *The Unbounded Community*, pp. 86–87; Charles Loring Brace, *The Dangerous Classes of New York City* (New York: Wynkoop and Hallenbeck, 1972), pp. 97–113 (quotation, 97); James F. Richardson, *The New York Police: Colonial Times to 1901* (New York: Oxford University Press, 1970), pp. 60–61; Clement, *Welfare and the Poor*, p. 30. For data on women police station lodgers during and after the Civil War, see chapter 6.

30. Robert W. Kelso, *The History of Public Poor Relief in Massachusetts, 1620–1920* (Boston: Houghton Mifflin, 1922), pp. 147–48; Oscar Handlin, *Boston's Immigrants* (Cambridge, Mass.: Harvard University Press, 1959), pp. 118, 162; Mohl, *Poverty in New York*, pp. 32–33; *Cleveland Herald*, August 5, 1842, in Works Projects Administration, *The Annals of Cleveland* (Cleveland, 1937–38), vol. 25, 437.

31. John C. Schneider, *Detroit and the Problem of Order, 1830–1880* (Lincoln: University of Nebraska Press, 1980), pp. 68–69, 78–79; Clement, "The Transformation of the Wandering Poor," pp. 60–61 (Figure 1).

32. Handlin, *Boston's Immigrants*, p. 119 (Chart D); Kelso, *History of Public Poor Relief*, pp. 146, 148 (quotation); Stephan Thernstrom, *Poverty and Progress: Social Mobility in a Nineteenth-Century City* (New York: Atheneum, 1969), pp. 21–22; *Cleveland Leader*, January 12, 1855, in Works Projects Administration, Annals, vol. 38, 24; *New York Times*, November 26, 1857; William Greenblatt, "Some Social Aspects of the Panic of 1857" (M.A. thesis, Columbia University, 1948), pp. 23–24 (quotation, p. 23); Kenneth M. Stampp, *America in 1857: A Nation on the Brink* (New York: Oxford University Press, 1990), pp. 221–30.

33. Mohl, *Poverty in New York*, pp. 20, 138–43, and chs. 10 and 15; Clement, *Welfare and the Poor*, pp. 150–61; M.J. Heale, "Humanitarianism in the Early Republic: The Moral Reformers of New York, 1776–1825," *Journal of American Studies* 2 (1968),

161–75 (quotation, 173); M. J. Heale, "The New York Society for the Prevention of Pauperism, 1817–1823," *New-York Historical Society Quarterly* 55 (1971), 153–76; Rosenberg, *Religion and the American City*; Elizabeth L. Bunkowsky, "The Church and the City: Protestant Concern for Urban Problems, 1800–1840" (Ph.D. dissertation, Boston University, 1973), pp. 147–60. On the AICP, see Paul Boyer, *Urban Masses and Moral Order in America, 1820–1920* (Cambridge, Mass.: Harvard University Press, 1978), pp. 86–93. For a succinct overview of these changes, see Michael B. Katz, *In the Shadow of the Poorhouse: A Social History of Welfare in America* (New York: Basic Books, 1986), pp. 58–66.

34. Benjamin Klebaner, "Poverty and Its Relief in American Thought, 1815–1861," *Social Service Review* 38 (1964), 384; Bunkowsky, "The Church and the City," p. 149 (quoting Stafford and Tuckerman); Heale, "The New York Society for the Prevention of Pauperism," 169–70; Rosenberg, *Religion and the Rise of the American City*, pp. 252–53; Brace, *The Dangerous Classes*, pp. 115–17.

35. See Eric Foner, *Free Soil, Free Labor, Free Men: The Ideology of the Republican Party Before the Civil War* (New York: Oxford University Press, 1970), esp. chs. 1 and 2.

36. See Barbara Bellows, *Benevolence Among Slaveholders: Assisting the Poor in Charleston, 1670–1860* (Baton Rouge: Louisiana State University Press, 1993), pp. 68–69, 74–77, 179–80.

37. Boyer, *Urban Masses*, pp. 86–89. On the contempt of reformers for traditional attitudes, see also Brace, *Dangerous Classes*, pp. 388–89.

38. New York Association for Improving the Condition of the Poor, *Fifth Annual Report, 1848*, 15; Leah H. Feder, *Unemployment Relief in Periods of Depression* (New York: Russell Sage Foundation, 1936), pp. 20–21 (quoting *Harper's*). For examples drawn from the 1807–1820 period, see Mohl, *Poverty in New York*, p. 20, 138–43; Clement, *Welfare and the Poor*, p. 150.

39. New York Association for Improving the Condition of the Poor, *Fifteenth Annual Report, 1858* (New York, 1858), pp. 57–58; Feder, *Unemployment Relief*, pp. 29–30.

40. The source for the following paragraphs is Bessie Boggs, "History of Western Community House" (unpublished manuscript, Urban Archives, Temple University, 1948).

41. Boggs, "History of Western Community House," p. 2.

42. Klebenar, "Poverty and Its Relief in American Thought," 385n; Heale, "The New York Society for the Prevention of Pauperism," 169–70; Mohl, *Poverty in New York*, pp. 255–56; Kelso, *History of Public Poor Relief*, pp. 146–48.

43. Katz, *In the Shadow of the Poorhouse*, p. 55 and 52–57 passim. For other examples of use of outdoor relief during the depression of the late 1850s, see Klebaner, "Public Poor Relief in America," ch. 6.

44. *Cleveland Daily True Democrat*, April 20, 1849, in Works Projects Administration, *Annals*, vol. 32, 189.

45. Walter Houghton, *The Victorian Frame of Mind* (New Haven: Yale University Press, 1957), pp. 273–81; Lisa N. Peters, "Images of the Homeless in American Art, 1860–1910," in *On Being Homeless: Historical Perspectives*, ed. Rick Beard (New York: Museum of the City of New York, 1987), pp. 43–53. E. Douglas Branch, *The Sentimental Years, 1836–1860* (New York: Hill and Wang, 1936), is still useful.

46. John G. Cawelti, *Apostles of the Self-Made Man* (Chicago: University of Chicago Press, 1966), pp. 62–73 (quotation, 62); Fitz James O'Brien, "Homeless," *The Knickerbocker* 52 (1858), 587; "Report of the Beggar Detectives," *Second Annual Message of [Mayor] Alexander Henry, with Accompanying Documents* (Philadelphia, 1860), pp. 77–79; data from unpublished vagrancy dockets of the Philadelphia County Prison, Philadelphia City Archives. For undertones of doubt about the success ethic in the antebellum United States, see also Bremer, *From the Depths*, p. 91; and Klebenar, "Poverty and Its Relief in American Thought," 384.

47. In researching this study, I discovered no examples of illegal train-riding by homeless men prior to the Civil War.

48. "Railroad Accidents," *American Railroad Journal* 29 (1856), 185; M. N. Forney, "American Locomotives and Cars," in *The American Railway: Its Construction, Development, Management, and Appliances*, ed. Thomas C. Clarke et al. (New York: Scribner's, 1889), pp. 100–141; Eugene Alverez, *Travel on Southern Antebellum Railroads, 1828–1860* (University: University of Alabama Press, 1974), pp. 68–106 (quotation, 68); L. K. Silcox, *Safety in Early American Railway Operation, 1853–1871* (Princeton: Princeton University Press, 1936), pp. 11–13; "Sketch of the Life and Experience of Charles H. Frisbie, for Forty-Seven Years a Railroad Engineer," in C. H. Salmons, *The Burlington Strike* (Aurora, Ill., 1889), pp. 468–69; Walter Licht, *Working for the Railroad: The Organization of Work in the Nineteenth Century* (Princeton: Princeton University Press, 1983), pp. 181–82.

49. See George Rogers Taylor, *The Transportation Revolution* (New York: Harper and Row, 1954), pp. 22–24, 26–31; Wiebe, *The Opening of American Society*, p. 259–60.

50. David E. Schob, *Hired Hands and Plowboys: Farm Labor in the Midwest, 1815–1860* (Urbana: University of Illinois Press, 1975), pp. 250–67; John Mack Faragher, *Sugar Creek: Life on the Illinois Prairie* (New Haven: Yale University Press, 1986); Stuart Blumin, *The Urban Threshold: Growth and Change in a Nineteenth-Century American City* (Chicago: University of Chicago Press, 1976), pp. 84–92.

51. Elizabeth Gaspar Brown, "Poor Relief in a Wisconsin County, 1846–1866: Administration and Recipients," *American Journal of Legal History* 20 (1976), 117; Mark Twain, *Life on the Mississippi* (New York, 1883), p. 82; Ben Reitman, "Following the Monkey" (unpublished autobiography, University of Illinois at Chicago Circle, 1932), p. 70.

52. Foner, *Free Soil, Free Labor, Free Men*, pp. 16–17, 25–26, 29–30, 37.

CHAPTER 3

1. Charles Astor Bristed, "The Probable Influence of the New Military Element on Our Social and National Character," *United States Service Magazine* 1 (1864), 601, 602. On the quest for "order" following the war, see George M. Fredrickson, *The Inner Civil War: Northern Intellectuals and the Crisis of the Union* (New York: Harper and Row, 1965); and David Thelen, *Paths of Resistance: Tradition and Democracy in Industrializing Missouri* (Columbia: University of Missouri Press, 1986), pp. 59–62.

2. Festus P. Summers, *The Baltimore and Ohio in the Civil War* (New York: Putnam's, 1939), p. 160–81; John F. Stover, *American Railroads* (Chicago: University of Chicago Press, 1961), pp. 58–60; Annie E. Foxon, "Sketches of Army Life," *United States Service Magazine* 4 (1865), 526; Dixon Wecter, *When Johnny Comes Marching Home* (Cambridge, Mass.: Harvard University Press, 1944), pp. 140–41; Charles George, *Forty Years on the Rail* (Chicago: Clarke, 1888), pp. 99–128; Russell F. Weigley, *Quartermaster General of the Union Army: A Biography of M. C. Meigs* (New York: Columbia University Press, 1959), p. 330.

3. Bell Irvin Wiley, *The Life of Billy Yank: The Common Soldier of the Union* (Baton Rouge: Louisiana State University Press, 1971), pp. 233–46; John D. Billings, *Hardtack and Coffee: The Unwritten Story of Army Life* (Chicago: R. R. Donnelly, 1887), pp. 112, 251–53, 263; Carlton McCarthy, *Minutiae of Soldier Life in the Army of Northern Virginia, 1861–1865* (Richmond, 1882), pp. 25–26, 62; Stephen Z. Starr, *Jennison's Jayhawkers: A Civil War Cavalry Regiment and Its Commander* (Baton Rouge: Louisiana State University Press, 1973), p. 200; Weigley, *Quartermaster General*, pp. 80–118, 199; J. Cutler Andrews, *The North Reports the Civil War* (Pittsburgh: University of Pittsburgh Press, 1955), pp. 577–78; John G. Barrett, *Sherman's March Through the Carolinas* (Chapel Hill: University of North Carolina Press, 1956), pp. 53–55, 96–105, 143–45, 189–91; Richard R. Duncan, *Lee's Endangered Left: The Civil War in Western Virginia, Spring of 1864* (Baton Rouge: Louisiana State University Press, 1998), pp. 152–56, 194–98.

4. Jack Black [pseud.], *You Can't Win* (New York: Macmillan, 1926), pp. 108–09; Thomas M. Page, *Bohemian Life; or, the Autobiography of a Tramp* (San Francisco: Sun Publishing Co., 1884), pp. 60–87; Ben L. Reitman, "Following the Monkey" (unpublished manuscript autobiography, University of Illinois at Chicago Circle, 1932), p. 70.

5. Wiley, *Life of Billy Yank*, p. 233; Billings, *Hardtack and Coffee*, pp. 118–19; "Not Pleasant Neighbors," *New York Times*, July 9, 1879, p. 3; Glen Mullin, *Adventures of a Scholar Tramp* (London: J. Cape, 1925), pp. 143–44; Josiah Flynt [Willard]. *Tramping with Tramps: Studies and Sketches of Vagabond Life* (New York: Century, 1899), p. 105. See also chapter 6.

6. Billings, *Hardtack and Coffee*, p. 267; *Eighth Annual Report of the State Board of Charities of Massachusetts*, 1872 (Boston, 1872), pp. 22–23.

7. Henry S. Commager, ed., *The Blue and the Grey: The Story of the Civil War as Told by Participants* (Indianapolis: Bobbs Merrill, 1950–), vol. 2, p. 952; James D. Burn, *Three Years Among the Working-Classes in the United States During the War* (New York: AMS Press, 1983 [1865]), p. 223; Wecter, *When Johnny Comes Marching Home*, p. 238; H. L. Mencken, with Raven I. McDavid, *The American Language*, 4th ed. (New York: Knopf, 1967), pp. 192–93; "The Bummers of New York," *New York Times*, November 29, 1868, p. 3; *Cleveland Leader*, December 16, 1868, in Works Projects Administration, *The Annals of Cleveland* (Cleveland: Works Projects Administration, 1937–38), vol. 51, p. 786; Charles Loring Brace, *The Dangerous Classes of New York* (New York: Wynkoop and Hallenbeck, 1872), pp. 101–02; Robert V. Bruce, *1877: Year of Violence* (Chicago: Quadrangle, 1959), p. 264.

8. Alexander Keyssar, *Out of Work: The First Century of Unemployment in Massachusetts* (Cambridge, Eng.: Cambridge University Press, 1986), p. 35; Wecter, *When*

Johnny Comes Marching Home, pp. 182, 183–85, 189–91; Don Ricky, Jr., *Forty Miles a Day on Beans and Hay: The Enlisted Soldier Fighting the Indian Wars* (Norman: University of Oklahoma Press, 1963), pp. 17–21, 137–55.

9. Wecter, *When Johnny Comes Marching Home*, pp. 234–36; *Third Annual Report of the State Board of Charities of Massachusetts, 1867*, pp. 194, 39–40, 128; *Fourth Annual Report . . . Massachusetts, 1868*, p. 127; "City Young Men," *Nation* 1 (1866), 201; *Cleveland Leader*, October 16, 1867, January 7, 1868, in Works Projects Administration, *Annals*, vol. 50, p. 416, LI, p. 785.

10. Trends in vagrancy from data in *Annual Reports of the State Board of Charities of Massachusetts* for 1867–1872; quotations from *Eighth Annual Report . . . Massachusetts, 1872* (Boston, 1872), p. 20. Similar trends are evident in New York City data in *Annual Reports of the Board of Commissioners of the Metropolitan Police*, for 1867–1872; "Our Vagrant Population," *New York Times*, December 28, 1873, p. 5.

11. Sidney Andrews, "Secretary's Report," *Tenth Annual Report of the State Board of Charities of Massachusetts, 1874* (Boston, 1875), p. 206. On the background of the depression of the 1870s, see Arthur Auble, "The Depression of 1873 and 1882 in the United States" (Ph.D. dissertation, Harvard University, 1949), chs. 1–3; Bruce, *1877*, and Nell Irvin Painter, *Standing at Armageddon: The United States, 1877–1919* (New York: Norton, 1987), pp. 1–18.

12. "Our Vagrant Population," p. 5; "Report of the Police Justices," *New York Times*, December 29, 1874, p. 8; "Police Statistics," ibid., January 12, 1878, p. 8; *Twelfth Annual Report of the State Board of Charities of Massachusetts, 1876* (Boston, 1876), p. 177; *Fifteenth Annual Report . . . Massachusetts, 1879* (Boston, 1879), pp. 101, 102. For Philadelphia statistics, see graph 6.3, chapter 6.

13. "A Farmer's Complaint," *New York Times*, June 3, 1875, p. 3; "The Tramp," ibid., August 8, 1875, p. 9.

14. Stover, *American Railroads*, pp. 143–48; "[John Douglas] Stewart's Journal— Railway Travel in 1869–1871," *Railroad History* 127 (October 1972), 59; [Willard], *Tramping with Tramps*, p. 355. In 1869 the average number of freight cars per train was 10 to 15; in 1880, about 30. By the end of the century 50 or more cars were not unusual. Charles Clark, "The Railroad Safety Movement in the United States: Origins and Development, 1869–1893" (Ph.D. dissertation, University of Illinois-Urbana, 1966), p. 16.

15. "Tramps in the West," *Railroad Gazette* 8 (1876), 309; "Tramps," ibid. 10 (1878), 338; "Train Wreckers Sentenced," ibid. 9 (1877), 295–96; "Train Wreckers," ibid. 15 (1883), 159; "A Tramp's Collision," ibid. 15 (1883), 621; "Tramps," ibid. 10 (1878), 423; Bruce, *1877*, p. 99; "Bold Tramps in Iowa," *New York Times*, July 12, 1878, p. 1; "Another Incursion of Tramps," ibid., July 13, 1878, p. 1; "The Tramp," ibid., August 8, 1875; *Philadelphia Inquirer*, May 28, 1885, p. 8; Paul T. Ringenbach, *Tramps and Reformers, 1873–1916: The Discovery of Unemployment in New York* (Westport, Conn.: Greenwood Press, 1973), p. 12.

16. "A Conductor on Tramps," *Railroad Gazette* 9 (1877), 460; "Tramps," ibid. 10 (1878), 406; "Tramps," ibid. 10 (1878), 348; "Tramps," ibid. 9 (1877), 224; "Tramps," ibid. 13 (1881), 439; Samuel Leavitt, "Tramps and the Law," *Forum* 14 (1886), 194–95.

17. "Tramps," *Railroad Gazette* 9 (1877), 309; "Tramps," ibid. 9 (1877), 578; "Tramps," ibid. 10 (1878), 67; "Washing a Tramp," ibid. 14 (1882), 554; "Tramps,"

ibid. 14 (1882), 568; "Tramps," ibid. 10 (1878), 363; *Railway Conductor's Monthly* 2 (1885), 193; George, *Forty Years on the Rail*, pp. 105–06.

18. Hobbs v. Texas and Pacific R. R. Co. 49 Ark. 357 (1887); Rounds v. Delaware, L. and W. R. R. Co. 64 N.Y. 129 (1876); Carter v. Louisville, N. A. and C. R. R. Co. 98 Ind. 552 (1882); Kansas City, Ft. S. and G. Ry. Co. v. Kelly 36 Kansas 655 (1887); Houston and T. C. Ry. Co. v. Grigsby 13 Tex. Civ. App. 639, 35 S. W. 815; *Railroad Gazette* 23 (1891), 371; ibid., 41 (1906), 32; "Trespassers on Trains," *Railway Age* 68 (1920), 330; "Tramps," *Railroad Gazette* 15 (1883), 602.

19. "A Tramp's Ingratitude," *New York Times*, April 26, 1879, p. 1; "Once More the Tramp," *Scribner's Monthly* 15 (1878–79), 882–83; John J. McCook, "Leaves from the Diary of a Tramp: Part IV," *Independent* 54 (1902), 24; Black, *You Can't Win*, p. 127.

20. "A Sign of the Times," *New York Times*, June 17, 1875, p. 4; "Playing with Fire," *New York Tribune*, November 28, 1877, p. 4. "A Very Interesting Report," *Nation* 20 (1878), 50; William Dean Howells, *The Vacation of the Kelwyns: An Idyl of the 1870s* (New York: Harper and Row, 1920), pp. 103, 193, 196; Howells, *The Undiscovered Country* (Boston: Houghton Mifflin, 1880), pp. 134–35; "Terrorized by Tramps," *New York Tribune*, May 4, 1884; Eugene Hayter, *The Troubled Farmer, 1850–1900: Rural Adjustment to Industrialism* (DeKalb: Northern Illinois State University Press, 1968), pp. 153–54.

21. Bruce, *1877*, pp. 186, 68–69; "Tramps," *Railroad Gazette* 10 (1878), 539; "Tramping the Gauntlet," *Philadelphia Inquirer*, May 1885, p. 1; "Severe Treatment for Tramps," *New York Times*, March 20, 1889, p. 2; "The Battle of the Tramps," *New York Tribune*, December 16, 1885, p. 1; Frank Leonard, "'Helping' the Unemployed in the Nineteenth Century: The Case of the American Tramp," *Social Service Review* 40 (1966), 430–32.

22. "Tramps," Clarion, Pa., *Democrat*, November 15, 1877, p. 1 (courtesy of Roberta A. Servey); *Second Annual Report of the Board of Commissioners of Public Charities of the State of Pennsylvania, 1872* (Harrisburg, 1872), p. 19.

23. "Tramps in Regiments," *New York Tribune*, July 28, 1876, p. 4; "Topics of the Times," *Scribner's Monthly* 13 (1876–77), 416; William H. Brewer, "What Shall We Do with Our Tramps?" *New Englander* 37 (1878), 526; Kenneth Allsop, *Hard Travellin': The Hobo and His History* (New York: New American Library, 1967), pp. 110–13; Howells, *Vacation of the Kelwyns*, p. 35.

24. "Playing with Fire," *New York Times*, November 28, 1877, p. 4; "Once More the Tramp," 883; "A Danger for Tramps," *New York Tribune*, March 19, 1882, p. 6; Francis Wayland, "The Tramp Question," *Conference of Boards of Public Charities Proceedings, 1877*, p. 113; Brewer, "What Shall We Do with Our Tramps?" p. 522; Tomás Almaguer, *Racial Fault Lines: The Historical Origins of White Supremacy in California* (Berkeley: University of California Press, 1994), pp. 133–34. This image of the Indian population in California was also applied to the indigenous Mexicans; an 1855 vagrancy law specifically targeted "idle" members of that racial group. Ibid., p. 57. On the conflation of images of striking workers, tramps, and "savage" Indians in 1876–77, see the brilliant study by Richard Slotkin, *The Fatal Environment: The Myth of the Frontier in the Age of Industrialization* (New York: Atheneum, 1985), pp. 476–97.

25. *Fourth Biennial Report of the Board of State Commissioners of Charities of the State of Illinois, 1876* (Springfield, 1877), p. 206; "The Tramp," *New York Times*, August 8, 1875, p. 9. Brewer, "What Shall We Do with Our Tramps?" pp. 521–32; Lee O. Harris, *The Man Who Tramps: A Story of Today* (Indianapolis, 1878), pp. 3, 20, 60–64, 72–73; Horatio Alger, Jr., *Tony, The Hero; or, A Brave Boy's Adventures with a Tramp* (New York, 1890), pp. 14–19, 37–45, 151. Amos Warner, in his standard *American Charities: A Study in Philanthropy and Economics* (New York: Thomas Crowell, 1894), p. 183, would also refer to Cain as "the proto-tramp."

26. Brace, *Dangerous Classes*, pp. 26–28; "Hard Winters," *Nation* 21 (1875), 396; *Fourth Biennial Report of the Board of Charities . . . Illinois, 1876*, pp. 200, 206, 209; *Eleventh Annual Report of the New York State Board of Charities* (Albany, 1878), pp. 260–21; [Willard], *Tramping with Tramps*, p. 391; Josiah Flynt [Willard], *Little Brother: A Story of Tramp Life* (Upper Saddle River, N.J.: Gregg Press, 1902), p. 83.

27. James D. McCabe, Jr., *Lights and Shadows of New York Life; or, Sights and Sensations of the Great City* (Philadelphia: Hubbard, 1872), p. 803; "Reports from States Represented," *Conference of Boards of Public Charities Proceedings, 1876*, p. 22; letter to the editor, *New York Tribune*, September 9, 1873, p. 4; "Immigration," *Philadelphia Inquirer*, May 20, 1885, p. 4. See also the discussion of the composition of the vagrant or homeless class in chapter 6.

28. On the low level of nativism in the immediate post–Civil War period, see John Higham, *Strangers in the Land: Patterns of American Nativism, 1865–1925* (New York: Atheneum, 1971 ed.), pp. 12–34. William G. McGloughlin, *The Meaning of Henry Ward Beecher: An Essay on the Shifting Values of Mid-Victorian America, 1840–1870* (New York: Knopf, 1970), pp. 149–51, is perceptive in analyzing a conservative commentator's view of poverty.

29. "Topics of the Times," p. 416; *Thirteenth Annual Report of the State Board of Charities of Massachusetts, 1877* (Boston, 1877), p. 91; Harris, *The Man Who Tramps*, p. 35; *National Conference of Charities and Correction Proceedings 1878*, p. 118; "Tramps Along the Hudson," *New York Times*, August 9, 1879, p. 5; "The Great American Tramp," *New York Tribune*, December 20, 1885, p. 4.

30. Brace, *Dangerous Classes*, pp. 390–91; Richard L. Dugdale, *The Jukes: A Study in Crime, Pauperism, Disease, and Heredity*, 4th ed. (New York: Putnam's, 1907), pp. 47, 59; Dugdale, "Hereditary Pauperism," *Conference of Boards of Public Charities Proceedings, 1877*, pp. 81–95; Brewer, "What Shall We Do with Our Tramps?" pp. 522–23, 528–30. On the development of hereditarian ideas in the late nineteenth century, see Mark H. Haller, *Eugenics: Hereditarian Attitudes in American Thought* (New Brunswick, N.J.: Rutgers University Press, 1963), chs. 3–4; Kenneth M. Ludmerer, *Genetics and American Society: A Historical Appraisal* (Baltimore: Johns Hopkins University Press, 1972); and Ian R. Dowbiggin, *Keeping America Sane: Psychiatry and Eugenics in the United States and Canada, 1880–1940* (Ithaca: Cornell University Press, 1997), chs. 1–2.

31. Haller, *Eugenics*, pp. 14–16; A. Reynolds, "The Prevention of Pauperism," *National Conference of Charities and Correction Proceedings, 1879*, pp. 213, 215. Harris, *The Man Who Tramps*, p. 22; Alger, *Tony, The Hero*, pp. 7–8, 22; John Hay, *The Bread-Winners*, ed. Charles Vandersee (New Haven: Yale University Press, 1973), p. 113.

32. "Not Pleasant Neighbors," p. 3; "The Tramp," *New York Times*, August 8, 1875, p. 9; "Tramps Again," *New York Tribune*, September 10, 1876, p. 4; "Playing with Fire," ibid., November 28, 1877, p. 4.

33. Dugdale, *The Jukes*, p. 59; *Eleventh Annual Report of the New York State Board of Charities* (New York, 1878), p. 261; Daniel T. Rodgers, *The Work Ethic in Industrial America, 1850–1920* (Chicago: University of Chicago Press, 1978), pp. 14, 22, and 1–22 *passim*; Alan Dawley and Paul Faler, "Working-Class Culture and Politics in the Industrial Revolution: Sources of Loyalism and Rebellion," *Journal of Social History* 9 (1976), 468–77; Walter Licht, *Working for the Railroad: The Organization of Work in the Nineteenth Century* (Princeton: Princeton University Press, 1983), ch. 5; Richard Oestreicher, *Solidarity and Fragmentation: Working People and Class Consciousness in Detroit, 1875–1900* (Urbana: University of Illinois Press, 1986), pp. 106–07. On the development of a northern "ideology" prior to the Civil War, see the classic work by Eric Foner, *Free Soil, Free Labor, Free Men: The Ideology of the Republican Party Before the Civil War* (New York: Oxford University Press, 1970), esp. pp. 111–39.

34. *Eleventh Annual Report of the New York State Board of Charities*, p. 261; Brace, *Dangerous Classes*, p. 98–100; Elizabeth Oakes Smith, *The Newsboy* (New York, 1854), p. 33; "Once More the Tramp," 883; "Topics of the Times," 417; Ringenbach, *Tramps and Reformers*, p. 4. Steady work at some task, however inconsequential, was considered the most important aspect of the treatment of the insane by nineteenth-century asylum managers. See David J. Rothman, *The Discovery of the Asylum: Social Order and Disorder in the Early Republic* (Boston: Little, Brown, 1971), pp.145–46.

35. Editorial, *New York Tribune*, January 13, 1876, p. 4; "Vilest of the Vile," *New York Times*, January 7, 1877, p. 5.

36. Allan Pinkerton, *Strikers, Communists, Tramps, and Detectives* (New York: G. W. Carleton, 1878), pp. 89–95, 307. George L. Cherry, "American Metropolitan Press Reaction to the Paris Commune of 1871," *Mid-America* 32 (1950), 3–12; Bruce, *1877*, pp. 225–29, 232, 237; Herbert G. Gutman, "The Tompkins Square 'Riot' in New York City on January 13, 1874: A Re-Evaluation of Its Causes and Its Aftermath," *Labor History* 6 (1965), 60; Painter, *Standing at Armageddon*, pp. 18–21.

37. "Once More the Tramp," 883; Editorial, *New York Tribune*, November 28, 1877, p. 4; "The Great American Tramp," ibid., December 20, 1885, p. 4; Brewer, "What Shall We Do with Our Tramps?" p. 532; letter to the editor, *New York Tribune*, September 9, 1876, p. 4; Ringenbach, *Tramps and Reformers*, pp. 13–14.

38. Pinkerton, *Strikers, Communists, Tramps, and Detectives*, p. 261; *Chicago Times*, quoted in Bruce, *1877*, pp. 242–43.

39. Harris, *The Man Who Tramps*, pp. 4, 17 19, 218.

40. Ibid., pp. 19–20, 28–29, 43–44, 112, 267–68.

41. Frank Bellew, *The Tramp: His Tricks, Tallies, and Tell-Tales, with All His Signs, Countersigns, Grips, Pass-Words, and Villainies Exposed. By an Ex-Tramp* (New York [1878]), pp. 16–30 passim.

42. Bruce, *1877*, pp. 99, 154, 173, 131, 187, 200, 214, 284; "Amateur Tramping," *New York Times*, January 21, 1878, p. 3.

43. Richard Hofstadter, *The Paranoid Style in American Politics and Other Essays* (New York: Vintage Books, n.d.), pp. 14–23; David Brion Davis, "Some Themes of

Counter-Subversion: An Analysis of Anti-Masonic, Anti-Catholic, and Anti-Mormon Literature," in Davis, *From Homicide to Slavery: Studies in American Culture* (New York: Oxford University Press, 1986), pp. 137–54; Foner, *Free Soil, Free Labor, Free Men*, pp. 9, 73, 97–102, 119–20; Larry Gara, "Slavery and the Slave Power: A Crucial Distinction," *Civil War History* 15 (1969), 5–18; Richard H. Sewell, *Ballots for Freedom: Antislavery Politics in the United States, 1837–1860* (New York: Norton, 1976), pp. 257–60, 267–68.

44. See Bruce, *1877*, pp. 20–21; Jules Tygiel, "Tramping Artisans: Carpenters in Industrial America, 1880–90," and Patricia A. Cooper, "The 'Travelling Fraternity': Union Cigar Makers and Geographic Mobility, 1900–1919," in Eric H. Monkkonen, ed., *Walking to Work: Tramps in America, 1790–1935* (Lincoln: University of Nebraska Press, 1984), pp. 87–138.

45. Bruce, *1877*, p. 68 (quoting *Iron Molders Journal*); Gutman, "The Tompkins Square 'Riot,'" 68–69; *Iron Age*, July 27, 1876; *National Labor Tribune*, August 14, 1875, p. 2; *Weekly Worker*, August 14, 1875, p. 3, quoted in Allsop, *Hard Travellin'*, pp. 113, 118; letter to the editor, *New York Tribune*, September 16, 1876, p. 4; Michael Davis, "Forced to Tramp: The Perspective of the Labor Press, 1870–1900," in Monkkonen, ed., *Walking to Work*, pp. 161–64; Terrance Powderly, *The Path I Trod* (New York: Columbia University Press, 1940), pp. 28–30. For references to Christ and the Apostles as tramps, see Herbert Gutman, "Protestantism and the American Labor Movement," in Gutman, *Work, Culture and Society in Industrializing America* (New York: Vintage Books, 1976), 96n.

46. *Twelfth Annual Report of the State Board of Charities of Massachusetts, 1876*, p. 173; *Eighth Annual Report . . . Massachusetts, 1872*, p. 24; "A Plea for the Tramp," *New York Tribune*, November 18, 1876, p. 4.

47. Sidney Andrews, "Secretary's Report," *Annual Report of the State Board of Charities of Massachusetts, 1874*, pp. 106–07; Leah Feder, *Unemployment Relief in Periods of Depression* (New York: Columbia University Press, 1936), pp. 47–48; Samuel Rezneck, "Distress, Relief, and Discontent in the United States During the Depression of 1873–78," in *Business Depressions and Financial Panics: Essays in American Business and Economic History* (Westport, Conn.: Greenwood Press, 1968), p. 134; Schneider, *Detroit and the Problem of Order*, p. 106.

48. New York Association for Improving the Condition of the Poor, *Thirty-First Annual Report, 1874* (New York, 1874), p. 33; "The Educational Influence of Free Soup," *Nation* 22 (1876), 156; "Soup in Boston," *New York Tribune*, January 13, 1876, p. 4; "A Model Lodging-House," *New York Times*, March 19, 1874, p. 8; Robert T. Davis, "Pauperism in the City of New York," *Journal of Social Science* 6 (1874), 77; *Annual Report of the State Board of Charities of Massachusetts, 1874*, pp. 111–12; David M. Schneider and Albert Deutsch, *The History of Public Welfare in New York State, 1867–1940* (Chicago: University of Chicago Press, 1941), pp. 35–37; *Cleveland Leader*, November 5, 1873, in Works Projects Administration, *Annals*, vol. 56, p. 662.

49. Schneider and Deutsch, *History of Public Welfare*, pp. 27–28; "Increasing Pauperism," *Philadelphia Inquirer*, January 4, 1876, p. 2. Ringenbach, *Tramps and Reformers*, pp. 16–18.

50. Andrews, "Secretary's Report," pp. 180–81; *Fourth Biennial Report of the Board ... of Public Charities ... Illinois, 1876*, p. 98; "The Treatment of Tramps," *New York Times*, December 24, 1877, p. 2; Feder, *Unemployment Relief*, p. 47; Robert H. Bremner, *From the Depths: The Discovery of Poverty in the United States* (New York: New York University Press, 1956), pp. 47–48.

51. Philadelphia Society for Organizing Charity, *Third Annual Report* (Philadelphia, 1881), p. 9; Edward T. Devine, *The Principles of Relief* (New York, 1904), pp. 294–97, 300–302; Schneider and Deutsch, *History of Public Welfare*, pp. 37–38; Feder, *Unemployment Relief*, pp. 31, 63–64; Kenneth L. Kusmer, "The Functions of Organized Charity in the Progressive Era: Chicago as a Case Study," *Journal of American History* 60 (1973), 659; Paul Boyer, *Urban Change and Moral Order in America, 1820–1920* (Cambridge, Mass.: Harvard University Press, 1978); Michael B. Katz, *In the Shadow of the Poorhouse: A Social History of Welfare in America* (New York: Basic Books, 1986), ch. 3.

52. F. D. Sanborn, "The Year's Work," *National Conference of Charities and Correction Proceedings, 1879*, p. 25; Dr. Luther, "Causes and Prevention of Pauperism," *National Conference of Charities and Correction Proceedings*, 1880, p. 248; Francis Wayland and F. B. Sanborn, "Report on Tramp Laws and Indeterminate Sentences," ibid., pp. 277–81; Ringenbach, *Tramps and Reformers*, pp. 23, 24.

53. "Tramps," *New York Tribune*, August 14, 1876, p. 4; *Philadelphia Inquirer*, June 9, 1876, p. 7.

54. "Wholesale Arrests," *Philadelphia Public Ledger*, May 29, 1876, p. 1; "No More Tramps," ibid., June 10, 1876, p. 4; *Philadelphia Inquirer* (1876), June 10, p. 3; June 12, p. 3; June 16, p. 7; June 17, p. 3; June 19, p. 3; June 22, p. 3; June 23, p. 3; June 24, p. 3; June 26, p. 3; June 27, p. 3.

55. *Twelfth Annual Report of the State Board of Charities of Massachusetts, 1876*, pp. 167–73, 176–77, 177–78.

56. "Tramps in Regiments," *New York Tribune*, July 28, 1876, p. 4. "Non-Resident and Alien Paupers," in *Thirteenth Annual Report of the New York State Board of Charities* (Albany, 1880), pp. 213–78, gives the minutes of an argumentative conference between New York and Massachusetts officials. Three examples of "solutions" to the tramp problem that were unacceptable were Brace's pass system, a compulsory registration bureau, and a state-controlled system of workhouses for vagrants. See Ringenbach, *Tramps and Reformers*, p. 20; *Philadelphia Inquirer*, January 5, 1876, p. 2; Dr. Luther, "Causes and Prevention," pp. 248–49. For an excellent example of the strong opposition of Americans to centralization of any kind, even at the local level, see Michael Frisch, *Town into City: Springfield, Massachusetts, and the Meaning of Community, 1840–1880* (Cambridge, Mass.: Harvard University Press, 1972), pp. 215–18.

57. "The Bummers of New York," *New York Times*, November 29, 1868, p. 3; "The Great American Tramp," *New York Tribune*, December 20, 1885, p. 4; *Fourth Biennial Report of the Board ... of Public Charities ... Illinois, 1876*, p. 204; Harris, *The Man Who Tramps*, p. 219; Davis, "Forced to Tramp," p. 164; *Annual Report of the State Board of Charities of Massachusetts, 1872*, pp. 24–25; Carroll D. Wright, "Labor, Pauperism, and Crime," *National Council of Charities and Correction Proceedings, 1878*, p. 162.

58. *Annual Report . . . of the Metropolitan Police, 1867* (New York, 1867), pp. 11, 28–29; Howard O. Sprongle, *The Philadelphia Police: Past and Present* (Philadelphia, 1888), pp. 219–20; Feder, *Unemployment Relief*, pp. 55, 321; "Where the Poor Lodge," *New York Times*, January 17, 1869, p. 3; Frisch, Town into City, pp. 223–24.

59. Warner, *American Charities*, p. 183; "A Growing Evil," *Nation* 26 (1878), 50; William Graham Sumner, "The Forgotten Man," *Social Darwinism: Selected Essays of William Graham Sumner*, ed. Stow Persons (Englewood Cliffs, N.J.: Prentice Hall, 1963), p. 122; "Tramps and Vagrants Not Criminals," *New York Tribune*, March 7, 1883, p. 3.

CHAPTER 4

1. *Railway Age Gazette* 55 (1913), 213. See chapter 6 for data on relative size of homeless population, 1870–1915.

2. For a sample of this literature see "Tramps," *Railroad Gazette* 14 (1882), 108, 336; "Tramps," ibid. 17 (1885), 148; "Tramps in Texas," ibid. 17 (1885), 70–71; *Philadelphia Inquirer*, May 28, 1885, p. 8; "Raid by Tramps," ibid., June 30, 1885, p. 2. See also B. B. Adams, "The Everyday Life of Railroad Men," in Thomas C. Clarke et al., *The American Railway: Its Construction, Development, Management, and Appliances* (New York: Scribner's, 1889), pp. 386–87; Josiah Flynt [Willard], *My Life* (New York: Outing Publishing Co., 1908), pp. 111–12.

3. "How to Deal with Tramps," *New York Times*, December 14, 1892, p. 2; C. G. Truesdale, "Treatment of the Poor in Cities," *Chautauquan* 15 (1892), 184.

4. For a discussion of the tumultuous political and social context of Coxey's "armies" in the 1890s, see Carlos Schwantes, *Coxey's Army: An American Odyssey* (Lincoln: University of Nebraska Press, 1985), and Nell Irvin Painter, *Waiting for Armageddon: The United States, 1877–1919* (New York: Norton, 1987), pp. 117–21 and ch. 4 passim.

5. Editorial, *New York Times*, May 1, 1894, p. 4; O. O. Howard, "The Menace of Coxeyism," *North American Review* 118 (1894), 454; On commandeering of trains (other than by Coxeyite groups), see "The Tramps and the Railroads," *Railroad Gazette* 28 (1894), 454; "The Scrap Heap," ibid. 28 (1894), 549. For typical newspaper stories on tramp attacks, see *Philadelphia Inquirer*, January 13, 1894, p. 5; May 2, 1894, p. 2; May 4, 1894, p. 2; January 27, 1894, p. 2; "The 'Whipping Post' for Tramps," *Century* 49 (1895), 794.

6. See, for example, "Tramps Infest Hudson Valley," *New York Tribune*, August 26, 1900, p. 10; "Tramps Terrorize Rockland County," ibid., September 1, 1900.

7. "Railroads Take Up the Tramp Problem," *New York Times*, September 20, 1907.

8. David G. McCullough, *The Johnstown Flood* (New York: Simon and Schuster, 1968), p. 26; William Aspinwall to John J. McCook, March 11, 1895, in the Social Reform Papers of John James McCook, Antiquarian and Landmarks Society, Hartford, Conn., Roll 12.

9. Robert Louis Stevenson, *Across the Plains, with Other Memories and Essays* (New York: Scribner's, 1898), p. 71; "Tramps," *Railroad Gazette* 15 (1883), 244; "Tramps," ibid. 17 (1885), 341.

10. Ben Reitman, "Following the Monkey" (unpublished manuscript autobiography, University of Illinois at Chicago Circle, 1932), p. 28. On the demographic characteristics of the homeless, see chapter 6.

11. See chapter 7 for examples.

12. James Stevenson, "The Brotherhood of Locomotive Engineers and Its Leaders, 1863–1920" (Ph.D. dissertation, Vanderbilt University, 1954), 170–72, 9–11; "Drunkenness," *Locomotive Engineers' Monthly Journal* 4 (1870), 200–202; "The Drunkard's Lament," ibid. 5 (1871), 16; "Temperance vs. Rum," ibid. 5 (1871), 549–50; "Firemen," ibid. 5 (1871), 8–12 (letter to the editor); "The Influence of Engineers," ibid. 6 (1872), 58–59; "Sobriety," ibid. 9 (1875), 89; Walter M. Licht, *Working for the Railroad: The Organization of Work in the Nineteenth Century* (Princeton: Princeton University Press, 1983), 240–42; Shelton Stromquist, *A Generation of Boomers: The Pattern of Railroad Labor in Nineteenth-Century America* (Urbana: University of Illinois Press, 1987), pp. 106–109. "Dead Beats," *Locomotive Firemen's Magazine* 13 (1889), 208, expresses a similar ideal for firemen.

13. "Hon. James F. Joy," *Locomotive Engineers' Monthly Journal* 3 (1869), 15–22; "Pittsburgh, Fort Wayne & Chicago Railway," ibid. 3 (1869), 85–86; "Correspondence," ibid. 8 (1874), 132; "Arbitration the True Method to Settle Labor Controversy," ibid. 20 (1886), 322; Stevenson, "The Brotherhood," 13 and passim; Robert V. Bruce, *1877: Year of Violence* (Chicago: Quadrangle, 1959), p. 224; Clyde E. Robbins, *Railway Conductors: A Study in Organized Labor* (New York: AMS Press, 1970 [1914]), 15–16, 20; Donald McMurry, *The Great Burlington Strike of 1888* (Cambridge, Mass.: Harvard University Press, 1956), p. 37; P. M. G. Arthur, quoted in Stromquist, *A Generation of Boomers*, p. 107.

14. "Honor of Labor" (letter), *Locomotive Engineers' Monthly Journal* 8 (1874), 77; "Be Not Idle," ibid. 10 (1876), 386; "Self-Made Man," ibid. 11 (1877), 345–46; "Locomotive, Past and Present," ibid. 7 (1873), 49; D. Everett, "Poverty," ibid. 22 (1888), 34–35; "Time Is Money," *Locomotive Firemen's Magazine* 13 (1889), 202–03; "Seniority in Promotion," ibid. 14 (1890), 41.

15. "Ability and Opportunity," ibid: 11 (1887), 265–66; "Seniority in Promotion," ibid. 14 (1890), 41; "Why Men Fail," *Locomotive Engineers' Monthly Journal* 22 (1888), 486.

16. For two general surveys of railroad labor, see David Lee Lightner, "Labor on the Illinois Central Railroad, 1852–1900" (Ph.D. dissertation, Cornell University, 1969), and Licht, *Working for the Railroad*, pp. 164–213 on negative aspects of railroad employment. For the period prior to 1880, Licht's study is nearly definitive.

17. Chauncey Del French, *Railroadman* (New York: Macmillan, 1938), p. 138; Stevenson, "The Brotherhood," p. 2; Charles Clark, "The Railroad Safety Movement in the United States: Origins and Development, 1869–1893" (Ph.D. dissertation, University of Illinois at Urbana, 1966), pp. 43–44; Licht, *Working for the Railroad*, p. 160.

18. Ibid., 241–42, 266–67; "Overwork and Railroad Accidents," *Locomotive Firemen's Magazine* 13 (1889), 200–201; ibid. 13 (1889), 203; K. C. B. to editor, *Locomotive Engineers' Monthly Journal* 27 (1893), 31; Clark, "The Railroad Safety Movement," pp. 50–57, 93–100; Bruce, *1877*, p. 304; McMurry, *Great Burlington Strike*, pp. 17, 28–35, 38–39, 42–44; Stromquist, *A Generation of Boomers*, pp. 113–30.

19. Stromquist, *A Generation of Boomers*, pp. 201–203; John F. Stover, *American Railroads* (Chicago: University of Chicago Press, 1961), 224.

20. Stover, *American Railroads*, pp. 151–52; Adams, "Everyday Life of Railroad Men," pp. 388–93; Bruce, *1877*, pp. 44–45; Clark, "The Railroad Safety Movement," pp. 18–26; "Brakeman's Narrow Escape," *New York Times*, August 21, 1900, p. 1; Stromquist, *A Generation of Boomers*, p. 109.

21. Massachusetts data reprinted in *Eleventh Annual Report of the Bureau of Labor Statistics . . . New Jersey, 1888* (Trenton, 1889), pp. 50–51. Walter Licht concludes that the accident rates were higher in 1889 than they had been before 1880 (he does not discuss post-1889 data) and that "over the course of the nineteenth century, accidents became more numerous and frequent both relatively and absolutely as the work became more hazardous." Licht, *Working for the Railroad*, pp. 194 and 190–94 passim.

22. Stover, *American Railroads*, p. 154; Clark, "Railroad Safety Movement," pp. 360–66; *Fifteenth Annual Report of the Bureau of Labor Statistics . . . Iowa, 1910–1911* (Des Moines, 1912), pp. 312, 313–14; Robert Hunter, *Poverty* (New York: Macmillan, 1904), pp. 36–39. See J. Harvey Reed, *Forty Years a Locomotive Engineer* (Prescott, Wash.: C. H. O'Neil, 1913).

23. Orlando F. Lewis, "Railroad Vagrancy," *Railway Age* 44 (August 2, 1907), 144; Lawrence M. Friedman and Jack Ladinsky, "Law and Social Change in the Progressive Era: The Law of Industrial Accidents," reprinted in Stanley N. Katz and Stanley Kutler, eds., *New Perspectives on the American Past* (Boston: Little, Brown, 1969), p. 188; Licht, *Working for the Railroad*, pp. 199–201; Thomas Schereth, *Victorian America: Transformations in Everyday Life* (New York: Harper and Row, 1991), p. 23.

24. Charles George, *Forty Years on the Rail* (Chicago: Clarke, 1888), p. 182 (see also pp. 197–98); "'Tramp' Railroad Men," *Railroad Gazette* 15 (1883), 121; Stevenson, "The Brotherhood," p. 194; Mrs. Henry B. Jones, "I Wonder Who Was Right," *Locomotive Engineers' Monthly Journal* 27 (1893), 30; H. P. Peebles, "A Solution of the Tramp Problem," *Railway Conductor* 12 (1895), 441–42. See also "Enforced Idleness," *Locomotive Firemen's Magazine* 13 (1889), 488; letter to the editor, *Locomotive Engineers' Monthly Journal* 18 (1884), 525–26.

25. "Tramp, Tramp, Tramp," *Railroad Trainman* 32 (1915), 994; Felix J. Koch, "The Bumper-Riders," *Railway Conductor* 32 (1915), 97–102. See also the letter to the editor, *Railway Conductor* 18 (1901), 221, which described how conductors could all too easily be "thrown out of the system" and find themselves part of the "army of tramps looking for work to make a little money to send home to feed loved ones."

26. "Tramps and Train Wrecking," *Railroad Gazette* 20 (1888), 773; Josiah Flynt [Willard], *Tramping with Tramps: Studies and Sketches of Vagabond Life* (New York: Century, 1899), p. 303; Jack Black [pseud.], *You Can't Win* (New York: Macmillan, 1926), pp. 196, 220–21; Orlando Lewis, "The Vagrant and the Railroad," *North American Review* 85 (1907), 605; Jack London, *The Road* (New York: Macmillan, 1908), pp. 200–201; Edwin Brown, *"Broke": The Man Without a Dime* (Boston: Four Seas, 1920), p. 276; Jim Tully, *Beggars of Life* (New York: J. Cape, 1925), pp. 68, 68–69; Bertha Thompson, *Sister of the Road*, ed. Ben Reitman (New York: Gold Label Books, 1937), pp. 36–37; McNamara v. Great Northern Ry. Co., 63 N. W. 726 (Minn., 1895).

27. [Willard], *Tramping with Tramps*, p. 292; Mullin, *Adventures of a Scholar Tramp*, pp. 225–26.

28. Dunham Walters, "Beating the Railroad," *Railroad Gazette* 36 (1904), 398; ibid. 32 (1901), 166; *The Hobo's Hornbook*, ed. George Milburn (New York: Washburn, 1931), p. 231.

29. Walters, "Beating the Railroad," 398; Thompson, *Sister of the Road*, p. 35; Glen Mullin, *Adventures of a Scholar Tramp* (London: J. Cape, 1925), p. 225; Arthur S. Haddaway, "The Bum and the Bumpers," *New York Times Review and Magazine*, October 8, 1922, p. 6.

30. Powers v. Boston & Maine R. Co., 153 Mass. 188, 26 N. E. 446 (1891); French, *Railroadman*, p. 262.

31. Thompson, *Sister of the Road*, p. 232; Mullin, *Adventures of a Scholar Tramp*, pp. 91, 190, 220; Brown, *"Broke,"* p. 267; [Willard], *Tramping with Tramps*, p. 288.

32. John J. McCook, "Tramps," *Charities Review* 3 (1893), 62–63; Mullin, *Adventures of a Scholar Tramp*, p. 47; Haddaway, "The Bum and the Bumpers," p. 6.

33. McCook, "Tramps," 63. For general background on the distinctive place of brakemen in the railroad hierarchy, see Licht, *Working for the Railroad*, pp. 82–83, 90–91, 182–85; Stromquist, *A Generation of Boomers*, p. 109.

34. On the distinctive status of brakemen in the railroad community, see Clark, "Railroad Safety Movement," pp. 9–10; Licht, *Working for the Railroad*, p. 234.

35. French, *Railroadman*, pp. 15–16, 18–20; Mullin, *Adventures of a Scholar Tramp*, p. 49; [Willard], *Tramping with Tramps*, p. 278.

36. Tully, *Beggars of Life*, pp. 114–15, 236.

37. George, *Forty Years on the Rail*, p. 232; John J. McCook, "Leaves from the Diary of a Tramp, Part II," *Independent* 53 (1901), 2882–83; Josiah Flynt [Willard], *My Life* (New York: Outing Publishing Co., 1908), p. 112.

38. Josiah Flynt [Willard], *Notes of an Itinerant Policeman* (New York, 1902), p. 239; "Tramps," *Railroad Gazette* 12 (1880), 37; "Tramps," ibid. 15 (1883), 602; Mullin, *Adventures of a Scholar Tramp*, p. 185.

39. [Willard], *Notes of an Itinerant Policeman*, pp. 234–37; Josiah Flynt [Willard] and Francis Walton [Alfred Hodder], *The Powers that Prey* (New York, 1900), p. 215; For an interesting example of a railroad worker who continued to identify completely with railroad management's philosophy of rules, regulations, and efficiency—and was greatly annoyed because most of his coworkers did not—see James O. Fagen, *Confessions of a Railroad Signalman* (New York: Houghton Mifflin, 1908), pp. 8–27, 40–43, 133–34.

40. John J. McCook, "The Tramp Problem," National Conference of Charities and Correction, *Proceedings, 1895*, p. 298; [Willard], *Tramping with Tramps*, p. 278.

41. Mullin, *Adventures of a Scholar Tramp*, pp. 36–38, 52–53, 285–87; Francis M. Bjorkman, "How Poughkeepsie Deals with Tramps," *Review of Reviews* 37 (1908), 211–12; "Tree Is His Lock-Up," *New York Times*, August 2, 1909, p. 6; Tully, *Beggars of Life*, p. 129; "Forty Tramps Rounded Up," *New York Tribune*, April 5, 1901, p. 4.

42. "Tramps and Wayfarers," American Statistical Association, *Publications 1900* (New York, 1900), p. 12; Harold Patten, "The Vagrant in California as Seen in the

Records of the Police Courts and County Jails" (Senior honors thesis, University of California at Berkeley, 1916), pp. 32–37, 39–41. See also "Reports of the States," National Conference of Charities and Correction, *Proceedings, 1908*, p. 402; David M. Schneider and Albert Deutsch, *The History of Public Welfare in New York State, 1867–1940* (Chicago: University of Chicago Press, 1941), p. 108.

43. "Tramp Catching Pays in Port Chester," *New York Tribune*, December 23, 1900, p. 14; "Tramps Lured by Prizes," *Philadelphia Inquirer*, January 8, 1894, p. 3; "The Tramp Nuisance," *Philadelphia Public Ledger*, January 13, 1894, p. 5.

44. "Refuge for Tramps," *New York Times*, May 25, 1883, p. 4; ibid., December 17, 1886, p. 4; "Bounty on Jersey Tramps," ibid., January 13, 1904, p. 2; W. H. Davies, *The Adventures of Johnny Walker, Tramp* (London: J. Cape, 1926), p. 63; "Tramp Nuisance in Nassau," *New York Tribune*, January 21, 1899, p. 5; John J. McCook, "A Tramp Census and Its Revelations," *Forum* 15 (1893), 765.

45. See Bruce Smith, *The State Police: Organization and Administration* (New York: Macmillan, 1925); Stanley L. Swart, "The Development of State-Level Police Activity in Ohio, 1802–1928" (Ph.D. dissertation, Northwestern University, 1974), pp. 39–46, 63.

46. W. L. Bull, "Tramping: Its Causes, Present Aspects, and Some Suggested Remedies," National Conference of Charities and Correction, *Proceedings, 1886*, p. 191; Bruce, *1877*, pp. 21–22, 262; Carlos C. Closson, "Unemployed in American Cities," *Quarterly Journal of Economics* 8 (1894); Closson, "Unemployed in American Cities, II," ibid. 8 (1894), 501–02; Donald L. McMurry, *Coxey's Army: A Study of the Industrial Army Movement of 1894* (Boston: Little, Brown, 1929), p. 127.

47. Closson, "Unemployed in American Cities," 201, 202; [Willard], *Tramping with Tramps*, pp. 10–11; Mullin, *Adventures of a Scholar Tramp*, p. 236.

48. Reitman, "Following the Monkey," p. 73; Harry Kemp, *Tramping on Life* (Garden City, N.Y.: Garden City Publishing Co., 1922), pp. 133, 138; Dean Stiff [Nels Anderson], *The Milk and Honey Route* (New York: Vanguard, 1931), pp. 43–44; "Would Repeal 'Hobo' Law," *New York Times*, January 15, 1933, p. 23; "Alabama's Tramp Law," *Railway Conductor* 18 (1901), 27–28; Mullin, *Adventures of a Scholar Tramp*, p. 229.

49. Relevant on this point are C. Vann Woodward, *The Burden of Southern History* (Baton Rouge: Louisiana State University Press, 1968), 29–30; John Higham, "Hanging Together: Divergent Unities in American History," *Journal of American History* 61 (1974), 8–9. The term "primordial" unity originated with Clifford Geertz, but Higham places the concept in the context of American history. John Hope Franklin, in "Public Welfare in the South during the Reconstruction Era, 1865–1880," *Social Service Review* 44 (1970), 385, notes the strength of localism in the South, especially in "a rather strong antipathy toward the kind of centralization represented by a state board of charities." Alan Dawley, in *Struggles for Justice: Social Responsibility and the Liberal State* (Cambridge, Mass.: Harvard University Press, 1991), persuasively argues that the "backward" nature of the American South made that section hostile to any reforms that would modify the nineteenth-century "liberal" state.

50. Black, *You Can't Win*, pp. 154–56; in re May, 1 Northeast Reporter 1021 (1879); "Tramps and Vagrants Not Criminals," *New York Tribune*, March 7, 1883, p. 3; John

Briggs, *History of Social Legislation in Iowa* (Chicago: University of Chicago Press, 1936), pp. 105–06; Kemp, *Tramping on Life*, p. 129; "Boston Driving Out Vagrants," *New York Tribune*, December 28, 1903, p. 9; Tully, *Beggars of Life*, 31–32; Forest W. Lacey, "Vagrancy Law and Other Crimes of Personal Condition," *Harvard Law Review* 66 (1953), 1203–19; Jeffrey S. Adler, "Vagging the Demons and Scoundrels: Vagrancy and the Growth of St. Louis, 1830–1861," *Journal of Urban History* 13 (1986), 3–30. See Arthur H. Sherry, "Vagrants, Rogues, and Vagabonds—Old Concepts in Need of Revision," *California Law Review* 48 (1960), 557–73, especially 561 for a listing of deviants and criminals arrested for vagrancy.

51. On Rybakowski's Army, see Sidney L. Harring, *Policing a Class Society: The Experience of American Cities, 1865–1915* (New Brunswick: Rutgers University Press, 1983), pp. 201–23. Harring gives more credence to the tramp laws as a means of labor discipline than I do.

52. "Slavery Days Recalled," *New York Times*, June 15, 1882, p. 5; Kenneth Allsop, *Hard Travellin': The Hobo and His History* (New York: New American Library, 1967), p. 121; John Dittmer, *Black Georgia in the Progressive Era, 1900–1920* (Urbana: University of Illinois Press, 1977), pp. 87–88; Carl V. Harris, *Political Power in Birmingham, 1871–1921* (Knoxville: University of Tennessee Press, 1977), pp. 198–202; William Cohen, *At Freedom's Edge: Black Mobility and the Southern White Quest for Racial Control, 1861–1915* (Baton Rouge: Louisiana State University Press, 1991), pp. 244–45. On the use of these laws in this manner outside the South, see Don Leschoier, "Harvesters and Hoboes," *Survey* 50 (1923), 504; "Raid on Pittsburgh Negroes," *New York Times*, February 3, 1909, p. 1.

53. *Eighth Annual Report of the State Board of Charities, Massachusetts, 1872* (Boston, 1873), p. 22; *Twenty-Sixth Annual Report of the State Board of Charities, Massachusetts, 1905* (Boston, 1905), vol. 3, p. 5; *Twelfth Annual Report of the State Board of Charities, 1876* (Boston, 1876), pp. 174–75. There are two series of Charities Board Reports; the renumbering of the volumes begins in 1880.

54. "Tramps and Wayfarers," American Statistical Association, *Publications, 1900*, pp. 12–13; H. C. Prentiss to John J. McCook, February 19, 1892, Series 11, Folder D, Social Reform Papers of John J. McCook, Connecticut Historical Society; *Seventeenth Annual Report of the State Board of Charities, Massachusetts, 1896* (Boston, 1896), p. 150; *Annual Report of the State Board of Charities for the Year 1899* (Albany, N.Y., 1900), p. 855; James F. Jackson, "The Rural Tramp," National Conference of Charities and Corrections, *Proceedings, 1903*, p. 402.

55. Information derived from "The American Tramp and What He Costs," *New York Times*, September 8, 1907, p. 10, and from the *Annual Reports* of the State Board of Charities of Massachusetts, 1901–1913. See also Orlando Lewis, "Vagrancy in the United States," National Conference of Charities and Correction, *Proceedings, 1907*, p. 56.

56. Schneider and Deutsch, *History of Public Welfare*, p. 108; Amos G. Warner, *American Charities: A Study in Philanthropy and Economics* (New York: Thomas Crowell, 1894), pp. 183–86; *Railroad Age Gazette* 46 (1909), 1105; *Railroad Age Gazette* 26 (1894), 288; Orlando Lewis, "Railroad Vagrancy," *Railway Age* 44 (1907), 144;

"Tramp Evil Grows; Railroads Suffer," *New York Times*, February 14, 1909, p. 9; "The American Tramp and What He Costs," p. 10; "Railroads Take Up the Tramp Problem," *New York Times*, September 20, 1907, p. 4.

57. Alice Willard Solenberger, *One Thousand Homeless Men* (New York: Survey Associates, 1914), p. 234; "Vagrants on the Pennsylvania," *Railroad Age Gazette* 46 (1909), 374; "Editorial," *Railroad Gazette* 42 (1907), 881; "Magistrates Do Not Punish Tramps," ibid. 71 (1921), 392; Alfred Crozier, "Organized and Unorganized Charity," National Conference of Charities and Correction, *Proceedings, 1897*, p. 157; Reitman, "Following the Monkey," p. 27.

58. Alan Trachtenberg, *The Incorporation of America: Culture and Society in the Gilded Age* (New York: Hill and Wang, 1982), ch. 2. On the railroads specifically, see Warren James Belasco, *Americans on the Road: From Autocamp to Motel, 1910–1945* (Cambridge, Mass.: MIT Press, 1979), pp. 19–25; Wolfgang Schivelbusch, *The Railway Journey: The Industrialization of Time and Space in the Nineteenth Century* (Berkeley: University of California Press, 1986).

59. Except for the issue of unfair hauling rates, negative response to, or reaction against, the railroads in late nineteenth-century America has usually been ignored by historians. See Thurman W. Van Metre, *Early Opposition to the Steam Railroad* (New York, 1929), p. 61, for the claim that all opposition to the railroad died off after the Civil War; and George R. Taylor, *The Transportation Revolution, 1815–1860* (New York: Harper and Row, 1951), p. 75, who argued that only "vested interests, timid individuals, and conservative communities fearful of innovation" opposed the railroad. One case study that provides a useful corrective is Charles Hirschfeld, *The Great Railroad Conspiracy: The Social History of a Railroad War* (East Lansing: Michigan Historical Commission, 1953).

60. See James Burn, *Three Years Among the Working-Classes in the United States During the War* (New York: AMS Press, 1983 [1865]), pp. 138–39; Charles Francis Adams, *Notes on Railroad Accidents* (New York: Putnam's, 1879), pp. 258–59; Eugene Alverez, *Travel on Southern Antebellum Railroads, 1828–1860* (University: University of Alabama Press, 1974), p. 19; "Accidents to Trespassers, Classified," *Railway Age Gazette* 58 (1915), 1131.

61. Seymour D. Thompson, "Railway Fires," *Central Law Review* 43 (1896), 71–74. See the comment in *Yale Law Journal* 147 (1906), 16: "The well settled rule is that railroads are liable for injuries to trespassers only when the railroad has been guilty of gross negligence." This rule was confirmed in Kentucky v. Jones, 188 Southwest Reporter 873 (1916).

62. See Hiram T. Gilbert, *The Railroads and the Courts* (Ottawa, Ill.: Published by author, 1885), pp. 9–10, 492–95. This is a neglected but important contemporary study.

63. Carlos Schwantes, *Coxey's Army: An American Odyssey* (Lincoln: University of Nebraska Press, 1985), pp. 88–103; *Railway Age Gazette* 55 (1913), 213; Orlando Lewis, "The Vagrant and the Railroad," *North American Review* 185 (1907), 606–07; Lewis, "Vagrancy in the United States," 59.

64. J. W. Bradshaw, "Treatment of Tramps in Small Cities," *Charities Review* 5 (1896), 336; Black, *You Can't Win*, pp. 121–22.

CHAPTER 5

1. On the Charity Organization Society (some local branches went under the names Society for Organizing Charity or Associate Charities), see Frank D. Watson, *The Charity Organization Movement in the United States* (New York: Macmillan, 1922); Robert H. Bremner, "Scientific Philanthropy, 1873–1893," *Social Service Review* 30 (1956), 168–73; Robert H. Bremner, *American Philanthropy* (Chicago: University of Chicago Press, 1960), 89–104; Roy Lubove, *The Professional Altruist: The Emergence of Social Work as a Career, 1880–1930* (Cambridge, Mass.: Harvard University Press, 1965), 1–21; and Michael B. Katz, *In the Shadow of the Poorhouse: A Social History of Welfare in America* (New York: Basic Books, 1986), pp. 66–80. My own perspective is presented in "The Functions of Organized Charity in the Progressive Era: Chicago as a Case Study," *Journal of American History* 60 (1973), 657–78. Thomas Bender's discussion of Charles Loring Brace and the Children's Aid Society in *Towards an Urban Vision: Ideas and Institutions in Nineteenth Century America* (Lexington, Ky.: University of Kentucky Press, 1975) is also relevant here. A valuable interpretation of attitudes toward, and responses to, urban poverty in the nineteenth century is Paul Boyer, *Urban Masses and Moral Order in America, 1820–1920* (Cambridge, Mass.: Harvard University Press, 1978).

2. Charles R. Henderson, "How to Care for the Poor Without Creating Pauperism," *Charities Review* 5 (1896), 184; Josephine Shaw Lowell, "Method of Relief of the Unemployed," *Forum* 16 (1894), 662; Albert O. Wright, "The New Philanthropy," National Conference of Charities and Correction, *Proceedings, 1896*, 7; Charles R. Henderson, "The Psychology of Pauperism," *Co-operation* [journal of the Chicago Charity Organization Society] 4 (March 17, 1904), 1–2; "A Strong Arm," *Cleveland Herald*, January 15, 1881, clipping in Family Service Association of Cleveland records, 1867–1976, Western Reserve Historical Society, Container 1; Philadelphia Society for Organizing Charity, *Third Annual Report, 1881* (Philadelphia, 1881), 10; Charles R. Henderson, *Introduction to the Study of the Dependent, Defective, and Delinquent Classes* (Boston: D. C. Heath, 1893), p. 56.

3. [P. W.] Ayres, "Relief in Work," National Conference of Charities and Correction, *Proceedings, 1892*, 438; Charles D. Kellogg, "Charity Organization in the United States," *idem, Proceedings, 1893*, 59; "Municipal Charities in the United States," *idem, Proceedings, 1898*, 118–69; "The Charity Organization Society in the City of Indianapolis," *idem, Proceedings, 1883*, 86; *Monthly Register of the Philadelphia Society for Organizing Charity* 5 (June 15, 1884), 1; "Wayfarers' Lodge," *Philadelphia Inquirer*, June 20, 1885, p. 2; Bradshaw, "The Treatment of Tramps in Small Cities," 230–31; Charles C. Canaday, "Weeding Out the Tramps," *American City* 14 (1916), 270.

4. A. O. Wright, "Vagrancy," National Conference of Charities and Correction, *Proceedings, 1896*, 233; Samuel Leavitt, "The Tramps and the Law," *Forum* 14 (1886), 195; "Tramps and Wayfarers," *American Statistical Association Publications, 1900*, 17; Joseph Lee, "Tramps," *Charities* 14 (1903), 501; David A. Schneider and Albert Deutsch, *History of Public Welfare in the State of New York, 1867–1940* (Chicago: University of Chicago Press, 1941), p. 108; "Organized Charity," *Cleveland Herald*, February 5, 1884, clipping in Family Services Association records, Container 1. See also

Philadelphia Society for Organizing Charity, *Fifth Annual Report* 1883, 10; Paul T. Ringenbach, *Tramps and Reformers, 1873–1916: The Discovery of Unemployment in New York* (Westport, Conn.: Greenwood Press, 1973), 50–52.

5. Philadelphia Society for Organizing Charity, *Sixth Annual Report, 1884* (Philadelphia, 1884), pp. 12–14; "Many Arrests for Vagrancy," *New York Times*, February 1, 1895, p. 6; "Free Lodgings in Station Houses," *Outlook* 53 (1896), 235–36; Leah Feder, *Unemployment Relief in Periods of Depression* (New York: Russell Sage, 1936), pp. 165–68, 212; Lewis, "Vagrancy in the United States," p. 57; Edwin Brown, *"Broke": The Man Without a Dime* (Boston: Four Seas, 1920), p. 122.

6. Philadelphia Society for Organizing Charity, *Eighth Annual Report, 1886* (Philadelphia, 1886), p. 11; *idem, Sixth Annual Report, 1884*, 10–11; *idem, Ninth Annual Report, 1887* (Philadelphia, 1887), p. 9; "A Wayfarers' Lodge," *Philadelphia Inquirer*, June 11, 1885, p, 2; "Beggars Going to the Fair," *New York Times*, May 11, 1893, p. 5; "The Charity Organization Society in the City of Indianapolis," 86.

7. A. F. Sanborn, "A Study of Beggars and Their Lodgings" *Forum* 19 (1895), 207–09.

8. Frances Kellor, *Out of Work: A Study of Unemployment* (New York: Putnam's, 1915), 406; Brown, *"Broke"*, pp. 57–58, 77–78, 86, 257–58; *New York Times*, May 15, 1910, p. 7; Admittance card for Washington, D.C., Municipal Lodging House, in 1901 file, Robins Papers.

9. Lowell, quoted in Lloyd C. Taylor, Jr., "Josephine Shaw Lowell and American Philanthropy," *New York History* 44 (1963), 338–39; Lowell, "Method of Relief," 661–62; John G. Brooks, "The Future Problem of Charity," *Annals of the American Academy of Political and Social Science* 5 (1894), 24–25; James Forbes, "Jockers and the Schools They Keep," *Charities* 14 (1903), 435; Charles R. Henderson, "Rural Police," *Annals of the American Academy of Political and Social Science* 40 (1912), 228–29; Eugene T. Lies, "The Homeless Man," *Co-operation* 5 (1905), 370. See also "Homeless Men in Chicago," ibid. 2 (1902), 3.

10. "To Reclaim the Beggar," *New York Tribune*, January 13, 1895, p. 13; "Beggars Must Work or Starve," ibid., July 19, 1896, p. 30; Edward T. Devine, "The Shiftless and Floating Population," *Annals of the American Academy of Political and Social Science* 10 (1897), 156; A. F. Weber, "The Tramp and the Labor Colony in Germany," *Chautauquan* 26 (1898), 605–10; Edmund Kelly, *The Elimination of the Tramp* (New York: Putnam's, 1908), p. 59.

11. Ibid., p. 72; "The Control of Vagrants," *New York Times*, March 28, 1909, p. 12; "Tramps Are Trumps," *Central Law Journal* 65 (1907), 428–29; *Report of the General Superintendent of Police, 1906* (Chicago, 1906), p. 100; Benjamin C. Marsh, "Causes of Vagrancy and Methods of Eradication," *Annals of the American Academy of Political and Social Science* 23 (1904), 452.

12. See Ringenbach, *Tramps and Reformers*, pp. 109–34, for a discussion of "back to the land" movements.

13. Lowell, quoted in Taylor, "Josephine Shaw Lowell," 345; Charles Loring Brace, *The Dangerous Classes of New York* (New York: Wynkoop and Hallenbeck, 1872), p. 395; Gustavus Myers, "Colonizing the Tramp," *American Review of Reviews* 39 (1909), 312–13; Robert W. Hebberd, letter to the editor, *New York Times*, March 9,

1909, p. 8; Harry R. Bogart, testimony, in *Industrial Relations: Final Report and Testimony Submitted to Congress by the Commission on Industrial Relations* (Washington, D.C., 1916), vol. 5, 5069.

14. Kellor, *Out of Work*, 4; "Address by Hon. James P. Baxter, Mayor of Portland," National Conference of Charities and Correction, *Proceedings, 1904*, 498–99; "Law Breakers," idem, *Proceedings, 1910*, 50; Solenberger, *One Thousand Homeless Men*, p. 237.

15. *Forty-Second Annual Report of the State Board of Charities* (Albany, 1909), 42; "Tramps in Denmark," *New York Times*, March 7, 1909, p. 5; "State Farm for Tramps," ibid., May 30, 1911, p. 5; "Colony Farm Proposed," ibid., May 21, 1911, pt. 5, p. 13; Charles K. Blatchly, "State Farm for Tramps and Vagrants," Survey 24 (1910), 87–89; Schneider and Deutsch, *History of Public Welfare*, 203–04.

16. *Plunkitt of Tammany Hall*, ed. Arthur Mann (New York: E. P. Dutton, 1963 ed.), p. 28; Karen Sawislak, *Smoldering City: Chicago and the Great Fire, 1871–1874* (Chicago: University of Chicago Press, 1995), pp. 85–87, 109–17.

17. Feder, *Unemployment Relief*, pp. 102, 105, 111–12, 132–33; Shelton, *Reformers in Search of Yesterday*, pp. 149–50; Ernest P. Bicknell, "Problems of Philanthropy in Chicago," *Annals of the American Academy of Political and Social Science* 21 (1903), 386.

18. Samuel Reznec, "Unemployment, Unrest, and Relief, . . . 1893–1897," in *Business Depressions and Financial Panics: Essays in American Business and Economic History* (Westport, Conn.: Greenwood Press, 1968), p. 183; Carlos C. Closson, "Unemployed in American Cities," *Quarterly Journal of Economics* 8 (1894), 191; Feder, *Unemployment Relief*, pp. 156–57, 196–97, 212, 261. See George Juergens, *Joseph Pulitzer and the New York World* (Princeton: Princeton University Press, 1966), chs. 8–10, and Michael Schudson, *Discovering the News: A Social History of American Newspapers* (New York: Basic Books, 1978), ch. 3, for comparisons of the style and content of the *New York Times* and the *New York World*.

19. *Monthly Register of the Philadelphia Society for Organizing Charity* 1 (June 15, 1880), 3; Barbour quoted in ibid. 2 (September 15, 1881), 7; Philadelphia Society for Organizing Charity, *Eighth Annual Report, 1886*, p. 12; Brace, *Dangerous Classes*, pp. 390–91; "Thy Neighbor the Beggar," *New York Tribune Supplement*, November 6, 1898, p. 15; Charles Hubbard, "Minutes and Discussion," National Council of Charities and Correction, *Proceedings, 1903*, 469; "The Beggar a Specialist," *Charities* 11 (1902), 365–66.

20. For examples, see "Rich Beggars," *New York Times*, July 23, 18, p. 4; "Rich Beggars," *New York Tribune Illustrated Supplement*, June 18, 1899, p. 1; "Beggars, Old and Young," *New York Tribune*, September 26, 1903, p. 26; "Plan Drive Against Wealthy Beggars," *New York Times*, September 3, 1922, pt. 2, p. 1; "Panhandler's Curse," ibid., September 3, 1922, p. 13; "Editorial," ibid., May 23, 1929, p. 28.

21. "The War on Beggars," *New York Times*, February 3, 1897, p. 12; H. V. R., "No Sinecure," ibid., May 14, 1905, p. 6; "Making the Life of Beggars More Difficult," *New York Tribune*, October 18, 1903, pt. 2, p. 3; Orlando Lewis, "Vagrancy in the United States," National Council of Charities and Correction, *Proceedings, 1907*, 61; "Organized to Prevent Mendicancy," *Survey* 23 (1909), 156; Solenberger, *One Thousand Homeless Men*, p. 168. For extreme fluctuations in arrests for begging in Chicago, see

data for 1901–04 in *Report of the General Superintendent of Police of the City of Chicago . . . 1904* (Chicago, 1905), p. 55.

22. Solenberger, *One Thousand Homeless Men*, pp. 171–72; "Vagrancy No Crime," *New York Times*, April 17, 1909; "Suppress the Beggars," ibid., February 21, 1911, p. 10.

23. Erving Goffman, *The Presentation of Self in Everyday Life* (Garden City, N.Y.: Doubleday, 1956), esp. ch. 2; Glen Mullin, *Adventures of a Scholar Tramp* (London: J. Cape, 1925), p. 138; "Begging as a Fine Art," *Nation* 79 (1904), 517.

24. "Beggars and Begging," *Harper's Weekly*, 46 (1902), 204; "Tricks of the Beggars," *New York Times*, June 8, 1884, p. 4; "Bums—By a Bum," *Saturday Evening Post*, 196 (1924), 173; Jack London, *The Road* (New York: Macmillan, 1908), p. 21. See also Josiah Flynt [Willard], *Tramping with Tramps* (New York: Century, 1899), p. 127.

25. "All 'Sisters' Who Beg in Saloons Are Frauds," *New York Times*, February 19, 1911, pt. 5, p. 11; Ben Reitman, "Following the Monkey" (unpublished autobiography [1932]), University of Illinois at Chicago Circle, p. 40; "C.O.S. Attitude Toward the Beggar," *Charities* 11 (1903), 159; [Willard], *Tramping with Tramps*, p. 128; "New York's Holiday Beggar and His 'Graft,'" *New York Times*, December 25, 1904, p. 3; Jack Black [pseud.], *You Can't Win* (New York, 1926), pp. 69–70; Document 89 ("Faker, Bulgarian, Forty-Five, Plays Deaf and Dumb"), unpag., Box 127, folder 1, Ernest W. Burgess Papers, University of Chicago Library.

26. "Beggars and Their Ways," *New York Times*, December 3, 1882, p. 14; "Concerning Beggars," *New York Tribune*, August 16, 1885, p. 4; "Mendicants in the Metropolis," *Harper's Weekly* 40 (1896), 302; *Literary Digest* (1914), 510; London, *The Road*, p. 17; "A New York Clergyman's Study of the Stranded," *World's Work* 4 (1902), 2510–2515; "Gentlemen Beggars Invade Fifth Avenue," *New York Times*, August 24, 1910, p. 18.

27. "City Beggars," *New York Times*, March 27, 1869, p. 12; C. G. Truesdale, "Treatment of the Poor in Cities," *Chautauquan* 15 (1892), 185; "Mendicants in the Metropolis," 302; Lee Meriweather, *The Tramp at Home* (New York, 1881), p. 50; London, *The Road*, p. 4; Mills quoted in Gregory Woirol, *In the Floating Army: F. C. Mills on Itinerant Life in California* (Urbana: University of Illinois Press, 1992), p. 83. See also [Willard], *Tramping with Tramps*, pp. 273–74; Edward Lee, *Prison, Camp, and Pulpit* (Oswego, N.Y.: R. J. Oliphant, 1889), p. 225; Document 9: "Englishman, Forty-One, Paralyzed Arm, . . . Mendicant," Box 127, folder 1, Burgess Papers.

28. Hutchins Hapgood, *The Spirit of the Ghetto: Studies in the Jewish Quarter of New York* (New York: Schocken, 1965 ed.), pp. 53 and 53–67 *passim*; "Schnorrers," *New York Tribune Supplement*, January 20, 1901, p. 13.

29. "Rich Beggars," *New York Tribune*, June 18, 1899, p. 1; "Beggar of 98 Had Money," *New York Times*, April 8, 1905, p. 6; "$1,727 on 'Starving' Pair," ibid., March 21, 1922, p. 17. The estimate of one hundred schnorrers was made by H. V. R. (not otherwise identified), "No Sinecure," p. 6.

30. Harvey Zorbaugh, *The Gold Coast and the Slum: A Sociological Study of Chicago's Near North Side* (Chicago: University of Chicago Press, 1929), p. 164; "Honorable Guild of Beggars," *New York Tribune*, June 23, 1899, p. 6; Shelton, *Reformers in Search of Yesterday*, pp. 131–32. Catholic charities generally had a more sympathetic attitude toward the homeless than did Protestant or German-Jewish charities. See John

Glenn, "Co-operation Against Begging," *Charities Review* 1 (1891), 70–71; "Tramp Reign of Terror," *New York Tribune*, August 23, 1903, p. 4; Shelton, *Reformers in Search of Yesterday*, pp. 133, 142; Ringenbach, *Tramps and Reformers*, pp. 84–85.

31. *Monthly Register of the Philadelphia Society for Organizing Charity* 1 (September 15, 1881), 7.

32. John J. McCook, "Leaves from the Diary of a Tramp [II]," *Independent* 53 (1901), 2885; [Willard], *Tramping with Tramps*, p. 105; Black, *You Can't Win*, p. 171.

33. The term "falling from grace" is taken from Katherine S. Newman's insightful study, *Falling from Grace: The Experience of Downward Mobility in the American Middle-Class* (New York, 1988).

34. Mariner J. Kent, "The Making of a Tramp," *Independent* 55 (1903), 677–70; Leonard U. Blumberg, Thomas E. Shipley, Jr., and Stephen F. Barsky, *Liquor and Poverty: Skid Row as a Human Condition* (New Brunswick: Rutgers Center of Alcohol Studies, 1978), pp. 50–51; Closson, "Unemployed in American Cities," 192; Carlos C. Closson, "Unemployed in American Cities, II," *Quarterly Journal of Economics* 8 (1894), 463–65; Jesse Dees, Jr., *Flophouse* (Francestown, N.H.: M. Jones, 1948), 21; Feder, *Unemployment Relief*, 258–61, 264; "Says Tramps Fill the 'Bread Line,'" New York Times, June 9, 1908, p. 7; "Plenty of Soup for the Hungry," *Philadelphia Inquirer*, January 6, 1897, p. 5.

35. Letter to the editor, *New York Tribune*, September 26, 1880, p. 6. See also Philadelphia Society for Organizing Charity, *Third Annual Report, 1881* (Philadelphia, 1881), p. 10; Lyman Abbott, "The Personal Problem of Charity," *Forum* 16 (1894), 665–66.

36. Shelton, *Reformers in Search of Yesterday*, pp. 128, 136, 142. On Protestant support for the charity reformers, see Nathan I. Huggins, *Protestants Against Poverty: Boston's Charities, 1870–1900* (Westport, Conn.: Greenwood Press, 1971); Kusmer, "Functions of Organized Charity in the Progressive Era," 673; Philip S. Benjamin, *The Philadelphia Quakers in the Industrial Age, 1865–1920* (Philadelphia: Temple University Press, 1976), pp. 106–07.

37. Perhaps because it was published by a theological publishing house, Norris Magnuson's important study, *Salvation in the Slums: Evangelical Social Work, 1865–1920* (Metuchen, N.J.: Scarecrow Press, 1977), has been neglected by historians. The publication of Diane Winston's *Red-Hot and Righteous: The Urban Religion of the Salvation Army* (Cambridge, Mass.: Harvard University Press, 1999) breaks new ground in understanding evangelical religion in its urban context.

38. S. H. Hadley, *Down in Water Street: A Story of Sixteen Years' Life and Work in Water Street Mission* (New York: F. H. Revell, 1902); Arthur Bonner, *Jerry McAuley and His Mission* (Neptune, N.J.: Loizeaux, 1967); Magnuson, *Salvation in the Slums*, pp. 2–8, 9–17, 30; E. H. McKinley, *Somebody's Brother: A History of the Salvation Army Men's Social Service Department, 1891–1985* (Lewiston: Mellen Press, 1986), p. 53; Closson, "Unemployed in American Cities," 214; Alvin F. Harlow, *Old Bowery Days* (New York, 1931), p. 405.

39. Henry A. Wisbey, Jr., *Soldiers Without Swords: A History of the Salvation Army in the United States* (New York: Macmillan, 1955), p. 97; Magnuson, *Salvation in the*

Slums, pp. 93, 101–02, 48–49; Winston, *Red-Hot and Righteous*, pp. 119–20; Shelton, *Reformers in Search of Yesterday*, p. 137.

40. Hulda Friedrichs, "The 'Bottom Dog,'" in *Selected Papers on the Social Work of the Salvation Army* (London: Salvation Army, 1907), pp. 8–9; Magnuson, *Salvation in the Slums*, pp. 48–50, 55–58, 82–83; Marion Louise Marshall, "The Salvation Army Women's Social Service for the Unmarried Mother" (M.A. thesis, Columbia University School of Social Work, 1943), pp. 18–19; W. H. J., "A Mighty Power for Good," *Demarest's Family Magazine* 32 (May 1896), pp. 394, 396, clipping in Salvation Army Archives, Alexandria, Virginia [hereafter SAA]; "Children's Bread Line Is Sad New York Spectacle," *Columbus [Ohio] Citizen*, March 21, 1905, clipping in Lawrence Castagna Papers, SAA; Marlise Johnston, "The Woman Out of Work," *Review of Reviews and the World's Work* 87 (1933), 31; Winston, *Red-Hot and Righteous*, pp. 128–29.

41. [Nels Anderson], *The Milk and Honey Route* (New York: Vanguard, 1931), pp. 54, 58; Theodore Dreiser, *The Color of a Great City* (New York: Boni and Liveright, 1925), pp. 205–06. Robert Wiebe, *The Search for Order, 1877–1920* (New York: Hill and Wang, 1967), identified the growth of bureaucratic thinking as a key feature of the Progressive era.

42. Dreiser, *Color of a Great City*, 207–08; Wyckoff, *The Workers, An Experiment in Reality: The West*, pp. 15–21; Lennox Kerr, *Back Door Guest* (New York: Arno Press, 1974 [1927]), pp. 55–60; Lee, *Prison, Camp, and Pulpit*, p. 191; Frank O. Beck, *Hobohemia* (Rindge, N.H.: R. R. Smith, 1956), p. 21.

43. Dees, *Flophouse*, p. 13. Keith Lovald, "From Hobohemia to Skid Row: The Changing Community of the Homeless Man" (Ph.D. dissertation, University of Minnesota, 1960), pp. 135–36; Wisbey, *Soldiers Without Swords*, p. 97; Ben Reitman, "Following the Monkey," pp. 49–52; Magnuson, *Salvation in the Slums*, pp. 92–93.

44. Taylor, "Josephine Shaw Lowell," 358–59; "Begging on Boston's Streets," *Survey* 23 (1909), 3; Devine, "The Shiftless and Floating Population," 162–63; Lewis, "Vagrancy in the United States," 64; "Minutes and Discussion," National Conference of Charities and Correction, *Proceedings, 1906*, pp. 506–09.

45. Freidenreich, "The 'Bottom Dog,'" p. 8; Wisbey, *Soldiers Without Swords*, pp. 102–05; Magnuson, *Salvation in the Slums*, pp. 96–101; McKinley, *Somebody's Brother*, pp. 41–42, 75–77.

46. McKinley, *Somebody's Brother*, p. 15.

47. Lee, *Prison, Camp, and Pulpit*, 225; Magnuson, *Salvation in the Slums*, pp. xiv–xv, 43; Lizabeth Cohen, *Making a New Deal: Industrial Workers in Chicago, 1919–1939* (Cambridge, Eng.: Cambridge University Press, 1990), p. 60. For a discussion of the use of Protestantism to further labor's goals in the late nineteenth century, see Herbert Gutman, "Protestantism and the American Labor Movement: The Christian Spirit in the Gilded Age," in Gutman, *Work, Culture, and Society in Industrializing America* (New York: Vintage, 1976), pp. 79–117.

48. Warner, *American Charities*, pp. 187–90. See also A. O. Wright, "The Defective Classes," National Conference of Charities and Correction, *Proceedings, 1891*, 227; Marsh, "Causes of Vagrancy and Methods of Eradication," 445–52.

49. Jeffrey Brackett, quoted in "Tramps," *Charities* 14 (1903), 500–501.

50. William H. Allen, "The Vagrant: Social Parasite or Social Product," National Conference of Charities and Correction, *Proceedings, 1903*, 379–86; Robert Hunter, *Poverty* (New York: Macmillan, 1904), 120–22, 124, 127, 131, 328, 336–37. For a discussion of Hunter's career, see Peter d'A. Jones's introduction to the Harper Torchbook edition of *Poverty*.

51. See, for example, the derogatory comments about Hunter made by Edward T. Devine in 1908, quoted in Ringenbach, *Tramps and Reformers*, 144.

52. Raymond Robins, "The One Main Thing," National Conference of Charities and Correction, *Proceedings, 1907*, 326–34; Raymond Robins, "The 'Spent Man,'" *Charities* 11 (1903), 237–38; Philip Davis, "Child Labor and Vagrancy," *Chautauquan* 50 (1908), 416–24; Allen F. Davis, "Raymond Robins: The Settlement Worker as Municipal Reformer," *Social Service Review* 33 (1959), 131–41.

53. Solenberger, *One Thousand Homeless Men*.

54. Ibid., pp. 187–88.

55. Roy P. Gates, "The Problem of Homeless Men," *The Family* 21 (1921–22), 85; Harold Patten, "The Vagrant in California as Seen in the Records of the Police Courts and County Jails" (Senior honors thesis, University of California at Berkeley, 1916), p. 43; Stuart Rice, "The Homeless," *Annals of the American Academy of Political and Social Science* 77 (1918), 147.

56. Frank Laubach, *Why There Are Vagrants* (New York: Columbia University Press, 1916); Nels Anderson, *The Hobo: The Sociology of the Homeless Man* (Chicago: University of Chicago Press, 1923), pp. 85–86 and passim. Laubach's study was a Ph.D. dissertation published in booklet form.

57. On variations in municipal facilities for the homeless and use of the work test, see *Report of the Superintendent of Police of Chicago, 1907* (Chicago, 1907), pp. 96–97; Laubach, *Why There Are Vagrants*, p. 101; Dees, *Flophouse*, pp. 25, 44; "Hobo Hotel Founded by Mayor of Buffalo," *New York Times*, January 13, 1926, p. 2; Pretzer, "Care of the Homeless in Cleveland," 43; Robert S. Wilson, *Community Planning for Homeless Men and Boys: The Experience of Sixteen Cities in the Winter of 1930–31* (New York: Family Welfare Association, 1931), *passim*; Brown, *"Broke"*, pp. 99, 103.

58. Feder, *Unemployment Relief*, p. 245; Katz, *In the Shadow of the Poorhouse*, p. 154.

59. Closson, "Unemployed in American Cities," 169–74, 179 181; "To Feed the Poor To-Day," *New York Tribune*, January 1, 1894, p. 5; Seymour Mandelbaum, *Boss Tweed's New York* (New York, 1965); Huggins, *Protestants Against Poverty*, pp. 139, 145–46; Lubove, *Professional Altruist*, p. 9; Kusmer, "Functions of Organized Charity," 667.

60. For an early example, see "Brief. Re. The Shelters" (March 2, 1904, memorandum), SAA. This is a very blunt appraisal of the physical condition of shelters in New York, Connecticut, New Jersey, and Philadelphia, and the characteristics of their managers. In almost every case the key question was whether the institution in question was operating in the black. (Most were.)

61. Feder, *Unemployment Relief*, pp. 246–47; Charles Richmond Henderson, "How Change Met the Unemployment Problem of 1915," *American Journal of Sociology* 20 (1915), 724–27; McKinley, *Somebody's Brother*, p. 88; Walter R. Hoy, "The Care of the

Homeless in St. Louis," *The Family* (1928), 216; Winston, *Red-Hot and Righteous*, pp. 173–77, 218–19.

62. Eugene Lies, "Public Outdoor Relief in Chicago," National Conference of Charities and Correction, *Proceedings, 1916*, 353; Stuart Rice, "The Homeless," *Annals of the American Academy of Political and Social Science* 77 (1918), 147; Fred Johnson, "The Division of Family Casework Between Public and Private Agencies, *idem, Proceedings, 1919*, 338; Philip Klein, *The Burden of Unemployment* (New York: Russell Sage, 1923), p. 166.

CHAPTER 6

1. The main problem with most historical data on the homeless is the anonymity of the people being counted. Officials seldom made an effort to record individual names of those seeking assistance, so the same homeless person might be recorded many times during the course of a year. As a result, yearly data on lodgings in police stations or shelters provide a fairly good idea of relative changes in homelessness, but they overestimate the absolute size of the homeless population at any point in time.

2. On increased police attention to vagrants in New York and Chicago at this time, see Amy Dru Stanley, "Beggars Can't Be Choosers: Compulsion and Contract in Postbellum America," *Journal of American History* 78 (1992), 1278–80.

3. In Massachusetts, between 1872–73 and 1874–75, the number of vagrants receiving public assistance increased from 88,037 to slightly over 200,000. After fluctuating again during the depression of the 1880s, however, the number declined to only 140,00 during the prosperous years of 1890–93, then rose to 226,679 in 1893–94 with the onset of another depression. *Annual Reports of the State Board of Public Charities [later State Board of Welfare] of Massachusetts*, 1874–1894. The numbers were much smaller in Pennsylvania, but followed a similar pattern, which continued into the World War I era. *Annual Reports of the Board of Commissioners of Public Charities of the Commonwealth of Pennsylvania.*

4. "Magistrates Do Not Punish Tramps," *Railway Age* 71 (1921), 423.

5. David Montgomery, "The 'New Unionism' and the Transformation of Workers' Consciousness in America, 1909–22," in Montgomery, *Workers' Control in America: Studies in the History of Work, Technology, and Labor Struggles* (Cambridge, Eng.: Cambridge University Press, 1979), p. 102; *Unemployment in the United States, Bureau of Labor Statistics, Bulletin No. 195* (Washington, 1916), pp. 6–7, 57–65; Davis R. Dewey, "Irregularity of Employment," *Publications of the American Economic Association* 9 (1894), pp. 525–39; John A. Fitch, *Causes of Industrial Unrest* (New York, 1917), pp. 137–64; Alexander Keyssar, *Out of Work: The First Century of Unemployment in Massachusetts* (Cambridge, Eng.: Cambridge University Press, 1986), ch. 3; Robert Hunter, *Poverty* (New York: Macmillan, 1904), p. 138. On packinghouse workers, see James R. Barrett, *Work and Community in the Jungle: Chicago's Packinghouse Workers, 1894–1922* (Urbana: University of Illinois Press, 1987), pp. 28–30; Rick Halpern, *Down on the Killing Floor: Black and White Workers in Chicago's Packinghouses, 1904–54* (Urbana: University of Illinois Press, 1997), pp. 29–30.

6. Stuart Rice, "The Homeless," *Annals of the American Academy of Political and Social Science* 77 (1918), 143; Nels Anderson, *The Hobo: The Sociology of the Homeless Man* (Chicago: University of Chicago Press, 1923), pp. 64–65; Keith A. Lovald, "From Hobohemia to Skid Row: The Changing Community of the Homeless Man" (Ph.D. dissertation, University of Minnesota, 1960), pp. 61–65. On the irregular nature of dock work, see David Montgomery, *The Fall of the House of Labor: The Workplace, the State, and American Labor Activism, 1865–1925* (Cambridge, Eng.: Cambridge University Press, 1987), pp. 98–99; Eric Arneson, *Waterfront Workers of New Orleans: Race, Class, and Politics, 1863–1923* (Urbana: University of Illinois Press, 1991), pp. 40–41.

7. Walter A. Wyckoff, in *The Workers, An Experiment in Reality: The West* (New York: Scribner's, 1898), pp. 40–85; Glen A. Mullin, *Adventures of a Scholar Tramp* (London: J. Cape, 1925), p. 88.

8. Robert H. Bremner, *From the Depths: The Discovery of Poverty in the United States* (New York: New York University Press, 1956), pp. 73–75, 250–56; Kurt Ketzel, "Railroad Management's Response to Operating Employees Accidents, 1890–1913," *Labor History* 21 (1980), 351–68; Robert Asher, "The Limits of Big Business Paternalism: Relief for Injured Workers in the Years Before Workmen's Compensation," in *Dying for Work: Workers' Safety and Health in Twentieth-Century America*, ed. David Rosner and Gerald Markowitz (Philadelphia: Temple University Press, 1987), pp. 19–33; Richard Oestreicher, *Solidarity and Fragmentation: Working People and Class Consciousness in Detroit, 1875–1900* (Urbana: University of Illinois Press, 1986), pp. 14–16. A valuable contemporary case study is Crystal Eastman, *Work-Accidents and the Law* (New York: Charities Publications Committee, 1910).

9. Solenberger, *One Thousand Homeless Men*, pp. 44, 48–49; Laubach, *Why There Are Vagrants*, pp. 60–63; *Report of the Police Department of New York City, 1902* (New York, 1902), pp. 27–31. The history of the employment—or lack of employment—of the physically handicapped remains to be written.

10. The Vagrancy Dockets are located in the Philadelphia City Archives. The sample was obtained by using data for all individuals arrested for vagrancy or idleness during the first two weeks of March, June, September, and December for both years.

11. The percentage of foreign-born among tramps in New York State during 1875–76 was similar, and like the Philadelphia vagrants, few were recent arrivals in the United States. See Michael B. Katz, *Poverty and Public Policy in American History* (New York: Academic Press, 1983), pp. 169–70.

12. Irish percentage estimated from data in Theodore Hershberg et al., "A Tale of Three Cities: Blacks, Immigrants, and Opportunity in Philadelphia, 1850–1880, 1930, 1970," in Hershberg, ed., *Philadelphia: Work, Space, Family and Group Experience in the Nineteenth Century* (New York: Oxford University Press, 1981), p. 465.

13. On the relative invulnerability of white-collar workers in the late nineteenth century to unemployment, see Keyssar, *Out of Work*, pp. 53–54. The number of clerical workers at this time, however, was much smaller than in subsequent decades. In Cleveland in 1870, only 7.4 percent of the males and 1.7 percent of females were clerical workers. Among Irish workers of both sexes, only 1.7 percent were lower-level white-collar workers. See comparative data by ethnic and racial group in Kenneth L.

Kusmer, *A Ghetto Takes Shape: Black Cleveland, 1870–1930* (Urbana: University of Illinois Press, 1976), p. 20.

14. Information on Callahan from Vagrancy Dockets, Philadelphia House of Correction, December 1875, registration no. 8801.

15. Population figures from Hershberg et al., "A Tale of Three Cities," p. 465.

16. Vagrancy Dockets, Philadelphia House of Correction, June 1875, registration no. 5419.

17. See Hasia Diner, *Erin's Daughters in America: Irish Immigrant Women in the Nineteenth Century* (Baltimore: Johns Hopkins University Press, 1983), pp. 108–09 and ch. 5 *passim*, and Kerby A. Miller, *Emigrants and Exiles: Ireland and the Irish Exodus to North America* (New York: Oxford University Press, 1985), pp. 318–19. On the negative consequences of male desertion on women and children, see *Annual Report of Bethel Associated Charities, . . . November to February, 1887* (Cleveland, n.p.), p. 7, in Family Service Association records, container 1, Western Reserve Historical Society, Cleveland, Ohio.

18. Nels Anderson, *The Homeless in New York* (New York: Welfare Council, 1934), p. 13. On the socioeconomic background of prostitutes, see Barbara Meil Hobson, *Uneasy Virtue: The Politics of Prostitution and the American Reform Tradition* (New York: Basic Books, 1987), ch. 4, and Timothy Gilfoyle, *City of Eros: New York City, Prostitution, and the Commercialization of Sex* (New York: Norton, 1992), pp. 49–72.

19. Vagrancy Dockets, House of Correction, June 1874; registration no. 1072. Record keepers listed the names of individual inmates only intermittently, and it was rare for them to provide the kind of detailed information used to describe Mary Carlin.

20. Almost a third of homeless Irish women in the Philadelphia Almshouse in 1874 were over age 50, compared to about 3 percent of homeless women born in Philadelphia. Data (not a sample) compiled from Philadelphia Almshouse Register, 1874, Philadelphia City Archives.

21. Alice Kessler-Harris, *Out to Work: A History of Wage-Earning Women in the United States* (New York: Oxford University Press, 1982), pp. 49–72; quotation from Leonard Blumberg, Thomas E. Shipley, Jr., and Stephen F. Barsky, *Liquor and Poverty: Skid Row as a Human Condition* (New Brunswick, N.J.: Rutgers Center of Alcohol Studies, 1978), p. 39.

22. A similar "masculinization" of the almshouse populations occurred during the post–Civil War decades. Michael B. Katz, *In the Shadow of the Poorhouse: A Social History of Welfare in America* (New York: Basic Books, 1986), pp. 90–91.

23. These generalizations draw on data from *Annual Reports of the Society for Organizing Charity* (Philadelphia, 1885–1908) and New York City, Department of Public Welfare, *Annual Reports, 1900–1910* (New York, 1901–1911).

24. Katz, *Shadow of the Poorhouse*, pp. 87–88; Karen Sawislak, *Smoldering City: Chicagoans and the Great Fire of 1871* (Chicago: University of Chicago Press, 1995), p. 87 (quotation); Philadelphia Society for Organizing Charity, *Concerning Tramps and Beggars: An Important Announcement* (Philadelphia, 1901 [pamphlet]), [p. 12].

25. Leah Feder, *Unemployment Relief in Periods of Depression* (New York: Russell Sage, 1936), p. 65; *Second Annual Report of the Bethel Associated Charities . . . 1886* (n.p., 1887), p. 3; "Semi-Annual Meeting of Board of Trustees of the Associated Charities,

Cleveland, Ohio, Nov. 20, 1905," in Family Services Association records, Container 1; *Monthly Register of the Philadelphia Society for Organizing Charity* 6 (1884), 1; Mary Conyton, quoted in Martha May, "The 'Problem of Duty': Family Desertion in the Progressive Era," *Social Service Review* 62 (1988), 44; Theda Skocpol, *Protecting Soldiers and Mothers: The Political Origins of Social Policy in the United States* (Cambridge, Mass.: Harvard University Press, 1992), ch. 6. For a superb case study of a private religious organization that worked with destitute or delinquent girls or young women, see Suellen Hoy, "Caring for Chicago's Women and Girls: The Sisters of the Good Shepherd, 1859–1911," *Journal of Urban History* 23 (1997), 260–94. On women's charitable endeavors in general, see Lori D. Ginzberg, *Women and the Work of Benevolence: Morality, Politics and Class in the Nineteenth-Century United States* (New Haven: Yale University Press, 1990).

    26. Jacob Riis, *How the Other Half Lives* (New York: Dover Press ed., 1971 [1890]), pp. 158–60; LeRoy Ashby, *Saving the Waifs: Reformers and Dependent Children, 1890–1917* (Philadelphia: Temple University Press, 1984); Katz, *In the Shadow of the Poorhouse*, pp. 119–20; Nurith Zmora, *Orphanages Reconsidered: Child Care Institutions in Progressive Era Baltimore* (Philadelphia: Temple University Press, 1994), pp. 47–50. For an excellent summary of child-saving activities, including institutions, see Priscilla Ferguson Clement, *Growing Pains: Children in the Industrial Age, 1850–1890* (New York: Twayne, 1997), ch. 4.

    27. See Skocpol, *Protecting Soldiers and Mothers*, ch. 8.

    28. Annual Reports of the Society for Organizing Charity (Philadelphia, 1894–1908). The 5–6 percent figure, from the printed census, is probably an underestimate of the actual black population. Regardless, blacks were no longer underrepresented among the homeless.

    29. Keyssar, *Out of Work*, pp. 88–89.

    30. For a case study of the economic decline for black northerners during this period, see Kusmer, *A Ghetto Takes Shape*, ch. 4.

    31. E. R. L. Gould, "How Baltimore Banished and Helped the Idle," *Forum* 17 (1894), 500; John J. McCook, "A Tramp Census and Its Revelations," ibid. 15 (1893), 756. Data on Irish lodgers from *Annual Reports* of the mayor of Philadelphia.

    32. *Annual Report of the Society for Organizing Charity* (Philadelphia, 1906); *Report of the Superintendent of Police of the City of Chicago . . . December 31. 1906* (Chicago, 1907), 35A; Solenberger, *One Thousand Homeless Men*, p. 20; Howard Mingos, "An Outdoor Lodging," *New York Times Review and Magazine* (October 16, 1921), 31. Annual Reports of the New York Municipal Lodging House, in New York City, Department of Public Welfare, *Annual Reports*, show an increase in native-born lodgers from 55 to 68 percent between 1902 and 1924.

    33. Solenberger, *One Thousand Homeless Men*, pp. 216–17; [Willard], *Tramping with Tramps*, p. 235; John J. McCook, "Leaves from the Diary of a Tramp: Part IV," *Independent* 54 (January 16, 1902), 154; Ben Reitman, "Following the Monkey" (unpublished autobiography, University of Illinois at Chicago Circle, 1932), pp. 5–6; John J. McCook, "Tramps," *Charities Review* 3 (1893), 66; Dean Stiff [Nels Anderson], *The Milk and Honey Route* (New York: Vanguard, 1931), p. 38; Walter Wyckoff, *A Day*

with a Tramp and Other Days (New York: Scribner's, 1901), 20; Jim Tully, *Beggars of Life* (New York: J. Cape, 1925), p. 72.

34. "The American Tramp," *New York Tribune*, August 13, 1891, p. 6; McCook, "Tramps," 66; Josiah Flynt [Willard], *Notes of an Itinerant Policeman* (Boston: L. C. Page, 1900), p. 127.

35. New York City, Department of Public Welfare, *Annual Report, 1906* (New York, 1907), p. 314; New York City, Department of Public Welfare, *Annual Report, 1908* (New York, 1909), p. 630; Department of Public Welfare, City of New York, *Annual Report, 1931* (New York, 1932), p. 82. The percentage of women who were native-born lagged behind not only homeless men but prostitutes also. By the World War I era, about 70 percent of prostitutes in New York were native-born. Gilfoyle, *City of Eros*, p. 292.

36. About 7 percent of the men interviewed by McCook in 1891–92 stated they were married, and Alice Solenberger recorded 8 percent married and another 6 percent divorced or separated. McCook, "A Tramp Census and Its Revelations," 757; Solenberger, *One Thousand Homeless Men*, 20.

37. See also Benjamin Marsh, "Causes of Vagrancy and Methods of Eradication," *Annals of the American Academy of Political and Social Science* 22 (1904), 454; Solenberger, *One Thousand Homeless Men*, p. 20; and, for data on Minneapolis, Keith A. Lovald, "From Hobohemia to Skid Row: The Changing Community of the Homeless Man" (Ph.D. dissertation, University of Minnesota, 1960), p. 170.

38. McCook, "Leaves from the Diary of a Tramp: Part IV," 28; John J. McCook, "Increase of Tramping: Cause and Cure," *Independent* 54 (1902), 624; "Tramp Reign of Terror," *New York Tribune*, August 23, 1903, p. 4; Solenberger, *One Thousand Homeless Men*, pp. 216–17; Nels Anderson, "Summary of a Study of Four Hundred Tramps, Summer 1921" (Ernest W. Burgess Papers, University of Chicago Library, Box 127, folder 2).

39. Laubach, *Why There Are Vagrants*, p. 69; John N. Webb, *The Transient Unemployed* (Washington: Government Printing Office, 1935), p. 121.

40. Vagrancy Dockets, Philadelphia House of Correction; Gould, "How Baltimore Banished and Helped the Idle," 500; Marsh, "Causes of Vagrancy and Methods of Eradication," 454; Solenberger, *One Thousand Homeless Men*, p. 135; data on lodgers from *Annual Reports of the Philadelphia Society for Organizing Charity, 1905–08*. McCook's survey in 1891 found 41.4 percent of tramps to be unskilled. McCook, "A Tramp Census and Its Revelations," 756–57.

41. Solenberger, *One Thousand Homeless Men*, p. 135.

42. Brenda Shelton, *Reformers in Search of Yesterday: Buffalo in the 1890s* (Albany: State University of New York Press, 1974), p. 141; Solenberger, *One Thousand Homeless Men*, pp. 20, 131–32; Marsh, "Causes of Vagrancy," 454; Laubach, *Why There Are Vagrants*, pp. 16–20; *Annual Message of the Mayor of Philadelphia, 1912*, p. 337.

43. An almost identical proportion of clerical workers used the wayfarers' lodges in Philadelphia at this time. In 1907 and 1908, 2.5 percent (283 individuals altogether) of the lodgers were clerks or salespeople, a group that charity officials included under the category "somewhat skilled." *Twenty-Ninth Annual Report of the Philadelphia*

Society for Organizing Charity, 1907 (Philadelphia, 1908), p. 38; *Thirtieth Annual Report of the Philadelphia Society for Organizing Charity, 1908* (Philadelphia, 1909), p. 34. Among males in Philadelphia, lower white-collar workers made up 11.1 percent of all workers in 1910, but only 2.8 percent of the vagrants in the House of Correction. For basic occupational data, see Ulf F. Balack, "The Structure and Development of the White Collar Group in the United States: A Study of Six Cities, 1900–1930" (M.A. thesis, Temple University, 1998), table A-30, p. 162.

44. Vagrancy Dockets, Philadelphia House of Corrections, 1874–75; Solenberger, *One Thousand Homeless Men*, 20; Laubach, *Why There Are Vagrants*, 16–20; Marsh, "Causes of Vagrancy and Methods of Eradication," 454. McCook found that less than 10 percent of the men in his sample were illiterate. McCook, "A Tramp Census and Its Revelations," 757.

45. Robert Hunter, *Poverty* (New York: Macmillan, 1904), p. 121. For early examples, see letter to the editor, *New York Tribune*, April 5, 1884, p. 7; C. W. Noble, "The Border-Land of Trampdom," *Popular Science Monthly* 50 (1896–97), 254.

46. Stephen Thernstrom, *The Other Bostonians: Poverty and Progress in the American Metropolis, 1880–1970* (Cambridge, Mass.: Harvard University Press, 1973), p. 73.

47. See Keyssar, *Out of Work*, pp. 77–88.

48. See Olivier Zunz, *The Changing Face of Inequality: Urbanization, Industrial Development, and Immigrants in Detroit, 1880–1920* (Chicago: University of Chicago Press, 1982), pp. 69–79.

49. Katz, *Shadow of the Poorhouse*, pp. 88–89.

50. For a general discussion of the ways in which workers coped with unemployment, see Keyssar, *Out of Work*, pp. 143–76. On the family economy among immigrants, see Zunz, *The Changing Face of Inequality*, pp. 227–40; and Ewa Morawska, *For Bread with Butter: Life Worlds of East Central Europeans in Johnstown, Pennsylvania, 1890–1940* (Cambridge, Mass.: Harvard University Press, 1985); Barrett, *Work and Community*, pp. 93–104.

51. E. Wight Bakke, *Citizens Without Work: A Study of the Effects of Unemployment Upon the Workers' Social Relations and Practices* (New Haven: Yale University Press, 1943), p. 237 and 226–42 *passim*. For evidence of this in the 1920s, see Cohen, *Making a New Deal*, pp. 61–62.

CHAPTER 7

1. "Tramps and 'Labor,'" *New York Times*, December 23, 1886, p. 4; *Philadelphia Inquirer*, editorial, January 5, 1876, p. 2; John J. McCook, "Increase of Tramping: Cause and Cure," *Independent* 54 (1902), 622; Edmund Kelly, *The Elimination of the Tramp* (New York: Putnam's, 1908), p. xviii; "The Organized Tramp," *Nation* 58 (1894), 306.

2. James Whittaker, "The Song of the Tramp," *American Federationist* 7 (1900), 155; Lizzie M. Holmes, "Two Types of Wasted Lives," ibid. 8 (1901), 407–08; Henry George, *Progress and Poverty* (New York: Robert Schalkenbach Foundation, 1979 [1879]); Terrence Powderly, *The Path I Trod* (New York: AMS Press, 1968 [1908]), p.

27; Michael Davis, "Forced to Tramp: The Perspective of the Labor Press, 1870–1900," in *Walking to Work*, ed. Eric Monkkonen (Lincoln: University of Nebraska Press, 1984), pp. 141–70; Alexander Keyssar, *Out of Work* (Cambridge, Eng.: Cambridge University Press, 1986), p. 141 (quotation). Keyssar's study is a fine history of unemployment in an important industrial state, but I disagree with his assessment of the causes and nature of tramping. For another example of the traditional perspective on tramping, see Paul T. Ringenbach, *Tramps and Reformers: The Discovery of Unemployment in New York* (Westport, Conn.: Greenwood Press, 1973), pp. xv, 36–38, 60–62.

3. See the fine case studies by Jules Tygiel, "Tramping Artisans: Carpenters in Industrial America," and Patricia A. Cooper, "The 'Travelling Fraternity': Union Cigar Makers and Geographical Mobility, 1900–1919," in *Walking to Work*, ed. Monkkonen, pp. 87–138; David Bensman, *The Practice of Solidarity: American Hat Finishers in the Nineteenth Century* (Urbana: University of Illinois Press, 1985), pp. 71–73; Daniel T. Rodgers, *The Work Ethic in Industrial America, 1850–1920* (Chicago: University of Chicago Press, 1978), pp. 163–65.

4. Benjamin Marsh, "Causes of Vagrancy and Methods of Eradication," *Annals of the American Academy of Social and Political Science* 22 (1904), 455; Montgomery, *The Fall of the House of Labor*, p. 239. On labor turnover, see also Montgomery, *Workers' Control in America*, pp. 32–33, 119; Keyssar, *Out of Work*, p. 268; and Lizabeth Cohen, *Making a New Deal: Industrial Workers in Chicago, 1919–1939* (Cambridge, Eng.: Cambridge University Press, 1990), 197–99.

5. Correspondence with Aspinwall in the Social Reform Papers of John J. McCook Papers, Connecticut Historical Society; Marsh, "Causes of Vagrancy and Methods of Eradication," 444; *Fourth Biennial Report of the Board of State Commissioners of Public Charities of the State of Illinois . . . 1876* (Springfield, Ill., 1876), p. 205.

6. John J. McCook, "Tramps," *Charities Review* 3 (1893), 65.

7. William Edge, *The Main Stem* (New York: Vanguard, 1927), p. 31; Laubach, *Why There Are Vagrants*, pp. 40, 41, 73–75; Floyd Dell, "'Hallelujah, I'm a Bum,'" *Century* 110 (1925), 139.

8. Laubach, *Why There Are Vagrants*, pp. 40–41, 44, 74; "The Great American Bum," in *The Hobo's Hornbook: A Repertory for a Gutter Jongleur*, ed. George Milburn (New York: Washburn, 1930), p. 73.

9. John N. Webb, *The Migratory-Casual Worker* (Washington, Government Printing Office [GPO], 1937), pp. 5–7; Stewart Holbrook, *Holy Old Mackinaw: A Natural History of the American Lumberjack* (New York: Macmillan, 1938); "Tramps Along the Hudson," *New York Times*, August 6, 1879, p. 5; Lennox Kerr, *Back Door Guest* (New York: Arno, 1974 [1927]), pp. 182–83, 209, 211–13. An excellent historical study of the wheat harvesters is Clayton Koppes, "Migratory Wheat Harvesters in the Great Plains, 1900–1930" (California Institute of Technology Social Science Working Paper No. 190, 1977).

10. Don Leschoier, "Harvesters and Hoboes in the Wheat Fields," *Survey* 50 (1923), 483–87 (quotation, 485); Josiah Flynt [Willard], *Notes of an Itinerant Policeman* (Boston: L. C. Page, 1900), pp. 118–19; Dean Stiff [Nels Anderson], *The Milk and Honey Route* (New York: Vanguard, 1931), p. 104; Solenberger, *One Thousand Homeless Men*, pp. 141–45.

11. Laubach, *Why There Are Vagrants*, pp. 44, 74; "The Great American Bum," *The Hobo's Hornbook*, ed. Milburn, p. 73; Solenberger, *One Thousand Homeless Men*, pp. 136–37.

12. W. J. Reveridge quoted in Lauck and Sydenstricker, *Conditions of Labor*, p. 120; Laubach, *Why There Are Vagrants*, p. 73; [Willard], *Notes of an Itinerant Policeman*, pp. 131, 133.

13. Laubach, *Why There Are Vagrants*, p. 42; Robert Herrick, Introduction to Jack Black [pseud.], *You Can't Win* (New York: Macmillan, 1926), p. xi.

14. Harry Kemp, *Tramping on Life* (Garden City, N.Y.: Garden City Publishing Co., 1922), pp. 8, 32–33, 26; Jim Tully, *Beggars of Life* (New York: J. Cape, 1925), pp. 11–12, 235, 13, 20, 21–22.

15. Edge, *The Main Stem*, pp. 1, 8–9, and *passim*; John Worby, *The Other Half: The Autobiography of a Tramp* (New York: L. Furman, 1937), pp. 24, 59.

16. Clifford Shaw, *The Jack-Roller: A Delinquent Boy's Own Story* (Chicago: University of Chicago Press, 1930), pp. 30–31, 62–63, 71–74, 84–85.

17. Ibid., pp. 90–91, 117–19, 125.

18. Ben Reitman, "Following the Monkey" (unpublished manuscript autobiography, University of Illinois at Chicago Circle, 1932), p. 27; Solenberger, *One Thousand Homeless Men*, pp. 216, 242.

19. Laubach, *Why There Are Vagrants*, pp. 67–71; Maury Graham and Robert J. Hemming, *Tales of the Iron Road: My Life as King of the Hobos* (New York: Paragon House, 1990); Josiah Flynt [Willard], *My Life* (New York: Outing Publishing Co., 1908), pp. 3–17. Nels Anderson, "The Juvenile and the Tramp," *Journal of Criminal Law, Criminology, and Police Science* 14 (1923–24), 290–300, stressed the combination of family troubles, work problems, and maladjusted personality as causes of boys becoming tramps.

20. Flynt, *Notes of an Itinerant Policeman*, pp. 122, 124; Shaw, *The Jack-Roller*, pp. 52–53; Reitman, "Following the Monkey"; Tully, *Beggars of Life*, pp. 13, 131; Thomas Philpott, *The Slum and the Ghetto* (New York: Oxford University Press, 1978), p. 65; Jacob Riis, *How the Other Half Lives: Studies Among the Tenements of New York* (New York: Dover Press edition, 1971 [1890]), p. 156; Laubach, *Why There Are Vagrants*, p. 80. On the attraction of tramping to boys, see also Nels Anderson's discussion of "The Juvenile and the Tramp," pp. 292–93.

21. "Juvenile Offenders and Vagrants," *Albany Law Journal* 4 (1871), 182; Karl Tilman Winkler, "Reformers United: The American and the German Juvenile Court, 1882–1923," in *Institutions of Confinement: Hospitals, Asylums, and Prisons in Western Europe and North America, 1500–1950*, ed. Norbert Finzsch and Robert Jutte (Cambridge, Eng.: Cambridge University Press, 1997), p. 255 (quotation); Eric Schneider, *In the Web of Class: Delinquents and Reformers in Boston, 1810s–1930s* (New York: New York University Press, 1992), pp. 101–07; Josiah Flynt [Willard], *Tramping with Tramps: Studies and Sketches of Vagabond Life* (New York: Century, 1899), p. 282; [Willard], *My Life*, pp. 86–99. The introduction of the juvenile court system, beginning in Illinois in 1899, was designed to provide more humane treatment for youthful offenders. Most youngsters were now put on probation, instead of being sent to reformatories. However, as David Rothman has explained, the new laws vastly increased

the power of the courts, and juveniles who broke parole were often sent to reformatories. See David Rothman, *Conscience and Convenience: The Asylum and Its Alternatives in Progressive America* (Boston: Little, Brown, 1980), ch. 6; Winkler, "Reformers United," pp. 256–61.

22. "Drawbacks of Being a Knight of the Road," *Literary Digest* 53 (1916), 1281; "Tramp Evangelist Restores Runaways," *New York Times*, April 4, 1904, p. 9; "Experiences of Boys as Tramps," *New York Tribune Supplement*, May 1, 1904, p. 5.

23. Ralph Chaplin, *Wobbly* (New York: Da Capo, 1972 [1948]), p. 87; Wyckoff, *The Workers, an Experiment in Reality: The West*, p. 23; Shaw, *The Jack-Roller*, p. 94; "Tramps and Their Travels," *New York Times*, May 24, 1906, p. 8; Edward P. Johanningsmeier, *Forging American Communism: The Life of William Z. Foster* (Princeton: Princeton University Press, 1994), pp. 26–27; "A Printer Stealing a Ride from San Francisco to New York," *Locomotive Engineers' Monthly Journal* 13 (1879), 67–70. See also *First Annual Report of the Bureau of Labor Statistics of the State of North Carolina for the Year 1887* (Raleigh, N.C., 1887), 35.

24. On the use of railroads by criminals, see Kemp, *Tramping on Life*, p. 129; Flynt, *Tramping with Tramps*, p. 307; Black, *You Can't Win*, pp. 80–83, 129. For examples of criminals impersonating tramps, see "Shot at His Post," *Philadelphia Inquirer*, May 1, 1885, p. 5; "Tramps with Pistols Invade a Meat Store," ibid., January 1, 1897, p. 5.

25. Sherwood Anderson, *A Story-Teller's Story* (New York: Huebsch, 1924), p. 278; Ernest Poole, *The Harbor* (New York: Macmillan, 1915), p. 60; Bertha Thompson, *Sister of the Road*, ed. Ben Reitman (New York: Gold Label Books, 1937), pp. 40–41; John Hayes, *James A. Michener: A Biography* (Indianapolis: Bobbs Merrill, 1984), pp. 21–22.

26. Koppes, "Migratory Wheat Harvesters," p. 10; Thompson, *Sister of the Road*; Kerr, *Back Door Guest*, p. 172.

27. Barrington Moore, Jr., *Injustice: The Social Basis of Obedience and Revolt* (New York: Pantheon, 1978), explores this issue.

28. On these trends, see Samuel P. Hays, *The Response to Industrialism, 1885–1914* (Chicago: University of Chicago Press, 1957); Hays, unpaginated "Preface to the Atheneum Edition," *Conservation and the Gospel of Efficiency: The Progressive Conservation Movement 1890–1920* (New York: Atheneum, 1969); Robert H. Wiebe, *The Search for Order, 1877–1920* (New York: Hill and Wang, 1967); Alan Trachtenberg, *The Incorporation of America: Culture and Society in the Gilded Age* (New York: Hill and Wang, 1982), ch. 2; Alfred Chandler, Jr., *Scale and Scope: The Dynamics of Industrial Capitalism* (Cambridge, Mass.: Harvard University Press, 1990), chs. 3–6; and Montgomery, *The Fall of the House of Labor*, ch. 5.

29. Edge, *The Main Stem*, pp. 151–52; Worby, *The Other Half*, p. 59; Tully, *Beggars of Life*, p. 20; "Beggars and Begging," *Harper's Weekly* 58 (1902), 221; Thompson, *Sister of the Road*, pp. 86–87. See also George Witten, "The Open Road: The Autobiography of a Hobo," *Century* 115 (1928), 353.

30. Pinkerton, *Strikers, Communists, Tramps, and Detectives*, p. 30; *Fourth Biennial Report of the Board of State Commissioners of Public Charities of the State of Illinois . . . 1876*, p. 205; Shaw, *The Jack-Roller*, p. 137. See also C. W. Noble, "The Border-Land of Trampdom," *Popular Science Monthly* 50 (1897–97), 252–58; Andress Floyd, *My Monks of Vagabondia* (n.p., 1913), pp. 135–36; [Willard], *Notes of an Itinerant Policeman*, p. 13.

31. Jack London, *The Road* (New York: Macmillan, 1908), p. 53; Hunter, *Poverty*, p. 129; Reitman, "Following the Monkey," pp. 1, 4, 72; Shaw, *The Jack-Roller*, p. 136; [Willard], *My Life*, p. 105.

32. [Anderson], *The Milk and Honey Route*, p. 15; Noble, "The Border-Land of Trampdom," 225; Carl Schockman, *We Turned Hobo* (Columbus, Ohio: F. J. Herr, 1937), pp. 65–66.

33. Hunter, *Poverty*, p. 130; Wyckoff, *The Workers, an Experiment in Reality: The West*, pp. 56, 64; Glen Mullin, *Adventures of a Scholar Tramp* (London: J. Cape, 1925), p. 76; Tully, *Beggars of Life*, p. 59; Edge, *The Main Stem*, p. 53, 61; Schockman, *We Turned Hobo*, pp. 44, 114; Worby, *The Other Half*, p. 108; London, *The Road*, pp. 53–54.

34. Data from *Annual Reports of the Philadelphia Society for Organizing Charity, 1887–1900* (Philadelphia, 1887–1900); Solenberger, *One Thousand Homeless Men*, p. 25; McCook tramp interview in Social Reform Papers of John James McCook, vol. 46 (1894), Box J-12; Hunter, *Poverty*, p. 129; London, *The Road*, p. 126; [Anderson], *The Milk and Honey Route*, pp. 35–38.

35. Schockman, *We Turned Hobo*, p. 77; [Willard], *Notes of an Itinerant Policeman*, p. 16; Josiah Flynt [Willard], *The Little Brother: A Story of Tramp Life* (New York: Century, 1902), p. 3; John J. McCook, Notebook J (1894), vol. 46, Social Reform Papers of John J. McCook, Connecticut Historical Society [hereafter McCook Papers]. McCook asked one tramp, "Where did you get that name?" The man answered honestly, "Oh, I made it [up]." For glossaries of terms used by tramps and hobos, see the appendix at the back of [Willard], *Tramping with Tramps; The Hobo's Hornbook*, ed. Milburn, pp. 283–88; and Irwin Godfrey, *American Tramp and Underworld Slang; Words and Phrases Used by Hoboes, Tramps, Migratory Workers, and Those on the Fringes of Society* (New York: Sears, 1931). For descriptive place-names, see David W. Maurer, "Underworld Place-Names," *American Speech* 15 (1940), 340–42; and Maurer, "More Underworld Place-Names," ibid. 17 (1942), 75–76.

36. Tully, *Beggars of Life*, p. 197.

37. Gregory R. Woirol, *In the Floating Army: F. C. Mills on Itinerant Life in California* (Urbana: University of Illinois Press, 1992), pp. 78–80, 106 (quotation, p. 80); "Tramps," *Railroad Gazette* 15 (1883), 244; [Anderson], *The Milk and Honey Route*, p. 20; Thompson, *Sister of the Road*, pp. 80, 233; Kemp, *Tramping on Life*, p. 133; Tully, *Beggars of Life*, p. 254; Worby, *The Other Half*, pp. 84–85, 99–100.

38. Kerr, *Back Door Guest*, pp. 167–68; Worby, *The Other Half*, p. 84; Woirol, *In the Floating Army*, p. 80. See also Tully, *Beggars of Life*, p. 254.

39. [Anderson], *The Milk and Honey Route*, p. 21; Reitman, "Following the Monkey," pp. 61–63; Tully, *Beggars of Life*, pp. 55–56, 253; Mullin, *Adventures of a Scholar Tramp*, pp. 295–97; [Willard], *Tramping with Tramps*, p. 148; Kemp, *Tramping on Life*, pp. 128, 132; Woirol, *In the Floating Army*, p. 79; Pinkerton, *Strikers, Communists, Tramps, and Detectives*, pp. 61–62; Lovald, "From Hobohemia to Skid Row," pp. 147–48; Graham and Hemming, *Tales of the Iron Road*, pp. 37–38.

40. See Carlos Schwantes, *Coxey's Army: An American Odyssey* (Lincoln: University of Nebraska Press, 1986).

41. Mullin, *Adventures of a Scholar Tramp*, p. 293. For examples, see *Philadelphia Inquirer*, June 9, 1885, p. 8; Kemp, *Tramping on Life*, p. 188; Black, *You Can't Win*, pp.

220–21; and, for a particularly brutal assault, William Aspinwall to John J. McCook, September 26/27, 1898, Roll 12, Series 12, McCook Papers.

42. Tully, *Beggars of Life*, p. 335; Shaw, *The Jack-Roller*, pp. 137–38; Black, *You Can't Win*, pp. 198–200; Worby, *The Other Half*, pp. 41–51; Kemp, *Tramping on Life*, p. 126; Anderson, *The Hobo*, pp. 18–22.

43. Charles H. Forster, "Despised and Rejected of Men," *Survey* 33 (1915), 671. This did not, it should be pointed out, prevent some residents of skid row from selling their votes for cash—a common practice in Chicago and some other cities. This hardly represented an assertion of political will on the part of the homeless, however.

44. Oestreicher, *Solidarity and Fragmentation*, pp. 60–67, 128–35, 172–221; Herbert Gutman, "Work, Culture, and Society in Industrializing America, 1815–1919," in Gutman, *Work, Culture, and Society in Industrializing America* (New York: Vintage, 1976), 32–47, 61–63; *The Tenant Movement in New York City, 1904–1984*, ed. Ronald Lawson (New Brunswick: Rutgers University Press, 1986), pp. 39–93; David Montgomery, *Workers' Control in America: Studies in the History of Work, Technology, and Labor Struggles* (Cambridge, Eng.: Cambridge University Press, 1979), pp. 40–44, 91–134; Gerald Sorin, *The Prophetic Minority: American Jewish Immigrant Radicals, 1880–1920* (Bloomington: Indiana University Press, 1985); John Bodnar, *The Transplanted: A History of Immigrants in Urban America* (Bloomington: Indiana University Press, 1985), pp. 90–92.

45. Chaplin, *Wobbly*, p. 180.

46. Peter Linebaugh, *The London Hanged* (Cambridge, Eng.: Cambridge University Press, 1992), p. 151. For examples of hostility to capitalism, see [Willard], *Itinerant Policeman*, pp. 126, 134–35, 198–99; Mullin, *Adventures of a Scholar Tramp*, p. 305; Edge, *The Main Stem*, pp. 41, 87; Tully, *Beggars of Life*, pp. 203–04. See also Robert Payne, *The Hobo Philosopher . . . or, The Message of Economic Freedom* (Puente, Cal.: Published by author, 1925).

47. Edwin D. Brown, *"Broke": The Man Without a Dime* (Boston: Four Seas, 1920), p. 37. For examples of the kangaroo court, see [Willard], *Tramping with Tramps*, pp. 81–83; Jim Tully, *Shadows of Men* (Garden City, N.Y.: Garden City Publishing Co., 1930), p. 102; Tully, *Beggars of Life*, 211–16; Kemp, *Tramping on Life*, p. 140. For English antecedents, see Linebaugh, *The London Hanged*, p. 150.

48. [Willard], *Itinerant Policeman*, p. 48.

49. Joel Williamson, *After Slavery* (Chapel Hill: University of North Carolina Press, 1965), pp. 34–39; Kolchin, *First Freedom*, pp. 4–7, 11, 23; Leon Litwack, *Been in the Storm So Long: The Aftermath of Slavery* (New York: Knopf, 1979), pp. 296–316; Lawrence Levine, *Black Culture and Black Consciousness: Afro-American Folk Thought from Slavery to Freedom* (New York: Oxford University Press, 1977), p. 263; Nell Irvin Painter, *Exodusters: Black Migration to Kansas after Reconstruction* (New York: Knopf, 1976); Eric Foner, *Reconstruction: America's Unfinished Revolution* (New York: Harper and Row, 1988), pp. 55, 57, 200–201; William Cohen, *At Freedom's Edge: Black Mobility and the Southern White Quest for Control, 1861–1915* (Baton Rouge: Louisiana State University Press, 1991), pp. 239–45.

50. Gavin Wright, *Old South, New South: Revolution in the Southern Economy Since the Civil War* (New York: Basic Books, 1986), pp. 159, 161–62; Jacqueline Jones, *The*

Dispossessed: America's Underclasses Since the Civil War (New York: Basic Books, 1992), pp. 141, 12–47, 155–65; Clyde V. Kiser, *Sea Island to City: A Study of St. Helena Islanders in Harlem and Other Urban Centers* (New York: Columbia University Press, 1932), pp. 174–76 and 145–90 *passim*; Michael W. Harris, *The Rise of Gospel Blues: The Music of Thomas Andrew Dorsey in the Urban Church* (New York: Oxford University Press, 1992), p. 20; William Aspinwall to John J. McCook, September 26, 1893, Reel 12, McCook Papers; Tully, *Beggars of Life*, pp. 142–45.

51. Schwantes, *Coxey's Army*, p. 62; *Tramping with Tramps*, p. 281; Louis L'Amour, *Adventures of a Wandering Man* (New York: Bantam, 1990), p. 30; Graham and Hemming, *Tales of the Open Road*, pp. 102–03 (quotation); Mullin, *Adventures of a Scholar Tramp*, pp. 48, 170–72, 189, 221, 259. The classic study of the Scottsboro case is Dan Carter, *Scottsboro: A Tragedy of the American South* (Baton Rouge: Louisiana State University Press, 1969). In my research, I have encountered no other incidents of this nature between black and white tramps in the South. Since, by the 1930s, both races had been using the trains illegally for over 50 years, it is probable that a good deal of toleration, if not acceptance, developed in white attitudes toward blacks on the trains.

52. F. C. Mills, quoted in Woirol, *In the Floating Army*, p. 79. On self-defense by black tramps, see "The Battle of the Tramps," *New York Tribune*, December 16, 1885, p. 1; "Tramps," *Railroad Gazette* 12 (1880), 217; "Tramps," ibid. 14 (1882), 336; "Tramp Catcher Shot Again," *New York Tribune*, August 21, 1903, p. 4; "Slain in Hobo Camp Row," *New York Times*, August 23, 1932, p. 15. For examples of acceptance of blacks in the hobo jungles, see London, *The Road*, pp. 69–70; Tully, *Beggars of Life*, pp. 141–45; Brown, *"Broke"*, pp. 275, 276–78; Reitman, "Following the Monkey," pp. 61–63, 104.

53. Kemp, *Tramping on Life*, pp. 133–34; Schockman, *We Turned Hobo*, pp. 70–72; Theodore Caplow, "Transiency as a Cultural Pattern," *American Sociological Review* 5 (1940), 737. Although there was little overt segregation on the road, this was not true of skid-row institutions. See ch. 8.

54. Solenberger, *One Thousand Homeless Men*, p. 190; Thompson, *Sister of the Road*, pp. 8–9, 13, 15; Noble, "The Border-Land of Trampdom," 255; John J. McCook, Notebook J, vol. 53 (1894), McCook Papers; Mrs. O. L. Amigh, "Minutes and Discussion," National Council of Charities and Correction, *Proceedings, 1903*, p. 517.

55. Thompson, *Sister of the Road*, pp. 8–9, 13, 15; William Aspinwall to John J. McCook, June 9, 1893, McCook Papers; Mrs. C. R. Lowell, "One Means of Preventing Pauperism," National Council of Charities and Correction, *Proceedings 1879*, pp. 189–93, 193n; John J. McCook, "Tramps," *Charities Review* 5 (1893), 63; Solenberger, *One Thousand Homeless Men*, p. 190. For other examples of female tramps, see *Railroad Gazette* 10 (1898), 374–75; Aspinwall to McCook, June 11, 1893, Reel 12, Folder B, and Aspinwall to McCook, Roll 12, Folder 1, in McCook Papers; and Lynn Weiner, "Sisters of the Road: Women Transients and Tramps," in *Walking to Work: Tramps in America, 1790–1935*, ed. Eric Monkkonen (Lincoln: University of Nebraska Press, 1984), pp. 175–79.

56. "Tramps," *Railroad Gazette* 12 (1880), 217; "An Unsophisticated Hobo," *Railway Conductor* 18 (1901), 26–27; "Tramps' Leader Found to Be a Woman," *New York Times*, August 7, 1902, p. 1.

57. See Gilfoyle, *City of Eros*, pp. 157, 160.

58. See, for example, "Boy Slaves of Tramp Masters," *New York Tribune*, November 15, 1903, pt. 2, p. 3; John J. McCook, "Leaves from the Diary of a Tramp, V," *The Independent* 54 (June 16, 1902), 154–55; Tully, *Beggars of Life*, pp. 15, 131–32; Black, *You Can't Win*, p. 129. Josiah Flynt [Willard] was particularly prone to play on this theme in his writings, which were pitched to a more popular audience than most tramp memoirs. See [Willard], *Tramping with Tramps*, pp. 56–57; [Willard], *Little Brother*, p. 201.

59. Nels Anderson, Document 115, Box 127, folder 2, Ernest W. Burgess Papers, University of Chicago Library.

60. Tully, *Beggars of Life*, p. 89; William Aspinwall to John J. McCook, June 11, 1893 (quotation), and Aspinwall to McCook, March 11, 1895, McCook Papers; Anderson interviews, Document 120 ("Young Man, Twenty-two, Well Dressed, Homosexual Prostitute"), p. 2, Box 127, folder 2, Burgess Papers; Anderson, "The Juvenile and the Tramp," 300–303.

61. In most cases, "boy" was used for anyone under age 21. I have encountered usages up to age 25, however.

62. Anderson interviews, Document 120, Burgess Papers, p. 2; George Chauncy, *Gay New York: Gender, Urban Culture, and the Making of the Gay Male World, 1890–1940* (New York: Harper and Row, 1994), pp. 88 and 76–97 *passim*.

63. Nels Anderson interviews, Document 120, Box 127, Burgess Papers; Aspinwall to McCook, March 11, 1895, McCook Papers; Worby, *The Other Half*, pp. 81–82.

64. London, *The Road*, pp. 24–52. For the larger cultural significance of London's book, see chapter 9.

65. Schockman, *We Turned Hobo*, pp. 81–85; Brown, *"Broke, "*p. 268; "He Does Not Want to Deadhead Again," *Locomotive Engineers' Monthly Journal* 10 (1876), 207–08; "A Printer Stealing a Ride from San Francisco to New York," 69; "Tramps," *New York Times*, June 7, 1926, p. 10; Mullin, *Adventures of a Scholar Tramp*, p. 22; Tully, *Beggars of Life*, p. 186; Tom Kromer, *Waiting for Nothing* (New York: Knopf, 1935), p. 141. See also railroad conductor Charles George's memoir, *Forty Years on the Rail* (Chicago, 1888), p. 232. For more on the various ingenious ways that tramps and hobos rode the trains, see Kenneth Allsop, *Hard Travellin': The Hobo and His History* (New York: New American Library, 1967), pp. 158–62.

66. Woirol, *In the Floating Army*, p. 96; Shaw, *The Jack-Roller*, p. 127; Tully, *Beggars of Life*, pp. 125–26; Reitman, "Following the Monkey," p. 79; John J. McCook, Notebook P (1894), McCook Papers; Mullin, *Adventures of a Scholar Tramp*, p. 32.

67. John J. McCook, "Leaves from the Diary of a Tramp: Part II," *Independent* 53 (1901), 2884–86; Mullin, *Adventures of a Scholar Tramp*, pp. 127–28, 130–31; "Tramps," *Railroad Gazette* 16 (1884), 602; Jack London, "Rods and Gunnels," *Bookman* 15 (1902), 541–44.

68. [Willard], *Tramping with Tramps*, p. 287. "Across the Continent Under a Car," *Locomotive Engineers' Monthly Journal* 13 (1879), 257; Tully, *Beggars of Life*, p. 305; Mullin, *Adventures of a Scholar Tramp*, pp. 149–60; Woirol, *In the Floating Army*, p. 96.

69. The Interstate Commerce Commission claimed that over 4,000 people were killed jumping or falling from trains over the five-year period 1901–05. "The American Tramp and What He Costs," *New York Times*, September 8, 1907, pt. 5, p. 10.

70. "A Lost Leg," *Railroad Gazette* 6 (1874), 250; "Tramps," ibid. 16 (1884), 895; Tully, *Beggars of Life*, pp. 271–72; Black, *You Can't Win*, p. 158; [Willard], *My Life*, p. 109; *The Hobo's Hornbook*, ed. Milburn, pp. 67–69, 131–33; McCook, "Leaves from the Diary of a Tramp, Part II," 2880; "Vagrancy—Discussion," National Council of Charities and Correction, *Proceedings, 1907,* p. 73.

71. Tully, *Beggars of Life*, p. 327; Laubach, *Why There Are Vagrants*, p. 21; Kemp, *Tramping on Life*, p. 105.

72. "Drawbacks of Being a Knight of the Road," 1781; "Reitman Talks in Mission," *New York Times*, December 5, 1907, p. 2; "Tramps Tell of Many Wanderings," ibid., December 15, 1907, pt. 2, p. 5; George Witten, "The Open Road: The Autobiography of a Hobo," *Century* 115 (1928), 353; Dell, "'Hallelujah, I'm a Bum,'" p. 139.

CHAPTER 8

1. On the development of skid rows in logging centers, see Stewart Holbrook, *Holy Old Mackinaw: A Natural History of the American Lumberjack* (New York: Macmillan, 1937).

2. For a general discussion of the evolution of spatial characteristics of cities in the mid-nineteenth-century decades, see David Goldfield and Blaine Brownell, *Urban America: From Downtown to No Town* (Boston: Houghton Mifflin, 1979), ch. 7; Olivier Zunz, *The Changing Face of Inequality: Urbanization, Industrial Development, and Immigrants in Detroit, 1880–1920* (Chicago: University of Chicago Press, 1982), chs. 2–4; and Howard P. Chudacoff and Judith E. Smith, *The Evolution of American Urban Society*, 4th ed. (Englewood Cliffs, N.J.: Prentice Hall, 1994), pp. 78–81.

3. Leonard U. Blumberg et al., *Liquor and Poverty: Skid Row as a Human Condition* (New Brunswick, N.J.: Rutgers Center of Alcohol Studies, 1978), pp. 7–9, 25. Despite its title, portions of this study are quite historical.

4. Ibid., pp. 9 (quoting Philadelphia Society for Organizing Charity, *Monthly Register* [18 January 1882]), and 38.

5. Ibid., pp. 18–21; vagrancy arrests calculated from data in Philadelphia Society for Organizing Charity, *Annual Report, 1895* (Philadelphia, 1895); John C. Schneider, *Detroit and the Problem of Order, 1830–1880* (Lincoln: University of Nebraska Press, 1980), pp. 107–09, 126–27. Schneider sees this process beginning before there were clearly demarcated areas for transient or homeless men. Such police activities certainly continued after the development of skid rows, however.

6. Schneider, *Detroit and the Problem of Order*, pp. 44–45, 93–95; Blumberg et al., *Liquor and Poverty*, pp. 54–56, 66–69; Nels Anderson, *The Hobo* (Chicago: University of Chicago Press, 1923), pp. 3, 14–15; Alice Willard Solenberger, *One Thousand Homeless Men* (New York: Survey Associates, 1914), p. 7; John C. Schneider, "Tramping Workers," in *Walking to Work*, ed. Eric Monkkonen (Lincoln: University of Nebraska Press, 1984), pp. 224–27; Paul Groth, *Living Downtown: The History of Residential Hotels in the United States* (Berkeley: University of California Press, 1994), p. 153. On Minneapolis, see Keith Lovald, "From Hobohemia to Skid Row: The Changing Community of Homeless Men" (Ph.D. dissertation, University of Minnesota, 1960). For

case studies of Omaha and San Francisco, see John C. Schneider, "Skid Row as an Urban Neighborhood, 1880–1960," *Urbanism Past and Present* 9 (1984), 11–13; and Alvin Averbach, "San Francisco's South of Market District, 1850–1950: The Emergence of a Skid Row," *California Historical Quarterly* 52 (1973), 201–06.

7. Alvin Harlow, *Old Bowery Days: The Chronicles of a Famous Street* (New York, 1931), pp. 190–234; William Haswell, *Reminiscences of New York by an Octogenarian* (New York: Harper, 1896), pp. 354–65; Edward R. Hewitt and Mary Ashley Hewitt, "The Bowery," in Maud Wilder Goodwin et al., eds., *Historic New York: Being the First Series of the Half Moon Papers* (New York: Putnam's, 1897), pp. 389–91; Christine Stansell, *City of Women: Sex and Class in New York, 1789–1860* (New York: Knopf, 1986), pp. 96–99; Timothy Gilfoyle, *City of Eros: New York City, Prostitution and the Commercialization of Sex, 1790–1920* (New York: Norton, 1992), pp. 89–91, 105–07; "New-York Dining Saloons," *New York Times*, April 5, 1866, p. 4; "Local Intelligence," ibid., January 16, 1866, p. 8; "How the Poor Lodge," ibid., January 17, 1869, p. 3; "Where the Poor Eat," ibid., February 21, 1869, p. 5; "The Bummers of New York," ibid., November 29, 1868, p. 3; James D. McCabe, Jr., *Lights and Shadows of New York Life* (Philadelphia: Hubbard, 1872), pp. 186–93 (quotation, 193); James D. McCabe, Jr., *New York by Sunlight and Gaslight* (Philadelphia: Hubbard, 1882), pp. 642–44; Kenneth T. Jackson, "The Bowery: From Residential Street to Skid Row," in Rick Beard, ed., *On Being Homeless: Historical Perspectives* (New York: Museum of the City of New York, 1987), pp. 72–73.

8. Jackson, "The Bowery," p. 75; Harlow, *Old Bowery Days*, pp. 388–89.

9. "Where the Beggars Sleep," *New York Tribune*, August 29, 1880, p. 5; Edward Lee, *Prison, Camp and Pulpit: The Life of a City Missionary in the Slums* (Oswego, N.Y.: R. J. Oliphant, 1889), p. 169; Thomas Byrnes, "Nurseries of Crime," *North American Review* 149 (1889), 356–57; Hewitt and Hewitt, "The Bowery," pp. 391–94; Ralph Julian, "The Bowery," *Century*, new ser., 21 (1890), 233–34; Alexander Irvine, "Bunk-House and Some Bunk-House Men," *McClure's* 31 (1908), 455; Ignatz L. Nascher, *The Wretches of Povertyville: A Sociological Study of the Bowery* (Chicago: University of Chicago Press, 1909).

10. "Shelter for the Idle," *New York Times*, February 12, 1877, p. 2; Byrnes, "Nurseries of Crime," 356–57; Jacob Riis, *How the Other Half Lives* (New York: Dover Press, 1971 [1890]), p. 72; [Dave Ranney], *Dave Ranney; Or Thirty Years on the Bowery* (New York: American Tract Society, 1910), pp. 87, 101–02; Rev. W. E. Paul, quoted in Lovald, "From Hobohemia to Skid Row," p. 107; Solenberger, *One Thousand Homeless Men*, p. 314. The rapid expansion of lodging houses in New York in the late 1880s is evident from the increase in number from 267 in 1888 to 345 a year later. *Report of New York City Police Department, 1888* (New York, 1888), pp. 76–77.

11. Harry M. Beardsley, "Along the Main Stem with Red" (manuscript [1917], p. 5), Box 126, Ernest W. Burgess Papers, University of Chicago Library; Anderson, *The Hobo*, pp. 27–33; William Edge, *The Main Stem* (New York: Vanguard, 1927), pp. 83–84; Robert Hunter, *Poverty* (New York: Macmillan, 1904), pp. 116, 128 (quotation); Solenberger, *One Thousand Homeless Men*, pp. 321–22; Paul Kennaday, "New York's One Hundred Lodging-Houses," *Charities and the Commons* 13 (1905), 486–92; Jesse Dees, Jr., *Flophouse* (Francestown, N.H.: M. Jones, 1948), pp. 137–38. On types of

lodging-house accommodations, see also Charles Hoch and Robert Slayton, *New Homeless and Old: Community and the Skid Row Hotel* (Philadelphia: Temple University Press, 1989), pp. 47–53; and Groth, *Living Downtown*, pp. 40–51.

12. Josiah Flynt [Willard], *Tramping with Tramps* (New York: Century, 1899), pp. 123–24; Solenberger, *One Thousand Homeless Men*, pp. 316–26; Anderson, *The Hobo*, pp. 30, 132; Hoch and Slayton, *New Homeless and Old*, pp. 48–49; Groth, *Living Downtown*, pp. 145–46.

13. Solenberger, *One Thousand Homeless Men*, p. 315; "How the Poor Lodge," *New York Times*, January 17, 1869, p. 3; Julian, "The Bowery," 231; [Willard], *Tramping with Tramps*, pp. 123–24; Riis, *How the Other Half Lives*, p. 72; Irvine, "Bunk-House and Some Bunk-House Men, 455; Lennox Kerr, *Back Door Guest* (New York: Arno, 1974 [1927]), p. 49 (quotation); Perry Duis, *The Saloon: Public Drinking in Chicago and Boston, 1880–1920* (Urbana: University of Illinois Press, 1983), p. 89.

14. Hunter, *Poverty*, pp. 118–19; Riis, *How the Other Half Lives*, p. 59; Lee, *Prison, Camp, and Pulpit*, pp. 172, 218, 224; Groth, *Living Downtown*, pp. 147–48.

15. Riis, *How the Other Half Lives*, pp. 61–64; Walter Wyckoff, *The Workers, A Study in Reality: The West* (New York: Scribner's, 1898), pp. 27–29.

16. Riis, *How the Other Half Lives*, p. 72; McCabe, *Lights and Shadows*, pp. 680–82; "Return of the Tramps," *New York Tribune*, October 18, 1876, p. 2; "The Tunnel Their Castle," ibid., April 26, 1896; Glen Mullin, *Adventures of a Scholar Tramp* (London: J. Cape, 1925), pp. 56–58. Howard Mingos, "An Outdoor Lodging for the Night," *New York Times Review and Magazine* (October 16, 1921), p. 5; Ben Reitman, "Following the Monkey" (unpublished manuscript autobiography [1932], University of Illinois at Chicago Circle), pp. 93–94.

17. Clifford R. Shaw, *The Jack-Roller: A Delinquent Boy's Own Story* (Chicago: University of Chicago Press, 1930), pp. 37–38.

18. On housing conditions in immigrant and black neighborhoods, see Riis, *How the Other Half Lives*, ch. 6; Philpott, *Slum and the Ghetto*, ch. 1; Allan H. Spear, *Black Chicago: The Making of a Negro Ghetto, 1890–1930* (Chicago: University of Chicago Press, 1967), pp. 24–26; E. Franklin Frazier, *The Negro Family in Chicago* (Chicago: University of Chicago Press, 1932), ch. 6.

19. On this trend, see A. B. Wolfe, *The Lodging House Problem in Boston* (Boston: Houghton Mifflin, 1906); Franklin K. Fretz, "The Furnished Room Problem in Philadelphia" (Ph.D. dissertation, University of Pennsylvania, 1911); Harvey Zorbaugh, *The Gold Coast and the Slum: A Sociological Study of Chicago's Near North Side* (Chicago: University of Chicago Press, 1929), chs. 3–5; Elizabeth Hawes, *New York, New York: How the Apartment House Transformed the Life of the City (1869–1930)* (New York: Knopf, 1993); Joanne J. Meyerowitz, *Women Adrift: Independent Wage Earners in Chicago, 1880–1930* (Chicago: University of Chicago Press, 1988); Groth, *Living Downtown*; Howard Chudacoff, *The Age of the Bachelor* (Princeton: Princeton University Press, 1999).

20. See Averbach, "San Francisco's South of Market District," p. 203.

21. Charles H. Forster, "Despised and Rejected of Men," *Survey* 33 (1915), 671–72 (quotation); Lovald, "From Hobohemia to Skid Row," pp. 88–89; Edge, *The Main Stem*, p. 19. For a general discussion of the growth of all types of employment agen-

cies, and efforts to regulate them, see Walter Licht, *Getting Work: Philadelphia, 1840–1950* (Cambridge, Mass.: Harvard University Press, 1992), pp. 123–28. Prior to 1933, when joint federal-state employment agencies came into being, Pennsylvania was the only state (beginning in 1915) to establish state-run employment agencies. Ibid., pp. 129–30.

22. Zorbaugh, *The Gold Coast and the Slum*, p. 107; [Dave Ranney], *Dave Ranney, or Thirty Years on the Bowery* (New York: American Tract Society, 1910), pp. 67–68 (quotation); Beardsley, "Along the Main Stem with Red," p. 6 (quotation); Owen Kildare, "The Drifters of 'The Valley of Never Care,'" *New York Times*, June 28, 1908, pt. 5, p. 6; Jack Black [pseud.], *You Can't Win* (New York: Macmillan, 1926), p. 153 (quotation); Blumberg et al., *Liquor and Poverty*, p. 9. In 1923, not a single grocery store existed on West Madison Street in Chicago. See Hoch and Slayton, *New Homeless and Old*, p. 93 (table 5-4).

23. Harlow, *Old Bowery Days*, p. 404; George Ade, *The Old Time Saloon: Not Wet—Not Dry, Just History* (New York: Long and Smith, 1931), pp. 34–48; Jim Tully, *Beggars of Life* (New York: J. Cape, 1925), p. 123; Black, *You Can't Win*, p. 195; Ralph Chaplin, *Wobbly* (New York: Da Capo, 1972 [1948]), p. 69; Wyckoff, *The Workers, A Study in Reality: The West*, pp. 54–55; Mullin, *Adventures of a Scholar Tramp*, pp. 18, 69–70; Duis, *The Saloon*, pp. 89–90.

24. [Ranney], *Dave Ranney*, p. 68; "West Madison Street" (Typescript report, January 7, 1934, Box 134, folder 2, Ernest W. Burgess Papers, University of Chicago Archives), p. 4 (quotation); Don Lescohier, *The Labor Market* (New York: Macmillan, 1917), pp. 157–58. For a parallel to taverns in immigrant neighborhoods, see Roy Rosenzweig, *Eight Hours for What You Will: Workers and Leisure in an Industrial City, 1870–1920* (Cambridge, Eng.: Cambridge University Press, 1983), p. 64.

25. Riis, *How the Other Half Lives*, p. 75; Julian, "The Bowery," 229–30 (quotation); Groth, *Living Downtown*, p. 155; Frank O. Beck, *Hobohemia* (Rindge, N.H.: R. R. Smith, 1956), p. 16; Hoch and Slayton, *New Homeless and Old*, p. 34 (Table 3–1).

26. Lovald, "From Hobohemia to Skid Row," pp. 121–22; Kildare, "The Drifters of the Valley of 'Never Care,'" p. 6; Zorbaugh, *The Gold Coast and the Slum*, p. 107; Beardsley, "Along the Main Stem with Red," p. 6.

27. Black, *You Can't Win*, p. 216; Zorbaugh, *The Gold Coast and the Slum*, p. 107; Groth, *Living Downtown*, p. 155; Kildare, "The Drifters of the 'Valley of Never Care,'" p. 6.

28. Harlow, *Old Bowery Days*, p. 389; Zorbaugh, *The Gold Coast and the Slum*, p. 108; Hunter, *Poverty*, pp. 110–11 (quotation); Julian, "The Bowery," 235; Wyckoff, *The Workers, An Experiment in Reality: The West*, pp. 2–3, 71.

29. Julian, "The Bowery," 235; Groth, *Living Downtown*, p. 55; Hunter, *Poverty*, p. 110 (quotation); Chaplin, *Wobbly*, p. 86; Zorbaugh, *The Gold Coast and the Slum*, 115–20; Schneider, *Detroit and the Problem of Order*, pp. 40–45; Blumberg et al., *Liquor and Poverty*, pp. 21, 25; Document 79 (Nels Anderson, "Report of Visit to Ten Gambling Houses of Hobohemia," January 1, 1923), Box 127, folder 1, Burgess Papers. On Towertown, see Zorbaugh, *The Gold Coast and the Slum*, pp. 87–104.

30. Document 105: "Casual Worker, Ex-Soldier, Twenty-eight," Box 127, Burgess Papers.

31. Document 105: "Casual Laborer, Ex-Soldier, Twenty-eight," Box 127, Burgess Papers; Riis, *How the Other Half Lives*; Theodore Dreiser, *The Color of a Great City* (New York: Boni and Liveright, 1923), pp. 206, 207; Zorbaugh, *The Gold Coast and the Slum*, pp. 108, 109, 129.

32. [Willard], *Tramping with Tramps*, pp. 118–19; "West Madison Street," pp. 4–5. On hobo migrations, see Edge, *The Main Stem*, p. 202; Anderson, *The Hobo*, pp. 12–13; Document 11: "Belgian, Fifty-Eight, Coal Miner, Lumber Jack [*sic*]," Box 127, folder 1, Burgess Papers; Nels Anderson, *Men on the Move* (Chicago: University of Chicago Press, 1940), pp. 269–70; Hoch and Slayton, *New Homeless and Old*, pp. 39–41.

33. "West Madison Street," p. 5 (quotation); Hunter, *Poverty*, p. 128; Irvine, "Bunk-House and Some Bunk-House Men," 455–56; Solenberger, *One Thousand Homeless Men*, pp. 91, 118–23, 124; Hunter, *Poverty*, p. 115; "Mills House a Year Old," *New York Tribune Illustrated Supplement*, November 6, 1898, p. 11; "Decent Lodgings for Poor Men," *Independent* 75 (1913), 638.

34. "West Madison Street," p. 2; Shaw, *The Jack-Roller*, pp. 80, 93. Although the origins of "skid row" (or "skid road," as Seattle's district was called) lie in the late nineteenth century, the term was little used prior to the 1920s.

35. Edge, *The Main Stem*, p. 18; "West Madison Street," pp. 1–2. On the significance of West Madison Street to hobos and tramps across America, see Beardsley, "Along the Main Stem with Red," p. 1; Wilfred S. Reynolds, "Report on . . . 50 Transient Men . . . ," July 10, 1933, unpag., Box 82, Federal Emergency Relief Administration files, Transient Division, Record Group 69, National Archives.

36. Jacob Riis, *The Children of the Poor* (New York: Scribner's, 1905), p. 271; Duis, *The Saloon*, p. 92 (Dawes quotation); "Beggar, Seventy-Two," Box 127, Burgess Papers; Frank Laubach, *Why There Are Vagrants* (New York: n.p., 1916), p. 64.

37. Edge, *The Main Stem*, p. 19.

38. Document 126: "Character Sketch of J. E. How," Box 127, Burgess Papers; Beck, *Hobohemia*, pp. 73–75; Bertha Thompson, *Sister of the Road*, ed. Ben Reitman (New York: Gold Label Books, 1937), p. 32; Roger Bruns, *The Damndest Radical: The Life and World of Ben Reitman* (Urbana: University of Illinois Press, 1987), pp. 22–25, 205–06 (quotation, 206); "Shipping Men to Farms," *New York Times*, July 21, 1913, p. 8; "Hobos Call Candidates," ibid., August 11, 1913, p. 14; "'Hobo College' Opens," ibid., June 11, 1919, p. 3; "Hobo College Specializes in Work for Vagrant Knights of the Road," ibid., August 19, 1923, pt. 7, p. 7; "Hoboes Meet Here Today," ibid., June 24, 1925, p. 19; Beardsley, "Along the Main Stem with Red," pp. 6, 11–12. On Reitman, see also Beck, *Hobohemia*, 34–39.

39. See, for example, "Hobo College Specializes," p. 7, and the statement by sociologist E. A. Ross, in Bruns, *The Damndest Radical*, p. 209.

40. "Hobo College Specializes," p. 7 (How quotation); Thompson, *Sister of the Road*, p. 33; A. E. Holt, "'Bos," *Survey* 60 (1928), 456 (quotation).

41. Thompson, *Sister of the Road*, pp. 51 (quotation), 67–68; Chaplin, *Wobbly*, 172, 174–78; Zorbaugh, *The Gold Coast and the Slum*, p. 115 (quotation); Beck, *Hobohemia*, p. 15; Document 60: "Notes on an Afternoon's Series of Talks on the Soap Box on Madison Street," Box 127, folder 1, Burgess Papers.

42. Beck, *Hobohemia*, pp. 51–60; Thompson, *Sister of the Road*, p. 60.

43. Mariner J. Kent, "The Making of a Tramp," *Independent* 55 (1903), 673; Hunter, *Poverty*, p. 111; Groth, *Living Downtown*, pp. 37–38; Riis, *How the Other Half Lives*, pp. 61 (quotation), 64; "New York Beggars," *New York Times*, July 17, 1898, p. 12.

44. "A Specialist in 'Down and Outing,'" *Literary Digest* 50 (1915), 268; Stephen Graham, "The Bowery Under Prohibition," *Harper's* 154 (1927), 341.

45. For case studies, see Kenneth L. Kusmer, *A Ghetto Takes Shape: Black Cleveland, 1870–1930* (Urbana: University of Illinois Press, 1976), chs. 3, 8; Richard W. Thomas, *Life Is What We Make It: Building Black Community in Detroit, 1915–1945* (Bloomington: Indiana University Press, 1992), ch. 5.

46. Dees, *Flophouse*, p. 29; W. S. Bixby, "Out of Work in Akron," *The Family* 2 (1921–22), 89; Robert Wilson, *Community Planning for Homeless Men and Boys: The Experience of Sixteen Cities in the Winter of 1930–31* (New York: Family Welfare Association, 1931), p. 103; Matthew Josephson, "The Other Nation," *New Republic* (May 17, 1933), 15; *Philadelphia Directory of Missions* (Philadelphia, 1894), pp. 46–69 *passim*; Magnuson, *Salvation in the Slums*, pp. 118–21; E. H. McKinley, *Somebody's Brother: A History of the Salvation Army's Men's Social Service Department, 1891–1985* (Lewiston, Me.: Mellen, 1986), pp. 184–85; Wells-Barnett quoted in Spear, *Black Chicago*, pp. 46–47; Winston, *Red-Hot and Righteous*, pp. 41–42, 60–61. In 1926, the Salvation Army in Cleveland established a separate black annex to their rescue home for women and girls. *Cleveland Gazette*, January 23, 1926, p. 1.

47. Anderson, *The Hobo*, p. 8; Groth, *Living Downtown*, p. 37; Spear, *Black Chicago*, chs. 1, 8; Kusmer, *A Ghetto Takes Shape*, chs. 2, 7; Joe Trotter, Jr., *Black Milwaukee: The Making of an Industrial Proletariat* (Urbana: University of Illinois Press, 1985); Thomas, *Life Is What We Make It*, pp. 135–43.

48. St. Clair Drake and Horace R. Cayton, *Black Metropolis: A Study of Negro Life in a Northern City* (New York: Harper and Row, 1945), pp. 600–603; Solenberger, *One Thousand Homeless Men*, p. 8; Spear, *Black Chicago*, pp. 148–49; Anderson, *The Hobo*, p. 8; Kusmer, *A Ghetto Takes Shape*, pp. 210–13.

49. See Mark H. Haller, "Policy Gambling, Entertainment, and the Emergence of Black Politics: Chicago from 1900 to 1940," *Journal of Social History* 17 (1991), 719–39, and the insightful discussion in Kevin J. Mumford, *Interzones: Black/White Sex Districts in Chicago and New York in the Early Twentieth Century* (New York: Columbia University Press, 1997), chs. 2 and 4.

50. See data on Chicago and Cleveland in Spear, *Black Chicago*, p. 149; Kusmer, *A Ghetto Takes Shape*, p. 227n.

51. Data from Evelyn Wilson, "Chicago Families in Furnished Rooms" (Ph.D. dissertation, University of Chicago, 1929), pp. 43–47, cited in Hoch and Slayton, *New Homeless and Old*, p. 25.

52. Laubach, *Why There Are Vagrants*, p. 59; Kildare, "Drifters of 'The Valley of Never Care,'" pt. 5, p. 6. Population data from Solenberger, *One Thousand Homeless Men*, and Anderson, *The Hobo*.

CHAPTER 9

1. Other studies that discuss the image of the tramp or hobo include Frederick Feied, *No Pie in the Sky: The Hobo as American Cultural Hero in the Works of Jack London, John Dos Passos, and Jack Kerouac* (New York: Citadel, 1964); John D. Seelye, "The American Tramp: A Version of the Picaresque," *American Quarterly* 15 (1963), 535–53; James Gilbert, *Work Without Salvation: American Intellectuals and Industrialization, 1880–1914* (Baltimore: Johns Hopkins University Press, 1977), pp. 23–30; and Benedict Giamo, *On the Bowery: Confronting Homelessness in American Society* (Iowa City: University of Iowa Press, 1989), which despite its title is primarily a literary analysis.

2. Edwin H. Cady, *The Realist at War: The Mature Years of William Dean Howells* (Syracuse: Syracuse University Press, 1958), pp. 65–80; Robert L. Hugh, *The Quiet Rebel: William Dean Howells as Social Commentator* (Lincoln: University of Nebraska Press, 1959), pp. 20–39; John Cawelti, *Apostles of the Self-Made Man* (Chicago: University of Chicago Press, 1966), pp. 152–58. Although I disagree with the author's portrayal of Howells as a protomodernist, the most insightful study is Kenneth Lynn, *William Dean Howells: An American Life* (New York: Harcourt, Brace, Jovanovich, 1971).

3. William Dean Howells, *The Undiscovered Country* (Boston: Houghton Mifflin, 1884), pp. 126–43.

4. William Dean Howells, *The Minister's Charge; Or, The Apprenticeship of Lemuel Barker* (Boston: Ticknor, 1887), pp. 89–96, 99.

5. Ibid., pp. 104–06, 110, 129; William Dean Howells, *A Hazard of New Fortunes* (New York: New American Library, 1965 [1890]), p. 382. Cady, *The Realist at War*, p. 4, concludes that these scenes from *The Minister's Charge* were "unprecedented in Howells's fiction."

6. William Dean Howells to W. C. Howells, November 19, 1893; Howells to W. C. Howells, April 1, 1894, William Dean Howells Papers, Harvard University; Cady, *The Realist at War*, pp. 139–63. For the background of Howells's turn toward radicalism, see William Alexander, *William Dean Howells: The Realist as Humanist* (New York: Burt Franklin, 1981), pp. 140–62.

7. William Dean Howells, "Are We a Plutocracy?" *North American Review* 158 (1894), 194; William Dean Howells, *A Traveler from Altruria* (New York, 1957 [1894]), pp. 22–23, 28, 34–35, 115; William Dean Howells, "Tribulations of a Cheerful Giver," in Howells, *Impressions and Experiences* (New York: Harper, 1896), pp. 182–84. See also Howells, *A Traveler from Altruria*, pp. 98–99.

8. For the context of Crane's career at the time these essays were published, see R. W. Stallman, *Stephen Crane: A Biography* (New York: George Braziller, 1968), pp. 95–98; and Linda H. Davis, *Badge of Courage: The Life of Stephen Crane* (New York: Houghton Mifflin, 1998), pp 79–81.

9. "The New Lawlessness," *Nation* 58 (1894), 340; Stephen Crane, "The Men in the Storm" and "An Experiment in Misery," both in *The New York City Sketches of Stephen Crane, and Related Pieces*, ed. R. W. Stallman and E. R. Hagemann (New York: New York University Press, 1966), pp. 315–22, 283–93 (quotation, p. 319).

10. Howells, *A Traveler from Altruria*, p. 116.

11. Crane, "The Men in the Storm," pp. 316–17. For a perceptive discussion of Crane's essay, see Giamo, *On the Bowery*, pp. 103–12.

12. K. K. Bentwick, "Street Begging as a Fine Art," *North American Review* 158 (1894), 125–28.

13. Henry B. Fuller, *With the Procession* (Chicago: University of Chicago, 1965 [1895]), p. 21. Compare, for contradictory impressions of the tramp, Henry E. Rood, "The Tramp Problem," *Forum* 26 (1898), 90–94, with E. L. Bailey, "Tramps and Hoboes," ibid., 26 (1898), 217–21. An early example of a highly sympathetic article in a popular magazine is M. I. Swift's significantly titled essay "Tramps as Human Beings," *Outlook* 52 (1895), 342–43.

14. Josiah Flynt [Willard], *Tramping with Tramps* (New York: Century, 1899), pp. 290, 313–14, 391; Josiah Flynt [Willard], "Railroad Police and the Tramp," *Railroad Gazette* 32 (1900), 579–80; Josiah Flynt [Willard], *Notes of an Itinerant Policeman* (Boston: L. C. Page, 1900), pp. 207–08; Anonymous review of *Tramping with Tramps*, in *New York Times Book Review*, March 31, 1900, p. 211; see also the anonymous review of Flynt's *Notes of an Itinerant Policeman*, in ibid., December 8, 1900, p. 902.

15. Such reportage was part of a larger journalistic trend to enlighten the middle class about the poor or working class at the turn of the century. See Mark Pittenger, "A World of Difference: Constructing the 'Underclass' in Progressive America," *American Quarterly* 49 (1997), 26–65.

16. Walter A. Wyckoff, *The Workers, A Study in Reality: The East* (New York: Scribner's, 1897), pp. viii–ix; Wyckoff, *The Workers, A Study in Reality: The West* (New York: Scribner's, 1899), pp. 88–89, 120; Wyckoff, "A Day with a Tramp," in Wyckoff, *A Day with a Tramp, and Other Days* (New York: Scribner's, 1901), p. 5.

17. Wyckoff, *The Workers, A Study in Reality: The West*, pp. 1,2; Wyckoff, *The Workers, A Study in Reality: The East*, pp. 23–24, 50; Davis, *Badge of Courage*, p. 80.

18. Robert Cowdrey, *A Tramp in Society* (Chicago: Frank Schwartz, 1891), pp. 46–47.

19. Richard Lingeman, *Theodore Dreiser: An American Journey* (New York: John Wiley, 1993), pp. 19–20, 87–89, 197–98.

20. Theodore Dreiser, *Sister Carrie*, ed. Catherine Simpson (Boston: Houghton Mifflin, 1959 [1900]), pp. 40–41, 43, 383, 416–17.

21. Prior to 1908, when a new American edition was published, few people had the opportunity to read *Sister Carrie*. Because of the objections of Doubleday and his wife to the book, only one thousand copies were printed in the original edition, and Doubleday did not advertise the book.

22. See Theodore Dreiser, *The Color of a Great City* (New York: Boni and Liveright, 1925), pp. 129–32, 222–27, 228–30. For a further discussion of the character of Hurstwood in *Sister Carrie*, see Giamo, *On the Bowery*, pp. 112–28.

23. Elizabeth Stuart Phelps, "Unemployed," *Harper's Monthly* 113 (1906), 904–07, 910, 912.

24. Stuart Rice, "Vagrancy," National Council of Charities and Correction, *Proceedings, 1916*, 458–59; A Matron Bum, "Keeping Up a Front on Thirty Cents," *New York Times Book Review*, April 9, 1922, p. 6.

25. Henry George, *Progress and Poverty: An Inquiry into the Causes of Industrial Depressions, and of Increase of Want with Increase of Wealth* (San Francisco: W. M. Hinton, 1879), pp. 6–9; Henry George, *Social Problems* (New York: Belford, Clarke, 1883), p. 129.

26. "Tramps and Millionaires," *New York Tribune*, July 26, 1887, p. 4.

27. See the classic study by Sigmund Diamond, *The Reputation of the American Businessman* (Cambridge, Mass.: Harvard University Press, 1955), pp. 53–106.

28. Mary A. Livermore, "Homes Builded by Women," *Chautauquan* 7 (1887), 408; Oscar Craig, "The Prevention of Pauperism," *Scribner's* 14 (1893), 121, quoted in Robert H. Bremner, *From the Depths: The Discovery of Poverty in the United States* (New York: New York University Press, 1956), p. 22; "A Tramp by Evolution," *New York Times*, December 23, 1888, p. 14; Cowdrey, *A Tramp in Society*, p. 236. On the "tramps and millionaires" theme in dime novels, see Michael Denning, *Mechanic Accents: Dime Novels and Working-Class Culture* (London: Verso, 1987), pp. 151–57. See also Thure De Thulstrup, "Where Two Ends Meet," *Harper's Weekly* 35 (1891), 616–17.

29. See Neil Harris, *The Artist in American Society, 1790–1860* (New York: Atheneum, 1966), chs. 2–3, for the impact of these values on art.

30. Mark Twain, *A Connecticut Yankee in King Arthur's Court* (New York: Harper, 1889), p. 159; Josiah Strong, *The Times and Young Men* (New York: Baker and Taylor, 1901), pp. 120–21.

31. "Roosevelt to Stop Big Man's Rascality," *New York Times*, August 27, 1908, p. 2; John D. Hicks, *The Populist Revolt* (Lincoln, Neb.: University of Nebraska Press, 1961 ed.), p. 436; S[amuel] M. Jones, "Charity or Justice—Which?" National Conference of Charities and Correction, *Proceedings, 1899*, p. 137; Robert Hunter, *Poverty* (New York: Macmillan, 1904), pp. 69–71; H. P. Peebles, "A Solution of the Tramp Problem," *Railway Conductor* 12 (1895), 443; Roger Payne, *The Hobo Philosopher; Or, the Message of Economic Freedom* (Puente, Cal.: Published by author, 1920), p. 10.

32. Lizzie M. Holmes, "Two Types of Wasted Lives," *American Federationist* 8 (1901), 407–08.

33. "The Great American Tramp," *New York Tribune*, December 20, 1885, p. 4; John J. McCook, "The Tramp Problem," National Conference of Charities and Correction, *Proceedings, 1895*, pp. 291–92; Francis G. Peabody, quoted in Gilbert, *Work Without Salvation*, p. 138; John J. McCook, "Leaves from the Diary of a Tramp: Part I," *Independent* 53 (1901), 2765; Benwick, "Begging as a Fine Art," 126–27.

34. George Beard, *American Nervousness: Its Causes and Consequences* (New York: Putnam's, 1881); Edward Wakefield, "Nervousness: The National Disease of America," *McClure's* 2 (1894), 302–04. For the context of this development, see Joseph Kett, *Rites of Passage: Adolescence in America, 1790 to the Present* (New York: Basic Books, 1977), pp. 160–61; and Thomas J. Schlereth, *Victorian America: Transformations in Everyday Life, 1876–1915* (New York: Harper and Row, 1991), pp. 289–90.

35. [Willard], *Tramping with Tramps*, p. 355.

36. "Wyckoff is not a tramp authority. He doesn't understand the real tramp. Josiah Flynt is the tramp authority." Jack London to Cloudesley Johns, December 6, 1901, *Letters from Jack London, Containing an Unpublished Correspondence Between Lon-*

don and Sinclair Lewis, ed. King Hendricks and Irving Shepard (New York: Odyssey, 1965), p. 126.

37. Jack London, *The Road* (New York: Macmillan, 1907), p. 34 and pp. 24–52 *passim*.

38. Ibid., pp. 21, 24, 32, 38, 47–48, 71, 173, 175; Andrew Sinclair, *Jack: The Biography of Jack London* (New York: Harper and Row, 1978), p. 89.

39. London, *The Road*, p. 50; Jack London, "A Jack London Diary: Tramping with Kelly Through Iowa," *Palimpsest* 8 (1926), 129–39; Sinclair, *Jack*, pp. 133–34; book reviews (only the third, positive review, from the *Washington Star*, is identified) quoted in King Hendricks, Introduction, Jack London, *The Road* (Santa Barbara, Peregrine ed., 1970), xv, xvi; Feied, *No Pie in the Sky*, p. 53.

40. Charles Ashleigh, *Rambling Kid* (London: Faber and Faber, 1930), quoted in Kenneth Allsop, *Hard Travellin': The Hobo and His History* (New York: New American Library, 1967), p. 245. For other examples, see Glen Mullin, *Adventures of a Scholar Tramp* (London: J. Cape, 1925), pp. 8–9; Jim Tully, *Beggars of Life* (New York: Boni, 1924), pp. 203–04; *The Hobo's Hornbook*, ed. Milburn, pp. xviii–xix, 237–38; Dean Stiff [Nels Anderson], *The Milk and Honey Route* (New York: Vanguard, 1931), p. 83. Particularly amusing is the story of a tramp who supposedly was "a specialist in speed," in Henri Tauscheraud, "The Passenger Stiff," *American Mercury* 5 (1925), 368–70.

41. "Walks 90 Miles in 24 Hours," *New York Times*, May 15, 1910, p. 1. Between 1906 and 1913 the *Times* published about 30 articles about Weston's walking tours.

42. Charles F. Lumis, *A Tramp Across the Continent* (New York, 1892), unpaginated preface preceding p. 1, pp. 1–2 and *passim*; "S" [William Suddards Franklin], *A Tramp Trip in the Rockies of Colorado and Wyoming* (Lancaster, Pa.: New Era, 1903), pp. 50–51. Numerous other books of this type were published during the 1890–1930 period.

43. Lumis, *A Tramp Across the Continent*, p. 8; London, *The Road*, p. 173.

44. "Laziness: Positive and Negative," *Independent* 91 (1917), 241; "Is Hard Work Healthful?" *Literary Digest* 52 (1916), 1775; S. G. Blyth, "Tapering Off on Work," *Saturday Evening Post* 198 (August 8, 1925), 3–4; F. C. Kelly, "Our Need for Wasting More Time," *Harper's Monthly* 150 (1925), 659–62; W. N. Polakov, "The Curse of Work," *Nation* 117 (1923), 506; William Hutchinson, "Balanced Work," *Saturday Evening Post* 194 (May 13, 1922), 40–46. Daniel Rogers's illuminating study, *The Work Ethic in Industrial America, 1850–1920* (Chicago: University of Chicago Press, 1978), chs. 4 and 8, may underestimate the growth of an ambivalent attitude toward the work ethic at the turn of the century.

45. "Tramps and Coxeyites," *New York Times*, May 5, 1894, p. 4; McCook, "The Tramp Problem," 298; C. Hanford Henderson, *Pay-Day* (New York: Houghton Mifflin, 1911), pp. 85, 88 (quotation). For examples of the perceived "monotony" of American life, see James F. Muirhead, *America: The Land of Contrasts* (New York: J. Lane, 1902), p. 38; Henry James, *The American Scene* (Bloomington: Indiana University Press, 1966 [1908]), p. 203.

46. For reference to "hobo kings," see "'The King of Tramps,'" *New York Times*, October 17, 1892, p. 1; "'King of Hoboes' in Cell," Ibid., July 13, 1919, p. 7; Bronson Batchelor, "The Hotel de Gink," *Independent* 81 (1915), 127–28; Bertha Thompson,

Sister of the Road, ed. Ben Reitman (New York: Gold Label Books, 1937), pp. 58–59; Nels Anderson, *The Hobo: The Sociology of the Homeless Man* (Chicago: University of Chicago Press, 1923), pp. 172–73; Paul T. Ringenbach, *Tramps and Reformers, 1873–1916: The Discovery of Unemployment in New York* (Westport, Conn.: Greenwood Press, 1973), pp. 166–67. On the Britt, Iowa, hobo convention, see Gretchen Carlson, "The Hobo Convention," *Palimpsest* 12 (1931), 257–72; and "How It All Began: A Historical Sketch of . . . the National Hobo Convention Held in Britt, Iowa" (undated pamphlet, Iowa Historical Society); Roger A. Bruns, *Knights of the Road* (New York: Methuen, 1980), pp. 123–24.

47. For examples, see "Tramps Along the Hudson," *New York Times*, August 6, 1879, p. 5; "Believe in Signs," *New York Tribune*, August 23, 1903, pt. 2, p. 14; Towne Nylander, "Tramps and Hoboes," *Forum* 71 (1925), 233–35; "Remember Those Old Hobo Signs?" (undated clipping in Iowa Clipping File, Iowa State Historical Society).

48. Thomas M. Page, *Bohemian Life: Or, The Autobiography of a Tramp* (St. Louis: Sun Publishing Co., 1884), p. 182; John J. McCook, "Leaves from the Diary of a Tramp: Part V," *Independent* 54 (1902), 154; London, *The Road*, p. 128; [Willard], *Notes of an Itinerant Policeman*, p. 167; [Anderson], *The Milk and Honey Route*, pp. 84, 85.

49. Anonymous review of *Adventures of a Scholar Tramp*, in *The Bookman* 41 (1925), 484; William Edge, *The Main Stem* (New York: Vanguard, 1927), p. 81; Anon., "Do You Give the Tramp a Ride?" *Sunset* 54 (1925), 79.

50. See William Brevda, *Harry Kemp: The Last Bohemian* (Lewisburg, Pa.: Bucknell University Press, 1986), pp. 111–29 for a discussion of Kemp and Dell. By embellishing and magnifying his early, fairly limited tramp exploits, Kemp came to be known as the "tramp poet" while still in college (ibid., pp. 32–33).

51. Knibbs, quoted in Allsop, *Hard Travellin'*, p. 234; Nylander, "Tramps and Hoboes," 229; Henri Tascheraud, "The Art of Bumming a Meal," *American Mercury* 5 (1925), 183–87; "An Amateur Hobo Finds the Road Not So Bad," *Literary Digest* 64 (June 9, 1928), 63.

52. On the importance of magazines in establishing new patterns of culture and consumption, see Jackson Lears, *Fables of Abundance: A Cultural History of Advertising in America* (New York: Basic Books, 1994), pp. 138–95, 210–34; and Richard Ohmann, *Selling Culture: Magazines, Markets, and Class at the Turn of the Century* (London: Verso, 1996), especially ch. 7. On the importance of nostalgia to the culture of the 1920s, see Lawrence W. Levine, "Progress and Nostalgia: The Self Image of the Nineteen Twenties," in Lawrence W. Levine, *The Unpredictable Past: Explorations in American Cultural History* (New York: Oxford University Press, 1993), pp. 189–205.

53. See Helen Lynd and Robert Lynd, *Middletown: A Study in Modern American Culture* (New York: Harcourt Brace and World, 1929), ch. 7; Whiting Williams, *What's on the Worker's Mind: By One Who Put on the Overalls to Find Out* (New York: Scribner's, 1921), p. 6; Robert McElvaine, *The Great Depression: America, 1929–1941* (New York: Times Books, 1984), pp. 22–23.

54. Clark D. Halker, *For Democracy, Workers, and God: Labor Song-Poems and Labor Protest, 1865–1895* (Urbana: University of Illinois Press, 1991), p. 123; "The Two Bums," in *The Hobo's Hornbook*, ed. Milburn, pp. 120–21; Allsop, *Hard Travellin'*, p. 176; Norm Cohen, *The Long Steel Rail: The Railroad in American Folksong* (Urbana:

University of Illinois Press, 1981), pp. 343–98 ("The Dying Hobo" is discussed on pp. 367–71).

55. Excerpts from blues songs quoted in Allsop, *Hard Travellin'*, pp. 280, 282; Cohen, *Long Steel Rail*, pp. 437–38. See also Paul Oliver, *Blues Fell This Morning: Meaning in the Blues* (Cambridge, Eng.: Cambridge University Press, 1990 [1960]), pp. 43–68.

56. Clark Kinnaird, "Cavalcade of the Funnies," in *The Funnies: An American Idiom*, ed. David M. White and Robert Abel (New York: Free Press, 1963), p. 91; White and Abel, Introduction, ibid., p. 9; Levy, pp. 286–87 (quotation); Maurice Horn, *The World Encyclopedia of Comics* (New York: Chelsea, 1976), pp. 693, 302–03; Charles Musser, *The Emergence of Cinema: The American Screen to 1907* (Berkeley: University of California Press, 1990), pp. 283, 316. See also the perceptive commentary on Happy Hooligan in Stephen Becker, *Comic Art in America* (New York: Simon and Schuster, 1959), p. 18.

57. Gilbert, *American Vaudeville*, pp. 269–75; Marian Spitzer, *The Palace* (New York: Atheneum, 1969), pp. 26, 40, 47; Bernard Sobel, *A Pictoral History of Vaudeville* (New York: Citadel, 1961), p. 47; White and Abel, Introduction, *The Funnies*, p. 9 (quotation); *The Hobo's Hornbook*, ed. Milburn, pp. 142–45. Occasionally, tramps were the lead characters in plays. For one extant example, a melodrama with comic overtones, see Robert J. Sherman, "The Tramp's Redemption: A Three-Act Comedy Drama" (Typescript manuscript, University of Chicago Library, 1915).

58. On the early development of American film and its audience, see Lewis Jacobs, *The Rise of the American Film* (New York: Harcourt Brace, 1939); Charles Musser, *The Emergence of Cinema: The American Screen to 1907* (Berkeley: University of California Press, 1990); Eileen Bowser, *The Transformation of Cinema: 1907–1915* (Berkeley: University of California Press, 1990); David Robinson, *From Peep Show to Palace: The Birth of American Film* (New York: Columbia University Press, 1996); and Steven J. Ross, *Working-Class Hollywood: Silent Film and the Shaping of Class in America* (Princeton: Princeton University Press, 1998), chs. 1–4.

59. David Nasaw, *Children of the City: At Work and at Play* (New York: Oxford University Press, 1985), pp. 120–27; Ross, *Working-Class Hollywood*, pp. 42–55, 79–80.

60. David Nasaw, *Going Out: The Rise and Fall of Public Amusements* (Cambridge, Mass.: Harvard University Press, 1993), pp. 144, 146, mentions the *Weary Willy* films. The other films are described (and sometimes depicted in stills) in Musser's authoritative *Emergence of Cinema*, pp. 226, 227, 393, 316, 400 (Musser quoted), 401, 487, 468.

61. For examples, see Charles Musser, "Work, Ideology, and Chaplin's Tramp," in *Resisting Images: Essays in Cinema and History*, ed. Robert Sklar and Charles Musser (Philadelphia: Temple University Press, 1990), pp. 36–37, 42–43.

62. On Chaplin's childhood, see Charlie Chaplin, *My Autobiography* (New York: Pocket Books, 1966), pp. 4–71; and David Robinson, *Chaplin: His Life and Art* (New York: McGraw Hill, 1985), pp. 10–42.

63. Review by Sime Silverman in *Variety*, excerpted in *Films of Charlie Chaplin*, ed. Gerald D. McDonald et al. (Secaucus, N.J.: Citadel, 1965), p. 99; also discussed in Musser, "Work, Ideology, and Chaplin's Tramp," pp. 53–54. Silverman's reviews of other Chaplin comedies struck a similar note.

64. In addition to the films themselves, unless otherwise indicated basic information is drawn from Uno Asplund, *Chaplin's Films: A Filmography*, trans. Paul B. Austin (London: David and Charles, 1971); and *The Films of Charlie Chaplin*, ed. McDonald et al.

65. Robert Sklar, *Movie-Made America: A Cultural History of American Movies* (New York: Vintage, 1975), pp. 112–16; Musser, "Work, Ideology, and Chaplin's Tramp," pp. 38–39, 46–48, 50–53. Both Sklar and Musser provide perceptive, thought-provoking analyses that have influenced my own interpretation of Chaplin. On *Work*, see also Robinson, *Chaplin*, pp. 144–45.

66. In addition to *Making a Living*, films that illustrate this include *Caught in a Cabaret* (1914), *Her Friend the Bandit* (1914), *A Jitney Elopement* (1915), *The Count* (1916), *The Adventurer* (1917), and, most impressively, *The Idle Class* (1921).

67. One of the best case studies of this transition is Roy Rosenzweig's study of Worcester, Massachusetts, *Eight Hours for What We Will: Workers and Leisure in an Industrial City, 1870–1920* (Cambridge, Eng.: Cambridge University Press, 1983), pp. 191–221.

68. See the reviews in *The Films of Charlie Chaplin*, ed. McDonald, p. 167.

CHAPTER 10

1. Glen Steele, *Temporary Shelter for Homeless and Transient Persons and Travelers Aid* (Washington: Government Printing Office [GPO], 1932), pp. 19–20 (table 5); "1,130,000 Lodgings by City This Year," *New York Times*, October 28, 1932, p. 2; "Aid to Homeless Over Nation Set a New High in February," ibid., May 15, 1933, p. 3; "City Faces Big Problem," *Philadelphia Record*, October 17, 1932, Philadelphia *Bulletin* Clipping Collection (BCC), Urban Archives, Temple University; Nels Anderson testimony, *Relief for Unemployed Transients: Hearings Before a Subcommittee of the Committee on Manufacturers, United States Senate*, S. 5121, January 13–15, 1933 [hereafter S.5121], p. 65.

2. John N. Webb, *The Transient Unemployed: A Description and Analysis of the Transient Relief Population* (Washington: GPO, 1935), p. 15; Maury Maverick, *A Maverick America* (New York: Covici, Friede, 1937), pp. 152–53 (quotation), 165; Kenneth Barnhart, "Supplement to a Study of the Transient and Homeless in Birmingham, Alabama, Jan.–July, [19]33," unpag., Box 3, State Series, Record Group 69, Federal Emergency Relief Administration Records, National Archives [hereafter, FERA-TD]; A Wayne McMillen, "An Army of Boys on the Loose," *Survey Graphic* 21 (1932), 390 (quotation).

3. Figures computed from data in FERA-TD, "State of Origin of Persons Receiving Transient Relief on September 30, 1934," New General Subject Series, February 1935, Box 67, RG69, NA. Data (such as Florida's 28 percent) on "state transients" do not, of course, take into account the large number of local homeless who never registered with the Federal Transient Service.

4. Walter R. Hoy, "The Case of the Homeless in St. Louis," *The Family* 9 (1928), 213; Thomas E. Murphy, "Elizabethan Hangover," *Survey* 70 (1934), 12–24; Joan M.

Crouse, *The Homeless Transient in the Great Depression: New York State, 1929–1941* (Albany: State University of New York Press, 1986), pp. 46, 196–99; Bertha McCall testimony, S.5121, p. 53.

5. [National] Committee on Care of Transient and Homeless, "Report on Census of Transient and Homeless for March, 1933," p. 3, Box 83, Transient General Correspondence, FERA-TD; S.5121, pp. 187–203. See also McMillan, "An Army of Boys on the Loose," 390.

6. Robert S. Wilson, *Community Planning for Homeless Men and Boys: The Experience of Sixteen Cities in the Winter of 1930–31* (New York: Family Welfare Association, 1931), pp. 113–18, 43 (quotation), 85 (quotation), 64 (quotation), 21.

7. Matthew Josephson, "The Other Nation," *New Republic* 75 (1933), 15; John Kazarian, "The Starvation Army" [pt. 2], p. 442; Carl Kolin interview, December 18, 1934, pp. 5–6, Box 134, folder 2, Ernest W. Burgess Papers, University of Chicago Library (quotation); Mary Heaton Vorse, "School for Bums," *New Republic* 69 (1931), 293; Wilson, *Community Planning*, pp. 34, 43, 86, 104; Maverick, *A Maverick American*, p. 155.

8. Crouse, *The Homeless Transient*, p. 82; Cheryl Lynn Greenberg, *"Or Does It Explode?" Harlem in the Great Depression* (New York: Oxford University Press, 1991), p. 57; Wilson, *Community Planning*, p. 114. On conditions in southern cities, see S.5121, pp. 187–203.

9. "Baldwins Offer to House Jobless," *Philadelphia Evening Bulletin*, November 29, 1930, BCC; Wilson, *Community Planning*, pp. 100–08 (quotation, p. 101); "City Faces Big Problem," *Philadelphia Record*, October 17, 1932, BCC; "Street Beggars Can Get Aid at City's Shelter," *Philadelphia Evening Bulletin*, February 18, 1933, BCC; Bonnie Fox Schwartz, "Unemployment Relief in Philadelphia, 1930–1932: A Study of the Depression's Impact on Volunterism," *Pennsylvania Magazine of History and Biography* 92 (1969), 86–108.

10. "Reds Lead Jobless in Lodging Demand," *New York Times*, January 4, 1931, p. 2 (quotation); "Mayor Has Snack at Lodging House," *New York Times*, July 1, 1934, pt. 2, p. 1.

11. "City Plans to Feed 12,000 Idle Daily," *New York Times*, October 24, 1930, p. 3; *The Salvation Army and the Present Crisis: Report of Unemployment Emergency Relief Work in Greater New York* (New York: Salvation Army, 1931); Committee on Care of Transient and Homeless, "Report of the Census of Transient and Homeless for March 22, 1933," unpag.; Wilson, *Community Planning*, p. 16; E. H. McKinley, *Somebody's Brother: A History of the Salvation Army's Social Service Department, 1891–1985* (Lewiston, Maine: Mellen, 1986), pp. 93–102 (quotations, pp. 94, 97); Crouse, *Homeless Transient*, pp. 80–92.

12. "Feeds Families of Unemployed," *Philadelphia Evening Bulletin*, December 18, 1930; "Man Out of Work Opens Soup Kitchen," ibid., March 17, 1931, BCC; "1,200 Hungry Get Noon Meal Daily," ibid., March 21, 1931, BCC; Gertrude Springer, "Well Advertised Breadlines," *Survey* 65 (1931), 545; Greenberg, *"Or Does It Explode?"* p. 60; Richard W. Thomas, *Life Is What We Make It: Building Black Community in Detroit, 1915–1945* (Bloomington: Indiana University Press, 1992), p. 177; Wilson, *Community Planning*, p. 16.

13. Garland O. Ethel, "Soup Line in Seattle," *Nation* 132 (1931), 209; Wilson, *Community Planning*, pp. 21–37, 44; Ewan Claque, "Philadelphia Studies Its Breadlines," *Survey* 67 (1931), 196–97; "1,200 Hungry Get Noon Meal Daily."

14. Ellen C. Potter, "Mustering Out the Migrants," *Survey* (1933), 411–12; Hoy, "The Case of the Homeless in St. Louis," 215; Wilson, *Community Planning*, pp. 45–46, 87 (quotation).

15. "Asks Public to Curb Begging in Streets," *New York Times*, January 4, 1932, p. 23; Wilson, *Community Planning*, pp. 45, 90 (quotation); Eric Marks testimony, S.5121, p. 165; "Men and Things," *Philadelphia Evening Bulletin*, May 4, 1934, p. 8, BCC.

16. "Report on 50 Transient Men Picked Up in Springfield, Ill.," attached to a letter from Wilfred S. Reynolds to Harry Hopkins, July 10, 1933, unpag., Box 82, State Series (Illinois), FERA-TD.

17. Mauritz A. Hallgren, "Mass Misery in Philadelphia," *Nation* 134 (1932), 275–76 (quotation, 275); "Street Beggars Can Get Aid at City's Shelter," *Philadelphia Evening Bulletin*, February 18, 1933, BCC; E. Wight Bakke, *The Unemployed Worker: A Study of the Task of Making a Living Without a Job* (New Haven: Yale University Press, 1940), pp. 26–27 (quotation); Nixon, quoted in Bruce Mazlish, *In Search of Nixon: A Psychohistorical Inquiry* (Baltimore: Penguin Books, 1972), p. 19. Maury Graham and Robert J. Hemming, *Tales of the Iron Road: My Life as King of the Hobos* (New York: Paragon, 1990), pp. 84–85. See also Studs Terkel, *Hard Times: An Oral History of the Great Depression* (New York: Pantheon, 1970), p. 35.

18. Mackey, quoted in Schwartz, "Unemployment Relief in Philadelphia," pp. 96–97; Jane Addams, "Social Consequences of Depression," *Survey* 67 (1932), 370–71; Aubrey W. Grossman, "Who Is a Vagrant in California," 23 California Law Review 506–18 (1935).

19. John Dos Passos, "Detroit: City of Leisure," *New Republic* 72 (1932), 281; Fred Gendral, "The Homeless Go to Camp," *Current History* 42 (1935), 489; "Jungle Life in New York," *Survey* (October 15, 1931), p. 91; Wilson, *Community Planning*, p. 67 (quotation); Boris Israel, "Shantytown, U.S.A.," *New Republic* 75 (1933), 40–41.

20. On the Bonus Army, see Roger Daniels, *The Bonus March: An Episode of the Great Depression* (Westport, Conn.: Greenwood Press, 1971); Donald Lisio, *The President and Protest: Hoover, Conspiracy, and the Bonus Riot* (Columbia: University of Missouri Press, 1974).

21. Terkel, *Hard Times*, pp. 13–14; Daniels, *The Bonus Army*, pp. 65–86. On Anacostia, see John Dos Passos, "The Veterans Come Home to Roost," *New Republic* 17 (1932), 177; William C. White, *B.E.F.* (New York: AMS Press, 1980 [1933]); Jack Douglas, *Veterans on the March* (New York: Workers' Library, 1934). On African Americans, see Terkel, *Hard Times*, p. 16; Roy Wilkins, *Standing Fast: The Autobiography of Roy Wilkins* (New York: Viking, 1982), pp. 118–19.

22. Testimony of J. Prentice Murphy, S.5121, pp. 94–103 (quotation, 102); Irving Bernstein, *The Lean Years: A History of the American Worker, 1920–1933* (Baltimore: Penguin Books, 1966), p. 454 (quotation).

23. Josephson, "The Other Nation," 14–15; Edward Dahlberg, *Bottom Dogs* (New York: AMS Press, 1976 [1930]); Tom Kromer, *Waiting for Nothing* (New York: Knopf, 1935); Nelson Algren, *Somebody in Boots* (New York, 1987 [1935]), p. 103; Richard

Pells, *Radical Visions and American Dreams: Culture and Social Thought in the Depression Years* (New York: Harper and Row, 1973), pp. 234–35.

24. Daniels, *Bonus March*, pp. 70, 186–87; Bernard Stershner, "Victims of the Great Depression: Self-Blame/Non-Self-Blame, Radicalism, and Pre-1929 Experiences," *Social Science History* 1 (1977), 145–48; Bertha Thompson, *Sister of the Road*, ed. Ben Reitman (New York: Gold Label Books, 1937), p. 52.

25. John C. Webb, *The Transient Unemployed: A Description and Analysis of the Transient Relief Population* (Washington: GPO, 1935), pp. 28–29 33, 35; [Elizabeth] Wickenden to [Harry] Hopkins, September 17, 1934, Old General Subject Series, March 1933–Jan. 1935, FERA Central Files, FERA-TD; George E. Outland, "Determinants Involved in Boy Transiency," *Journal of Education and Society* 11 (1938), 364; Herbert J. P. Schubert, *Twenty Thousand Transients: A Year's Sample of Those Who Apply for Aid in a Northern City* (Buffalo: Emergency Relief Bureau, 1935), pp. 12, 18–21; Thomas Minehan, *Boy and Girl Tramps of America* (New York: Farrar and Rinehart, 1934), p. 253.

26. Wickenden to Hopkins, September 17, 1924, FERA General Files; *Pennsylvania Monthly Relief Bulletin* 1 (June 1935), 27; Robert Lynd and Helen Merrell Lynd, *Middletown: A Study in Modern American Culture* (New York: Harcourt Brace and World, 1929), pp. 34–35; Lizabeth Cohen, *Making a New Deal: Industrial Workers in Chicago, 1919–1939* (Cambridge, Eng.: Cambridge University Press, 1990), 246, 320–21. In Buffalo, 8.6 percent of transient males were over age 50. Schubert, *Twenty-Thousand Transients*, p. 12.

27. Webb, *The Transient Unemployed*, pp. 25, 29; Edwin H. Sutherland and Harry J. Locke, *Twenty Thousand Homeless Men* (Chicago: University of Chicago Press, 1936), p. 36; [Elizabeth] Wickenden to [Harry] Hopkins, September 17, 1934 ("Summary of Transient Program"), Old General Subject Series, March 1933–January 1935 (Transients), FERA Central Files, FERA-TD; Carl F. Schockman, *We Turned Hobo: A Narrative of Personal Experience* (New York: Century, 1937), p. 16 (quotation); Broadus Mitchell, *Depression Decade: From New Era through New Deal, 1929–1941* (New York: Harper and Row, 1967), p. 328; Minehan, *Boy and Girl Tramps*, p. 26; McMillan, "An Army of Boys on the Loose," 391; Outland, "Determinants Involved in Boy Transiency," 365–66, 369–70 (quotation); George Outland, *Boy Transiency in America* (Santa Barbara: Santa Barbara State College Press, 1939), pp. 104–14; Lowell A. Norris, "America's Homeless Army," *Scribner's* 93 (1933), 316–18.

28. Sutherland and Locke, *Twenty Thousand Homeless Men*, pp. 70–92; "Report on 50 Transient Men Picked Up in Springfield, Ill.," unpag. For another case study, see Carl Kolins interview, December 18, 1934, p. 4, Burgess Papers. See also Minehan, *Boy and Girl Tramps*, pp. 21–53.

29. Warren James Belasco, *Americans on the Road: From Autocamp to Motel, 1910–1945* (Cambridge, Mass.: MIT Press, 1981), p. 109–12 (quotation, 110); Hoy, "The Care of the Homeless in St. Louis," 211; Webb, *The Transient Unemployed*, p. 24.

30. [Eliabeth] Wickenden to [Harry] Hopkins, September 17, 1934 ("Summary of Transient Program"), Old General Subject Series, March 1933-January 1935, FERA Central Files, FERA-TD; "Census Report on Age, Race and Sex . . . December 31, 1934," FERA New General Subject Series, FERA-TD; Webb, *Transient Unemployed*,

pp. 31–33; *Unemployment Relief in PA, Sept. 1–August 31, 1934: Second Annual Report of the Executive Division of the State Employment Relations Board of Pennsylvania* (Harrisburg, 1935), p. 53; *Pennsylvania Monthly Relief Bulletin* 1 (June 1935), 27; Cook County Service Bureau for Transients, "Summary of Mid-Monthly Censuses, July–December 1934," unpag., State Series (Illinois), Box 81, FERA-TD; Anderson testimony, S.5121, p. 65.

31. Emily Hahn, "Women Without Work," *New Republic* 75 (May 31, 1933), 63–65 (quotation, 64); Marlise Johnston, "The Woman Out of Work," *Review of Reviews and the World's Work* 87 (February 1933), 30.

32. "Charlie" interview, November 28, 1934, Burgess Papers; Minehan, *Boy and Girl Tramps*, pp. 133–35; Walter Reckless, "Why Women Become Hoboes," *American Mercury* 31 (1934), 176, 178 (quotations); Graham, *Tales of the Open Road*, pp. 99–101 (quotation, 99); "Report on 50 Transient Men Picked Up in Springfield, Ill.," unpag.

33. Reckless, "Why Women Become Hoboes," 176; Thompson, *Sister of the Road*, pp. 16, 251–52.

34. [National] Committee on Care of Transient and Homeless, "Report of the Census of Transient and Homeless for March 22, 1933," p. 5; Alice Kessler-Harris, *Out to Work: A History of Wage-Earning Women in the United States* (New York: Oxford University Press, 1982), pp. 229, 258–59; Claudia Goldin, *Understanding the Gender Gap: An Economic History of American Women* (New York: Oxford University Press, 1990), pp. 16–21; Webb, *The Transient Unemployed*, p. 36.

35. FERA Transient Division, "Census Report on Age, Race and Sex of All Individuals under the Care of the Federal Transient Division on December 31, 1934," Box 67, New General Subject Series, FERA-TD; FERA, Transient Division, "Census Report, . . . June 30, 1935," Box 67, New General Subject Series, FERA-TD; Alabama Relief Administration, "Report of the . . . Transient Bureau, December, 1933," Box 3, State Series (Alabama), FERA-TD; *Negroes on the Road: A Survey of the Transient Negro in New Jersey* (New Jersey: Emergency Relief Administration, 1935), p. 6; Nels Anderson, *The Homeless in New York City* (New York: Welfare Council, 1934), pp. 134, 137; "Just Another Day for Them," *Philadelphia Record*, Nov. 27, 1931, p. 2. For data on population of northern cities, see St. Clair Drake and Horace R. Cayton, *Black Metropolis: A Study of Negro Life in a Northern City* (New York: Harper and Row, 1945), p. 9; Kenneth L. Kusmer, *A Ghetto Takes Shape: Black Cleveland, 1870–1930* (Urbana: University of Illinois Press, 1976), p. 10; Richard W. Thomas, *Life Is What We Make It: Building Black Community in Detroit, 1915–1945* (Bloomington: Indiana University Press, 1992), p. 26; Greenberg, *"Or Does It Explode?"* p. 225.

36. Kusmer, *A Ghetto Takes Shape*, p. 205; Cohen, *Making a New Deal*, pp. 242–43; Greenberg, *"Or Does It Explode?"* pp. 65–69; Drake and Cayton, *Black Metropolis*, pp. 214–18, 84 (quotation); Rick Halpern, *Down on the Killing Floor: Black and White Workers in Chicago's Packinghouses, 1904–1954* (Urbana: University of Illinois Press, 1997), p. 105; FERA-TD, "Census Report . . . June 30, 1935," unpag.

37. Data from Webb, *The Transient Unemployed*, pp. 48–50. Only 21 percent of Pennsylvania transients were unskilled; 45 percent were "skilled or semi-skilled," 14 percent were domestic servants, and 9.4 percent were white-collar. *Pennsylvania*

Monthly Relief Bulletin 1 (June 1935), p. 28. For parallel unemployment data by occupation for Chicago, see Cohen, *Making a New Deal*, p. 240.

38. "West Madison Street" (typescript report, January 7, 1934), p. 5, Box 127, Ernest W. Burgess Papers; Alvin Roseman, *Shelter Care and the Local Homeless Man* (Chicago: Public Administration Service, 1935), p. 9; "Hartford House," *The Transient* 2 (January 1935), 4; Vorse, "School for Bums," 293–94; Ethel, "Souplines in Seattle," 209.

39. Daniels, *The Bonus March*, pp. 140–81; Lisio, *The President and Protest*, 56.

40. Elizabeth Wickenden, "Reminiscences of the Program for Transients and Homeless in the Thirties," in *On Being Homeless: Historical Perspectives*, ed. Rick Beard (New York: Museum of the City of New York, 1987), p. 83; Roseman, *Shelter Care and the Local Homeless Man*, p. 13.

41. Webb, *The Transient Unemployed*, pp. 96–99.

42. Anderson testimony, S.5121, p. 69; Helen S. Hawkins, "A New Deal for the Newcomer: The Federal Transient Service" (Ph.D. dissertation, University of California-San Diego, 1975), pp. 173–77.

43. National Council of Social Work, National Committee on Care of Transient and Homeless, "Report on Program and Standards of the CCTH," April 17, 1933, FERA Central Files, FERA-TD, p. 5.

44. Wickenden to Hopkins, September 17, 1934; Webb, *The Transient Unemployed*, pp. 11, 28; Hawkins, "A New Deal for the Newcomer," pp. 189–92; Crouse, *The Homeless Transient*, pp. 136–41.

45. Wickenden to Hopkins, September 17, 1934; Elizabeth Wickenden, "Transiency = Mobility in Trouble," *Survey* 73 (1937), 308; Reed, *Federal Transient Program*, p. 53; Wickenden, "Reminiscences," pp. 81–82; Fred Gendral, "The Homeless Go to Camp," *Current History* 42 (1935), 488; Hawkins, "A New Deal for the Newcomer," pp. 196–98, 213–14.

46. Computed from data in Webb, *The Transient Unemployed*, pp. 22–24, 27–28.

47. "Diary of James Carlone and Bob O'Hare," pp. 14–15 (quotation), Narrative Reports and Correspondence, 1933–36, Box 32, FERA-TD; Crouse, *Homeless Transient*, pp. 143–44.

48. *Unemployment Relief in Pennsylvania, September 1, 1932–August 30, 1934*, pp. 52–53; "Diary of James Carlone and Bob O'Hare," pp. 11–13; Wickenden, "Reminiscences," p. 82; Terkel, *Hard Times*, p. 33.

49. Reed, *Federal Transient Program*, pp. 53–58.

50. Reed, *Federal Transient Program*, pp. 57–58, 66–69, 15–16 (quotations), 70–72; Crouse, *Homeless Transient*, pp. 139–40; Wickenden, "Reminiscences," pp. 85–86; Gendral, "The Homeless Go to Camp," 490–91 (quotation).

51. Reed, *Federal Transient Program*, pp. 74–78; Hawkins, "A New Deal for the Newcomer," pp. 246–52; Crouse, *Homeless Transient*, 144–45; Elizabeth Wickenden to Sen. Hugo Black, December 26, 1933, Old General Subject Series, FERA Central Files, March 1933–January 1935, FERA-TD.

52. On the U.S.S. Mercy's program, see "Congregate Shelter Aboard the U.S.S. Mercy," p. 2, Narrative Reports and Correspondence, Box 32, FERA-TD; Reed, *Federal Transient Program*, p. 85.

53. Reed, *Federal Transient Program*, pp. 83–86; *Quaker City Trumpet*, September 1, 1935, unpag. ("Educational" section); William Weathersby and Emily Smith, "Journalism in Transient Bureaus," *The Transient* 2 (May 1935), pp. 8–9; Gendrel, "The Homeless Go to Camp," 492. Basic information on educational programs is drawn from the large selection of transient bureau papers located in FERA-TD files.

54. For an oblique discussion of the organizational structure of transient camps, see Reed, *Federal Transient Program*, pp. 61–62.

55. In 1935 in New York State, transient workers helped communities affected by severe flooding. Such emergency work was relatively unusual, however. See Crouse, *Homeless Transient*, pp. 161–64.

56. Reed, *Federal Transient Program*, p. 61; Gendral, "The Homeless Go to Camp," 491–92; "Camp McMahon Will Quarter Transients," Narrative Reports and Correspondence, 1934, Box 32, 1933–36, FERA-TD; Gertrude Springer, "Men Off the Road," *Survey Graphic*, 23 (1934), 422–26; Schubert, *Twenty Thousand Homeless Men*, pp. 124–27; Hawkins, "A New Deal for the Newcomer," pp. 277–80; Crouse, *Homeless Transient*, pp. 154–59; "Diary of James Carlone and Bob O'Hare," p. 12.

57. Reed, *Federal Transient Program*, p. 57.

58. "Hartford House: A Unique Housing Unit of the New York State Transient Division," *The Transient* 2 (January 1935), 4–5; Crouse, *The Homeless Transient*, pp. 172–76.

59. Schubert, *Twenty Thousand Transients*, p. 127; Hawkins, "A New Deal for the Newcomer," p. 276; "Diary of James Carlone and Bob O'Hare"; Reed, *Federal Transient Program*, pp. 26–27; "Diary of James Carlone and Bob O'Hare," p. 9; Harriet E. Anderson, "The Philadelphia Shelter for Homeless Men," *The Family* (1931), 76.

60. Wickenden to Hopkins, September 17, 1934; [National] Committee on Care of Transient and Homeless, "Report on Program and Standards," p. 1; Agnes V. O'Shea, "Development of the Care of Transient Women," *The Transient* 1 (November 1934), 3; *Unemployment Relief in Pennsylvania, September 1, 1932–August 31, 1934*, p. 53; Crouse, *Homeless Transient*, pp. 180–81.

61. "Diary of James Carlone and Bob O'Hare," p. 3; Harry L. Hopkins, *Spending to Save: The Complete Story of Relief* (New York: Norton, 1936), p. 127; Crouse, *Homeless Transient*, pp. 140–41, 150–52.

62. Hawkins, "A New Deal for the Newcomer," pp. 2, 363–76; Memorandum from Josephine C. Brown to All Regional Social Work Staff, June 28, 1935, New General Subject Series, Box 67, Folder B, FERA-TD.

63. For a discussion of this shift in the broader context of New Deal welfare policies, see James T. Patterson, *America's Struggle Against Poverty, 1900–1980* (Cambridge, Mass.: Harvard University Press, 1981), ch. 4; Michael B. Katz, *In the Shadow of the Poorhouse* (New York: Basic Books, 1986), pp. 206–34.

64. Elizabeth Wickenden testimony, *Interstate Migration: Report of the Select Committee to Investigate the Interstate Migration of Destitute Citizens, H. Res. 63, 491, 629* (Washington: GPO, 1941), pp. 604, 605 [hereafter H. Res. 63]; M. Starr Northrup, et al., *A Survey of the Transient and Homeless Population in 12 Cities, September 1935 and September 1936* (Washington: GPO, 1937), p.7. An additional 8 percent left for "miscellaneous reasons." Only 2 percent found refuge with family or friends.

65. The administrative history of the disbanding of the program is surveyed in Hawkins, "A New Deal for the Newcomer," pp. 359–96.

66. "Recent Observations on the Transient Problem," *Public Welfare News* 4 (January 1936), 6; "Transients Refused Relief," *Philadelphia Evening Bulletin*, October 7, 1935 (quotation), BCC; "Ban on Transients Arouses Protests," *Philadelphia Inquirer*, October 9, 1935, BCC; "Shelter Houses Fewest Residents," *Philadelphia Evening Ledger*, November 1, 1935, BCC; "Shelter Reopens to Homeless Men," ibid., January 24, 1936 (quotation), BCC; "Shelter Reopened as Cold Weather Snaps Red Tape," *Philadelphia Record*, January 24, 1936 (quotation), BCC; "City Must Move Shelter Inmates to Another Site," *Philadelphia Evening Bulletin*, March 17, 1936, BCC; "Wilson Orders Shelter Closed," ibid., October 28, 1936, BCC; "City Turns 248 Out of Shelter,"ibid., January 11, 1937, BCC; "New City Shelter Planned by Mayor," *Philadelphia Evening Ledger*, January 19, 1937 (quotation), BCC.

67. Northrup et al., *A Survey*, p. 44 (quotation), 31; "One-Man Drive Nets Subway Vagrants," *New York Times*, January 11, 1937, p. 40; "Padlocks Ordered for Playgrounds," ibid., February 16, 1937, p. 25; "41 Seized as Park Loiterers," ibid., August 15, 1938, p. 2; H. Res. 63, pp. 608–11; "The Meaning of the Houston Survey," *The Transient* 4 (September 1937), 1; Robert Lynd and Helen Merrell Lynd, *Middletown in Transition* (New York: Harcourt Brace and World, 1937), pp. 135–36; "Recent Observations on the Transient Problem," 4.

68. On the background and limitations of the original Social Security legislation, see Patterson, *America's Struggle Against Poverty*, pp. 67–77; Katz, *In the Shadow of the Poorhouse*, pp. 234–42; Edward D. Berkowitz, *America's Welfare State: From Roosevelt to Reagan* (Baltimore: Johns Hopkins University Press, 1991), pp. 13–28.

69. [Charles Alspach] to Frank Bane, September 21, 1935, Box 67, "B" Files, New General Subject Series, FERA-TD. On the New Deal relationship with the states, see James T. Patterson, *The New Deal and the States: Federalism in Transition* (Princeton: Princeton University Press, 1969).

CHAPTER 11

1. "Transient Jobless Interstate Puzzle," *New York Times*, March 8, 1936, pt. 4, p. 6; "Unwanted Visitors," *Survey* 72 (1936), 111; Carey McWilliams, *Factories in the Field: The Story of Migratory Farm Labor in California* (Boston: Little, Brown, 1939), pp. 310–11; Tim O'Brien, "Move On, You!" *Commonweal* 28 (1938), 607–09; Walter Stein, *California and the Dust Bowl Migration* (Westport, Conn.: Greenwood Press, 1973), pp. 73–74; Helen S. Hawkins, "A New Deal for the Newcomer: The Federal Transient Service" (Ph.D. dissertation, University of California at San Diego, 1975), pp. 401–19. The blockade in California was actually carried out by the Los Angeles police, even though such actions were far beyond their normal jurisdiction, and the state courts refused to intervene.

2. M. Starr Northrup et al., *A Survey of the Transient and Homeless Population in Twelve Cities* (Washington: Government Printing Office [GPO], 1937), pp. 18–19; "East River 'Jungle' to be Razed Today," *New York Times*, January 1, 1937, p. 22.

3. "Transient Order Arouses Protest," *Survey* 71 (1935), 303–04; Elizabeth Wickenden, "Transiency = Mobility in Trouble," *Survey* 73 (1937), 307–09; Ellen C. Potter, *After Five Years: The Unsolved Problem of the Transient Unemployed* (New York, 1937 [pamphlet]); George Outland, *Boy Transiency in America* (Santa Barbara: Santa Barbara State College Press, 1939), pp. 22–23; Theodore Caplow, "Transiency as a Cultural Pattern," *American Sociological Review* 5 (1940), 733–34; Stein, *California and the Dust Bowl Migration*, pp. 192–201; John Benton, "Rest for Weary Willy" [pt. 1], *Saturday Evening Post* 209 (1936), 5 (quotation), 5–6, 79, 81–82; [pt. 2], ibid. (1936), 14–15, 87, 90; [pt. 3], ibid. (1936), 23, 90–95 (quotation, 95).

4. McWilliams, *Factories in the Field*; U.S. Congress, House of Representatives, *Select Committee to Investigate the Interstate Migration of Destitute Citizens*, H. Res. 63 and 491, 76th Congress, 3rd session, 1940–41; U.S. Congress, House of Representatives, Select Committee Investigating Defense Migration, *National Defense Migration*, H. 113, 77th Congress, 1st session, 1941–42; Stein, *California and the Dust Bowl Migration*, pp. 210–15. For a perceptive assessment of the cultural impact of the Okies, see Charles J. Shindo, *Dust Bowl Migrants in the American Imagination* (Lawrence: University of Kansas Press, 1997).

5. Stein, *California and the Dust Bowl Migration*, p. 215 (quotation); Shindo, *Dust Bowl Migrants*, p. 9. For the political mood of the 1938–41 period, see Robert McIlvaine, *The Great Depression: America, 1929–1941* (New York: Times Books, 1984), ch. 14; and Michael S. Sherry, *In the Shadow of War: The United States Since the 1930s* (New Haven: Yale University Press, 1995), pp. 29–63.

6. "Railroad Boomer Passing," *New York Times*, September 15, 1929, pt. 10, p. 13; T. Lynn Smith, *The Sociology of Rural Life* (New York: Harper's, 1953), p. 192; "The Bowery Sends Its Drunks to the War," *New York Times*, February 2, 1943, p. 21; Robert M. Yoder, "Bum's Rush: Milwaukee's Hoboes Recruited for Labor," *Saturday Evening Post* 216 (March 11, 1944), 34–36; Samuel E. Wallace, *Skid Row as a Way of Life* (Totowa, N.J.: Bedminster Press, 1965), pp. 22–24.

7. Caplow, "Transiency as a Cultural Pattern," 734; Alvin Averbach, "San Francisco's South of Market District, 1850–1950: The Emergence of a Skid Row," *California Historical Quarterly* 52 (1973), 214. The generalizations in this paragraph are based largely on Anderson's interviews, conducted in 1923 (Documents 1 through 126) in Box 127, Ernest W. Burgess Papers, University of Chicago Library.

8. John N. Webb, *The Transient Unemployed* (Washington: GPO, 1935), p. 29; Nels Anderson, *The Homeless in New York City* (New York: Welfare Council of New York, 1934 [mimeograph]), pp. 165–66; Leonard Blumberg et al., *The Men on Skid Row: A Study of Philadelphia's Homeless Man Population* (Philadelphia: Temple University Department of Psychiatry, 1960 [typescript]), p. 4. Keith Lovald, "From Hobohemia to Skid Row: The Changing Community of the Homeless Man" (Ph.D. dissertation, University of Minnesota, 1960), pp. 246, 248; Donald Bogue, *Skid Row in American Cities* (Chicago: University of Chicago Press, 1963), p. 91; Averbach, "San Francisco's South of Market District," 215; John C. Schneider, "Skid Row as an Urban Neighborhood, 1880–1960," *Urbanism Past and Present* 9 (1984), 15.

9. "Tour of Lodging Houses a Panorama of Misery," *Philadelphia Bulletin*, December 20, 1946, Philadelphia *Bulletin* Clipping Collection (BCC), Urban

Archives, Temple University; Blumberg et al., *The Men on Skid Row*, pp. 76–77, 177; George Nash, *The Habitats of Homeless Men in Manhattan* (New York: New York City Department of Public Welfare, 1964 [typescript]), pp. E3–4; Lovald, "From Hobohemia to Skid Row," pp. 395–96; Bogue, *Skid Row*, pp. 49, 82; Wallace, *Skid Row*, p. 39; Charles Hoch and Robert A. Slayton, *New Homeless and Old: Community and the Skid Row Hotel* (Philadelphia: Temple University Press, 1986), pp. 96–97, 101–02; Averbach, "San Francisco's South of Market District," p. 218.

10. Bogue, *Skid Row*, pp. 5–6; Nash, *Habitats*, pp. C4, A11 (quotation), D8, E23; Leonard U. Blumberg et al., *Liquor and Poverty: Skid Row as a Human Condition* (New Brunswick: Center for Alcohol Studies, 1973), pp. 132–35; George Garrett and Howard M. Bahr, "Women on Skid Row," *Quarterly Journal of Studies of Alcohol* 34 (1973), 1228–43.

11. Bogue, *Skid Rows*, pp. 245–59; Nash, *Habitats*, pp. C3–4, D-10, E20–33, 38–43; Lovald, "From Hobohemia to Skid Row," pp. 234–41; Hoch and Slayton, *Old Homeless and New*, pp. 91–92; Schneider, "Skid Row as an Urban Neighborhood," 15–16; Averbach, "San Francisco's South of Market," 217–18; Nash, *The Habitats of Homeless Men*, pp. D10, D16–17.

12. Blumberg et al., *Men on Skid Row*, pp. 51–52, 57, 62; Lovald, "From Hobohemia to Skid Row," pp. 268–71; Bogue, *Skid Row*, pp. 174–77.

13. Blumberg et al., *Men on Skid Row*, p. 79; Bogue, *Skid Row*, pp. 186–87; Mark Stern, "Poverty and Family Composition Since 1940," in *The "Underclass" Debate: Views from History*, ed. Michael B. Katz (Princeton: Princeton University Press, 1993), pp. 237 and 220–53 *passim*; Lovald, "From Hobohemia to Skid Row," p. 274. See also Hoch and Slayton, *New Homeless and Old*, pp. 94–97.

14. Blumberg et al., *Men on Skid Row*, pp. 62–63; Lovald, "From Hobohemia to Skid Row," pp. 254–55; Bogue, *Skid Row*, pp. 194, 309–11. The Philadelphia study seriously underestimates the number of white-collar workers on skid row (3.3 percent) by categorizing clerks as semiskilled workers. Better estimates are provided by Lovald (12.6 percent) and Bogue (14.1 percent). Howard Bahr, "Worklife Mobility Among Bowery Men," *Social Science Quarterly* 49 (1968), 128–41, questioned Bogue's conclusion that homeless men typically had experienced downward mobility during their lives. The data by Blumberg et al. and Lovald (not cited by Bahr), however, strongly support Bogue.

15. Bogue, *Skid Row*, pp. 180–82, 193–94, 410–18; Jerome Ellison, "The Shame of Skid Row," *Saturday Evening Post* 225 (December 20, 1952), 48. For further confirmation of skid-row men's desire for retraining, see Blumberg et al., *Men on Skid Row*, p. 62.

16. Collins, *America's Own Refugees*, pp. 140–43 (Mexican farm workers), 130–31 (hitchhikers).

17. William H. Whyte, *The Organization Man* (New York: Simon and Schuster, 1956).

18. "Hard Times on Skid Row," *Time*, 48 (July 22, 1946), 20; "Land of the Living Dead," ibid., 54 (August 29, 1949), 48; Hoch and Slayton, *New Homeless and Old*, p. 109.

19. Ellison, "The Shame of Skid Row," 14; Meyer Berger, "The Bowery Blinks in the Sunlight," *New York Times Magazine*, May 20, 1956, p. 28; Elmer Bendiner,

"'Immovable Obstacle,' in the Way of a New Bowery," ibid., January 21, 1962, p. 22; Elmer Bendiner, *The Bowery Man* (New York: Thomas Nelson, 1961), p. 38.

20. Bogue, *Skid Row*, p. 174; Howard M. Bahr, ed., *Disaffiliated Man: Essays and Bibliography on Skid Row, Vagrancy, and Outsiders* (Toronto: University of Toronto Press, 1970); Howard M. Bahr and Theodore Caplow, *Old Men Drunk and Sober* (New York: New York University Press, 1973); Wallace, *Skid Row as a Way of Life*, p. 144; Kim Hopper, "Homelessness Old and New: The Matter of Definition," *Housing Policy Debate* 2 (1991), 776. See also the critique of the disaffiliation theorists in Hoch and Slayton, *Old Homeless and New*, pp. 107–110.

21. These include Lovald, "From Hobohemia to Skid Row"; Blumberg et al., *Men on Skid Row*; and Nash, *Habitats*.

22. "Explorers Find Bowery Stratified," *New York Times*, November 1, 1952, p. 23; Nash, *Habitats*, pp. D5–6; John McKeon, "The Bowery Today," *Commonweal* 57 (1952), 252; Hoch and Slayton, *Old Homeless and New*, pp. 98–100, 155–62.

23. Blumberg et al., *Men on Skid Row*, pp. 41–42; Lovald, "From Hobohemia to Skid Row," pp. 400–401; Nash, *Habitats*, pp. D16–17; Bogue, *Skid Row*, pp. 144–45.

24. Bogue, *Skid Row*, pp. 144–45; Michael Harrington, *The New American Poverty* (New York: Holt, Rinehard, and Winston, 1984), p. 97; Jane Jacobs, *The Death and Life of Great American Cities* (New York: Vintage, 1961), pp. 99–100.

25. Lovald, "From Hobohemia to Skid Row," 248–49; Blumberg et al., *Men on Skid Row*, p. 6; Bogue, *Skid Row*, pp. 6, 106–07, 256–60; Blumberg et al., *Liquor and Poverty*, pp. 125–26.

26. Nash, *Habitats*, C16, D27; Blumberg, et al., *Liquor and Poverty*, pp. 123–26. Because he used city burial records to estimate the homeless population, Nash's raw figures are undoubtedly too high. Not everyone who died without having their body claimed was homeless. As a measure of the racial identity of the homeless, however, the use of city burial statistics is much more reliable. The 31 percent figure was calculated from Nash's estimate that 35 percent of the homeless outside the Bowery were Negro.

27. See Jon C. Teaford, *The Rough Road to Renaissance: Urban Revitalization in America, 1940–1985* (Baltimore: Johns Hopkins University Press, 1990), chs. 1–4; Robert A. Beauregard, *Voices of Decline: The Postwar Fate of US Cities* (Oxford: Blackwell, 1993), chs. 5–6.

28. "19 Vagrants Jailed as City Pushes Drive," *Philadelphia Bulletin*, July 5, 1949, BCC; "15 Vagrants Seized in Franklin Square," ibid., June 27, 1949, BCC; "Three Midcity Squares Raided for Vagrants," ibid., July 14, 1954, BCC; "24 Sent to Jail Here in Drive," ibid., May 2, 1955, BCC; Nash, *Habitats*, p. E64.

29. Lovald, "From Hobohemia to Skid Row," pp. 311, 313, 318–24 (quotation, 318), 327, 345; Bogue, *Skid Rows*, p. 416.

30. "Face-Lifting Campaign Along the Bowery," *New York Times*, November 11, 1946, p. 29; "Bowery Clean-Up Under Way," ibid., June 24, 1949, p. 48; "New Group Will Aim to Improve Bowery," ibid., April 30, 1953, p. 36; "Bowery Clean-Up Planned," ibid., October 31, 1961, p. 21; Peter S. McGhee, "Bowery Bums' Rush," *Nation* 198 (1964), 435; McKeon, "The Bowery Today," 252.

31. "7 'Skid Row' Hotels Warned," *Philadelphia Bulletin*, January 20, 1956, BCC; Larry R. Ford, *Cities and Buildings: Skyscrapers, Skid Rows, and Suburbs* (Baltimore: Johns Hopkins University Press, 1994), p. 68.

32. John H. Mollenkopf, *The Contested City* (Princeton: Princeton University Press, 1983), chs. 4–5; Nancy Kleniewski, "From Industrial to Corporate City: The Role of Urban Renewal," in *Marxism and the Metropolis*, rev. ed., ed. William K. Tabb and Larry Sawers (New York: Oxford University Press, 1984), pp. 205–22; Teaford, *Rough Road*, ch. 4; *Unequal Partnerships: The Political Economy of Urban Redevelopment in Postwar America*, ed. Gregory D. Squires (New Brunswick: Rutgers University Press, 1989).

33. "Grim Problems of the Bowery," *New York Times*, November 20, 1961, p. 36; Lovald, "From Hobohemia to Skid Row," p. 448; Stephen Metraux, "Waiting for the Wrecking Ball: Skid Row in Postindustrial Philadelphia," *Journal of Urban History* 25 (1999), 704–05; Teaford, *Rough Road*, pp. 148–49; Hoch and Slayton, *New Homeless and Old*, pp. 119–22, 175; Kenneth Jackson, "The Bowery: From Residential Street to Skid Row," in *On Being Homeless: Historical Perspectives*, ed. Rick Beard (New York: Museum of the City of New York, 1987), p. 78.

34. Lovald, "From Hobohemia to Skid Row," p. 448; Metraux, "Waiting for the Wrecking Ball," 704–05; Hoch and Slayton, *New Homeless and Old*, p. 119; Chester Hartman, *Yerba Buena: Land Grab and Community Resistance* (San Francisco: Glide, 1974).

CHAPTER 12

1. Mark Stern, "The Emergence of the Homeless as a Social Problem," *Social Service Review* 58 (1984), 291–301. On methodological problems of counting the homeless, see Peter Rossi, *Down and Out in America: The Origins of Homelessness* (Chicago: University of Chicago Press, 1989), pp. 50 (quotation), 48–70, 93–97; Kim Hopper, "Homelessness Old and New: The Matter of Definition," *Housing Policy Debate* 2 (1991), 773–80; Joel Blau, *The Visible Poor: Homelessness in the United States* (New York: Oxford University Press, 1992), pp. 22–24; "Deep Poverty and Illness Found Among Homeless," *New York Times*, December 8, 1999, A-16. The Urban Institute report, based on data for 1995–96, was not released until 1999.

2. On the "housing squeeze" as a cause of homelessness, see Kim Hopper and Jill Hamberg, "The Making of America's Homeless: From Skid Row to New Poor, 1945–1984," in *Critical Perspectives on Housing*, ed. Rachael G. Bratt et al. (Philadelphia: Temple University Press, 1986), pp. 20–23; Charles Hoch and Robert A. Slayton, *New Homeless and Old: Community and the Skid Row Hotel* (Philadelphia: Temple University Press, 1989), ch. 9; Blau, *The Visible Poor*, ch. 5; Michael E. Stone, *Shelter Poverty: New Ideas on Housing Affordability* (Philadelphia: Temple University Press, 1998), chs. 5–6. For a superb case study of the growing inequality of housing in postindustrial Philadelphia, see David W. Bartelt, "Housing the 'Underclass,'" in *The "Underclass" Debate: Views from History*, ed. Michael B. Katz (Princeton: Princeton University Press, 1993), pp. 118–57.

3. Leonard Blumberg et al., *The Men on Skid Row: A Study of Philadelphia's Homeless Man Population* (Philadelphia: Temple University, Department of Psychiatry, 1960 [typescript]), p. 75; Donald Bogue, *Skid Row in American Cities* (Chicago: University of Chicago, 1963), p. 184; Rossi, *Down and Out*, p. 104–06; The Urban Institute, *Homelessness: Programs and the People They Serve* (Washington: GPO, 1999), preface, p. 11. Income levels of the homeless are difficult to determine, partly because income from illegal activities is often not reported to interviewers. This is as true for the skid-row era as today, however, so the relative difference in incomes between the two periods is probably roughly accurate.

4. Bennett Harrison and Barry Bluestone, *The De-Industrialization of America: Plant Closings, Community Abandonment, and the Dismantling of Basic Industry* (New York: Basic Books, 1982), chs. 2–3; David Bensman and Roberta Lynch, *Rusted Dreams: Hard Times in a Steel Community* (New York: McGraw Hill, 1987); Carolyn T. Adams et al., *Philadelphia: Neighborhoods, Division, and Conflict in a Postindustrial City* (Philadelphia: Temple University Press, 1991); Dale Maharidge and Michael Williamson, *Journey to Nowhere: The Saga of the New Underclass* (Garden City, N.Y.: Dial Press, 1985), pp. 11–49; Rossi, *Down and Out*, pp. 108–16; Kim Hopper et al., "Economies of Makeshift: Homelessness and Deindustrialization in New York City," *Urban Anthropology* 14 (1985), 183–236; David A. Snow and Leon Anderson, *Down on Their Luck: A Study of Homeless Street People* (Berkeley: University of California Press, 1993), pp. 145–70, 249–51.

5. Edward D. Berkowitz, *America's Welfare State: From Roosevelt to Reagan* (Baltimore: Johns Hopkins University Press, 1991), pp. 70–72; Mark J. Stern, "Poverty and Family Composition Since 1940," in *The "Underclass" Debate*, p. 241; Hopper and Hamberg, "Making of America's Homeless," pp. 27–28; Rossi, *Down and Out*, pp. 190–94, 196–97; Snow and Anderson, *Down on Their Luck*, pp. 251–52. As Peter Rossi has pointed out, many homeless persons do not get welfare support even if they are eligible because they do not understand or fail to follow through on the rules for receiving benefits. The homeless are an easy target for bureaucratic budget-cutters. Even if they did receive benefits, however, the income would not be enough to support either a single person or family at the most basic level.

6. "We Can't Pay the Rent," *Washington Post Parade Magazine*, January 10, 1988, pp. 4–6; "Institute Finds a Number That Adds Up, Has Meaning on the Streets," *Washington Post*, May 16, 1994, p. 3; Rossi, *Down and Out*, p. 118; Urban Institute, *Homelessness*, ch. 3, p. 1; "More Homeless Families are Searching for Shelter," *New York Times*, September 17, 1992, pp. B1, 8; "Homeless Families Increase in Cities," ibid., December 22, 1993, p. 4; Institute for Children and Poverty, *The Cycle of Family Homelessness* (New York: Institute for Children and Poverty, 1998), pp. 3–4. On the difficult struggles of homeless single women with families, see the fine ethnographic study by Alisse Waterston, *Love, Sorrow, and Rage: Poor Women's Lives and Stories of the Street, Etched into a Narrative of the Heart* (Philadelphia: Temple University Press, 1999).

7. The Urban Institute, *Homelessness: Programs and the People They Serve* (Washington: GPO, 1999), ch. 3, p. 4. For other data on ages, see Ira Goldstein et al., *Homelessness in Philadelphia: Roots, Realities, and Resolutions* (Philadelphia: Coalition on Homelessness in Pennsylvania, 1989), p. 14.

8. Kim Hopper, "Margins Within Margins: Homelessness Among African American Men," in *Marginality*, ed. Sam Nolutshungu (Rochester: University of Rochester Press, 1996), p. 224; Rossi, *Down and Out*, pp. 122–25; Urban Institute, *Homelessness*, ch. 3, p. 16. In Philadelphia, racial minorities made up 87 percent of the homeless population in 1989. Goldstein et al., *Homelessness in Philadelphia*, p. 13.

9. Hopper, "Margins," pp. 227, 230–31; Adams et al., *Philadelphia*, pp. 60–61; Hoch and Slayton, *New Homeless and Old*, pp. 188–89; Thomas J. Sugrue, "Carter's Urban Policy Crisis," in *The Carter Presidency: Policy Choices in the Post–New Deal Era*, ed. Gary M. Fink and Hugh Davis Graham (Lawrence: University of Kansas Press, 1998), pp. 137–57; Raymond A. Mohl, "Shifting Patterns of American Urban Policy Since 1900," in *Urban Policy in Twentieth-Century America*, ed. Raymond A. Mohl and Arnold Hirsch (New Brunswick: Rutgers University Press, 1993), pp. 20–29; Helene Slessarev, *The Betrayal of the Urban Poor* (Philadelphia: Temple University Press, 1997), p. 38.

10. "Institute Finds a Number," p. 3; David A. Snow et al., "The Myth of Pervasive Mental Illness Among the Homeless," *Social Problems* 33 (1986), 407–13; David A. Snow et al., "Criminality and Homeless Men: An Empirical Assessment," ibid. 36 (1989), 532–49; Rossi, *Down and Out*, ch. 6; Blau, *Visible Poor*, pp. 26–27; Snow and Anderson, *Down on Their Luck*, pp. 256–59, 165–67; Urban Institute, *Homelessness*, ch. 3, p. 12; Marybeth Shinn, Beth C. Weitzman, and Kim Hopper, "Homelessness," *Encyclopedia of Mental Health* (New York: Academic Press, 1998), pp. 395–98.

11. For these trends, see Kenneth L. Kusmer, "African Americans in the City: From the Industrial to the Post-Industrial Era," *Journal of American History* 21 (1995), 458–504; Thomas J. Sugrue, *The Origins of the Urban Crisis: Race and Inequality in Postwar Detroit* (Princeton: Princeton University Press, 1996); Jon Teaford, *The Rough Road to Renaissance: Urban Revitalization in America, 1940–1985* (Baltimore: Johns Hopkins University Press, 1990), p. 155; Raymond A. Mohl, "Race and Space in the Modern City: Interstate-95 and the Black Community in Miami," in *Urban Policy*, ed. Hirsch and Mohl, pp. 100–158.

12. "Crime Problems in the Bowery," *New York Times*, November 20, 1961, p. 36; Blumberg et al., *Homeless Men*, p. 7.

13. Marjorie Robertson, "Homeless Veterans: An Emerging Problem?" in *The Homeless in Contemporary Society*, ed. Richard D. Bingham et al. (Newbury Park, Calif.: Sage, 1987), pp. 64–81; "New York Is Facing 'Crisis' of Vagrants," *New York Times*, June 28, 1981, p. 1. On the recruitment of blacks, Hispanics, and poor whites into the army during the Vietnam War, see Lawrence M. Baskir and William A. Strauss, *Chance and Circumstance: The Draft, the War, and the Vietnam Generation* (New York: Vintage, 1978), pp. 124–31.

14. Blumberg et al., *Homeless Men*, p. 8; Bogue, *Skid Row*, p. 110; Rossi, *Down and Out*, p. 127; Blau, *Visible Poor*, pp. 27–28; Snow and Anderson, *Down on Their Luck*, pp. 278–79; Urban Institute, *Homelessness*, ch. 3, p. 7. A careful survey of the mostly white homeless population of Santa Cruz in 1984–85 found that half had attended college and 10 percent were college graduates. Robert A. Marotto and William H. Friedland, "Homelessness in Santa Cruz, California," *Humanity and Society* 14 (1990), 373–94.

15. "Deep Poverty and Illness Found Among Homeless," p. A-16; Snow and Anderson, *Down on Their Luck*, p. 265.

16. Blau, *Visible Poor*, ch. 8; "Report to Clinton See Vast Extent of Homelessness," *New York Times*, February 17, 1994, p. 1; Michael B. Katz, *The Undeserving Poor: From the War on Poverty to the War on Welfare* (New York: Pantheon, 1989).

17. Urban Institute, *Homelessness*, preface, pp. 10–11. On the early development of advocacy groups, see Blau, *Visible Poor*, ch. 7.

18. M. Magnet, "Homeless: Craziness, Dope, and Danger," *New York Times*, January 26, 1990, quoted in Kim Hopper, "Marginalia: Notes on Homelessness in the United States, 1992," in *Hemloeshet i Norden*, ed. M. Jaervinen and C. Tigerstedt (Helsinki: NAD, 1992), p. 143; Dale Maharidge, "I Find the Homeless Hateful," *New York Times*, December 8, 1991, p. 17; Anna Quindlen, "The Unworthy," ibid., December 16, 1993, p. 29; Peter Marin, "Helping and Hating the Homeless," *Harper's* 274 (January 1987), 39–49; "Homeless Seeing Less Apathy, More Anger," *New York Times*, February 25, 1994, p. B1, 2; Lynn Sharon Schwartz, "Beggaring Our Better Selves," *Harper's* 278 (December 1991), 65.

19. "Homeless Ask Court to Halt City Crackdown," *New York Times*, November 26, 1993, p. 27; "Cities Crack Down on Homeless," *Christian Science Monitor*, January 21, 1994, p. 4; "Homeless Defy Cities' Drive to Move Them," *New York Times*, December 7, 1999, pp. 1, 18; "Good Works Engender Bad Blood," ibid., March 31, 1997, p. 10.

20. Elliot Liebow, *Talley's Corner* (Boston: Little, Brown, 1967); "In Sea of Wealth, Homeless Defy the Cold," *New York Times*, January 21, 1994, pp. 1, B6; "Fleeing the World Underneath," ibid., March 28, 1994, p. B-3; "At the End of the Tunnel, a Home," ibid., April 15, 1996, pp. B1, 6.

Index

Bahr, Howard, 230, 315n14
Baltimore, Maryland, 75
Baptists, 88
  black, 198
Barbour, Levi, 82
Barnes, Paul, 186
Bartelt, David, 317n.2
Beck, Paul, 29
Beggars
  in antebellum period, 24, 30–31
  in colonial period, 15–16, 20
  during Great Depression, 199–200
  immigrant, 86–87
  numbers in late nineteenth century,
    82
  and public's response to, 83–87
  on skid row, 159, 161, 227
  studied by Solenberger, 93
  women, 84, 163
  See also Charity Organization Society,
    Police
Bellew, Frank, 48–49
Bendiner, Elmer, 230
Benton, John, 222
Beveridge, W. H., 127
Biegler, Martha, 163
Billings, John, 36–37
Birmingham, Alabama, 69
"Black Jack" [pseud.], 63
Blau, Joel, 320n.17
Bloom, Lew, 186
Blues, the, 185
Bogue, Donald, 230, 232, 315n14
Bohemian districts in cities, 157
Bonus Army, 9, 202–04, 209
Booth, William, 165
Booth-Tucker, Frederick, 88–89
Boston, 15, 21, 22, 51, 54
  increases public relief, 96
  Salvation Army in, 89
  treatment of homeless women in, 112
Bowery, the
  blacks living in, 233

decline of, 225–26, 234–36
lodging houses in, 152
origins of, 149–50
during World War II, 224
Boyer, Paul, 274n.1
Brace, Charles Loring, 27, 37, 45, 47, 80
Brackett, Jeffrey, 92
The Bread-Winners (Hay), 46
Brewer, William H., 43
Britt, Iowa "hobo convention" 181–82
Brooklyn, New York, 52
Brown, Edwin, 78, 144
Bryn Mawr College, 95
Buffalo, New York
  hostility of police in, 68
  sympathy for tramps in, 81
Burgess, Ernest W., 158–60
Bush, George, 245
California
  transients in 1930s, 194, 215,221–23,
    313n.1
  vagrancy arrests in, 66
  See also San Diego, San Francisco,
    Santa Cruz
Callahan v. Carrey (1979), 246
Camden, New Jersey
  and fees system for tramps, 66–67
  and Tramp Act of 1876, 54
Caplow, Theodore, 140, 224
Carlone, James, 212, 217–18
Carr, Jeff, 66
Carter, Jimmy, 242
Cartoons of homeless, 185–86
Catholics
  attitude toward homeless, 19, 86, 88,
    277–78n.30
  and employment bureaus, 90
  among homeless population, 106
Cawelti, John, 31
Cayton, Horace, 208
Central Soup House (Philadelphia), 87
Chaplin, Charlie, 188–91

Great Awakening, the, 22
Guthrie, Woodie, 223, 228
Gutman, Herbert, 252n.12

Hadley, S. H., 89
Hamberg, Jill, 317.n.2
Hannibal, Missouri, 33
Hapgood, Hutchins, 85
Harlow, Alvin, 155
Harrington, Michael, 232
Harris, Lee, 44, 48–49
Harris, Neil, 302n.29
"Harry" (a slave), 16
Hartley, Robert, 28
Hawkins, Helen S., 313n.65
Hay, John, 46
A Hazard of New Fortunes (Howells), 171
Henderson, Charles Richmond, 74, 96
Higham, John, 271n.49
Hispanics, 241, 243, 318–19n.8, 319n.13.
    See also Mexicans
The Hobo (Anderson), 94
Hobo "jungles," 135–36
Hobos. *See* Migratory labor
Hoch, Charles, 231, 316n.20
Homeless, the
    centrality to American history, 7–12
    children, 25, 27, 47, 93, 113, 128–30,
        204–05, 218, 241–42, 283n.17,
        218nn.19–21
    crime by, 37, 121, 237, 242–43
    defined, 4–5, 251nn.2–3
    demographic characteristics of,
        104–19, 204–09, 224–25, 227–28,
        241–44
    elderly, 159, 161, 225, 241
    hostility toward, 43–44, 66, 67–69,
        246
    native-born, 114–16, 119–21
    negative image of, 43–50, 58, 142,
        242–43, 293n.58
    numbers, 38–39, 99–103, 193–94,
        223–24, 239, 261n.10

occupations of, 105, 107, 108–10,
    118–19, 208–09, 310–11n.37,
    225–27, 285n.43
portrayed in popular culture, 169–91,
    203, 209–10
problems of counting, 5–6, 281n.1
in rural areas and small towns, 18, 33,
    40, 42–43, 59, 242
and social workers, 91–95, 195–97
as symbol of social/economic
    change, 8, 169–91, 193, 202–03,
    229
sympathy for, 21–22, 27–32, 50–51, 55,
    62–66, 71–72, 87–91, 200–01,
    269n.25
terminology used to describe, 3, 37,
    209
urban origins of, 105, 204
white-collar workers, 105, 118–19,
    208–09, 216, 282n.13, 285–86n.43,
    315n.14
women, 10–11, 107–113
See also African Americans,
    Almshouses, Beggars, Immi-
    grants, the South, Tramps
Homelessness, causes of, 8–9
colonial era, 37
1865–1930 period, 100–04, 107–110,
    113–14, 120–21
1930s, 205–06, 207–09
post-World War II era, 224–25,
    227–28
after 1975, 240–42
See also African Americans, Women
Homosexuals, 141–43
Hoover, Herbert, 201, 203, 210
Hoovervilles. *See* Shantytowns
Hopkins, Harry, 210–11, 217–18
Hopper, Kim, 230, 317n.2
House of Corrections
    characteristics of vagrants in, 104–111
    before 1800, 15–16, 20–21
    in 1930s, 219

Minneapolis, Minnesota
  homeless in, 117, 231, 234, 285n.37
  lodging house district (skid row), 150,
    225
  skid row demolished, 236
Minnesota
  migrant workers in, 102, 228
Mississippi, 36
Mobile, Alabama, 68
Mobility. *See* Social mobility
Monkkonen, Eric, 6
Montgomery, Alabama, 68
Montgomery, David, 102, 124, 282n.6
Moore, Barrington, 131–32
Morgan, Edmund, 254n.10
Mornington, Ohio, 127
Mullin, Glen, 67, 182
Mumford, Kevin, 299n.49
Muncie, Indiana, 220
Municipal lodging houses, 75, 77–78, 93,
    94–95, 100, 102–03, 164, 166, 280n.57
Musser, Charles, 305n.60, 306n.65

Nasaw, David, 305n.60
Nash, George, 230–31, 233, 316n.26
National Committee on Care of Tran-
    sient and Homeless (NCCTH),
    210–11, 217
National Committee to End Homeless-
    ness, 245
National Law Center on Homelessness,
    246
Native Americans
  homeless, 232, 241–42
  image of, 44, 262n.24
Nebraska, 33
New Brunswick, New Jersey, 67
New Deal, the, 193, 210, 218, 220, 222–23
New Hampshire, 53
New Jersey, 105, 280n.60
  anti-tramp campaign of 1876, 53–54
  Federal Transient Service camps in,
    212, 215, 217

  See also Camden, New Brunswick,
    Trenton
Newman, Katherine S., 278n.33
New Mexico, 213
New Orleans, 67, 219
Newport, Rhode Island, 14
Newsboys, 47
Newspapers
  and exposés about beggars, 82
  supportive of homeless, 81–82
New York City, 4, 8, 52, 55, 775
  Federal Transient Service center in,
    216
  hobo college in, 162
  homelessness before 1860, 14–15,
    22–26
  migration of homeless from, in 1870s,
    105
  municipal lodging house policies, 94,
    97, 100–02
  and native-born homeless, 115
  in 1930s, 197–98, 200, 202, 209,
    220–22
  response to homeless in nineteenth
    century, 26–28, 51, 79
  Salvation Army in, 89, 280n.60
New York Society for the Prevention of
    Pauperism (NYSPP), 26–27, 51–52
New York State
  Federal Transient Service centers in,
    216, 218
  and Great Depression transients, 194
  and proposed institution for tramps,
    79–80
  and social workers and beggars in
    1930s, 200
New York University, 234
Nietzsche, Friedrich, 179
Nixon, Richard, 201, 242

O'Hara, Bob, 212, 217–18
Ohio, 18, 128
  and Great Depression transients, 194

migrant workers in, 228
See also Cincinnati, Cleveland, Mornington, Youngstown
"Okies," 223
Oklahoma, 222. *See also* Oklahoma City
Oklahoma City, 95
and Great Depression, 8
Omaha, Nebraska, 144
The Other Bostonians (Thernstrom), 120
Outdoor relief
in colonial era, 15
crusade to eliminate, 30, 52, 81
expanded after 1907, 95–96

Painter, Nell Irvin, 48
Paley, William, 188
Palmer, Eddie, 198
Parsons, Lucy, 163
Patterson, James T., 313n.69
Pawnshops, 155–56
Payne, Roger, 177
Peabody, Francis, 178
Pennsylvania, 131
Federal Transient Service centers in, 212
vagrants in almshouses in, 100, 281n.3
See also Allentown, Philadelphia, Pittsburgh
Phelps, Elizabeth Stuart, 175–76
Philadelphia, 8, 15, 53, 280n.60
beggars in, 82
black homeless in, 113–14
demolition of skid row, 236
Federal Transient Service centers in, 212, 214, 219
"function shops" in, 155
growth of homeless before 1860, 22–26
homelessness after 1945, 226–28, 231–32, 318n.7
lodging house district (skid row) in, 147–48, 225–26, 233

police station lodgers in, 100
small charities in, 28–30, 87
Philadelphia Society for Organizing Charity (PSOC), 29, 74, 75–76
Pinkerton, Allen, 132
Pittenger, Mark, 301n.15
Pittsburgh, 202
Plunkitt, George Washington, 80–81, 96
Plymouth Colony, 20
Police, 251n.4, 313n.1
and "containment" of skid row after 1945, 233–35
and station house "tramp rooms," 6, 55–56, 70
and street beggars, 11, 24–26, 32, 82–83
vagrancy arrests by, 1860–1900, 99–100
See also Vagrancy laws
Poole, Ernest, 131
Populist Party, the, 177
Port Chester, Pennsylvania, 66
Potter, Ellen, 211, 222
Poverty (Hunter), 92
Powderly, Terrance, 51, 123
Presbyterians, 88
Progress and Poverty (George), 176
Prostitutes, 108–09, 256n.23, 283n.18, 285n.35
Protestants
homeless, 106, 120–21
support charity reformers, 87–88
and working-class sympathy for tramps, 279n.47
See also Puritans, Salvation Army, Urban missionaries, *specific denominations*
Providence, Rhode Island, 15
Puerto Ricans, 232
Puritans, the, 19–22

Quakers, 88
Quindlen, Anna, 246